Power and
Influence in
Organizations

To Maureen, Matthew, and Catherine
from Rod,
and
Al, CJ and Maddie
from Maggie

Power and Influence in Organizations

Roderick M. Kramer
Margaret A. Neale
Editors

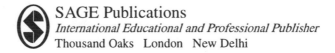
SAGE Publications
International Educational and Professional Publisher
Thousand Oaks   London   New Delhi

For information:

SAGE Publications, Inc.
2455 Teller Road
Thousand Oaks, California 91320
E-mail: order@sagepub.com

SAGE Publications Ltd.
6 Bonhill Street
London EC2A 4PU
United Kingdom

SAGE Publications India Pvt. Ltd.
M-32 Market
Greater Kailash I
New Delhi 110 048 India

Printed in the United States of America

Library of Congress Cataloging-in-Publication Data

Main entry under title:

Power and influence in organizations / edited by Roderick M. Kramer
    and Margaret A. Neale.
        p. cm.
    Includes bibliographical references and index.
    ISBN 0-7619-0860-9 (acid-free paper)
    ISBN 0-7619-0861-7 (pbk : acid-free paper)
    1. Communication in organizations. 2. Communication in
management. I. Kramer, Roderick Moreland, 1950- II. Neale, Margaret Ann.
    HD30.3 .P68 1998
    302.3′5—ddc21   98-19776

This book is printed on acid-free paper.

98 99 00 01 02 03 04 7 6 5 4 3 2 1

Acquisition Editor:	Marquita Flemming
Editorial Assistant:	Maryann Vail
Production Editor:	Astrid Virding
Editorial Assistant:	Nevair Kabakian
Typesetter/Designer:	Christina M. Hill
Indexer:	Will Ragsdale

Contents

Introduction

This edited volume is the end product of a conference, "Power and Influence in Organizations," that was held at the Stanford University Graduate School of Business in May 1996. The goal of the conference was to bring together leading scholars in organizations theory who were interested in exploring new perspectives on the role of power and influence in organizations.

The idea for this book originated at a prior conference that focused on exploring the implications of conceptualizing negotiation as fundamentally, rather than only incidentally, a social process. A goal of this conference was to document some of the enormous contributions that negotiation theory and research had made to a wide variety of fundamental topics in organizational studies, including understanding of organizational decision making, resource allocation, social exchange, dispute resolution, and even the notion of the organization as a negotiated social order. We published the results of this conference in a previous Sage book (Kramer & Messick, 1995).

One result of the rich discussions during the first conference was an appreciation of the simple fact that, no matter how important the topic of negotiation, there are other forms of social influence that are also widely used in organizational settings. Although negotiation is indisputedly a central and pervasive form of influence, it is only one among many such processes found in organizations. Moreover, it can be a highly scripted and ritualized form of organizational encounter, invoking its own unique tacit and explicit norms and expectations about appropriate or effective behaviors. Because negotiation theory and research had gained prominence in organizational science, we observed that other forms of social influence had received less serious scrutiny—regarding both theory development and empirical investigations.

Accordingly, one of the primary goals of the second conference was to explore some of these other facets of the social influence process. In fact, the original, and intendedly provocative, theme of our conference was "Beyond Bargaining: Exploring Alternative Perspectives on the Influence Process." In suggesting the need to move "beyond bargaining," we hoped to stimulate renewed attention to some of the subtle psychological, social, and structural bases of power and influence in organizations.

Another reason the conference was held was a conviction that the "basic research" literature on power and social influence—especially contributions from the basic social science disciplines, such as social psychology and sociology—was not receiving the kind of sustained attention it merited from organizational theorists. Although most leading business schools in the United States offer courses on power and influence in organizations, unlike negotiation, there were virtually no current, readily accessible compilations of original, scholarly writings reflecting emerging trends and new perspectives in theory and research. This conference was intended to address this problem.

In attempting to explore new ideas about the role of power and influence in organizations, we used a three-pronged approach. First, we approached some of the major contemporary intellectual pioneers in research on power and influence, including Samuel Bacharach, Robert Cialdini, Edward Lawler, and Jeffrey Pfeffer, and asked them to think about what is new, either in terms of their own original research ideas or, more broadly, in terms of general trends they have observed, as well as where future research might be headed. We wanted to do more than round up the usual suspects, however. Thus, we also invited leading scholars in organizational behavior theory and research whose work touched on themes related to power and influence, even if they themselves or others might not necessarily categorize their work in this way. Thus, we invited scholars such as Philip Tetlock, Tom Tyler, and Robert Sutton to offer their thoughts about how their work on such diverse topics as accountability, trust in authorities, and impression management might connect with and inform thinking about the conference themes. Third, we sought young scholars working in this area who might offer fresh or unusual perspectives on this problem.

To catalyze this diverse brew, we invited Mayer Zald to serve as discussant and occasional referee. He graciously consented to take on this role and provided his usual deft blend of scholarly acumen, historical perspective, and humorous insight. He helped us take our efforts more seriously while not allowing us to take ourselves too seriously.

With all these elements in place, we launched into our collective endeavors with high expectations. We were not disappointed. The end result was a wonderfully engaging and intellectually lively conference in which social psychologists, sociologists, and organizational theorists challenged, cajoled, and critiqued each others' thinking and work.

The result of these collective labors is this book, which we hope produces intellectual fodder and enjoyment. We also hope the chapters in this book provide a useful road map and stimulus for future research in this area.

Reference

Kramer, R. M., & Messick, D. M. (Eds.). (1995). *Negotiation as a social process.* Thousand Oaks, CA: Sage.

1

Illusions of Influence

JEFFREY PFEFFER
ROBERT B. CIALDINI

The idea of influence is ubiquitous in organizational analysis. Efforts to understand the causes of organizational actions and outcomes inevitably lead to concern with the causal factors responsible for those outcomes—who or what has influence in the situation. Some of the relevant literature pursues the direction set by the demonstration of the fundamental attribution error (Ross, 1977) and explores when observers attribute influence to persons, for instance, in leadership roles in contrast to situational factors. Thus, some research asks the question: In what circumstances do observers attribute influence over events and outcomes to individual leadership (Calder, 1977; Pfeffer, 1977)? Meindl, Ehrlich, and Dukerich (1985) argued that leadership effects would be attributed more under conditions of organizational performance extremes—either very good or very poor performance—and when economic stress was high because of poor macroeconomic conditions. In other literature, the following question is asked: What do individuals do to acquire actual influence over situations? This focus on how individuals develop influence is evident, for instance, in

1

the literature on leadership (House & Baetz, 1979) and interpersonal power (Cialdini, 1988; Pfeffer, 1992).

This chapter focuses on inferences about influence made not by observers but by those who are actually in managerial or super-visorial—in other words, potentially influential—roles. The attributional approach taken in some, although not all, of the relevant literature implies that both actors and observers are engaged in a process of inferring causality (Kelley, 1971) and potentially taking subsequent actions based on these attributions. Observers' attributions of influence and causality, the focus of much of the existing literature, are interesting and relevant for understanding individual causal schema and interpersonal perception. The attributions about personal influence developed by the actors themselves, however, are possibly even more consequential because these individuals are likely to act on the basis of their beliefs and thereby affect both themselves and others through their actions.

To the extent that attributional processes are involved in inferring who or what has influence over events and outcomes and how much influence various parties possess, it is possible and perhaps even in-evitable that attribution errors will occur. The fundamental attribution error (Ross, 1977) is one example of an error in causal reasoning in which outcomes are overattributed to individual characteristics such as personality while the effects of situational constraints are errone-ously underestimated. This error in causal reasoning, however, is not the only, or perhaps even the most consequential, error in under-standing organizational dynamics. Another possible inference error involves an illusion of influence—the belief that one has influence over a behavior or outcome even when one does not or, at a minimum, overestimating one's degree of influence and control in a particular setting or situation. For example, the literature on the illusion of control (Langer, 1983) shows that people come to believe they actually have influence over chance events. When people are more actively involved in the activity and therefore both committed and behaving as though they might have influence, they are likely to believe that they have causal control over random outcomes. Thus, individuals who throw dice or draw colored balls out of urns rather than just watching some-one else do these things, thereby having more involvement in the situation, are willing to bet more on the outcome because they feel they have more control over it.

The illusion of influence is probably quite widespread in organizations, with important effects on both those who harbor these illusions and the organizations in which they work. This chapter seeks to understand the factors that can produce an illusion of influence and some of the effects of such illusions. We then discuss possible ways of overcoming illusions of influence in organizational settings under the presumption that by so doing, some of the dysfunctional consequences of influence illusions can be avoided.

Where Does the Illusion of Influence Come From?

There are a number of psychological factors that would cause someone to believe he or she had influence over a situation in which there was little or none or to overestimate the amount of influence possessed. One such factor is the motivational bias for individuals to want to see themselves in the most favorable light possible, the so-called self-enhancement bias. Myers (1996) has reviewed the extensive literature documenting the tendency of individuals to regard themselves as more intelligent, skilled, ethical, honest, persistent, original, friendly, reliable, attractive, fair-minded, and even better drivers than others. In the negotiations literature, this self-enhancement effect has been shown to lead to overconfidence—for instance, in a situation of final-offer arbitration, the individuals involved thought their offer had a 68% chance of winning (Bazerman & Neale, 1982). This overconfidence often hinders the willingness to make concessions (Neale & Bazerman, 1985), find integrative solutions, or negotiate rationally (Neale & Bazerman, 1991).

Unrealistic and ego-enhancing self-perceptions can be maintained by selectively processing and interpreting information in ways that promote the person's self-concept. Thus, people (and organizations) are more likely to attribute success to internal factors, such as hard work and intelligence, and poor outcomes to factors such as chance or environmental perturbations over which they had no control (Brown & Rogers, 1991; Fletcher & Ward, 1988). Studies of the accounts for organizational performance provided in annual reports have consistently observed this effect—poor performance is attributed to general economic or industry conditions, whereas good performance is cred-

ited to management and other internal organizational factors (Salancik
& Meindl, 1984, p. 246). Individuals may believe that tests on which
they have done well are more valid (Shepperd, 1993). Also, people
believe that others who accept rather than resist their persuasive arguments are more intelligent (Cialdini, Braver, & Lewis, 1974; Cialdini &
Mirels, 1976).

Possessing influence is, at least in the United States and most other
Western countries, seen as something that is desirable. Being powerful
rather than powerless, being influential, and being efficacious are all
valued and complimentary appellations. Consequently, one way for
individuals to engage in self-enhancement is to overestimate their
influence and power—to believe that they have more control over
others and situations than they actually do. Indeed, the preoccupation
with leadership, training in leadership, becoming a leader, and so forth
leads to a heightened veneration of those in influential positions. Thus,
it is reasonable to expect that, as part of a process of self-enhancement
motivated by the desire to have as favorable a self-concept as possible,
individuals will overestimate not only their leadership abilities but
also the results of their attempts to act as a leader and to influence
others.

There are experimental data consistent with these self-enhancement arguments. Pfeffer, Cialdini, Hanna, and Knopoff (in press) conducted an experiment using Stanford MBA students, all of whom have
had work experience and some of whom have had supervisory experience—in other words, a reasonably sophisticated subject pool. In the
experiment, subjects were told that they would be randomly assigned
to one of two roles—either someone given the task of preparing a draft
advertisement for a new watch or someone in the position of oversee-
ing that other person's efforts. In actuality, all subjects were in the role
of the manager, and the materials they received that were supposedly
"prepared" by their colleague in the other room were actually supplied
by the experimenters. In the lowest involvement and control condition,
subjects spent the time filling out personality questionnaires, were told
that, as is often the case, they were too busy to closely oversee the work
of their subordinate, and saw only a final advertisement. In an inter-
mediate condition, subjects saw a rough draft of the advertisement and
filled out a feedback form (to ensure that they spent time thinking
about it) but were told that, again as is the case in the real world, the
subordinate would not be able to receive the feedback because of time

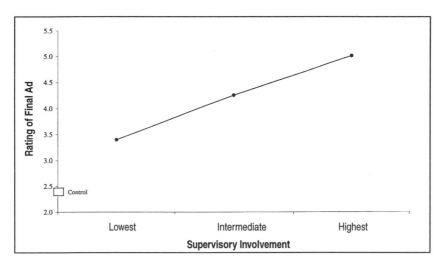

Figure 1.1. Rating of the Final Ad

limitations. In the highest involvement condition, subjects saw the identical rough draft, filled out the feedback form, and believed that the person working on the advertising campaign had seen their advice.

All subjects rated the identical final advertisement on four dimensions: its creativity and originality, its demonstrated business sense, its interest level, and overall quality of the final advertisement. These four items were used to construct an index measuring the overall quality of the advertisement as assessed by the various subjects. Subjects also provided other ratings, such as for the competence of the person doing the work and their own effectiveness as a manager, and answered other questions about the study. The study results were dramatic. The greater the degree of perceived control and involvement, the more highly subjects rated the advertisement. The differences were substantial: The subjects in the highest involvement condition rated the advertisement about twice as favorably (on a 7-point scale) as those in the lowest involvement and control condition. Moreover, the study found that merely being involved in the experiment tended to inflate evaluations of the work. A control group that simply saw the advertisement rated it the least favorable of all. These results are shown in Figure 1.1.

Moreover, in addition to evaluating the advertisement more favorably, subjects evaluated their own managerial effectiveness substan-

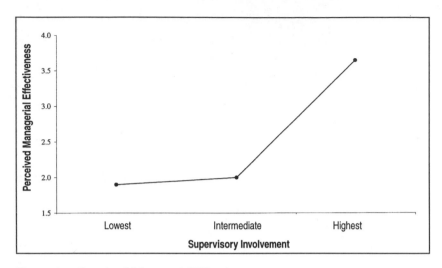

Figure 1.2. Perceived Managerial Effectiveness

tially more favorably to the extent that they were more involved in the activity of supervising and, therefore, felt that they had more control over the final outcome. Also, it is striking how easy it was for a subject population with some work and in many cases actual supervisory experience to come to believe that they had influence over an outcome for which there was minimal supervision and actually no effect on the final product. The results of the experimental manipulations on subjects' ratings of their own managerial effectiveness are shown in Figure 1.2.

To the extent that the illusion of influence is fostered by a motivation for self-enhancement, conditions that affect either the content of what is self-enhancing or the motivational importance of self-enhancement would be expected to affect the magnitude of the influence illusion. Cultural values and beliefs are one such moderating condition (Markus & Kitayama, 1991; Triandis, 1989). As Heine and Lehman (1995, p. 595) noted, "Evidence suggests that self-enhancing tendencies can be culturally variant; they may, in fact, be less prominent in the motivational repertoire of people from cultures outside of North America." Their study, which compared levels of unrealistic optimism—"The tendency for people to believe that they are more likely to experience positive events, and less likely to experience negative events, than similar others" (p. 596)—between samples of Canadians and Japanese, found that the Canadians showed higher levels of unrealistic optimism.

The idea of individual, compared to group or collective, influence and efficacy is a particularly Western idea. Singelis (1994), in developing a scale measuring independent versus interdependent construals of the self, wrote,

> People in the West hold an independent view of the self that emphasizes the separateness, internal attributes, and uniqueness of individuals (the independent self-construal) and . . . many non-Western peoples hold an interdependent image of self stressing connectedness, social context, and relationships (the interdependent self-construal). (p. 580)

As Morris and Peng (1994) have demonstrated, Chinese are much less likely to make causal attributions to the individual, in part because they have been culturally conditioned to more often subordinate themselves to the group and to view the group as being a more focal social unit. Other cultural distinctions in addition to the Western/non-Western distinction are relevant, including organizational cultures that also obviously vary in the extent to which they emphasize individual as opposed to more collective bases and causes of action. We expect that there is less tendency to observe people holding illusions of individual influence, and therefore overrating themselves and what they are associated with producing, in more collectivist organizational or national cultures. Since collectivist orientations vary across individuals even within cultures, this argument suggests that measures of collective versus individual orientation (such as those developed by Hofstede, 1980, or Singelis, 1994) could be useful in studies exploring this idea.

When we described results of our Stanford study to colleagues, a frequent response was the following:

> Of course your student subjects saw both their effectiveness and the quality of the work product as being better the more they were apparently involved in the process that produced the advertisement. After all, they are students in an elite MBA program in which they are learning both how to manage and that, by their very selection into the school, they have managerial skills and talents.

It is certainly plausible to believe that one consequence of going to business school or going through any form of management training is to
heighten the importance of being an effective and efficacious manager
for an individual's self-concept. After all, the very behavior of investing
time and other resources in training means that the individual's self-
concept is more closely linked with and committed to being an effective
manager.

If this line of argument is correct, it suggests that the illusion of
influence, in which one inflates one's own effectiveness and the quality
of work that one has been involved in producing, should be greater
among business students or, for that matter, managers than in a population with a self-concept less directly tied to being an effective leader.
Moreover, it is reasonable to hypothesize that one important consequence of going to business school or going through other forms of
management training is to increase the likelihood that the person will
see himself or herself as effective and influential. The more such training one has, the more one's self-concept is tied with being a "good
manager," which at least in Western cultures means being able to get
things done and having influence.

Although our subject population was too small for definitive tests,
trends in the data are consistent with these arguments. When the same
study was conducted using Arizona State University undergraduates
as subjects, the effects were somewhat attenuated. Also, there is evidence that the longer the MBA subjects had been in business school at
the time of the experiment, the more they tended to view the advertisement as being better and their own management competence as
being better in the high-involvement condition.

We have argued that any circumstance that increases the importance of being influential to the self-concept should increase the
strength of the illusion of influence and the corresponding inflation of
both the perceived quality of the work product and one's own self-
evaluation of effectiveness as a manager. Factors that can increase the
importance of being influential to the self-concept include anything
that elevates a person's status in an organizational hierarchy and, as a
consequence, implicates the person's sense of self with his or her
success in that hierarchy. Such status markers include increased salary
differentials across organizational levels, formal office arrangements
that connote status, and job titles—indeed, even the title manager or
supervisor. Each of these would be expected to increase the motivation

for self-enhancement and, consequently, the strength of the illusion of influence. In this sense, many of the arrangements that rank individuals hierarchically—differences in offices, wages, and job titles— become self-reinforcing in that they produce behavior motivated to enhance the self by believing that one's own actions are important and effective. Consequently, it is not surprising that many high-commitment workplaces and organizations that have implemented total quality management approaches have attempted to do away with, at least to some degree, these status markers (Pfeffer, 1994, 1998). With the status distinctions in place, the motivation for self-enhancement is increased and, as a result, the tendency to credit or even involve others or view them as being important in affecting the work process is diminished.

Regarding this point, we have argued that a motivation for self-enhancement leads to the development of an illusion of influence, and this motivation is particularly strong under conditions in which the self-concept is highly implicated—when the individual is a manager, has gone through some sacrifice or behavioral commitment to become one, and has other status distinctions that both make being influential important and create markers that signify influence. Individual motivation for self-enhancement, although important, is not likely to be the only factor involved in the illusion of influence. After all, one of the most reliable findings of social psychology concerns the potency of social influences, including informational social influence (Cialdini, 1988; Deutsch & Gerard, 1955; Festinger, 1954; Salancik & Pfeffer, 1978). As briefly mentioned, people in different social environments vary in their beliefs about the efficacy and importance of individual leadership and personal (compared with more social or group) efficacy (Morris & Peng, 1994; Triandis, 1989).

As the research by Meindl and colleagues (1985) indicates, not only do socially constructed beliefs about the efficacy and potency of individual leaders vary across broad cultural contexts but also these beliefs vary across time and may vary across organizations or even organizational subunits at a single point in time within a single national culture. The research by Meindl et al. suggests that illusions of influence are likely to be particularly potent at times of extreme performance—when the unit or organization is doing either very well or very poorly. Recently, an article in the *Wall Street Journal* noted the rise of the chief executive in U.S. firms as a public figure. In contrast to the situation in, perhaps, the 1950s and 1960s, currently executives write books, are focal in news stories, and have become almost cultural icons (e.g., Bill Gates of Microsoft, Andrew Grove of Intel, and Steve Jobs of Apple and Pixar). When a business newspaper finds the veneration and visibility of executives worthy of comment, something of social importance is occurring. Part of the explanation lies in the exceptional economic performance, as reflected in the stock market, of the past half decade and the apparent attribution of this exceptional performance to the skills of senior business leaders (as contrasted, for instance, with the environment). Part of the explanation must also lie in the fact that senior executive salaries and executive wealth have increased disproportionately, which also makes these individuals more visible, focal, and noteworthy.

It is important to note, however, that the executives and their organizations can either emphasize or deemphasize their individual influence, and by so doing cause others to ascribe more or less influence to them as individuals. Toyota Motors has certainly been among the most successful and admired companies in the world, but its chief executive officer receives limited media attention. In the United States, there are successful organizations, such as USAA in finance and insurance, MBNA in credit cards and banking, Norwest in banking, AES in the production of electric power, and numerous others, in which there is less of an emphasis on the efficacy of individual leadership and, we predict, as a consequence less of a tendency to observe illusions of influence. Our prediction is straightforward. There is a social contagion effect such that persons placed in an information environment in which self-enhancing motivation is emphasized and the independent, rather than the interdependent, self-construal is dominant will over time exhibit more tendency to demonstrate illusions of influence—overvaluing things they have had more ostensible involvement in or control over and overvaluing their own efficacy as leaders or managers.

Some Consequences of the Illusion of Influence

We have already discussed one important consequence of the illusion of influence—the inflated evaluation of work output produced under more supervisory involvement and the more positive self-evaluation of the person's managerial competence and ability. It is implicit that this inflated evaluation of the quality of work produced under more supervisory control is more likely to occur to the extent that the work product itself has some uncertainty or ambiguity associated with it. Allison, Messick, and Goethals (1989), in a study of positive illusions, found smaller effects for ratings of intelligence than morality. They argued that this was because of "the greater publicity, specificity, and/or objectivity of behaviors signaling intelligence than of behaviors indicating morality" (p. 289). In the experiment described previously, evaluating an advertisement for a new watch inherently involves taste and judgment as opposed to the simple application of a formula. Situations of ambiguity and uncertainty are not infrequent in organizations and are particularly prominent the higher one rises in the hierarchy and in staff rather than line positions.

The following question was also addressed in the experimental study: What was the consequence of the illusion of influence for the rating of the presumed subordinate doing the work? There are two different predictions that can be made. Some research (Kipnis, 1972; Strickland, 1958) would predict that the competence of the subordinate would not be rated highly. Kipnis found that the more someone had power over others, the less likely that person was to want to interact with those others and they were less favorably evaluated. Strickland described the supervisor's dilemma: If someone works under supervision, how can the supervisor know whether or not the person can be trusted or is competent because there is no opportunity in such circumstances to observe the subordinate's trustworthiness or skill at working without direction?

Using the concepts of commitment and consistency, the opposite prediction can be made. If the subjects evaluate the advertisement more favorably with increasing involvement, then a halo or consistency effect (Heider, 1958) to maintain cognitive balance should indicate that they also evaluate the person producing that work more favorably. Moreover, more involvement is more committing, and research shows that the more involvement a person has—in this instance, in making the decision to hire someone—the more favorable will be the evaluation of that individual because of the person's commitment (Bazerman, Beekun, & Schoorman, 1982; Schoorman, 1988).

In the Pfeffer et al. (in press) study, the data supported the consistency prediction. Not only did the degree of supervisory involvement

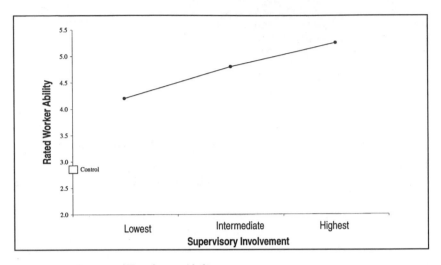

Figure 1.3. Rating of Employee Ability

relate to the rating of the advertisement and the self-evaluation of managerial competency but also it significantly related to the evaluation of the subordinate doing the work, with the greater the level of supervisory involvement and control, the more favorable the evaluation of the subordinate's competence (Figure 1.3). Given the absence of actual interpersonal interaction in the experimental situation, it is perhaps not surprising that the consistency effect predominated. In other contexts, interaction can produce self-fulfilling cycles of behavior (Snyder, 1982) in which subordinate competence may be devalued over time, which could not happen in this instance.

There are important implications of this result and the studies by Schoorman for the performance appraisal or evaluation process. If supervisorial involvement in a task inflates the supervisor's opinion not only of the work product but also of the subordinates, there should be serious concern about the extent to which such appraisals will be fair or the likelihood that this bias will encourage decentralization and delegation of decision making. Evaluations that entail obtaining information from peers and subordinates as well as from supervisors— so-called 360-degree feedback—would be preferable because they reduce the effect of supervisory bias while maintaining the involvement of the manager in the evaluation and appraisal process—necessary for maintaining commitment.

The illusion of influence may have other, even more profound, consequences and implications. The following question motivated the Pfeffer et al. (in press) experiment: Given the documented positive effects of participation on organizational performance, why is it that true empowerment (through the use of things such as self-managed teams) is so rare? The study provides one answer: If work produced under more control is evaluated more favorably, the person supervising the work has an enhanced opinion of himself or herself, and the supervisor also rates the subordinate more favorably, there is little in the situation to induce delegation. Control brings its own reward in a more favorable view of almost all aspects of the work setting.

The illusion of influence produces a false sense of self-confidence and security in work produced with one's direct involvement and a corresponding diminished confidence in work produced without one's involvement. Both effects may be harmful to organizations. As one observes organizations making mistakes that seem obvious to outsiders—for instance, airlines' pursuing low-service strategies that result from too fierce cost-cutting, companies foregoing investment in and development of new product technologies as in the case of a number of computer firms that missed the personal computer revolution, and so forth—what is striking is not just the initial judgmental error but also the persistence in seemingly failing decisions. This phenomenon has typically been described as an example of escalating commitment to a failing course of action, with the commitment arising because of the failure and the need, therefore, to justify one's initial decision by investing more resources (Ross & Staw, 1993; Staw, 1976). The illusion of influence perspective offers a complementary view of the same observed phenomenon. There is persistence with flawed decisions not simply as a way of justifying one's previous commitments but also because, given the level of involvement in the decision-making process, the decision maker does not accurately perceive the outcomes and therefore never really apprehends the true extent of the problem or failure. What appears to be escalating commitment to the outside observer may appear to be persistence with a successful course of action to the decision maker, who is subject to self-enhancement-induced motivations to see decision outcomes as more favorable than they are in reality.

By the same token, the readiness to see problems in work produced without the manager's direct involvement leads to a derogation of the abilities of subordinates that makes delegation difficult. Moreover, the subordinates must certainly learn about the illusion of influence over time from a trial-and-error process. When they do work on their own, the work is not evaluated nearly as favorably as when they involve their supervisor or at least cause that individual to believe that he or she has had control over the work process. Therefore, over time, people will look up the hierarchy for supervision, and supervisors will wonder why they cannot get their subordinates to accept responsibility, thus creating a self-reinforcing, albeit less than healthy, cycle of behavior.

There are two sides to the illusion of influence. Writing about self-enhancing illusions more generally, Taylor and Brown (1988, p. 193) noted that such illusions "can serve a wide variety of cognitive, affective, and social functions." Tyler and Hastie (1991) have also noted that some motivationally based forms of self-enhancement may be good for the individual's mental health as well as for stimulating more effort directed toward achievement. The illusion of influence is associated with inflated evaluations of work that one is involved with, and this very overconfidence may be useful in stimulating entrepreneurial decision making. Many organizational decisions, and certainly decisions associated with starting a new business or launching a new product, are inherently risky and there are limits as to how much data and analysis can reduce that uncertainty. Without some perhaps unjustified sense of control and influence over events, decisions that are required for launching new activities would be more difficult to make and it is less likely that decision makers would get beyond the risk and uncertainty to make these decisions.

A prominent and successful South Korean graduate of Stanford Business School was asked about his experience at the school and what he learned. After graduating, this individual worked at a family-owned company and expanded its scope dramatically, with a particularly bold and successful expansion into financial services. He said that what he had gained most from business school was a sense of self-confidence and, as a consequence, the willingness and ability to take prudent business risks and to lead the firm on a much more aggressive expansion path than it had followed in the past. Therefore, on the one hand, the illusion of influence produces the overconfidence that makes everything one is involved in look better. On the other hand, that same illusion of influence encourages entrepreneurial decision making that might be less evident if one had a more realistic sense of one's own abilities and influence over decisions and outcomes.

Reducing the Illusion of Influence

What does our research suggest about how to ameliorate some of the negative effects of the illusion of influence while not losing some of the positive consequences? In other words, how can organizations reduce the biasing effects of the influence illusion without undermining the commitment of managers to the organization's tasks and performance? Because we were interested in understanding how to overcome some of the resistance to delegation, in the Pfeffer et al. (in press) experiment we ran the same three conditions of increasing involvement, altering the managerial orientation through a simple change in language. In the hierarchical managerial orientation, subjects were consistently referred to as "manager" or "supervisor" and were told that they would be "responsible for supervising while the other person prepares a solution." In a team-based managerial orientation, subjects were told that the company stressed a team approach; they were called "team leaders," and the other person was called a "team member" throughout the experiment. Furthermore, their instructions stated that they were "responsible for assisting while the other person prepares a solution."

This is a relatively subtle manipulation of orientation because in neither case was there any actual contact between the subject and the person presumably preparing the advertisement—people in the "team" orientation did not, in fact, work in teams. Previous research, however, has shown that assigning controlling labels, such as "managing director" or "group supervisor," to people with oversight responsibilities produced more self-oriented behavior than assigning less controlling labels, such as "group leader" (Messe, Kerr, & Sattler, 1992; Samuelson & Allison, 1994).

In the experiment we conducted, the tendency for the advertisement to be rated more positively under conditions of more supervisory involvement was reduced under the team-based managerial orientation, with this effect being observed primarily for the condition of greatest involvement. This is not surprising because it is only under some degree of involvement in the activity that self-enhancement motivations would be activated.

Although our research does not provide conclusive evidence on
the mechanisms explaining why simply invoking a team orientation
through a fairly subtle language manipulation had an effect, there are
a number of plausible reasons for this result. The term team, particularly when used with a subject population that is itself involved in
management training and education, probably conjures up a set of
associations and cognitive scripts about what it means to be part of a
team compared with being a supervisor, even if the objective differences in the experimental conditions are fairly minor. Being on a team
has implications for who gets credit for the work—the team as a whole
rather than just a single individual—as well as implications for who is
responsible and accountable for the work—once again, the team as a
whole rather than the manager or supervisor. One of the most reliable
findings in social psychology concerns the effects of expectations on
behavior (Eden, 1990; Jones, 1977). Simply using the term team changes
people's orientations, expectations, and, thus, their behavior, including the behavior of overvaluing work and holding an illusion of
influence. Language and terminology make some behaviors and expectations comparatively more salient, and what is salient and prominent in consciousness directs behavior.

Salience, although very important in directing and affecting behavior, is fragile and readily altered. This implies that in organizations
in which there are multiple sources of information, multiple labels, and
multiple messages on an ongoing basis, for one to observe the effects
of the team idea in overcoming the illusion of influence, the team
concept must be pervasive in all aspects of the organization and its
operations. Simply using the term team without also changing rewards, measurements and evaluations, social interactions, and work
organization to reinforce the concept is unlikely to be effective, as many
organizations have learned through experience. Compensation
schemes that do not isolate and reward individual performance but
instead reward group performance should reduce the overvaluation
and biasing effects of the illusion of influence. More social events
attended by people at different levels and functions in the organization
should have much the same effect, as would physical design that
deemphasizes status distinctions and, instead, reinforces a common
social identity. To maintain the team concept, particularly in Western
cultures that emphasize the individual, requires maintaining the idea

on a chronic basis and ensuring that virtually all the environmental cues are consistent with a team-based orientation.

In the Pfeffer et al. (in press) study, although the team-based managerial orientation did reduce the inflated evaluation of the quality of the advertisement, the orientation did not undermine subjects' estimate of their managerial effectiveness. This is an important result because it is crucial to be able to overcome the illusion of influence, thereby encouraging delegation and participation, without undermining managers' feeling of commitment or efficacy. What one wants is leaders committed to the organization or the group rather than to individual efforts. There is evidence that this is accomplished in a team-based orientation, in which subjects feel effective but that undermines their belief in the efficacy of personal, individual control, and involvement.

Conclusion

Much of the research on decentralization and delegation has examined the effects of these management practices on people exposed to them. Much of the research based on attribution theory has explored how observers make attributions about causality. Much of the research on power has taken a similar, outside-in approach, asking what factors and behaviors create power and influence. The premise of this chapter and our research is that although each of these perspectives is useful and important, each omits certain significant social psychological processes.

To understand why decentralization and delegation of decision-making authority has diffused so slowly and with such great difficulty, it is important to explore its effects on supervisors and managers, not just those exposed to that type of management. Managerial centralization and involvement are consistent with beliefs about the potency and efficacy of management and, significantly, lead to an overvaluation of the work produced under tighter managerial control. In a similar fashion, it is important to understand the factors that tend to cause individuals in managerial positions to develop illusions of influence and control, and why and how they see more personal efficacy in situations than may be warranted.

Once one understands the social and social psychological factors that produce illusions of influence, one can begin to develop strategies for mitigating some undesirable consequences while still maintaining commitment and involvement. Our research has suggested that team-based managerial orientations, and elements in the management system that reinforce a team-based orientation, can be helpful in this regard.

Much research remains to be done, however. Although the findings of our experiment and the arguments mustered may be persuasive, they are incomplete as an empirical foundation on which to rest either a complete theory of how illusions of influence develop or the managerial implications of this phenomena. This particular area of inquiry seems to be one in which cultural issues loom large because the independent and interdependent conceptions of the self vary dramatically across contexts. As such, the questions and issues posed in this chapter would particularly benefit from a comparative frame and program of research.

References

Allison, S. T., Messick, D. M., & Goethals, G. R. (1989). On being better but not smarter than others: The Muhammad Ali effect. *Social Cognition, 7,* 275-296.

Bazerman, M. H., Beekun, R. I., & Schoorman, F. D. (1982). Performance evaluation in a dynamic context: A laboratory study of the impact of prior commitment to the ratee. *Journal of Applied Psychology, 67,* 873-876.

Bazerman, M. H., & Neale, M. A. (1982). Improving negotiator effectiveness under final offer arbitration: The role of selection and training. *Journal of Applied Psychology, 67,* 543-548.

Brown, J. D., & Rogers, R. J. (1991). Self-serving attributions: The role of physiological arousal. *Personality and Social Psychology Bulletin, 17,* 501-506.

Calder, B. J. (1977). An attribution theory of leadership. In B. M. Staw & G. R. Salancik (Eds.), *New directions in organizational behavior* (pp. 179-204). Chicago: St. Clair Press.

Cialdini, R. B. (1988). *Influence: Science and practice.* Glenview, IL: Scott, Foresman.

Cialdini, R. B., Braver, S. L., & Lewis, S. K. (1974). Attributional bias and the easily persuaded other. *Journal of Personality and Social Psychology, 30,* 631-637.

Cialdini, R. B., & Mirels, H. L. (1976). Sense of personal control and attributions about yielding and resisting persuasion targets. *Journal of Personality and Social Psychology, 33,* 395-402.

Deutsch, M., & Gerard, H. (1955). A study of normative and informational social influences on individual judgment. *Journal of Abnormal and Social Psychology, 51,* 629-636.

Eden, D. (1990). *Pygmalion in management: Productivity as a self-fulfilling prophecy.* Lexington, MA: Lexington Books.

Festinger, L. (1954). A theory of social comparison processes. *Human Relations, 7,* 117-140.

Fletcher, G. J. O., & Ward, C. (1988). Attribution processes: A cross-cultural perspective. In M. H. Bond (Ed.), *The cross-cultural challenge to social psychology* (pp. 230-244). Newbury Park, CA: Sage.

Heider, F. (1958). *The psychology of interpersonal relations.* New York: John Wiley.

Heine, S. J., & Lehman, D. R. (1995). Cultural variation in unrealistic optimism: Does the West feel more invulnerable than the East? *Journal of Personality and Social Psychology, 68,* 595-607.

Hofstede, G. (1980). *Culture's consequences.* Beverly Hills, CA: Sage.

House, R. J., & Baetz, M. L. (1979). Leadership: Some generalizations and new research directions. *Research in Organizational Behavior, 1,* 341-423.

Jones, R. A. (1977). *Self-fulfilling prophecies: Social, psychological, and physiological effects of expectancies.* Hillsdale, NJ: Lawrence Erlbaum.

Kelley, H. H. (1971). *Attribution in social interaction.* Morristown, NJ: General Learning Press.

Kipnis, D. (1972). Does power corrupt? *Journal of Personality and Social Psychology, 24,* 33-41.

Langer, E. J. (1983). *The psychology of control.* Beverly Hills, CA: Sage.

Markus, H. R., & Kitayama, S. (1991). Culture and the self: Implications for cognition, emotion, and motivation. *Psychological Review, 98,* 224-253.

Meindl, J. R., Ehrlich, S. B., & Dukerich, J. M. (1985). The romance of leadership. *Administrative Science Quarterly, 30,* 78-102.

Messe, L. A., Kerr, L., & Sattler, D. N. (1992). "But some animals are more equal than others": The supervisor as a privileged status in group contexts. In S. Worchel, W. Wood, & J. A. Simpson (Eds.), *Group processes and productivity.* Newbury Park, CA: Sage.

Morris, M. W., & Peng, K. (1994). Culture and cause: American and Chinese attributions for social and physical events. *Journal of Personality and Social Psychology, 67,* 949-971.

Myers, D. G. (1996). *Social psychology.* New York: McGraw-Hill.

Neale, M. A., & Bazerman, M. A. (1985). The effects of framing and negotiator overconfidence on bargainer behavior. *Academy of Management Journal, 28,* 34-49.

Neale, M. A., & Bazerman, M. A. (1991). *Cognition and rationality in negotiation.* New York: Free Press.

Pfeffer, J. (1977). The ambiguity of leadership. *Academy of Management Review, 2,* 104-112.

Pfeffer, J. (1992). *Managing with power.* Boston: Harvard Business School Press.

Pfeffer, J. (1994). *Competitive advantage through people.* Boston: Harvard Business School Press.

Pfeffer, J. (1998). *The human equation: Building profits by putting people first.* Boston: Harvard Business School Press.

Pfeffer, J., Cialdini, R. B., Hanna, B., & Knopoff, K. (in press). Faith in supervision and the self-enhancement bias: Two psychological reasons why managers don't empower workers. *Basic and Applied Social Psychology.*

Ross, J., & Staw, B. M. (1993). Organizational escalation and exit: Lessons from the Shoreham nuclear power plant. *Academy of Management Journal, 36,* 701-732.

Ross, L. D. (1977). The intuitive psychologist and his shortcomings: Distortions in the attribution process. In L. Berkowitz (Ed.), *Advances in experimental and social psychology, Vol. 10* (pp. 173-220). New York: Random House.

Salancik, G. R., & Meindl, J. R. (1984). Corporate attributions as strategic illusions of management control. *Administrative Science Quarterly, 29,* 238-254.
Salancik, G. R., & Pfeffer, J. (1978). A social information processing approach to job attitudes and task design. *Administrative Science Quarterly, 23,* 224-253.
Samuelson, C. D., & Allison, S. T. (1994). Cognitive factors affecting the use of social decision heuristics in resource-sharing tasks. *Organizational Behavior and Human Decision Processes, 58,* 1-27.
Schoorman, F. D. (1988). Escalation bias in performance appraisals: An unintended consequence of supervisor participation in hiring decisions. *Journal of Applied Psychology, 73,* 58-62.
Shepperd, J. A. (1993). Student derogation of the Scholastic Aptitude Test: Biases in perceptions and presentations of college board scores. *Basic and Applied Social Psychology, 14,* 455-473.
Singelis, T. M. (1994). The measurement of independent and interdependent self-construals. *Personality and Social Psychology Bulletin, 5,* 580-591.
Snyder, M. (1982, July). Self-fulfilling stereotypes. *Psychology Today, 16,* 60-68.
Staw, B. M. (1976). Knee deep in the big muddy: A study of escalating commitment to a chosen course of action. *Organizational Behavior and Human Performance, 16,* 27-44.
Strickland, L. H. (1958). Surveillance and trust. *Journal of Personality, 26,* 200-215.
Taylor, S. E., & Brown, J. D. (1988). Illusion and well-being: A social psychological perspective on mental health. *Psychological Bulletin, 103,* 193-210.
Triandis, H. C. (1989). The self and social behavior in differing cultural contexts. *Psychological Review, 96,* 506-520.
Tyler, T., & Hastie, R. (1991). The social consequences of cognitive illusions. In M. H. Bazerman, R. J. Lewicki, & B. H. Sheppard (Eds.), *Research in negotiation in organizations, Vol. 3.* Greenwich, CT: JAI.

Simmelian Ties

Super Strong and Sticky

DAVID KRACKHARDT

The importance of informal relations in organizations has been a well-established theme in the organizational literature, dating back to Mayo's famous Hawthorne experiments (Roethlisberger & Dickson, 1939). Most of the work in this area since that time has underscored how the structure of such relations can have profound implications for the members of the organization (Burt, 1992; Krackhardt & Brass, 1994). A small number of scholars have forced attention on the overlooked fact that the content of these relations should be taken into account when making substantive predictions about their consequences (Krackhardt, 1992; Lincoln & Miller, 1979). The purpose of this chapter is to combine both these perspectives and show that the quality of a dyadic relationship fundamentally changes as a function of the overall structure in which the relationship is embedded. To do this, I build on Granovetter's theory of weak ties and on Simmel's classic discussion of the social triad.

Strong Versus Weak Ties

There is perhaps no more cited work in the literature on networks than Granovetter's (1973) "The Strength of Weak Ties." He proposed that weak, infrequent ties are often more influential and critical than strong ties in assisting an individual in gathering and taking advantage of information that is disseminated through the social network. His seminal paper has generated years of mostly confirmatory research (Granovetter, 1982, 1994).

Recently, however, some have questioned this diversion from research on the strong ties that are critical links in systems under some conditions (Krackhardt, 1992; Krackhardt & Stern, 1988; Nelson, 1989).[1] I draw from this discussion to build in a new direction. Granovetter (1973, p. 1361) suggested that strong ties are composed of four elements: (a) the amount of time spent interacting, (b) emotional intensity in the interaction, (c) the extent of "mutual confiding," and (d) the degree of "reciprocal services" performed. Krackhardt (1992) amended this set of criteria, suggesting that trust is the key element that makes strong ties important. He asserted that the strong tie requires simultaneously (a) frequent interaction, (b) affection, and (c) a history of a relationship (i.e., there is no such thing as an instant strong tie). To differentiate his definition from Granovetter's, he used the term *Philos*, the Greek word for "friend," to identify a relationship that had all three of these qualities.

These concepts have in common a focus on the dyad. Both Granovetter and Krackhardt suggested that, to determine whether a tie is strong or not, one has only to observe the interactions and sentiments between a pair of people. I extend this thinking about the importance of a strong tie by broadening the focus beyond the isolated dyad.

Simmel's Triadic Model

Simmel also focused attention on social relationships as a key to understanding how and why people behave and think as they do. Also, while others have examined structural units larger than dyads (e.g., Kadushin's [1968] "social circles"; Alba & Moore, 1983), Simmel (1950, pp. 135-169) provided the first and most thorough theoretical foundation for the idea that social triads are fundamentally different in charactor from dyads. This difference is not due simply to the fact that triads have more participants. Rather, the difference is one of quality, of dynamics, and of stability. Because this difference is key to motivating this chapter, I briefly describe the main arguments in Simmel's model.

Simmel (1950) distinguished dyads from triads on several grounds. First, he noted that dyads preserve much more individuality than triads because, within a dyad, no majority can be mustered to outvote any individual. In any group of three or larger, an individual can be outvoted by the other group members, suppressing individual interests for the interests of the larger group.

Second, individuals have much more bargaining power in a dyad than in a triad. When faced with only one other partner, the dyadic group can be dissolved if the demands of one of its members are not met. In a triad, the demanding individual can withdraw, but the group still remains as a dyad. The withdrawing individual has the most to lose by withdrawing, isolating himself or herself while the others retain each other's company. Thus, the threat of withdrawal carries less weight.

Third, conflict is inevitable in any relationship over time and is more readily managed and resolved in a triad. In a standard dyadic arrangement, conflicts escalate and positions harden. In the presence of a third party, such positions are more likely to be moderated. The third party can reformulate and present the concerns of the other parties without the harsh rhetoric and emotional overtones. As Simmel (1950, p. 145) stated, "The appearance of the third party indicates transition, conciliation, and abandonment of absolute contrast." Even if a third party does not act decisively in resolving a conflict between two parties, his or her mere presence can ameliorate dissension: "Such mediations need not occur in words: A gesture, a way of listening, the quality of feeling which proceeds from a person, suffices to give this dissent between two others a direction toward consensus" (p. 145).

Simmel (1950) focused on the triad, then, as distinct from the dyad as a unit of analysis and representative of larger structures. By defining the specific features of dyads, he was able to demonstrate how the addition of a third party produced a fundamental change in the dynamics between the original two actors. He argued, however, that adding more people to the group did not change the dynamics commensurately: "[Adding a third party to a dyad] completely changes them, but . . . the further expansion to four or more persons by no means correspondingly modifies the group any further" (p. 138). Thus, the key to understanding the quality of a tie between two actors can be reduced to asking whether it is part of a strong triad or not.

All three of the forces—toward reduced individuality, reduced individual power, and moderated conflict—contribute to the group's survival and preserve its identity at the expense of the individual, at least when compared with the isolated dyad. Thus, as a consequence of this theory, one would expect that individuals who are a part of a three-person (or more) informal group are less free, less independent, and more constrained than a person who is only part of a strong dyadic relationship.

Simmelian Tie Defined

Based on Simmel's (1950) theory of triadic structures, I define a "Simmelian tie" as follows: Two people are Simmelian tied to one another if they are reciprocally and strongly tied to each other and if they are each reciprocally and strongly tied to at least one third party in common.

This definition resembles the concept of a clique (Luce & Perry, 1949), and there is a strong symmetry between the two ideas. Cliques are defined on a graph as a maximal set of three or more nodes (people, in this case), all of whom are directly and reciprocally connected to each other. Thus, each pair of people in a clique are Simmelian tied to each other; conversely, any pair of individuals who are Simmelian tied are comembers of at least one clique. Thus, I argue here that a coclique relationship—the existence of a strong tie that is reinforced through a common tie to at least one third person—is a qualitatively different tie that deserves attention and analysis in its own right, just as Simmel (1950) argued that triads are a fundamental sociological unit. I call such a coclique relationship "Simmelian" to differentiate it from Granovetter's (or Krackhardt's) definition of a strong tie.

Durability of Simmelian Ties

Simmelian ties might be best thought of as "super-strong" ties, ties that qualitatively add durability and power beyond that found in sim-

ply strong dyads. Thus, the primary proposition that emerges from a
theory of Simmelian ties is that, once formed, Simmelian ties are
"sticky"—that is, they will last longer than other forms of merely strong
ties. Because a person Simmelian tied is less independent and less powerful, and because interpersonal conflict is more likely attenuated, people are less likely to want to or be able to sever a Simmelian tie. This
leads to two immediate predictions.[2] The first easily follows directly
from the primary proposition:

> *Prediction 1:* A Simmelian tie from actor A to actor B at any point in
> time will more likely be followed by a tie from actor A to actor
> B at a subsequent point in time than will a non-Simmelian tie.

Scott Feld (1997), in an exploration of Granovetter's concept of embeddedness, made a similar prediction. He operationalized the concept
of embeddedness between two actors as the extent to which others
nominated both actors. This is a modification of the Simmelian tie, as
defined here, for two reasons. First, Feld counts the number of alters
who nominate the two parties. The Simmelian argument, as mentioned
previously, suggests that the effect of groups larger than three is not
substantive, and therefore only a dichotomous value is used; a tie is
either Simmelian or it is not. Second, for any given pair of nodes, A and
B, Feld counts the set of third others who jointly nominate A and B; thus,
asymmetric ties are allowed. The argument here is that ties from third
others should be strong ties (reciprocated ties) to enforce "group"
norms and values. Scott did show, however, a small correlation between
the extent of embeddedness and the probability that a tie would continue to exist for 6 months.

Although it is true that one could predict specifically the subsequent existence of Simmelian ties (rather than the simple existence
of any tie), it is sufficient to show that the Simmelian ties are more likely
to be followed by any kind of tie to support the proposition. For
purposes of this chapter, I focus only on this definition of stability.

The second prediction also follows from the primary proposition
but requires more explanation:

> *Prediction 2:* Simmelian ties will occur with greater frequency than
> would be expected by chance, given the overall structure of the
> relations.

This prediction derives from two reasonable assertions about Simmelian ties. First, one may easily see that, given equal opportunity for different ties to come into existence, those that last longer will be observed more frequently at any given moment. As an analogy, suppose one were to throw a set of tennis balls in rapid succession at two walls, one green and one red. Suppose further that the green wall was covered with a particularly sticky surface such that once the balls hit the surface they stuck to the surface for as much as a minute before falling to the ground. The red wall, however, was covered with a less sticky substance so that the balls fall relatively quickly to the ground. At any given time, one would expect to see more balls on the green wall than on the red wall.

This assumes that balls are thrown equally frequently to each wall. If the number of balls thrown at the red wall far exceeds the number of balls thrown at the green wall, we may not observe more balls on the green wall despite the advantage of having a sticky surface. Also, given that Simmelian ties have more stringent requirements for their existence (there must exist three individuals, each mutually tied to each other, for even one Simmelian tie to exist from one actor to another), one might posit that they are relatively rare to begin with, thus concluding that even with relative staying power they would not overcome this initial disadvantage.

The second critical assertion, then, is that we have reason to expect from other theoretical and empirical work that Simmelian ties compensate for this initial frequency deprivation. In particular, balance theory (Heider, 1958) indirectly predicts the existence of Simmelian ties in a social system. Heider's argument is psychological in nature: People feel more comfortable with balanced triads than they do with unbalanced ones. Heider further points out that balance in social relations implies both symmetry in the relation (p. 205) and transitivity in the relation (p. 206). Thus, as people strive to make their world balanced, more transitive-symmetric triads should be observed. Davis (1968) argues that the explanation for this occurrence is even simpler: People are forced together by time and space constraints. That is, if you spend time with a friend, and the friend spends time with his or her friend, then you and that second friend are likely to find yourselves in the same place at the same time with the mutual friend, creating an opportunity for another friendship link with that second friend. Thus, without relying on Heiderian psychology, Davis also predicts Simmelian ties will tend to occur relatively frequently.

Whatever the true underlying mechanism, the empirical work of Davis and others (Davis, 1979; Davis & Leinhardt, 1972; Doreian, Kapuscinski, Krackhardt, & Sczypula, 1996; Holland & Leinhardt, 1970, 1972, 1977) has shown that transitive-symmetric triads tend to occur much more often than we would expect by chance, given the density of ties. For example, Davis (1970) reports in an overall study of hundreds of groups of people that the existence of the 3-0-0 triad (defined as all three actors mutually linked to each other) appeared statistically more frequently (relative to chance appearance given the density and reciprocity in the matrix of relations) than any of the other 15 kinds of triads that might have existed.

Although these authors did not explore the relative probability of particular kinds of ties within these structures, I take this as evidence that Simmelian ties are not so disadvantaged at the start that they cannot capitalize on their durability to be seen more frequently than would be expected by chance. Thus, I predict Prediction 2 will hold.

To examine these predictions, I analyzed the data Newcomb (1961) collected over a 15-week period in a college living group composed of 17 undergraduates. Newcomb asked each member of this group to rank order each of the other 16 people on how much they liked them (Nordlie, 1958) (a rank of "1" was assigned to the person the respondent liked best, and a rank of "16" was assigned to the person the respondent liked least). Although the rank orders are less than ideal for purposes of this chapter, the fact that they were replicated systematically for 15 weeks allows exploration of the stability of the relations over that time.

To determine if the Simmelian ties were stable over time, I had to define a tie as existing if it exceeded an arbitrary ranking threshold. In some sense, they were all friends, although Newcomb (1961) recounts that some friction developed among some of the people during parts of the study. For any given threshold, a binary friendship matrix **F** may be constructed as follows:

$$\mathbf{F}_{ij}^{t} = \begin{cases} 1 & \text{If } \mathbf{FR}_{ij}^{t} \leq \text{threshold} \\ 0 & \text{otherwise,} \end{cases} \tag{2.1}$$

where $\mathbf{FR}_{ij}{}^t$ is the ranking that person i gave to person j at period t (lower rankings indicate stronger liking).

For comparative purposes, I separated the ties into three mutually exclusive and exhaustive categories:

1. A tie $(\mathbf{F}_{ij})$ is asymmetric if and only if $\mathbf{F}_{ij} = 1$ and $\mathbf{F}_{ji} = 0$.
2. A tie $(\mathbf{F}_{ij})$ is Simmelian if and only if $\mathbf{F}_{ij} = 1$ and $\mathbf{F}_{ji} = 1$ and there exists at least one k such that all four of the following statements are true:
    i. $\mathbf{F}_{ik} = 1$
    ii. $\mathbf{F}_{ki} = 1$
    iii. $\mathbf{F}_{jk} = 1$
    iv. $\mathbf{F}_{kj} = 1$
3. A tie $(\mathbf{F}_{ij})$ is sole symmetric if and only if $\mathbf{F}_{ij} = 1$ and $\mathbf{F}_{ji} = 1$ and the tie is not Simmelian.

These definitions count ties as a set of ordered pairs of nodes. It is worth pointing out that one could have counted ties here as a set of unordered pairs of nodes, similar to the way in which Holland and Leinhardt (1972, 1975) counted unordered sets of triads in their triad census. This choice affects the counts in significant ways. For example, in the simplest case, consider the following triad:

$$A \leftrightarrow B \leftarrow C$$

One method is to claim that there are two ties represented in this equation, one symmetric (A,B) and one asymmetric (B,C). Another method is to state that there are three ordered ties: A,B and B,A, both of which are reciprocated, and B,C, which is not reciprocated. Our natural intuition is to go with the first method because our eye sees only two lines and because the latter seems to "double count" the symmetric ties. If we consider what each individual in the equation is experiencing, however, the second interpretation makes more sense. That is, in this equation, there are three critical events: (a) A sends (with commensurate intention, risk, and all that the act of sending entails) a tie to B, and A *experiences the reciprocated tie from B*; (b) B sends a tie to A, and B experiences the tie being reciprocated; and (c) B sends another tie to C, but in this case B experiences a nonreciprocation. Thus, from the actors' point of view, we count clearly three events, not two.

In the case of Simmelian ties resulting from a clique of three actors, we count six events (ordered pairs) at a time, not three. That is, the existence of a Simmelian tie embedded in a group of three, *A, B,* and *C*, requires that each of the three actors experience the constraint of the Simmelian tie with the two other actors, for a total of six events. Person *A* experiences the Simmelian constraint when considering whether to continue his or her relationship with Person *B*; separately, Person *B* experiences the Simmelian constraint when considering whether to continue his or her relationship with Person *A*. These are separate experiences and separate choices, and thus they constitute separate countable predictions. Thus, I differ with the tradition that treats un-ordered ties as countable events because the Simmelian theory, which focuses on the asymmetric action and choice of its actors, guides me to do so.

Static Test Against a Random Model

The first test was simply to determine whether Simmelian ties occurred with frequencies greater than one would expect by chance, given the structure of the Newcomb (1961) friendship patterns, and to compare these frequencies with those of other types of non-Simmelian ties. It is important to control for the structure in these comparisons because the frequency of types of ties would be heavily influenced by density (e.g., denser matrices will create more Simmelian ties by chance). To get a sense of how frequent each type of tie would be under a random model, I generated a set of 1,000 matrices[3] of several moderate thresholds (5-10).[4]

Table 2.1 shows the observed number of ties averaged across all 15 weeks for each type (asymmetric, sole symmetric, and Simmelian), the expected number of ties of each type (the mean occurrence of each type across the 1,000 simulated matrices), and the probability of finding more than the observed number of the tie type among the 1,000 randomly generated matrices (this latter number serves as a one-tailed significance test).

An interesting and consistent pattern emerges among these results. First, we compare the frequency of Simmelian ties with the frequency of non-Simmelian ties. In absolute terms, asymmetric ties were more frequent than Simmelian ties when the density was low (outdegree = 5 or 6). For all outdegrees (or densities), the appearance

TABLE 2.1 Observed and Expected Number of Ties of Each Type

	Asymmetric			Sole Symmetric			Simmelian		
Outdegree	Observed	Expected	p	Observed	Expected	p	Observed	Expected	p
5	41.13	58.61	1.000	17.07	24.13	.919	26.80	2.26	.001
6	45.20	63.89	1.000	13.87	30.61	1.000	42.93	7.50	.001
7	48.87	67.01	.999	9.47	32.92	1.000	60.67	19.08	.001
8	50.80	68.10	.999	7.33	29.13	1.000	77.87	38.78	.001
9	50.47	66.91	.994	6.40	19.91	.980	96.13	66.18	.002
10	51.33	63.73	.993	5.87	9.79	.799	112.80	96.47	.022

NOTE: The observed number of ties is the number of ties of that type observed averaged across all 15 weeks of data for the particular outdegree threshold. The expected number is the number of ties of that type averaged across all 1,000 randomly generated matrices with that particular outdegree. The p value is calculated by observing how often the number of ties in the randomly generated matrices exceeds the number of observed ties. The formula for $p = N_o + 1/N_r + 1$, where N_r is the number of randomly generated matrices and N_o is the number of those matrices in which the number of ties exceeded the number of observed ties.

of Simmelian ties was more frequent than sole-symmetric ties. Thus, under most conditions, Simmelian ties outnumber other kinds of ties, with the exception that under conditions of low density, asymmetric ties outnumber Simmelian ties.

If we compare the observed frequencies relative to what we would expect to find by chance, however, we find a much stronger picture in support of Prediction 2. In all cases, the number of occurrences of asymmetric ties and sole-symmetric ties is substantially less than we expect by chance, given the structure of the matrices. These numbers, for the most part, are strongly statistically significant. For example, the estimated expected number of asymmetric ties given an outdegree of 6 was 63.89, the average (across all 15 weeks) observed number of asymmetric ties was only 48.87, and all 1,000 randomly generated matrices exceeded this observed mean. Similarly, the estimated number of expected sole-symmetric ties with an outdegree of 6 was 30.61, the average number of observed sole-symmetric ties was only 13.87, and all 1,000 randomly generated matrices exceeded this observed mean.

By contrast, the number of observed Simmelian ties exceeded the expected number for all outdegrees reported in Table 2.1. For example, the estimated number of expected Simmelian ties when the outdegree

is 6 was 7.5; the observed average number of Simmelian ties in the
Newcomb (1961) data, however, was 42.93; and this observed value
exceeded the number of Simmelian ties in all 1,000 randomly generated matrices.

The fact that asymmetric ties do not appear in the Newcomb (1961)
data as often as would be predicted by chance is not a surprise given
the strength of the norm of reciprocity (Gouldner, 1960). That sole-symmetric ties are so statistically rare, however, is surprising. Because the
three types of ties are mutually exclusive and exhaustive, one interpretation of this finding is that Simmelian ties so dominate the landscape
that little room is left for the occurrence of sole-symmetric ties. Sub-
stantively, perhaps people tend to look not just for individual friends
but also for groups of friends with whom to associate.

Dynamic Test Against a Random Model

I now discuss the test of Prediction 1, which directly addresses the
stability of each kind of tie. Specifically, we are concerned here with
the following question: What is the probability that a tie at time t will
still be there at time t + lag?

To examine temporal stability, I calculated a conditional probability over a lagged period of time for each type of tie:

$$P_{(type;\ t;\ lag)} = \frac{N_c}{N_p} \tag{2.2}$$

where N_p is the number of ij ordered pairs wherein a tie of the desig-
nated type exists at time t (these ties are predicting the existence of a
subsequent tie), and N_c is the number of these ties that correctly predicted the existence of a tie F_{ij} at period t + lag.

Table 2.2 shows these conditional probabilities for each type of tie
when outdegree threshold = 8^5 and lag = 1 for all 14 available time
periods (Time 1 to Time 2, Time 2 to Time 3, . . . Time 14 to Time 15). In
addition to the conditional probability, the significance of this probability is reported against the null hypothesis that the results could
have been generated randomly.[6]

As Table 2.2 shows, Simmelian ties have a substantially greater
chance of predicting ties at t + 1 week than either asymmetric or
sole-symmetric ties. An asymmetric tie has an average probability of
.80 of continuing at period t + 1. Sole-symmetric ties have an average

TABLE 2.2 Proportion of Correctly Predicted Ties at $t + 1$ Weeks

	Asymmetric			Sole Symmetric			Simmelian		
Week	Proportion Correct	p	n Predicted	Proportion Correct	p	n Predicted	Proportion Correct	p	n Predicted
1	.629	.0131	62	.688	.1280	16	.845	.0001	58
2	.780	.0001	50	.800	.0856	10	.868	.0001	76
3	.795	.0001	44	.667	.2281	12	.900	.0001	80
4	.729	.0010	48	.600	.3926	10	.962	.0001	78
5	.827	.0001	52	.500	.6320	6	.974	.0001	78
6	.827	.0001	52	.750	.3366	4	.962	.0001	80
7	.827	.0001	52	1.000	.3135	2	.939	.0001	82
8	.800	.0001	50	.833	.0311	12	.959	.0001	74
9	.783	.0001	46	.750	.3409	4	.895	.0001	86
10	.760	.0001	50	1.000	.3264	2	.929	.0001	84
11	.875	.0001	48	.750	.1762	8	.913	.0001	80
12	.833	.0001	54	.833	.1420	6	.974	.0001	76
13	.875	.0001	48	.667	.3681	6	.976	.0001	82
14	.900	.0001	50	.750	.1642	8	.897	.0001	78

Average proportion correct and n predicted across all 14 weeks of predictions
    Asymmetric: proportion correct = .8029, n = 50.43
    Sole-Symmetric: proporation correct = .7562, n = 7.57
    Simmelian: proporation correct = .9281, n = 78.00

NOTE: Proportion correct is the fraction of the tie type in period t that corresponded to an existing tie at time period $t + 1$. p is the significance level as determined by the number out of 999 random permutations of the matrix of ties at $t + 1$ that equaled or exceeded the proportion of correctly predicted ties. n Predicted is the total number of ties of a particular type at time t—which equals the number of ties conditionally predicted to exist at time $t + 1$.

probability of continuing at period $t + 1$ of .76, which is slightly less than that of asymmetric ties. Simmelian ties, however, have an average probability of continuing of .93, which is substantially higher than those of either asymmetric or sole-symmetric ties. The probability of asymmetric ties ranged in predictive probability from .63 (Week 1) to .9 (Week 14). The probability of sole-symmetric ties varied much more, ranging from .5 to 1.0. Simmelian ties, however, had the narrowest range of predictive ties: .85 (Week 1) to .98 (Week 13). Indeed, in all but 1 of the 14 time periods, Simmelian ties predicted better than asymmetric ties; in all but 2 of the 14 time periods, Simmelian ties predicted better than sole-symmetric ties.

TABLE 2.3 Proportion of Correctly Predicted Ties at $t + 8$ Weeks

	Asymmetric			Sole Symmetric			Simmelian		
Week	Proportion Correct	p	n Predicted	Proportion Correct	p	n Predicted	Proportion Correct	p	n Predicted
1	.516	.4515	62	.563	.4131	16	.741	.0009	58
2	.640	.0187	50	.500	.5996	10	.737	.0002	76
3	.636	.0426	44	.333	.8877	12	.825	.0001	80
4	.750	.0002	48	.500	.6163	10	.821	.0001	78
5	.712	.0007	52	.500	.6379	6	.897	.0001	78
6	.750	.0001	52	.500	.6466	4	.925	.0001	80
7	.808	.0001	52	1.000	.2986	2	.866	.0001	82

Average proportion correct and n predicted across all 7 weeks of predictions
    Asymmetric: proportion correct, .6874, $n = 51.43$
    Sole symmetric: proportion correct = .5565, $n = 8.57$
    Simmelian: proportion correct = .8303, $n = 76.00$

NOTE: Proportion correct is the fraction of the tie type in period t that corresponded to an existing tie at time period $t + 8$. p is the significance level as determined by the number out of 999 random permutations of the matrix of ties at $t + 8$ that equaled or exceeded the proportion of correctly predicted ties. n Predicted is the total number of ties of a particular type at time t—which equals the number of ties conditionally predicted to exist at time $t + 8$.

When t – lag = 8 (Table 2.3), one finds fewer predictive successes, as one would expect. It is more difficult for any tie to remain predictive over 8 weeks than over 1 week. Asymmetric tie predictive rate drops to .69, sole-symmetric tie predictive rate drops to .56, and Simmelian tie predictive rate drops to .83. The differential advantage of Simmelian ties over the other two types of ties, however, increases substantially.

The advantage that Simmelian ties have over asymmetric ties and sole-symmetric ties in predicting future ties appears to have increased as the time between periods expands. To demonstrate this further, I plotted in Figure 2.1 predictive probabilities for each type of tie for each lag (lag = 1-14) averaged across the weeks for which predictions could be made. Note that as the time interval increases, the rate at which Simmelian ties reduce their predictive power does not diminish as quickly as the rate at which either the asymmetric or the sole-symmetric ties reduce their predictive power. The durability advantage that Simmelian ties enjoyed holds with the passage of time.[7]

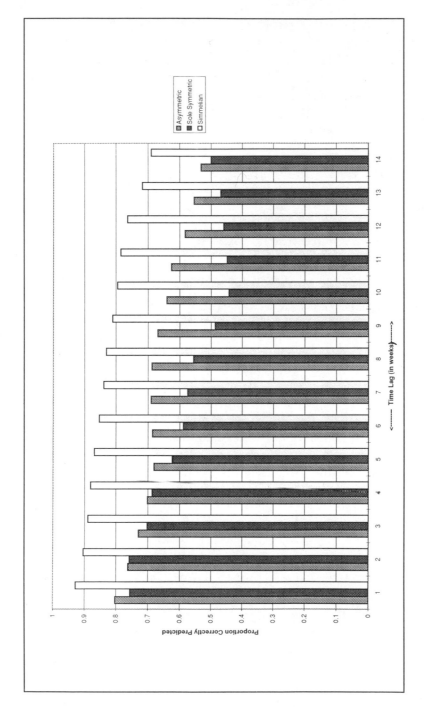

Figure 1. Proportion of Each Type of Tie Correctly Predicting Ties at *t* + lag

Concluding Remarks

In this chapter, I have argued that Simmelian ties are qualitatively different from simple, dyadic ties that networkers normally focus on. They represent more than strong ties consistent with Granovetter's theory. They are ties backed up by the normative power of groups, providing stability beyond that experienced by bridges or isolated dyads. We should expect stronger predictions from these ties when compared to sole-symmetric ties, a distinction ignored by Granovetter's (1973) strong ties or Krackhardt's (1992) Philos ties.

One should not consider this chapter an argument for doing away with traditional analysis on raw network relations. Such analyses are necessary to uncover weak ties and bridges between groups. As Burt (1992) has so ably demonstrated, those actors who are not embedded in cliques may find themselves in particularly advantageous positions. Rather, I believe that we enhance our chances of understanding organizational systems by separating out Simmelian ties and making separate predictions about them. In pursuing both the very strong ties and the bridging ties Granovetter and Burt emphasize, we may find that structural analysis provides us with more insight into organizational phenomena.

Notes

1. Even Granovetter (1982) admitted that there are reasons to view strong ties as providing, at a minimum, more motivation than weak ties in many cases.

2. I use the term *prediction* instead of the more formal *hypothesis* because of the technical difficulty in formally testing these predictions. The technical difficulty stems from the age-old problem of dyadic network data not obeying the critical independence-of-observations assumption required of all standard hypothesis tests (Laumann & Pappi, 1976; Proctor, 1975). Although I will employ permutation tests that will address some of these problems (Krackhardt, 1988), one might quibble with whether the null hypothesis in these tests is appropriate, given that the comparison of interest is between Simmelian ties and other kinds of ties and not simply against a random null model. This is particularly true of Prediction 1. Thus, the reader should keep in mind that these predictions will be "tested" in a less formal sense. A true statistical test of these predictions awaits further development of these statistical techniques.

3. Each 17×17 matrix was generated by randomly and independently permuting each row of 0's and 1's. Each random matrix not only contained the same density for a given threshold but also contained the same outdegree for each row. For example, in the case in which the threshold = 8, each row of each simulated matrix contained exactly eight

1's and eight 0's. This method most closely approximates the constraints on the values the Newcomb (1961) data could take on.

4. This range of threshold values was selected because they provided a reasonable stability to the results. Thresholds of less than 4 resulted in some of the observed matrices containing no Simmelian ties, and therefore no test of stability could be computed. Thresholds of more than 10 resulted in the opposite problem: In some of the observed matrices, no sole-symmetric ties were observed, meaning that no comparative assessment could be performed. The threshold values between 5 and 10 gave predominantly similar results to each other, indicating a fair degree of robustness. Thus, I restricted the current analysis to thresholds between 5 and 10 in this chapter, and so I report only these frequencies and expected frequencies in Table 2.1.

5. I chose a threshold of 8 to simply demonstrate the effect. Any reasonable value could have been used. Other neighboring threshold values did not make appreciable differences in the results. I calculated the numbers in Tables 2.2 and 2.3 and Figure 2.1 of all threshold values from 5 to 10, and the overall results obtain.

6. The exact test of this prediction was conducted by permuting the rows and columns of the matrix of observed relations at Time t + lag and recalculating p (as given in Eq. [2.2]) under each permutation. The observed p was compared to this reference distribution of P's calculated under 999 permutations of the target matrix. This test not only preserves the outdegree of the matrix for each permutation but also preserves the entire structure of the matrix—including the extent to which choices are reciprocated and the extent to which some choices are more popular than others. This type of test has been shown to be generally applicable to a wide range of statistical problems (Hubert, 1987) and robust against such structural features in the data (Krackhardt, 1988). As noted earlier, however, it is only a test against a random null; it is not a test that allows us to state statistically that Simmelian ties last significantly longer than other ties.

7. The average was calculated for all available weeks for which a prediction can be made. For example, for lag = 1, 14 different prediction probabilities were made (Week 1 predicting Week 2 . . . Week 14 predicting Week 15). The average is across these 14 weeks of predictions. For lag = 14, however, there was only 1 week of prediction (Week 1 predicting Week 15), so the "average" is based on 1 week's set of observations.

References

Alba, R. D., & Moore, G. (1983). Elite social circles. In R. S. Burt & M. J. Minor (Eds.), *Applied network analysis: A methodological introduction* (pp. 245-261). Beverly Hills, CA: Sage.

Burt, R. S. (1992). *Structural holes: The social structure of competition.* Cambridge, MA: Harvard University Press.

Davis, J. A. (1968). Social structures and cognitive structures. In R. P. Albelson, E. Aronson, W. J. McGuire, T. M. Newcomb, M. J. Rosenberg, & P. H. Tannenbaum (Eds.), *Theories of cognitive consistency: A sourcebook.* Chicago: Rand McNally.

Davis, J. A. (1970). Clustering and hierarchy in interpersonal relations: Testing two theoretical models in 742 sociograms. *American Sociological Review, 35,* 843-852.

Davis, J. A. (1979). The Davis/Holland/Leinhardt studies: An overview. In P. W. Holland & S. Leinhardt (Eds.), *Perspectives on social network research* (pp. 51-62). New York: Academic Press.

Davis, J. A., & Leinhardt, S. (1972). The structure of positive interpersonal relations in small groups. In J. Berger et al. (Eds.), *Sociological theories in progress* (Vol. 2). Boston: Houghton-Mifflin.

Doreian, P., Kapuscinski, R., Krackhardt, D., & Sczypula, J. (1996). A brief history of balance through time. *Journal of Mathematical Sociology, 21*, 113-131.

Feld, S. L. (1997). Structural embeddedness and stability of interpersonal relations. *Social Networks, 19*, 91-95.

Gouldner, A. W. (1960). The norm of reciprocity: A preliminary statement. *American Sociological Review, 25*, 161-179.

Granovetter, M. (1973). The strength of weak ties. *American Journal of Sociology, 78*, 1360-1380.

Granovetter, M. (1982). The strength of weak ties: A network theory revisited. In P. Marsden & N. Lin (Eds.), *Social structure and analysis*. Beverly Hills, CA: Sage.

Granovetter, M. (1994). *Getting a job* (2nd ed.). Cambridge, MA: Harvard University Press.

Heider, F. (1958). *The psychology of interpersonal relations*. New York: John Wiley.

Holland, P. W., & Leinhardt, S. (1970, November). A method for detecting structure in sociometric data. *American Journal of Sociology, 70*, 492-513.

Holland, P. W., & Leinhardt, S. (1972). Some evidence on the transitivity of positive interpersonal sentiment. *American Journal of Sociology, 72*, 1205-1209.

Holland, P. W., & Leinhardt, S. (1975). Local structure in social networks. In D. R. Heise (Ed.), *Sociological methodology*. San Francisco: Jossey-Bass.

Holland, P. W., & Leinhardt, S. (1977). Transitivity in structural models of small groups. In S. Leinhardt (Ed.), *Social networks* (pp. 49-66). New York: Academic Press.

Hubert, L. J. (1987). *Assignment methods in combinatorial data analysis.* New York: Dekker.

Kadushin, C. (1968). Power, influence, and social circles: A new methodology for studying opinion makers. *American Sociological Review, 31*, 786-802.

Krackhardt, D. (1988). Predicting with networks: A multiple regression approach to analyzing dyadic data. *Social Networks, 10*, 359-381.

Krackhardt, D. (1992). The strength of strong ties: The importance of philos in organizations. In N. Nohria & R. Eccles (Eds.), *Networks and organizations: Structure, form, and action* (pp. 216-239). Boston: Harvard Business School Press.

Krackhardt, D., & Brass, D. (1994). Intra-organizational networks: The micro side. In S. Wasserman & J. Galaskiewicz (Eds.), *Advances in the social and behavioral sciences from social network analysis* (pp. 209-230). Thousand Oaks, CA: Sage.

Krackhardt, D., & Stern, R. (1988). Informal networks and organizational crises: An experimental simulation. *Social Psychology Quarterly, 51*, 123-140.

Laumann, E. O., & Pappi, F. U. (1976). *Networks of collective action: A perspective on community influence systems*. New York: Academic Press.

Lincoln, J. R., & Miller, J. (1979). Work and friendship ties in organizations: A comparative analysis of relational networks. *Administrative Science Quarterly, 24*, 181-199.

Luce, R. D., & Perry, A. D. (1949). A method of matrix analysis of group structure. *Psychometrika, 14*, 95-116.

Nelson, R. E. (1989). The strength of strong ties: Social networks and intergroup conflict in organizations. *Academy of Management Journal, 32*, 377-401.

Newcomb, T. N. (1961). *The acquaintance process*. New York: Holt, Rinehart & Winston.

Nordlie, P. H. (1958). *A longitudinal study of interpersonal attraction in a natural group set-ting*. Unpublished doctoral dissertation, University of Michigan, Ann Arbor.

Proctor, C. H. (1975). Graph sampling compared to conventional sampling. In P. W. Holland & S. Leinhardt (Eds.), *Perspectives on social network research* (pp. 301-318). New York: Academic Press.

Roethlisberger, F. J., & Dickson, W. J. (1939). *Management and the worker*. Cambridge, MA: Harvard University Press.

Simmel, G. (1950). Individual and society. In K. H. Wolff (Ed.), *The sociology of Georg Simmel*. New York: Free Press.

3

Sticky Ties and Bad Attitudes

*Relational and Individual Bases
of Resistance to Change in
Organizational Structure*

KATHLEEN L. VALLEY
TRACY A. THOMPSON

Dictating formal structure is a critical medium of control in complex organizations. Through prescribed reporting and production structures, management compels certain ways of getting the work of the organization accomplished and imposes certain constraints on the other ways of completing that same work. Although management

AUTHORS' NOTE: The authors are grateful to James Evans for his very able research assistance. We could not have completed this research without him. We are also thankful to John Morford, Maggie Neale, Jim Sebenius, Dick Walton, FSC, and numerous participants in seminars at which this work was presented for their honest and insightful suggestions. This research was funded by a research grant from the Harvard Business School.

39

has the legitimate power to dictate and change formal organizational structure, employee resistance to change can hinder management's structuring and restructuring efforts. In this chapter, we investigate the extent to which management's power to set a new organizational structure is checked by employee resistance, and we explore both individual and relational sources of resistance. Several questions form the basis of our inquiry: Will the emergent, task-based social structure after a restructuring be more closely related to management's ideal or to the social structure in place prior to the restructuring efforts? In addition, we explore specific individual and relational sources of resistance to structural change: What individual and relational forces determine resistance? How do the forces at the individual level interact with those at the relational level?

Scholars of organizational structure have long debated the relationship between formal, prescribed structure and informal, emergent structure (Blau, 1955; Giddens, 1977; March & Olsen, 1976; Ranson, Hinings, & Greenwood, 1980; Weick, 1976). Early research on structure was often founded in Weber's (1947) treatise on bureaucracy and offered formal structure as the determining influence on organizational functioning. Little, if any, attention was given to the emergent structure arising out of the day-to-day operations of the organization. Alternatives to the Weberian view (Blau, 1955; Crozier, 1964; Merton, 1940) pointed out the extent to which emergent patterns of interaction differed from formal structure, reflecting instead the wills and preferences of individual members. Bringing the two views into one frame, Weick (1976) and March and Olsen (1976) argue that the actual pattern of interaction within an organization results from a complex recursive relationship between formal (prescribed) structure and the informal (emergent) behavior of the organization's members.

Although inroads have been made, the views are not yet fully reconciled or integrated beyond general agreement that (a) the two forms of structure influence and are influenced by one another and (b) longitudinal, empirical work is needed to clarify the complex interweaving of prescribed and emergent structure. In this chapter, we use longitudinal data from one organization to explore the "constituted and constitutive" (Ranson et al., 1980, p. 3) connection between prescribed and emergent structures.

Individual and Relational Sources
of Resistance

Resistance can result from either active opposition or passive friction. Although some resistance is conscious and intentional (Barbalet, 1985), other types of resistance may occur without active intent simply because of the difficulty in changing "routine-based and history-dependent" behavior (Levitt & March, 1988). Diamond (1986, p. 544) argues that human behavior in times of change is "compulsive, repetitive, security-oriented, and self-sealing." Building from these observations, we argue that active and passive resistance can stem from both individual and relational variables.

Resistance at the individual level can come from at least two sources: attitudes toward the change and the extent to which a person's new job includes new task demands. Diamond (1986) argues that resistance is ignited when attitudes are negative, or competence and security are threatened. Although organizational research has explored how social interaction and structure influence attitudes (Berger & Cummings, 1979; Dean & Brass, 1985; Erickson, 1988; Ibarra & Andrews, 1993; Salancik & Pfeffer, 1978) and how attitudes affect behaviors (Bell & Staw, 1989), this research provides little guidance as to how held attitudes will affect social structure. An early social psychological theory sheds some light on the question: Sarnoff, Katz, and McClintock (1965) assert that individual attitudes serve as the link between a person's feelings and perceptions regarding a change or novel object and the behavior displayed toward that change or object. Attitudes help people make sense of new facets of their environment, linking each new item into a belief set that transmits value and drives behavior. This view of attitudes suggests that in times of change, if members of the organization embrace the change or believe the change will benefit them, they may quickly adapt to new working systems in line with management's dictate. Negative attitudes toward the change should have the opposite effect, decreasing the likelihood that the new social structure will be adapted as prescribed.

The extent to which an individual is subjected to new task demands can also create resistance. Some people's jobs are objectively more affected by an organizational restructuring than are others'. The more an individual's tasks are altered, the more likely skills will be underdeveloped and the greater the need for acquiring competence. Tichy (1983) and Diamond (1986) both argue that these conditions will increase the likelihood of individual resistance to change. Resistance as ego defense is tapped into when one is faced with new tasks, decreasing the likelihood of compliance in individuals facing major job changes.

In addition to individual level sources of resistance, we also explore two relational influences on resistance: previous ties that run counter to management's planned structure—"sticky ties"—and previous ties that are congruent with management's planned structure—"greasy ties." Resistance at the relational level is founded in the ingrained habits of past social interaction. Mandating changes in social ties create passive resistance or inertia—that is, resistance that results naturally whenever attempts are made to change the pattern of interacting away from the currently stable social structure. Prescribed changes demand alterations or adaptations in social routines, which normally evolve very slowly. In many organizational routines, people rely on one another for successful completion of individual tasks; they interact with certain people in certain ways during the passage of a workday. Trust and reliability are built up over time, and even when management dictates otherwise, people may continue to "stick" to their old task-based social ties to help them get things done rather than turning to new, untried partners for support. Thus, resistance results to the extent that the new organizational structure requires people to sever existing task-based relationships.

Not only are the old relations hard to let go, it is also difficult to develop new ones. If the new formal structure builds on existing task-based ties, this existing "social grease" will make it easy for workers to increase the frequency or strength of interaction within those ties. In contrast, if the new structure requires interaction where there was no previous task-based relationship, the initial passive resistance may be substantial as individuals take time to test the reliability of new relations.

There is likely to be an interaction between the individual and relational sources of resistance, but it is difficult to predict the direction of these effects. Organizational research provides strong evidence of the effects of social interaction and structure on attitudes (Berger &

Cummings, 1979; Dean & Brass, 1985; Hartman & Johnson, 1989; Ibarra & Andrews, 1993; Rice & Aydin, 1991) but gives little guidance for predicting the potential interaction between the two levels of variables and the resultant effects on compliance with organizational change. Studies investigating the effects of individual variables in strong versus weak situations provide some insight, suggesting that group influence on behavior will be more influential in strong situations than in weak situations, in which individual attributes will be more determinate (Mischel, 1977). In times of organizational restructuring, however, the social structure and social demands of the situation are changing. It is difficult to ascertain, a priori, how strong the situation is likely to be. We therefore treat the investigation into interaction effects as exploratory: We expect individual and relational sources to have interactive effects on resistance but make no predictions regarding directionality.

To summarize our approach, the research questions addressed in this chapter concern the tension between management's power to prescribe organizational structure and individual and relational sources of resistance. We attempt to answer these questions through longitudinal field research in a metropolitan newspaper undergoing a change in organizational structure—a move from traditional hierarchical departments to more focused "teams."

Study Background

We investigate the attempts of one organization to alter its organizational routines and structures. To examine our questions about resistance to change, we use data from a longitudinal field study of a newspaper called *The Range*,[1] a metropolitan newspaper with a daily circulation of approximately 130,000 and an additional 20,000 readers on Sunday. *The Range* is owned by a large, publicly traded newspaper group. Although there is no direct newspaper competition in the metropolitan area, management is concerned with other competitive media products and the decline of readership penetration (percentage of the adult population in the area that subscribes). In the year prior to the reorganization, circulation growth had not kept up with population growth.

We took advantage of a "natural experiment" at *The Range,* in which, literally overnight, members of the newsroom were placed into a new organizational structure. Management established "topic teams" and eliminated the traditional "desks" or "beats" that had constituted the organizational structure since the birth of the newspaper. The stated goals of this shift to a team-based production model were to democratize content decisions and to encourage reporters and editors to think more strategically. In the words of the executive editor, the restructuring was an attempt to help reporters "think more like publishers." In this way, the restructuring efforts represent a philosophical change as well as a structural change.

The restructuring efforts at *The Range* mirror those at many other newspapers across the country. Revolutions in technology and changing consumer tastes have led newspapers to adopt new, more reader-oriented strategies. Newspapers are gradually moving from a journalism model, in which the reporters and editors decide what the reader "should" want, to a marketing model, in which customer tastes and preferences drive the selection and placement of news stories. In the spirit of Chandler's (1962) "structure follows strategy" model, newspapers have begun to change the production process of news, presumably in an attempt to better execute a new, more reader-oriented strategy.

The Change Process

The process of planning the changes in structure began 6 months prior to the final restructuring. A majority of employees in the newsroom participated, studying structural changes in other newsrooms and making recommendations regarding the substance of topic teams' coverage. Social psychology research (Coch & French, 1948; Lewin, 1965) provides unambiguous evidence that active group participation in decisions regarding change facilitates successful adaptation. The high level of participation in the planning process should decrease the aggregate level of resistance to the change because the substance of the change will reflect more of the preferences of those affected and because the process of the change is likely to be viewed more positively. The active participation of newsroom members was a process consciously chosen by management to increase buy-in and to help ensure that the policies chosen were optimal.

There was general, although not universal, agreement among the members of the newsroom that the new topic teams better reflected reader interests than did the traditional beats. Despite active engagement in the planning process, however, many of the newsroom employees, especially reporters, were skeptical of the move toward a marketing-based strategy. Left largely unsaid during the planning process was the reality that restructuring into teams would take away much of the coveted individualism of the reporters within the newsroom.

Viewed from an external perspective, resistance to the change in formal structure was to be expected, but the sources and extent of that resistance were not immediately clear. Our theoretical investigation into the issue and our observation of the newsroom suggested that a member's resistance to the change in formal structure would be influenced by his or her individual attitude toward the change, the extent to which his or her tasks were altered in the change, and the structure of his or her prior task-based ties.

Changes in Structure and Work Flow

Before the restructuring, the executive editor oversaw two managing editors, who, in turn, oversaw the reporting desks and functional departments. The newsroom had four desks, each composed of one to three layers of desk editors (supervisors) and reporters covering a basic type of news story—metropolitan news, business, features, and general assignment. In addition, there were three functional departments—copyediting, art, and photography.

The work flow was sequential across desks and functional departments. Within a desk, the reporter received an assignment from a desk editor, wrote the story with input from the editor, and then passed it back to the editor. At this point, when the editor sent the text to the copy department, the story left the reporter and the desk. Copy editors worked in isolation from the desk as they tightened prose and added headlines. The copy department also included page designers who added graphics and photos and formatted the article onto the page. Assistant managing editors were then responsible for getting the paper to production by deadline. Overall, decisions at each step were made independently by whomever was controlling the story at that stage.

In the new formal structure, the newsroom is overseen by two "coordinators" who report to the executive editor. The layers of desk editors have been eliminated and replaced with one supervisory layer, "topic team leaders." The functional departments still exist, but copyediting has been split into two distinct teams—presentation and editing.

The traditional content areas were modified to focus the reporters on the interests of local readers. Nine new topic teams were created to sharpen this focus. Each team is assigned a specific type of story and point of view to emphasize. For example, one team is assigned to report on jobs, employment, and work in the metropolitan area, and its charter is to focus on issues of interest to a consumer (i.e., a reader) rather than report generally about the larger economy.

Work flow in the newsroom was modified so that the emphasis is on integration rather than sequential access. Reporters are more involved with the production of the story and are encouraged to work collectively with their team members and functional staff when making decisions about stories. Similarly but to a lesser degree, functional staff are expected to make their decisions about editing and presentation in concert with reporters and team leaders. Concurrent with the dictate of a new organizational structure, members of the newsroom moved into a new seating arrangement so that the members of each team were in close proximity to one another.

A critical feature of the work in this newsroom, as in all daily newspapers, is the extreme time sensitivity of most tasks. At the beginning of the 10-hr shift in which a newspaper is produced, only advertisements are already produced and placed; at the end of the shift, more than 100,000 copies of the paper are shipped out across the distribution area. A few news stories and editorials are complete before a shift begins, but the vast majority of the editorial content of a newspaper is created within a single shift. (Observing this rate of production is a humbling experience for academics used to 2-year turnarounds.) There are numerous deadlines within a shift: photo deadlines, color deadlines, "wire" deadlines,[2] inside story deadlines for reporters and for copy editors, front page deadlines for reporters and copy editors, layout deadlines, and production deadlines. Content and placement of stories are discussed or argued by editors and representatives of each team in two daily news meetings, but final decisions are often made minutes before each deadline. Although there is a general mood of congeniality in the newsroom studied, there is little idle conversation.

Design and Data Collection

The findings presented in this chapter are part of a larger longitudinal study of relational and individual influences on organizational functions across time. The data used in answering the questions presented in this chapter were gathered through observation, interviews with management, attitude surveys, and sociometric surveys. Employees were surveyed at two points in time: 2 weeks before the organizational restructuring (Time 1) and 2 months after the change (Time 2).[3]

Sixty-four people were physically present in the central part of the newsroom at the time of the study. This number excludes those whose primary office was outside the central newsroom and those who operated solely out of satellite offices. Survey response rates at Times 1 and 2 were 94.9% and 86.5%, respectively. Responses from the executive editor and the coordinating editors were omitted from the analyses because these editors were the management representatives dictating the change and would not be expected to resist. Two reporters worked as rovers and did not have clearly prescribed interaction structures; their data were also not used in the analyses. Because the analyses require data from both time periods, we include only those observations in which all survey data are complete at both collection periods; thus, 14 observations were removed. In the final analyses, we use data from 46 observations or 76.7% of the central newsroom employees.

Independent Measures

We develop independent measures at two levels to operationalize the individual and relational constructs in our theoretical arguments. At the individual level, we create measures of the attitudes regarding the change and of the extent to which the tasks carried out by each individual were altered in the reorganization. At the relational level, we develop two measures reflecting the prechange social structure of the newsroom.

Data on individual attitudes were collected via a survey given to members of the newsroom 2 weeks prior to the reorganization. The members responded to the following statements:[4]

1. "In your opinion, the change to a team structure in the newsroom is a good idea" (1-7 scale, where 1 = strongly disagree, 4 = neutral, and 7 = strongly agree).
2. "In your opinion, the change to a team structure in the newsroom will result in" (1-7 scale, where 1 = a much worse news product, 4 = no noticeable change in news product, and 7 = a much better news product).
3. "In your opinion, the change to a team structure in the newsroom will result in" (1-7 scale, where 1 = a much worse working environment, 4 = no noticeable change in working environment, and 7 = a much better working environment).

A Cronbach's alpha test showed the three statements could reliably be treated as one scale (α= .858). Therefore, we averaged the responses from the three statements to produce one measure of attitude regarding the upcoming change. The resulting measure of attitudes toward the change in organizational structure varies from 1 (consistent and strong negative attitudes toward the change) to 7 (consistent and strong positive attitudes toward the change). We expect resistance to the new formal structure to be negatively associated with individual attitudes regarding the change—that is, more positive attitudes toward the change will decrease resistance.

To measure individual job change, we created an individual level measure of the extent to which the tasks required for a person's job prior to the restructuring matched those required subsequent to the change. Job change is a trichotomous measure, where 1 is no change in job assignment; 2 is a moderate change in job, such as shifting to a new and unfamiliar reporting beat; and 3 is a significant change in job, such as moving from being a reporter to being a team leader. These data were gathered through personnel records and interviews with the coordinators prior to the reorganization, after all job assignments had been determined. Of the 64 newsroom staff, 12 faced significant job change subsequent to the reorganization, and 25 faced moderate job change. Because significant job change decreases feelings of competence and increases ego-enhancing defenses, we expect greater job change to result in higher levels of resistance.

The relational-level independent variables were derived from self-reports of interaction with others in the newsroom. In sociometric surveys distributed 2 weeks prior to and 2 months after the reorganization, each person was asked to consider his or her interaction with others in the newsroom and then to answer the following questions:

1. "At work, in person, how often do you interact with this person on job-related issues?"
2. "How often do you rely on this person for task-related support?"
3. "How significant is this person to your overall productivity in the newsroom?"[5]

The first two questions were answered on a 1 to 7 Likert scale, where 1 = never, 3 = a few times weekly, 5 = a few times daily, and 7 = constantly. The third question was answered on a 1 to 7 Likert scale, where 1 = not at all and 7 = critical. Thus, the sociometric data are valued (i.e., scores vary by the strength of the relationship) rather than dichotomous (i.e., scores = 1 if a tie is present and = 0 if no tie is present). Across both time periods, the data revealed high correlations between task-based interaction, helping interaction, and critical work interaction (Cronbach's alpha = .932 at Time 1 and .941 at Time 2). Therefore, at each time period we averaged the scores from these three measures into a single measure reflecting task-based ties.

The two relational independent variables were derived from this three-item average of task-based ties. The first measure, sticky ties, uses a modified form of a centrality measure and thus operationalizes the overall structure of an individual's relationships prior to the change. To calculate sticky ties, we summed each worker's task-based ties with all others in the newsroom, excluding task-based ties with those who will be in the actor's team subsequent to the change. A high value indicates that the individual is closely tied with a relatively large number of others outside his or her new team, whereas a low value indicates few strong ties to others outside the new team. This measure is called sticky ties to indicate that we expect strong ties to people other than one's new team members to increase resistance to the change. Sticky ties present a source of friction to the prescribed structural change, making compliance less likely. Subsequently, we predict that resistance to the new formal structure will be positively associated with the value of sticky ties.

The second independent measure at the relational level, greasy ties, operationalizes the preexisting task-based social ties that provide avenues for compliance to a new social structure. We calculated greasy ties as the average of reported task-based ties, prior to the reorganization, between an actor and all other actors assigned to the same Time 2 team (i.e., the average strength of the task-based ties with all future teammates, as reported by a focal actor at Time 1). This measure is called greasy ties to indicate that we expect strong prior ties to future team members to provide social grease, reducing friction and decreasing passive resistance to the change. Thus, we predict that resistance will be negatively associated with the strength of greasy ties.

To control for spurious association between Time 1 interaction and Time 2 compliance, created by possible variance in similarities between past workplace ties and postchange prescribed interaction, we also created a control variable from the sociometric data. The control variable, "Time 1 actual with Time 2 prescribed," is the correlation between actual interaction at Time 1 and prescribed interaction at Time 2. Alternatively, we could have calculated the correlation between Time 1 prescribed structure and Time 2 prescribed structure, but this would be misleading and would underestimate the similarities across the two time periods: For example, the prescribed structure for a reporter was to talk only with his or her immediate superior and no one else, but this was not the normal method of accomplishing tasks for any of the reporters. "Time 1 actual with Time 2 prescribed" controls for the possibility that there were differences in the extent to which the restructuring actually placed demands on newsroom employees to change their task-based interaction.

Dependent Measures

We created two dependent measures to operationalize resistance or the extent to which the members of the newsroom followed management's dictate. The first measure, within-team compliance, operationalizes resistance to the mandate to interact actively within teams. We calculated the strength of each worker's task-based ties within his or her newly assigned team 2 months after the change, relative to his or her task-based ties in the newsroom as a whole. Specifically, we measure within-team compliance as the average strength (1-7, where 7 is strongest) of the individual's task-based ties with others in his or her team divided by the average strength of his or her task-based ties outside the team. This provides an estimate of the extent to which each individual is working within the team structure dictated by management while controlling for overall sociability or involvement in the task network of the newsroom. High scores on this variable indicate low levels of resistance, whereas low scores indicate high levels of resistance.

The second dependent measure, match, operationalizes resistance to the broader change in organizational structure. We calculated match as a correlation between an individual's prescribed interaction in the new formal structure and his or her actual task-based ties subsequent to the change. This quantifies the extent to which the individual's overall interaction complies with management's dictate. Prescribed interaction patterns were determined through an iterative interview process with the executive editor and one of the two newsroom co-ordinators. We asked them to describe what the task-based interaction in the newsroom would be if the restructuring were completely successful. Using their answers, we created a sociomatrix, in which the value in each cell reflected the intended level of interaction between the row actor and the column actor. The executive editor and one coordinator then reviewed the matrix and suggested changes where our interpretations did not meet their intentions. We revised the sociomatrix according to their suggestions and used this revised matrix as our "prescribed" matrix. The dependent variable, match, is the correlation between an individual's prescribed interaction vector and his or her reported task-based ties. Consistent with the interpretation of within-team compliance, high scores on the match variable indicate low levels of resistance, whereas low scores indicate high levels of resistance.

Results

Before discussing our research questions, we first present the means, standard deviations and the simple pairwise correlations across all variables (Table 3.1). Greasy ties, average strength of Time 1 ties to Time 2 team members, are highly and positively correlated with the

TABLE 3.1 Variable Descriptives and Correlations

Descriptive statistics	Mean (N = 46)	SD
T1 actual correlation with T2 prescribed	.326	.247
Job change (1–3)	1.956	.918
Attitudes (1–7)	4.710	1.190
Sticky ties (sum)	131.116	35.567
Greasy ties (average)	3.066	1.306
Attitude[a] × sticky[a] interaction	13.112	42.975
Attitude[a] × greasy[a] interaction	.136	1.890
T2 within team compliance	2.293	.752
Match-T2 actual and prescribed	.616	.140

Correlations	1	2	3	4	5	6	7
1. T1 actual with T2 prescribed	1.000						
2. Job change	−.241	1.000					
3. Attitudes	.248*	.169	1.000				
4. Sticky ties	.237	−.165	.381**	1.000			
5. Greasy ties	.638**	−.396**	.161	.479**	1.000		
6. Within team compliance	.060	.207	−.062	−.270*	.145	1.000	
7. Match-T2 actual and pre-scribed	.120	.466**	.242	−.030	−.018	.495**	1.000

a. Normalized variable.
*Correlation is significant at the .10 level (two-tailed).
**Correlation is significant at the .01 level (two-tailed).

control variable, Time 1 actual with Time 2 prescribed. This is to be expected because individuals with higher levels of prechange interaction with their soon-to-be team members have a closer fit between what they were actually doing in Time 1 and what the restructuring prescribes for them in Time 2. Similarly, job change is negatively and significantly correlated with greasy ties; higher values of job change result when an actor is taken out of his or her current position and assigned to interact with a new task group. Attitudes at Time 1 are positively and significantly correlated with sticky ties at Time 1: Those who are more central in the task-based network are more likely to have a positive attitude about the change. Sticky ties are positively and significantly correlated with greasy ties, suggesting that some people are generally more social than others. Job change has significant pairwise correlations with the match-dependent variable.

The two dependent variables were designed to operationalize the same construct, resistance to (or, conversely, compliance with) the new organizational structure. Within-team compliance operates at the within-team level, whereas match operates at the newsroom level. As expected, the two dependent variables operationalizing the emergent structure are significantly correlated, although they are far from identical. Those who resist working closely with their new team members also tend to resist working within the dictates of the newly organized larger structure.

The first question we explore in the analysis is whether employee resistance can neutralize management's power to change emergent structure through a change in formal structure. To investigate this, we computed the correlation between self-reported task-based ties and prescribed interaction at Time 2 and compared this association to the correlation between self-reported task-based ties across Time 1 and Time 2. In other words, we checked to see whether emergent task-based structure subsequent to the change is more like the newly prescribed structure or more like the informal task-based structure of the past. If employee resistance outweighs management's power, the correlation of actual interaction across time should be noticeably greater than the cross-sectional correlation between actual and prescribed structures at Time 2. At the newsroom level, the correlation between actual interaction at Time 2 and prescribed interaction at Time 2 is .617 ($SD = .140$, $p < .01$), suggesting that employees are complying to a significant degree with the dictates of management. Also at the newsroom level, the correlation between self-reported interaction at Times 1 and 2 is .578 ($SD = .244$, $p < .01$), suggesting there is also a substantial overlap between one's pattern of task-based interaction before the restructuring and one's pattern after the restructuring. The correlation between Time 1-reported task-based ties and prescribed interaction at Time 2 at the newsroom level is .314 ($SD = .259$). Hence, the overlap is due partially to similarities in past interaction and present formal structure but also partially to resistance. The power of management has not been completely thwarted, but there does appear to be resistance in action.

To address the questions regarding the roles of individual and relational influences on resistance, we tested four models for each dependent variable (Tables 3.2 and 3.3). Because of high multicollinearity when multiplicative terms are used in regression analyses with

TABLE 3.2 Regression Models Explaining Within-Team Compliance

| | Model | | | | | | | |
| | 1 | | 2 | | 3 | | 4 | |
	B Coefficient (SE)	β (t)	B Coefficient (SE)	β (t)	B Coefficient (SE)	β (t)	B Coefficient (SE)	β (t)
(Constant)	1.644 (.371)	(4.432)***	1.875 (.346)	(5.416)****	1.868 (.356)	(5.254)****	1.796 (.320)	(5.617)****
T1 fit with T2 prescribed	.528 (.496)	.174 (1.065)	−.340 (.568)	−.112 (−.598)	−.330 (.580)	.109 (−.570)	−.135 (.527)	−.045 (−.257)
Job change	.242 (.134)	.295 (1.798)*	.271 (.130)	.331 (2.091)**	.275 (.136)	.336 (2.029)**	.288 (.119)	.351 (2.410)**
Attitudes[a]	−.104 (.104)	−.165 (−.999)	−.005 (.102)	−.007 (−.044)	−.007 (.105)	−.001 (−.064)	−.025 (.094)	−.039 (−.262)
Sticky ties[a]			−.010 (.004)	−.458 (−2.753)***	−.009 (.004)	−.459 (−2.721)***	−.007 (.003)	−.322 (−2.005)*
Greasy ties[a]			.327 (.119)	−.568 (2.737)***	.328 (.121)	.570 (2.702)***	.196 (.119)	.340 (1.647)
Attitudes[a] × sticky[a]					−.000 (.003)	−.017 (−.119)		
Attitudes[a] × greasy[a]							−.158 (.055)	−.398 (−2.874)***
F — model	$F_{(3, 42)} = 1.178$		$F_{(5, 40)} = 2.932$*		$F_{(6, 39)} = 2.386$*		$F_{(6, 39)} = 4.264$***	
R^2	.078		.268		.268		.396	
F change			5.210***		.014[b]		8.262***	

a. Normalized variable.
b. Relative to Model 2.
*$p < .10$; **$p < .05$; ***$p < .01$; ****$p < .001$

54

TABLE 3.3 Regression Models Explaining Match Between Prescribed and Actual Structure

	Model							
	1		2		3		4	
	B Coefficient (SE)	β (t)	B Coefficient (SE)	β (t)	B Coefficient (SE)	β (t)	B Coefficient (SE)	β (t)
(Constant)	.440 (.060)	(7.294)****	.449 (.063)	(7.134)***	.473 (.060)	(7.858)****	.456 (.062)	(7.296)****
T1 fit with T2 prescribed	.111 (.081)	.197 (1.383)	.080 (.103)	.142 (.780)	.049 (.098)	.086 (.496)	.062 (.103)	.109 (.599)
Job change	.072 (.022)	.474 (3.296)***	.073 (.024)	.479 (3.095)***	.059 (.023)	.388 (2.567)**	.071 (.023)	.469 (3.058)***
Attitudes[a]	.017 (.017)	.145 (1.003)	.021 (.019)	.177 (1.120)	.029 (.018)	.243 (1.604)	.023 (.018)	.193 (1.229)
Sticky ties[a]			-.000 (.0001)	-.094 (-.575)	-.000 (.001)	-.077 (-.501)	-.001 (.001)	-.161 (-.955)
Greasy ties[a]			.012 (.022)	.110 (.543)	.007 (.021)	.067 (.346)	.024 (.023)	.223 (1.024)
Attitudes[a] × sticky[a]					.001 (.000)	.319 (2.492)**		
Attitudes[a] × greasy[a]							.015 (.011)	.197 (1.349)
F — model	$F_{(5, 42)} = 5.777$***		$F_{(5, 40)} = 3.424$**		$F_{(6, 39)} = 4.186$***		$F_{(6, 39)} = 3.215$**	
R^2	.292		.300		.392		.331	
F change			.217		5.900**[b]		1.821[b]	

a. Normalized variables.
b. Relative to Model 2.
*$p < .10$; **$p < .05$; ***$p < .01$, ****$p < .001$

main effects, Cronbach (1987) and Jaccard, Turrisi, and Wan (1990) suggest using normalized main effect variables in the multiplicative term and the associated main effect terms. Following this method, we normalized the attitude, sticky ties, and greasy ties variables by subtracting the respective mean from each observation. The regressions reported throughout this section use the normalized variables as the main effect terms and their products as the interactive terms.

Model 1 tested the prediction that resistance to management's power to determine emergent structure lies fundamentally at the individual level. Job change and individual attitudes regarding the change are entered along with the control for the correlation between Time 1 interaction and the new prescribed structure.[6] Model 2 tested the prediction that resistance to management's power has important determinants at both individual and relational levels. Sticky ties and greasy ties are entered simultaneously with the individual level variables in the equations. Finally, Models 3 and 4 tested the prediction that individual attitudes interact with relational variables to create significant resistance to management's power to change interaction patterns. In Model 3, the interaction between individual attitudes and sticky ties is added and the results are compared to those of the main effect model (Model 2). Similarly, in Model 4, the interaction between individual attitudes and greasy ties is added to the equation and the results are compared to those of the main effect model.[7]

Table 3.2 shows the effects of individual and relational variables on "within-team compliance," the strength of individuals' Time 2 ties to their newly assigned team members, relative to their overall levels of task-based interaction within the newsroom. Low levels of compliance with the dictate to interact as a team are indicative of higher levels of resistance. In Model 1, the overall regression testing the effects of individual variables alone is not significant. Individual variables appear to have little independent effects on resistance within a newly formed team. Model 2 produces a significant increase in fit compared to model 1 (F change $[2, 40] = 5.210$, $p < .01$). The overall regression is significant, explaining 26.8% of the variance in the strength of within-team ties. The change in squared multiple correlations indicates that 19% of the variance in within-team compliance is due to one's prior relations with others in the organization. Sticky ties have a significant and negative effect, as predicted, indicating that strong prior ties with many people outside one's new team are likely to inhibit within-team interaction. Greasy ties have a significant and positive effect, also as predicted, indicating that within-team interaction is facilitated by prior ties with new team members. Both these effects are very strong despite the control for the amount of overlap between one's prior overall task network and one's prescribed task network subsequent to the restructuring. With the inclusion of the relational variables, job change now exhibits a significant effect in a positive direction, opposite that hypothesized. In Model 3, we added the interaction term between attitudes and sticky ties. The variance explained remains at 26.8%, and the regression is only marginally significant, indicating that the main effects model (Model 2) is a better fitting model.

In Model 4, we added the interaction term between attitudes and greasy ties to the main effects model. The results show this to be the best fitting model of the four. This interaction model produces significantly better fit than the main effects model (F change [1, 39] = 8.262, $p < .01$) and increases the variance explained to 39.6%. The strength of the interaction effect can be seen in the difference between the squared multiple correlation for the interaction model and that of the main effects model: The interaction between greasy ties and attitudes accounts for a notable 12.8% of the variance in within-team compliance. The main effects for greasy ties and attitudes are not significant. The main effect for sticky ties remains negative and marginally significant ($p = .052$). Effects for job change remain positive and significant.

To examine the interaction more closely, we treated attitudes as the moderator variable and trichotomized it at one standard deviation above and below the mean and then graphed the effects on within-team tie strength at Time 2 (Figure 3.1). The results are striking: The effects of greasy ties on within-team compliance are flat for those with neutral or positive attitudes, but for those with negative attitudes more greasy ties lead to significantly higher levels of compliance.

Table 3.3 shows the effects of individual and relational variables on match, the correlation between prescribed interaction and emergent interaction across the newsroom. Model 1 shows strong support for the effects of individual variables. The overall regression is highly significant, explaining 29.2% of the variance in the dependent measure. The effects are driven by the strong, positive influence of job change on match—that is, once again contrary to predictions, job change

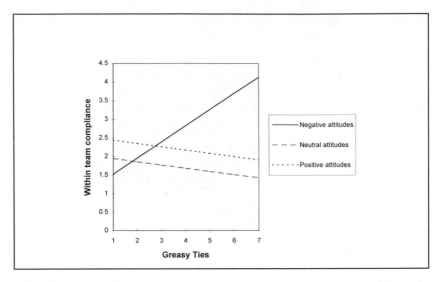

Figure 3.1. Within-Team Compliance: The Interactive Effects of Attitudes and Greasy Ties

decreases resistance. Adding the relational variables in Model 2 provided no additional explanatory power over the individual variables alone (F change $[2, 40] = .217, p > .1$).

The fit is significantly increased when the interaction between attitudes and sticky ties is added in Model 3 (F change $[1, 39] = 5.900$, $p < .05$). The interaction explains an additional 9.2% of the variance, raising the R^2 to .392. Job change remains positive and significant. Once again, we treated attitudes as the moderator variable, trichotomizing it one standard deviation above and below the mean to index the interaction effect. The results are presented graphically in Figure 3.2. For those with average attitudes toward the change, prior ties have no effect on the match between prescribed structure and actual task-based interaction. For those with strongly positive or negative attitudes, however, sticky ties have a significant effect on match. For individuals with positive attitudes toward the change, many strong prior ties to nonteam members increase the match between prescribed and emergent interaction; in contrast, many sticky ties decrease the match when attitudes toward the change are negative. Model 4, which adds the interaction between attitudes and greasy ties to Model 2, provides no significant increase in fit over the main effects model.

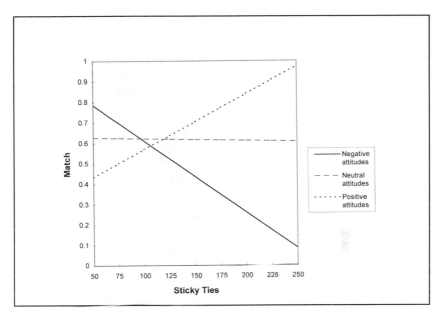

Figure 3.2. Match Between Time 2 Actual Ties and Prescribed Structure: The Interactive Effects of Attitudes and Sticky Ties

In summary, for both dependent variables, the best fitting model is one that includes the effects of an interaction between individual attitudes and a social variable. The associated social variable differs across the two dependent variables. An interaction model including the interaction between greasy ties and attitudes provides the best fit when the dependent variable is within-team compliance, explaining 39.6% of the variance in resistance to the team structure. When the dependent variable is the post-restructuring correlation between actual interaction and prescribed interaction across the newsroom, the best fit is provided by an interaction model including the interaction between sticky ties and attitudes. This model explains 39.2% of the variance in resistance to the larger formal structure.

Discussion

We began our study by asking two basic questions: Can employee resistance neutralize management's power to change social structure by changing the formal organizational structure? and What roles do individual sources and relational sources of resistance play? Our results provide strong support for the contention that employee resistance plays an important role in power relations during organizational change. Employee resistance counters, but does not eliminate, management's power to change social structure. The analyses we present illustrate clearly that resistance stems from both individual and relational sources, and that these sources interact with one another to shape the emergent social structure within the organization.

Regarding the first question, our data show that actual interaction patterns are a function of both formal organizational arrangements (in this case, management's changes in those arrangements) and the existing social structure. Patterns of task-based interaction are not completely impervious to manipulation, but neither are they completely malleable. The relative success of this restructuring effort may be, in part, due to the high level of group involvement in the change process because groups that participate in change efforts are more likely to comply with the new order (Coch & French, 1948). Because of this, we present a conservative test of employee resistance and a generous test of compliance: Resistance in organizations in which the changes are determined less participatively is likely to be greater, whereas compliance is likely to be reduced. Returning to our original question about power and resistance, management appears to possess some power to alter routines, but that power is limited by resistance rooted in the deep structure of the organization.

Having established that at least some resistance is present, using our second set of analyses we attempted to understand more about the various sources of that resistance. Just as researchers have challenged the notion of power being an individual trait or characteristic (Pfeffer, 1981), we challenge the notion that resistance stems only from individual factors or only from structural factors. Our data show sources of resistance at the two levels have an interactive effect on management's ability to implement structural change.

We proposed two individual-level predictors—attitudes regarding the restructuring and the amount of job change experienced in the tasks performed by the individual. We also proposed two relational predictors—sticky ties, prechange ties with others who are not on one's team subsequent to the reorganization, and greasy ties, prechange ties to one's future team members. To isolate individual and relational sources of resistance to change, we developed two correlated but distinct measures of employee adaptation. Within the team, we examined individual and relational influences on the degree to which individuals were in fact interacting more closely with their new team members than with other newsroom members subsequent to the reorganization. Across the organization (the newsroom in this case), we tested for effects on the correlation between prescribed and actual task-based ties. Not only were individuals asked to interact intensely with the members of their new team but also they were expected to develop different relationships with others in the newsroom—for example, copy editors, other team leaders, the newsroom coordinators, and the executive editor. Our second measure of compliance takes this broader mandate into account.

Employee attitudes toward management's change initiatives showed little effect on resistance when considered independently of social variables. The influence of attitudes becomes clear only when simultaneously considering the individual's location in the prior social network. At the within-team level, strong prior ties to new team members facilitate interaction within the new team for those with negative attitudes toward the change. At the newsroom level, prior ties to others in the newsroom facilitate acceptance of the larger formal structure for those with positive attitudes toward the change but decrease acceptance for those with negative attitudes toward the new structure. Taken together, these results suggest that a full understanding of resistance must include a consideration of how relational and individual sources of resistance interact to influence the emergent structure of a changing organization.

Examining the interactions in more detail provides some insights into the mechanisms behind these effects. Greasy ties and attitudes interact to create a substantial effect on resistance to the team structure: A history of strong social ties to one's new teammates mitigates the effects of individually held negative attitudes. In fact, those with highly negative attitudes toward the change and strong prior ties to new team members exhibited the least resistance to working within their new teams. These people did not "buy in" to the change overall, but they found it comfortable to work with others whom they already knew well. Although the change whirled about them, they found solace in the familiarity of their new team. One reporter who was strongly against the change but knew most of the people in her new team stated, "I personally feel more isolated from the rest of the news-room, except within my team."

In contrast to the interactive effects of greasy ties and attitudes on within-team compliance, it is sticky ties and attitudes that interact to determine compliance with the larger organizational structure. For those individuals who report positive attitudes toward the change, strong prechange ties to people outside one's future team increase the match between prescribed and emergent structures. For people with negative attitudes toward the change, the opposite is true—stronger external relations decrease compliance. They seem to resent the man-date to interact less with their tried and true coworkers. One person stated, "Restructuring has made me feel more competitive . . . against other people and other teams." Although strong and wide-ranging task-based ties provide a mechanism for compliance for those who are accepting of a change, for those who are negative toward a change these ties provide an anchor for resistance.

Changes in workers' tasks had the opposite effect of what we predicted: More change in tasks led to greater acceptance of the new structure. Many reporters in the newsroom underwent significant change in job tasks. Some reporters changed to new and unfamiliar beat topics, areas of expertise with which they had little familiarity. Others moved from being a reporter to being a team leader and there-fore had to learn a new set of managerial tasks. We expected that these changes would generate anxiety over a potential lack of skills and fear of incompetence. Such changes have been found in prior studies to lead to strongly held ego-enhancing attitudes (Sarnoff et al., 1965) and have been argued to lead to increased resistance (Tichy, 1983). Instead, we found a slight positive correlation between job change and attitude and a strong negative relationship between job change and resistance.

To obtain a finer, and possibly more revealing, analysis of the effects of job change, we ran additional regressions representing job change with two dummy variables in the fully fitted models. The results revealed that for both within-team compliance and across-newsroom match, those with little or no change in their specific task were significantly more likely to resist the new structure than were those facing moderate or significant change. Post hoc, there appear to be several factors that can explain these effects, factors that we failed to consider in our initial assessment. First, the job assignments were voluntary in nature: Individuals listed their top three job choices in the newsroom, and estimates given by management indicate that nearly 60% got their first or second choice. Second, for individuals voluntarily taking on a new job, being asked to interact with new people in a new structure was only an incremental adjustment. Both types of adjustment were likely seen as parts of a larger change. In contrast, those who remained in their current job were doing the same things, so asking them to do it in a different way with different people was likely to be more ego threatening and create greater resistance. Finally, many of these reporters had been doing essentially the same job for years. Perhaps these reporters were bored and a change in task was welcomed, irrespective of their attitudes toward the larger structural change. Our understanding of resistance would be enhanced if future research could tease apart the different effects of change in the task itself versus change in the larger structure. The voluntary nature of changes in individual job assignments may be an important contingent variable.

Because organizational change occurs across time, the analyses we performed have important temporal components that could only have been addressed using longitudinal data. Attitude and relational variables were based on survey and sociometric responses gathered 2 weeks prior to the restructuring, whereas the dependent measures of postchange structure were collected through sociomatrices completed 2 months after the change. Job change compares tasks being performed by individuals prior to the change to those assigned in the restructured organization. Similarly, the control variable for overlap in social structure across time correlates past task-based ties with ties prescribed in the new structure. It is often necessary to collect network data at one point in time and ask people to recall whether the ties were present or absent at some given point in the past (Podolny & Baron, 1997) or how long the tie has been in place (Burt, 1992). This is appropriate for many questions but is problematic for tracing changes in social structure. Our data offer significant advantages beyond the typical cross-sectional investigations of power and influence in exploring structural change across time and sorting out direction of causation. Even two time periods, however, can be problematic. Because difficulties in causal inference may exist when only two time periods are used (Finkel, 1995), future research on structural change should test the robustness of these effects by collecting data at multiple time periods.

This research contributes useful knowledge about power and resistance during times of organizational change. It also provides new insights into emergent social structure. Results reveal a complex relationship between emergent social structure and prescribed social structure, with management's power being limited by individual factors as well as relational factors. Important interactions across levels further influence power relations. Information regarding individuals' attitudes toward change as well as information about the routines embedded in the workplace can be used to inform the prescribed changes in structure. These efforts can minimize resistance and, in turn, may lead to an emergent structure that more closely follows the prescribed formal structure.

If a reorganization requires deep shifts away from current social structures, the social system may create blocks in the implementation of management's prescriptions, most notably for those individuals who do not believe in the value of the change. Influencing behavior entails more than formal power and more than just winning over people's minds; it depends on understanding how current social structure interacts with minds and hearts to influence people's ability and willingness to do things a different way.

Notes

1. The name of the paper has been changed to provide confidentiality to the organization and the individual respondents.

2. "Wire" stories are those purchased from one of the major national wire services (e.g., the *New York Times* and Associated Press). Wire stories are adapted by staff at the local paper to fit the local reader and space requirements.

3. Data from three subsequent time periods were also collected but were not used in this study.

4. Two open-ended questions were also asked. The responses to these questions are not used in this analysis.

5. Three other questions regarding expressive interaction and use of alternative media were also included in the survey. The responses to these questions are not used in this study.

6. Because job change is a trichotomous measure, we tested for linearity. The results show that there is significant linearity in the variable. We also tested all the models using two dummies for the job change variable. The results were not qualitatively different: All the same variables were significant at approximately the same level in all eight equations. We therefore chose to present the less complex equations, treating job change as an interval variable.

7. The correlation between the two interactions terms is .758, suggesting that multicollinearity, and hence interpretability, would be a problem if both were entered in the same equation.

References

Barbalet, J. M. (1985). Power and resistance. *British Journal of Sociology, 36,* 531-548.

Bell, N. E., & Staw, B. M. (1989). People as sculptors versus sculpture: The roles of personality and personal control in organizations. In M. B. Arthur, D. T. Hall, & B. S. Lawrence (Eds.), *Handbook of career theory* (pp. 232-251). Cambridge, UK: Cambridge University Press.

Berger, C. J., & Cummings, L. L. (1979). Organizational structure, attitudes, and behaviors. In B. M. Staw (Ed.), *Research in organizational behavior* (Vol. 1, pp. 169-208). Greenwich, CT: JAI.

Blau, P. M. (1955). *The dynamics of bureaucracy.* Chicago: University of Chicago Press.

Burt, R. (1992). *Structural holes.* Cambridge, MA: Harvard University Press.

Chandler, A. D., Jr. (1962). *Strategy and structure.* Cambridge: MIT Press.

Coch, L., & French, J. R. P., Jr. (1948). Overcoming resistance to change. *Human Relations, 1,* 512-532.

Cronbach, L. (1987). Statistical tests for moderator variables: Flaws in analysis recently proposed. *Psychological Bulletin, 102,* 414-417.

Crozier, M. (1964). *The bureaucratic phenomenon.* Chicago: University of Chicago Press.

Dean, J., Jr., & Brass, D. (1985). Social interaction and the perception of job characteristics in an organization. *Human Relations, 38,* 571-582.

Diamond, M. A. (1986). Resistance to change: A psychoanalytic critique of Argyris and Schon's contributions to organization theory and intervention. *Journal of Management Studies, 23,* 543-562.

Erickson, B. H. (1988). The relational basis of attitudes. In B. Wellman & S. D. Berkowitz (Eds.), *Social structures: A network approach* (pp. 99-121). New York: Cambridge University Press.

Finkel, S. E. (1995). *Causal analysis with panel data.* Thousand Oaks, CA: Sage.

Giddens, A. (1977). *Studies in social and political theory.* London: Hutchinson.

Hartman, R. L., & Johnson, D. J. (1989). Social contagion and multiplexity: Communication networks as predictors of commitment and role ambiguity. *Human Communication Research, 15,* 523-548.

Ibarra, H., & Andrews, S. B. (1993). Power, social influence, and sense making: Effects of network centrality and proximity on employee relations. *Administrative Science Quarterly, 38,* 277-303.

Jaccard, J., Turrisi, R., & Wan, C. K. (1990). *Interaction effects in multiple regression.* Newbury Park, CA: Sage.

Levitt, B., & March, J. G. (1988). Organizational learning. *Annual Review of Sociology, 14,* 319-340.

Lewin, K. (1965). Group decision and social change. In H. Proshansky & B. Seidenberg (Eds.), *Basic studies in social psychology* (pp. 423-437). New York: Holt, Rinehart & Winston.

March, J. G., & Olsen, J. P. (1976). *Ambiguity and choice in organizations.* Bergen, Norway: Universitetsforlaget.

Merton, R. K. (1940). Bureaucratic structure and personality. *Social Forces, 18,* 560-568.

Mischel, W. (1977). The interaction of person and situation. In D. Magnusson & N. S. Endler (Eds.), *Personality at the crossroads: Current issues in international psychology.* Hillsdale, NJ: Lawrence Erlbaum.

Pfeffer, J. (1981). *Power in organizations.* Marshfield, MA: Pitman.

Podolny, J. M., & Baron, J. N. (1997). Relationships and resources: Social networks and
    mobility in the workplace. *American Sociological Review, 62,* 673-693.
Ranson, S., Hinings, B., & Greenwood, R. (1980). The structuring of organizational struc-
    tures. *Administrative Science Quarterly, 25,* 1-17.
Rice, R. E., & Aydin, C. (1991). Attitudes toward new organizational technology: Network
    proximity as a mechanism for social information processing. *Administrative Sci-
    ence Quarterly, 36,* 219-244.
Salancik, G., & Pfeffer, J. (1978). A social information processing approach to job attitudes
    and task design. *Administrative Science Quarterly, 23,* 224-253.
Sarnoff, I., Katz, D., & McClintock, C. (1965). Attitude-change procedures and motivating
    patterns. In H. Proshansky & B. Seidenberg (Eds.), *Basic studies in social psychology*
    (pp. 121-129). New York: Holt, Rinehart & Winston.
Tichy, N. (1983). *Managing strategic change: Technical, political and cultural dynamics.* New
    York: John Wiley.
Weber, M. (1947). *The theory of social and economic organization.* New York: Oxford Univer-
    sity Press.
Weick, K. E. (1976). Educational organizations as loosely coupled systems. *Administrative
    Science Quarterly, 21,* 1-19.

Political Alignments in Organizations

Contextualization, Mobilization, and Coordination

SAMUEL B. BACHARACH
EDWARD J. LAWLER

This chapter develops a framework for conceptualizing and analyzing enduring political alignments in organizations. We address the following key questions: (a) What processes promote political alignments, in particular ones that are likely to be recognized and identifiable by members of an organization? and (b) What are the major forms of political alignment? Repeated coalitions among the same actors are the central mechanism that generates enduring, identifiable political alignments. The power relations within and between coalitions determine the nature of the political alignments. Overall, political alignments are construed as microinstitutions that generate coordinated efforts to influence organizational strategy, policies, and practices.

AUTHORS' NOTE: The authors thank Valerie McKinney for critical assistance and comments on the manuscript.

Defining Organizational Politics

It is probably an understatement to say that the existing literature on organizational politics is highly fragmented and piecemeal. Although there have been a number of broad theoretical works (Bacharach & Lawler, 1980; Clegg, 1990; Minztberg, 1983; Pettigrew, 1973; Pfeffer, 1981), they all approach organizational politics from their own perspective, without taking account of each other. Unlike many other areas of organizational theory (e.g., institutional theory and organizational ecology), there is little active dialogue across the various perspectives and no core set of problems or issues that have been subjected to empirical analysis or theoretical debate. As a result, there is relatively little coherence, much less cumulative theory and research, within the organizational politics tradition.

There is an array of interesting empirical works on organizational politics in a number of disciplinary areas, including political science, education administration, international relations, and social work, but there is little dialogue or cross-fertilization across these disciplines. "Organizational politics" in this literature is a broad rubric of disconnected concepts and research studies, unified primarily by the vague notion that power and influence are important issues for research and theorizing. After more than 30 years of periodic bursts of interest—at least since Cyert and March (1963)—there are few hints of an emerging or developing "political theory of organizations" or an approach that stands alongside resource-dependence, institutional, or organizational ecology theories.

A pervasive problem for scholars interested in organizational politics is the conception of the phenomenon itself. What are the domain boundaries of organizational politics? What is not subsumed by this term? How does one discern what is and is not political action? Answers to these questions have run the gamut. Some approaches cast organizational politics as the use of "nonsanctioned" means and ends; others treat it as upward forms of influence or as self-serving tactics of influence such as ingratiation (Ferris et al., 1993; Ferris, Russ, & Fandt, 1989; Mayes & Allen, 1977; Mintzberg, 1983; Porter, Allen, & Angle, 1981); still others conceptualize politics as decision criteria that produce departures from rational decision making (Pfeffer, 1981). All these definitions treat organizational politics as beyond or on the fringe of formally rational and legitimate modes of operation in an organization. We define organizational politics more broadly as follows: Organizational politics are the efforts of individuals or groups in organizations to mobilize support for or opposition to organizational strategies, policies, or practices in which they have a stake or interest.

Organizational politics, therefore, are at the center of organizational processes and a principal way that "people things get done" in organizations rather than being limited to the unsanctioned or nonrational domains. "Power" is the key resource used and the "objects" it is directed at are longer term organizational directions (strategy), rules for achieving shorter term objectives (policy), and the informal, customary "ways of doing things" in the organization (practices).

We have argued elsewhere (Bacharach & Lawler, 1980) that any broad theory of organizational politics should be based on the analysis of power, power perception, and power tactics. Thus, our perspective on organizational politics is embedded in a power framework; that is, we accept that power is the critical niche for any political theory of organizations, and that any such theory must be explicit on the role of power. Also, we accept that intentional, goal-directed action in organizations is based partly on the desire to enhance power capabilities and to use these power capabilities to impact strategies, policies, and practices. Accordingly, we treat political action as purposive behavioral moves or countermoves to influence the perceptions of others and thus, at least indirectly, to influence organizational policies, strategies, and practices.

From a political perspective, organizations are arenas in which actors are interdependent, purposive (instrumental or goal-oriented), and take into account the actual and prospective actions of others inside and outside of the organization (responsiveness). Organizations are created to serve some sort of collective purpose or interest (Olson, 1965), however, and as a result, organizational members do not just take account of their own interests and those on which they are dependent; they also take account of the collective endeavor, whether they work in support or in opposition to prevailing collective goals. Indeed, the cognitive aspects of taking the collective into account—namely, the organization as a whole—differentiate political action taken by an actor as a member of an organization from many other forms of political action. That is, our analysis of political action in organizations is based on three key assumptions: (a) Actors (individuals or groups) want to influence strategies, policies, and practices likely to impact their interests; (b) their interests and their view of what is collectively rational for the organization are intertwined; and (c) they develop, maintain, and use power to promote strategies, policies, and practices viewed by them as in their own or the organization's interests or both.

Embedded in these three assumptions is an "action" orientation rather than a purely structural orientation to organizational politics. In the tradition of Max Weber, we view organizational politics as the actions of actors that, although framed by the structural context and often constrained by personality, exist in the domain of volitional action. For Weber, the key to organizational politics is the notion of "meaningful social action" (the basic unit of Weberian sociology)—that is, the subjective meaning that actors give to their positive and negative decisions (Aron, 1987, p. 282). The meanings of these social actions are constantly negotiated and renegotiated within organizations. A Weberian might claim that organizations are political because structures cannot predict all situations, leaving much uncertainty in the midst of which meaning and action are negotiated by the participants. Thompson (1967) placed such uncertainty at the center of organizational life:

> Uncertainty appears as a fundamental problem for complex organizations, and coping with uncertainty, as the essence of the administrative process. Just as complete uncertainty and randomness is the antithesis of purpose and of organization, complete certainty is a figment of the imagination. (p. 159)

The combination of uncertainty and bounded rationality (i.e., the fact that cognitive limits make it impossible for any individual to make purely rational decisions on the basis of complete information) has important consequences. The criteria that are applied in making decisions and the methods used to carry out tasks are always the source of ambiguity and conflict and subject to negotiation. Furthermore, under the assumption of bounded rationality, it becomes difficult to specify all goals and means; therefore, ambiguous goals and means become subject to negotiation by organization members. The selection of goals, means, and the strategy to achieve them becomes a source of ambiguity and thus a potential focus for political action within organizations (Bacharach & Mundell, 1993; Bacharach, Mundell, & Masters, 1995; Pfeffer, 1981).

Many tactics for using power involve acting alone (Blegen & Lawler, 1989; Kipnis & Schmidt, 1983; Lawler & Bacharach, 1976), but many also involve acting in concert with others. Our focus is the latter—joint action with others. The primary purpose of this chapter is to theorize how political alignments come about, what forms they take, and what consequences they have for those included in them and for the larger organization. Political alignments are emergent microinstitutions. We specifically develop the concept of "political alignments" to capture the enduring relations that promote action in concert with the same others repeatedly.

Political alignments constitute a structural or relational context for mobilizing joint, collective action in support of certain organizational strategies, policies, or practices over others and for combating efforts of competitors to achieve advantageous power positions in the organization. Individuals are the catalysts or key actors in political processes, but subgroups and the alignments among them are a critical foundation. Individuals have goals, are responsive to others, and are aware of their identity and responsibility as organizational members. Political action essentially promotes collective goals and interests in line with those of individuals and their subgroups. Thus, it is important to stress that organizational politics are manifest, empirically, in the actions of individuals. To influence organizational strategies, policies, or practices, individuals make several decisions or choices: whether to act alone or with others, how to mobilize resources or others, and how to coordinate or align their actions with others. There are three main problems: contextualization, mobilization, and coordination.

The first problem faced by an individual attempting to influence the organization is whether to act alone or in a group. We term this "contextualization." The power and influence of any single actor—whether a group or individual—is limited by the fact that there are many individuals and groups in organizations, and each needs the support and cooperation of at least some others to significantly shape organizational strategies, policies, or practices toward their own interests. This, of course, may be more characteristic of decentralized than centralized organizations, but it likely applies to the latter as well. Finding others with similar values or policy preferences, anticipating where opposition will come from, and devising tactics that will overcome or mitigate that opposition are essential tasks for actors attempting to change or, for that matter, prevent changes in, organizational strategy, policy, or practices. We term this the "problem of contextualization," the process by which individuals take into account the context of the actions of others and the organization itself and assess the utility of not acting, acting alone, or acting in concert with others.

The mobilization issue is essentially a question of how to use the resources available for the purpose of influencing organizational policies. The resources involved in acting alone include individual properties, such as knowledge, experience, and persuasiveness, and positional properties, such as authority. The mobilization question is how to put these to use, tactically, for the desired ends. The resources involved in acting with others are known social similarities, interpersonal ties, and social networks. Coalitions are the primary method of collective mobilization, and they essentially transform adherents or proponents (e.g., those individuals "on similar wavelengths") into allies or constituents—that is, individuals who recognize their common interests and are willing to devote resources (time, phone calls, and contacts) to a common effort (McCarthy & Zald, 1977). Coalitions develop against a backdrop of structural differentiations, including departmental or divisional memberships, job categories or hierarchies, professional affiliations, seniority, demographics (age distributions), and social identities (ethnicity and gender), all of which constrain and define the interests and preferences that actors have regarding the organizational strategies, policies, or practices. Many coalitions are tacit and hidden from view (Bacharach & Lawler, 1980; Cyert & March, 1963).

The third problem faced by actors is coordination—how to align individual or coalitional actions with anticipated actions (or reactions) from other individuals, groups, or coalitions in the organization. For coalitions to form and be effective, they need to solve the problem of how to produce enough joint benefit in terms of influence in the organization beyond what individual actors anticipate they could receive from going it alone. Coordination entails transaction costs. Minimally, these are the time and effort that could be devoted elsewhere, but greater transaction costs may be incurred to resolve disagreements, to introduce more explicitness into tacit understandings, or to guard against opportunism by one or more participants. Political alignments are a microinstitutional "solution" to the coordination problem. Such alignments are defined as ongoing alliances involving mutual expectations of joint action among the same actors on multiple issues over time. Alignments emerge from repeated coalitions among the same actors across time, and they are likely to be widely inferred (or suspected) but unacknowledged patterns of coordination built on perceived similarities, ties, and trust. Alignments economize on transaction costs by being readily available means for individual actors to jointly influence organizational strategies, policies, and practices and do so without much explicit negotiation or exchange. They can be construed as informal, subtle institutions that regularize coalitional responses to future issues. Political alignments essentially are an institutionalized substratum of organizations.

In our framework, contextualization, mobilization, and coordination are key moments in an organizational political process, indicating how individual interests are transformed into coordinated group action that affects the strategies, policies, and practices of an organization. Contextualization, mobilization, and coordination are key junctures or crossroads leading toward or away from organizational change. We address these three moments on a theoretical level, asking three questions: (a) What are the bases on which actors form or join coalitions in organizations? (b) How do coalitions mobilize resources (people, effort, and ties)? and (c) How do coalitions transform interdependent actors with differential power into ongoing political alignments that can be called on easily and quickly when important issues emerge in an organization? To address the first question, we integrate and apply notions of subjective expected utility to decisions about whether to attempt influence. To address the second question, we distinguish four coalition processes: insulation, cooperative exchange, absorption, and negotiated exchange. To answer the third question, we suggest how coalitions and political alignments are promoted by relative and mutual dependencies among potential allies.

Expected Utility Theory

A simple way to examine why individuals join coalitions is to compare the magnitude of the resources controlled by individual actors to that of the resources controlled by the coalition. In this context, we could easily hypothesize that the greater the proportion of total organizational resources controlled by an actor, the less likely it is for that actor to join a coalition. An actor who is critical to the production process (e.g., one who has control of a key technology and is not easily replaceable) may be very influential in organizational decisions and therefore not likely to join a coalition. High resources imply high influence, which is inversely proportional to the likelihood of joining a coalition. Only when actors are convinced that a coalition will have greater influence in organizational decisions than they would individually are they likely to join the coalition. This rational-choice process can be captured parsimoniously by treating expected utility as a cognitive schema by which actors make this calculation.

Subjective expected utility theory assumes that in any relationship, parties attempt to maximize their gains, but built into this assumption is the idea that actors in organizations operate, for the most part, in a "live-and-let-live" world. As long as their gain is maximized, they care little about the gains of others. They cooperate when needed and compete when needed. In an analysis of organizational politics, such an orientation seems particularly important. On the one hand, it assumes that no organizational actor is particularly interested in the total annihilation of other actors in the organization. On the other hand, it assumes that actors will not go out of their way to cooperate on every issue for the sake of organizational harmony and the gain of the total organization. Some issues will push actors to close cooperation or to competition. We assume, however, that organizational actors generally operate somewhere between cooperation and competition. This means that actors will view resources as neither zero-sum nor infinite.

A second assumption of subjective utility theory is that actors will subjectively attach a utility to different lines of action by estimating the magnitude of outcomes attached to each option and weighing these magnitude estimates by the probability of achieving these outcomes. In Weberian terms, parties will synthesize and summarize the "meaning" of the key aspects of the situation and the potential relationship in terms of outcome magnitudes and outcome probability estimates. The choice of option is not based simply on magnitude but rather on the magnitude multiplied by probability. In an organizational context, subjective expected utility theory suggests that actors in organizations compare the magnitude of working within a coalition to working outside a coalition. If, for example, the resource involved is a pay increase, the magnitude may be viewed as the expected pay increase if an actor works outside versus inside a coalition. The probability factor is the probability of achieving the magnitude expected as a member of a coalition versus the probability of achieving the magnitude expected as an individual actor. Therefore, actors will form a coalition when the magnitude of outcomes expected as part of a coalition, multiplied by the probability of achieving these outcomes as a coalition, exceeds the magnitude of outcomes expected when operating as a single actor multiplied by the probability of achieving these outcomes as a single actor. This is a straightforward application of rational-choice principles (Elster, 1986).

Although, on the one hand, applying subjective expected utility theory to the question of whether actors join coalitions may seem to provide a somewhat standard rational-choice answer, on the other hand, the components of this theoretical approach crystallize how actors socially construct the political environment in which they operate as well as the political opportunities and obstacles that they may face. For example, workers who engage in nonroutine decision-making activities may view their control of uncertainty as critical to the organization and thus feel that they have such a strong power base that they need not join any coalition. Alternatively, workers engaged in highly routine, non-problem-solving activities may view themselves as expendable and therefore feel a greater need to join a coalition. Furthermore, the very probability of achieving one's goal may be constrained by historical and environmental conditions. For example, the past success or failure of particular coalitions, in changing environmental conditions, may not predict future success or failure. Therefore, subjective expected utility offers a useful way of identifying relevant components (e.g., magnitude and probability) that are socially constructed with the historical and cultural materials embedded in the organization.

Coalition Processes

By definition, coalitions include some actors and exclude others. They simultaneously (a) bind some actors together within the coalition and (b) divide or distinguish them from actors outside the coalition. In this sense, coalition processes in organizations should generate patterns of inclusiveness and exclusiveness, and one result is the partitioning of organizational members into distinct informal groupings. To the extent that these groupings recur and are perceived by members as real, they become organizationally situated political identities that structure social contacts and interaction within and outside the organization. Examples of such political identities are "old guard," "young turks," "central office," and "Day Hall." These are meaningful and important identities that have associated expectations about attitudes, orientations, allegiances, competencies, and behaviors. An organizational political identity is a social identity in Tajfel and Turner's (1986) terms, but the bases of social categorization are perceived strategy and policy stances or orientations within the organization. Borrowing from social identity theory, the impact of coalitions on the relations of actors within the coalition (forms of inclusion) should be related to the effects on relations to those outside (forms of exclusion). The distinction between being included and excluded is critical to the strength of the social identity (Brewer, 1993; Kramer, 1993).

Once actors have joined a coalition, what remains problematic is how the coalition will enhance the actors' commitment to collective action—that is, how the coalition will ensure that it is capable of mobilizing the resources of all constituent actors. The decision to join does not guarantee mobilization of one's resources for the coalition. That is, the rational calculation made on the basis of subjective expected utility theory to join the coalition (the contextualization issue) does not preclude the need for a coalition to normatively integrate an actor into its distinctive social category (the mobilization issue).

The mobilization question often depends on whether actors identify with the coalition, and as such, successful coalitions are those that establish mechanisms that enhance this collective identity. A clear example comes from the labor movement. By distinguishing between union membership and union participation, often members will be able to calculate, using the schema of expected utility, that joining a union is in their benefit. Because they do not identify with the union beyond this rational calculation, however, they are unlikely to give of their time and labor (i.e., resources) unless there are dire circumstances (i.e., a major strike). In this instance, the union as a coalition has failed to bind the actors together within the coalition and, at the same time, divide or distinguish them from actors outside the coalition. They identify with the union some of the time, but most of the time they identify with the work organization.

Overcoming the problem of coalition mobilization through the enhancement of identification is the sociological mechanism by which coalitions overcome the free-rider phenomenon (Kramer, 1993). The more individuals identify with an individual subgrouping (i.e., a coalition), the more likely they are to commit resources to that group and the greater that group's collective power becomes. Specifically, when individuals feel a sense of social identity, this will inevitably enhance the solidarity of the group and thus enhance group power (Hechter, 1987). If organizations are viewed as being composed of social categories that stand in power and status relation to one another (Hogg & Abrams, 1990, p. 14), and coalitions are viewed as one of these social categories, we accept that these categories do not exist in isolation but rather in contrast to one another (Brewer, 1993). To transform the power of individuals into collective power through identity and group solidarity, coalitions establish mechanisms of inclusion and exclusion of members, which sharpen the boundaries of inclusion and exclusion between coalitions.

There are conceivably two basic relations of inclusion and two basic relations of exclusion that coalitions can produce. For inclusion, the two relations are absorption and cooperative exchange. Absorption refers to a situation in which one group essentially absorbs another, making it indistinguishable within the political processes of the organization. A small subunit, not central to the organization, may routinely ally with a larger, more central unit and thereby be perceived as "in the camp" of the larger unit whenever relevant policies are at issue. The smaller unit would remain distinct organizationally but not be perceived as a distinct, independent actor on the political landscape of the organization. Absorption occurs when there is highly unequal power dependence that effectively subordinates one group to another. Cooperative exchange is based on reciprocity and refers to relations in which actors or groups achieve mutual, joint gains through social exchange. Mutual dependencies provide each actor or group of actors the potential to offer and receive something important from joint action. Neither is subordinate to the other, and both retain a separate political identity in the organization beyond the joint one that could be generated if they coalesce frequently with each other. A coalition between finance and marketing to influence the development of a new product, for example, would tend to involve cooperative exchange rather than absorption and call on existing organizational identities without creating a new one.

In addition to relations of inclusion within the coalition, there are relations of exclusion between members of the coalition and outsiders. Insulation and negotiated exchange are two important relations of exclusion. Insulation refers to the degree of distinct separation and independence between those inside and outside the coalition. Coalitions insulate their members by accentuating task, functional, or other organizationally relevant differences, making it legitimate for those subunits to "go their own way" and operate with nearly complete autonomy. Insulation reflects and strengthens low interdependencies between subunits of an organization and is especially common in highly decentralized and loosely coupled organizations. All things being equal, insulation should strengthen the distinctiveness of the coalition members' political identities, a condition that produces stronger favoritism toward one's own group and discrimination toward those outside (Brewer, 1993). Negotiated exchange between the coalition and outside individuals or groups tends to occur when mutual dependencies are high and the policy issues have mixed-motive properties. Here, the connections between the coalition and those outside are likely to involve relatively explicit agreements or understandings.

Inclusion and exclusion imply a range of tactical options for those forming coalitions to use them to influence organizational policies. Absorption is a tactic for larger, more central units to build stronger and stronger power bases vis-à-vis other contender units in the organization. Insulation is a tactic for maximizing autonomy and may be common for units at the technical core, given their centrality, or for those on the periphery of the organization with narrowly specified purposes. Finding areas of common fate or joint benefit with others and forming coalitions on the basis of cooperative (reciprocal) exchange is particularly useful for units attempting to manage unpredictability in dense networks of interdependence. Negotiated exchanges are tactics for groups facing major adversaries with relatively equal power. Negotiated exchange is a way to manage or resolve policy disputes and to protect one's interests while accommodating the interests of powerful others.

The crucial underlying condition for relations of inclusion and exclusion is the power or dependence relation. The tendency of repeated coalitions to generate different forms of inclusion and exclusion is contingent on the degree of power-dependence inequality within the coalition and mutual or total dependence outside the coalition. Power is defined here as a capability or potential that may or may not be used by actors and, if used, may or may not be effective (Bacharach & Lawler 1980, 1981; Molm, 1990). Using power-dependence theory, the power of A is based on the dependence of B on A and vice versa (Bacharach & Lawler, 1981; Cook & Emerson, 1978; Emerson, 1972; Lawler, 1992; Molm, 1987). The relative power of actors (or power differences) within the coalition is distinguished from the total power in these relations (average power or cohesion in Emerson's terms). The distinction of relative and total power applies to the capability only, and it integrates zero-sum and non-zero-sum features. Relative power is the zero-sum dimension, and total or mutual power is the non-zero-sum dimension. The importance of the non-zero-sum component is that it incorporates the idea that actors can each increase their power simultaneously—that is, an increase in one actor's power does not by definition produce a decrease in the power of others. The fundamental reason for this is that the relations in question are embedded in a larger social context involving actual and potential relations with others.

We suggest that relative dependencies or power differences are of prime import within the coalition, whereas mutual dependencies are of prime import to relations with those outside the coalition. This makes sense because the fact of repeated coalitions implies mutual dependence beyond some minimal threshold; the issue within the coalition is how its constituent groups or actors deal with equalities or inequalities of power dependence. The issue with regard to relations outside the coalition is whether there is sufficient mutual dependence to provide an incentive to negotiate accommodative agreements. It should also be noted that the relations within and outside are theoretically orthogonal. Absorption or cooperative exchange within the coalition has no necessary bearing on whether relations to the outside are insulated or negotiated. One reason for this is that different dimensions of power—relative versus total (mutual)—relate to different processes.

The power relations among recurring allies should have important effects on the forms of inclusion. Absorption will be a primary integrative mechanism that sustains the coalition when coalitions reemerge from issue to issue, and those who form them have unequal relative power. Cooperative exchange, however, will be a primary integrative mechanism when the actors or groups that form the coalition have equal relative power. This may be stated in propositional form as follows:

> *Proposition 1:* Repeated coalitions among actors or groups with unequal relative power produce the absorption of the least powerful actor or group by the more powerful actor or group within the coalition.
>
> *Proposition 2:* Repeated coalitions among actors or groups with relatively equal power produce cooperative exchange relations between the actors or groups within the coalition.

Propositions 1 and 2 deal with the internal dynamics of the coalition (specifically regarding whether inclusion entails absorption or cooperative exchange) based on the relative power of its constituent actors or groups. What also must be specified, however, is how the coalition postures itself vis-à-vis other actors, groups, or coalitions in the organization. That is, will the coalition insulate itself or will it engage in negotiated exchange? This can be predicted best by examining the degree to which a coalition that forms repeatedly has high or low mutual dependence vis-à-vis other actors, groups, or coalitions in the organization. A coalition with high mutual dependence is more likely to feel a need to negotiate with other actors, groups, or coalitions, whereas a coalition with low mutual interdependence will be more likely to turn inward and insulate itself. This may be summarized by the following propositions:

> *Proposition 3:* Low mutual (total) dependence with other actors or groups in the organization will lead a repeated coalition to insulate itself from other actors, groups, or coalitions in the organization.
>
> *Proposition 4:* High mutual (total) dependence with other actors or groups in the organization will lead a repeated coalition to engage in negotiated exchange with other actors, groups, or coalitions in the organization.

Political Alignments

Alignments emerge as microinstitutions if the same coalitions re-peatedly form over time to deal with political issues. The impact of repetition is crucial but also a matter of degree. An alignment begins to exist when the actors in it expect to collaborate on such issues in the future, and it is reified and objectified when those inside and outside of it perceive its existence and likely persistence. Although this requires repeated coalitions among the same actors, the following question arises: How many instances of the same coalition are necessary? Berger and Luckmann (1967) suggest that only one repetition of a behavior is necessary to generate "incipient institutionalization," and if we can view the early stage of political alignments similarly, two instances will start the process. This may be more likely for strategy issues because these tend to arise less often than policy disputes and to be more im-portant when they do arise. Thus, we surmise that one repetition of a coalition is sufficient for strategy issues, but more than one is necessary for political alignments organized around policies or practices.

The general hypothesis is that predominant forms of political alignment in an organization vary with the degree of power inequality in relations of the organization and the average degree of interde-pendence among these relations. Power inequality derives from the degree that (a) actors provide resources of unequal value or impor-tance to others in the organization and the organization as a whole, (b) they have differential access to alternative or substitutable sources of value, or both. The average or total dependence is based on the degree that actors are linked together in complex webs of interdependence, such that they cannot accomplish their tasks without support from or coordination with many other individuals or groups in the organiza-tion. Using power-dependence theory, we argue that variations in power inequality and interdependence will jointly determine the pre-dominant form of political alignment. For example, organizations composed of distinct centers or separate business units with relatively equal power and low interdependencies among them should promote different kinds of political alignment than organizations with large power inequalities and high degrees of interdependence among subunits.

TABLE 4.1 Types of Political Alignment by Relative and Total Power

		Total Power	
Power Inequality		*Low*	*High*
	Low	Confrontative alignment	Accommodative alignment
	High	Patronage alignment	Cooptive alignment

To specify fundamental effects of power on political alignments, we dichotomize the dimensions of power dependence into low versus high unequal power and low versus high total power and then cross-classify these dimensions. This yields four forms of political alignment that we term confrontational, accommodative, patronage, and cooptive (Table 4.1).

Confrontational Alignments

Alignments tend to be confrontational when a few actors with relatively equal power contend repeatedly over the basic strategies and direction of an organization. If coalition processes create distinct, hostile "camps" with relatively equal power, confrontations often may produce "crises" when important policy or strategy issues are debated. This type of political alignment is grounded in the insulation processes that ostensibly occur when the actors have relatively equal power and neither is highly dependent on the other (i.e., low average dependence on one another). The ideal type is a highly decentralized organization in which there are relatively few actors vying for power and influence, and the actors are not very interdependent. In this context, (a) political alignments pit the same actors against one another over time, creating distinct political camps; (b) none of the alliances achieve dominance or do so for any length of time; (c) conflicts are typically more serious than the policy issues that produce them because actors are prone to view them in distributive (zero-sum) terms; and (d) the actors develop distinct political identities that are recognized and that create widely shared expectations for those actors in the organization. In this context, third-party interventions from within or outside the organization are prime means of managing conflicts and keeping them within acceptable bounds, although if interdependence is very low, they tend to avoid conflict by minimizing contacts.

Accommodative Alignments

This form of alignment results from power conditions that promote cooperative exchanges among actors in the coalition: highly interdependent actors with relatively low power inequalities. The ideal type is a highly decentralized organization in which the distinct subunits have strong incentives to collaborate in mutually acceptable and satisfying ways. Under such conditions, conflicts occur periodically, but these are likely to be resolved through negotiation by the actors themselves, without the need for third parties. Political alignments will tend to congeal actors with the greatest incentives to exchange information, resources, and so on, and informal divisions and distinct political identities will take shape around these "pockets of cooperation." Generally, when conflicts occur, they tend to involve misinformation, miscommunication, or misperception rather than fundamental differences of interest among aligned groups. Areas of common ground can typically be built on through negotiated exchange and used to minimize the effects of distributive issues. Thus, if negotiation is needed for some conflicts, it will be integrative rather than distributive in form. The cooperative exchange within coalitions under these conditions is likely to set the stage for negotiated exchange between coalitions.

Patronage Alignments

This form of political alignment develops out of the absorption processes that ostensibly occur when there are large relative power inequalities and low interdependencies on average among actors. The prototype is a centralized, hierarchical organization in which those with little power have few ties to each other but strong ties of dependence to superiors. Superiors are analogous to "patrons," who serve the needs of subordinates in return for strong loyalty. The internal political identity is transformed into an organizational identity that patrons and subordinates share. This kind of alignment should crosscut the higher and lower levels of the organization, induce high degrees of voluntary compliance, create the appearance of little or no conflict, and foster myths of unity and consensus. At the extreme, this type of political alignment entails a "personality cult" around the leader that infuses the entire organization. Less extreme forms include a recurrently enacted pattern or norm of paternal superordinate-subordinate relations, manifest in familial metaphors for the organization. With a patronage alignment, the most problematic conflicts occur among multiple patrons, but these tend to be resolved behind the scenes to sustain myths of unity and consensus. If the number of powerful actors becomes large, this alignment could evolve toward the confrontational form because patrons will build independent power bases.

Cooptive Alignments

In the context of large power differences, those with greater power may elicit and maintain cooperation through selective incentives. Cooptive alignments also have their source in absorption processes but, in this case, higher power inequality is combined with higher degrees of mutual dependence within and across organizational levels. Those with greater power have an incentive to coopt select actors with lower power to solidify their power position vis-à-vis other high-power actors and to prevent collective mobilization by those with less power. Cooptation divides or forestalls potential opposition while also strengthening each higher-power actor's dealings with other powerful actors in the organization. Importantly, those coopted have alternatives and, therefore, can change allegiances in the future; this creates a defection problem for those with greater power, but it is solvable with selective incentives. Coalitions that produce cooptation alignments tend to require periodic, if not continual, negotiation, and the power inequality should make them somewhat more fragile than accommodative alignments.

Given the previous characterization of each form of political alignment, we can specify four more propositions based in part on the earlier propositions:

> *Proposition 5:* Power-dependence conditions (low power inequality and low interdependence) that produce cooperative exchange within coalitions and insulation from outside actors, respectively, will generate confrontational political alignments. (This proposition combines Propositions 2 and 3.)

Proposition 6: Power-dependence conditions (low power inequality and high interdependence) that produce cooperative exchange within coalitions and negotiated exchanges with those outside will generate accommodative political alignments. (This proposition combines Propositions 2 and 4.)

Proposition 7: Power-dependence conditions (high power inequality and low interdependence) that produce absorption within coalitions and insulation from those outside will generate patronage forms of alignment. (This proposition combines Propositions 1 and 3.)

Proposition 8: Power-dependence conditions (high power inequality and high interdependence) that produce absorption within coalitions and negotiated exchanges with those outside will generate cooptive political alignments. (This proposition combines Propositions 1 and 4.)

Conclusion

Unlike structuralists, who emphasize the rational order of organizations, or reductionists, who marvel that organizations can actually sustain themselves (Weick, 1976), a political perspective views the organizational system as a process of power-based negotiation and re-negotiation (Strauss, 1978). The failure to develop a theory of organizational change may in fact be explained by the tendency of having ignored the volitional actor within an organizational setting and the microinstitutional processes that emerge from volitional actors and action. Barley and Tolbert (1997) have argued that the history of institutions can often be cast as the history of negotiations. Similarly, DiMaggio (1988) has maintained that if we want to understand institutional change, we need to focus on the role of interests—that is, we need to focus on how interests play themselves out through the negotiations and politics in the organizational arena. It is through political process that volitional actors pursue their interests in concert or in conflict with other actors. Indeed, to pursue political action, it is inevitable that actors in the organization align themselves with others. The history of such alignments becomes the history of organizational change (Michels, 1962).

Underlying our argument is the notion that organizational life cannot be explained effectively by either (macro)structures or (micro)phenomena alone. One way of bridging the micro-macro distinctions is to examine under what conditions actors join coalitions and when these coalitions will be institutionalized through the emergence of enduring political alignments. As such, the political perspective we offer in this chapter contends that individual interests and schema, although constrained by the structures and environments of organizations, are the beginning of an institutionalization process, and that coalitions and alignments transform these cognitions into organizational forms and structures (DiMaggio & Powell, 1991). A theory of change that is therefore political in its nature must, in our opinion, be both micro and macro in its orientation. Thus, we return to the basic assumption that has guided most of our work—that is, that for organizational politics the Weberian notion of "social action" is a crucial theoretical frame.

References

Aron, R. (1987). *Main currents of sociological thought.* New York: Basic Books.
Bacharach, S. B., & Lawler, E. J. (1980). *Power and politics in organizations.* San Francisco: Jossey-Bass.
Bacharach, S. B., & Lawler, E J. (1981). *Bargaining, power, tactics, and outcomes.* San Francisco: Jossey-Bass.
Bacharach, S. B., & Mundell, B. (1993). Organizational politics in schools: Micro, macro and logics of action. *Education Administration Quarterly, 29,* 423-452.
Bacharach, S. B., Mundell, B., & Masters, F. (1995). Institutional theory and the politics of institutionalization. In R. Ogawa (Ed.), *Advances in theory and practice of educational policy.* Greenwich, CT: JAI.
Barley, S., & Tolbert, P. (1997). Institutionalization and structuration: Studying the link between action and institution. *Organizational Studies, 18*(1), 93-118.
Berger, P., & Luckmann, T. (1967). *The social construction of reality.* New York: Doubleday.
Blegen, M. A., & Lawler, E. J. (1989). Power and bargaining in authority-client relations. In R. G. Braungart & M. M. Braungart (Eds.), *Research in political sociology* (pp. 168-186). Greenwich, CT: JAI.
Brewer, M. B. (1993). Social identity, distinctiveness, and in-group homogeneity. *Social Cognition, 11,* 150-164.
Clegg, S. R. (1990). *Modern organizations.* London: Sage.
Cook, K. S., & Emerson, R. M. (1978). Power, equity, and commitment in exchange networks. *American Sociological Review, 27,* 721-739.
Cyert, R., & March, J. (1963). *Behavioral theory of the firm.* Englewood Cliffs, NJ: Prentice Hall.

DiMaggio, P. (1988). Interest and agency in institutional theory. In L. Zucker (Ed.), *Institutional patterns in organizations: Culture and environment* (pp. 3-21). Cambridge, MA: Ballinger.

DiMaggio, P., & Powell, W. (1991). Introduction. In W. Powell & P. DiMaggio (Eds.), *The new institutionalism in organizational analysis* (pp. 1-38). Chicago: University of Chicago Press.

Elster, J. (1986). Introduction. In J. Elster (Ed.), *Rational choice theory* (pp. 1-34). New York: NYC Press.

Emerson, R. (1972). *Sociological theories in progress.* Boston: Houghton Mifflin.

Ferris, G. R., Brand, J. F., Brand, S., Rowland, K. M., Gilmore, D. C., King, T. R., Kacmar, K. M., & Burton, C. A. (1993). Politics and control in organizations. In E. Lawler, B. Markovsky, K. Heimer, & J. O'Brien (Eds.), *Advances in group processes* (pp. 83-111). Greenwich, CT: JAI.

Ferris, G. R., Russ, G. S., & Fandt, P. M. (1989). Politics in organizations. In R. A. Giacalone & P. Rosenfeld (Eds.), *Impression management in the organization* (pp. 143-170). Hillsdale, NJ: Lawrence Erlbaum.

Hechter, M. L. (1987). *Principles of group solidarity.* Berkeley: University of California Press.

Hogg, M., & Abrams, D. (1990). *Social identifications: A social psychology of intergroup relations and group processes.* London: Routledge.

Kipnis, D., & Schmidt, S. (1983). An influence perspective on bargaining within organizations. In M. Bazerman & R. J. Lewicki (Eds.), *Negotiating in organizations* (pp. 303-319). Beverly Hills, CA: Sage.

Kramer, R. M. (1993). Cooperation and organizational identification. In J. K. Murnighan (Ed.), *Social psychology in organizations* (pp. 244-248). Englewood Cliffs, NJ: Prentice Hall.

Lawler, E. J. (1992). Power processes in bargaining. *Sociological Quarterly, 33,* 17-34.

Lawler, E. J., & Bacharach, S. B. (1976). Outcome alternatives and value as criteria for multistrategy evaluations. *Journal of Personality and Social Psychology, 34,* 885-894.

Mayes, B. T., & Allen, R. W. (1977, October). Toward a definition of organizational politics. *Academy of Management Review 2*(4), 672-678.

McCarthy, J. D., & Zald, M. N. (1977). Resource mobilization and social movements: A partial theory. *American Journal of Sociology, 82,* 1212-1241.

Michels, R. (1962). *Political parties: A sociological study of the oligarchical tendencies of modern democracy.* New York: Free Press.

Mintzberg, H. (1983). *Power in and around organizations.* Englewood Cliffs, NJ: Prentice Hall.

Molm, L. (1987). Power dependence theory: Power processes and negative outcomes. In E. J. Lawler & B. Markovsky (Eds.), *Advances in group processes* (pp. 171-198). Greenwich, CT: JAI.

Olson, M., Jr. (1965). *The logic of collective action.* Cambridge, MA: Harvard University Press.

Pettigrew, A. M. (1973). *The politics of organizational decision marking.* London: Tavistock.

Pfeffer, J. (1981). *Power in organizations.* Marshfield, MA: Pitman.

Porter, L. W., Allen, W., & Angle, H. L. (1981). The politics of upward influence in organizations. In B. M. Staw & L. L. Cummings (Eds.), *Research in organizational behavior* (Vol. 3, pp. 109-149). Greenwich, CT: JAI.

Strauss, A. (1978). *Negotiations: Variety, context, processes and social order.* San Francisco: Jossey-Bass.

Tajfel, H., & Turner, J. C. (1986). The social identity theory of intergroup behaviour. In
    S. Worchel & W. G Austin (Eds.), *Psychology of intergroup relations*. Chicago:
    Nelson-Hall.
Thompson, J. (1967). *Organizations in action*. New York: McGraw-Hill.
Weick, K. (1976). Educational organizations as loosely-coupled systems. *Administrative
    Science Quarterly, 21,* 1-19.

5

The Power of Resistance

Sustaining Valued Identities

BLAKE E. ASHFORTH
FRED A. MAEL

Sometimes . . . when I make something, I put a little dent in it. I like to do something to make it really unique. Hit it with a hammer. I deliberately f*** it up to see if it'll get by, just so I can say I did it. It could be anything. . . . I'd like to make my imprint. . . . A mistake, mine.
       —Steelworker (Terkel, 1975, pp. 9-10)

A scenario I personally saw acted out . . . by several different workers involved a foreman stopping to talk to a worker in a non-work-related, seemingly friendly conversation. The worker would be smiling and conversing congenially, yet the moment the foreman turned to walk away, the worker would make an obscene gesture (usually involving the middle finger) behind the foreman's back, so that all other workers could clearly see.
       —Beef processing plant (Thompson, 1983, p. 222)

There is an incredibly rich lore on workplace resistance, from the fiercely violent strikes earlier in this century to the sabotage of computers in recent years. Whether resistance is epic or everyday, it would be a mistake to assume that it simply reflects irrationality or pathology, laziness or surliness, or boredom or vindictiveness—

although at times it may reflect any of these. As we will argue, acts of resistance are inherently *meaningful* to the actors and their peers. In particular, resistance is often prompted by a perceived threat to *identity*, to a valued conception of self.

Defining Resistance

By *resistance*, we mean intentional acts of commission or omission that defy the wishes of others. The term *intentional* signifies that one's motive is central to the dynamics of resistance but does not mean that resistance is necessarily premeditated or rational. In this chapter, we do not consider acts of resistance that are purely psychological (e.g., revenge fantasies) or are driven by unconscious motives, although these are worthy topics in their own right.

The notion of resistance implies opposition *against* something, usually the exercise of power—the attempt to influence or control the resister. It is somewhat arbitrary, however, to label one behavior an act of power or control and another as an act of resistance. As we contend, power and resistance are embedded in a dynamic relationship that tends to be mutually reinforcing: An exercise of control may engender resistance, and resistance may engender countercontrol or "resistance to resistance," triggering further iterations of resistance and control. Indeed, as Knights and Vurdubakis (1994, p. 191) argue, "Acts of resistance are also exercises of power." Nevertheless, we follow the convention of referring to acts by those in authority—typically managers and members of what Mintzberg (1979) refers to as the technostructure (e.g., industrial engineers, budget analysts, trainers)—as acts of "control." Acts of control are usually intended to create and maintain the conditions of employment and to craft meaning for organizational members (e.g., the organization as a caring family). Conversely, employee responses that are intended to oppose these acts are referred to as resistance.

Studies of resistance typically focus on organizational members at the nonsupervisory level, presumably because they are more likely to be the target rather than the instigator of acts of control, and they have less power to affect the goals, policies, and operating routines of the organization. Labor process and radical or critical views of resistance, inspired by Marxism, are in fact predicated on a great divide between rank-and-file members and capitalist owners and their representatives (managers) (Brower & Abolafia, 1995). However, because every organizational member—including owners—becomes embedded over time in a more or less structured context with webs of membership obligations, the dynamics of everyday resistance are applicable to anyone. Indeed, because the obligations of managers (and other salaried employees) are diffuse and open-ended and involve not only behavior but also modes of thinking and feeling, it could be argued that managers have a greater need to resist the intrusions of organizational life (Jackall, 1988). Thus, although most of our examples are derived from studies of nonsupervisory members, our arguments are relevant to all organizational members.

We do not assume a particular evaluative stance toward resistance: Whether acts of defiance are seen as positive or rational rather than negative or irrational depends largely on one's perspective. For example, whistle-blowing is usually viewed as negative by senior executives and positive by the general public. Furthermore, we recognize that acts of resistance often have multiple causes of varying legitimacy, from alleviating boredom and gaining peer approval to avoiding unfair demands and ill-conceived changes.

Overview

The discussion is divided into three parts. The first, identity as a motive for resistance, argues that organizations can be characterized as systems of domination that seek to impose definitions of the organizational self and desirable conduct. These impositions may threaten existing self-conceptions and trigger ambivalence and a desire to resist. The second part, nature of resistance, provides a three-dimensional typology of acts of resistance. We also maintain that asserting one's desired self-conception(s) through resistance has symbolic value beyond any substantive outcomes, that resistance is often a collective product, performed with and legitimated by peers, and that resisters tend to have very little difficulty in justifying their defiance. The third part, the resistance cycle, outlines an iterative process of control → resistance → countercontrol, ultimately leading to a more or less stable state of mutual accommodation. This state, however, is inherently fragile and subject to renegotiation as new issues arise.

Thus, the power of resistance lies at least partly in its potential to contest *meaning*, specifically the definition of the individual derived from organizational membership.

Identity as a Motive for Resistance

Organizations as Systems of Domination

In Coser's (1974) terms, many organizations are inherently "greedy institutions" in that their demands on the person are "omnivorous": They take as much behavioral and psychological involvement as they can, even if members cannot afford it. This is particularly applicable to managers and other salaried employees whose membership obligations are, as noted, typically open-ended.

Edwards (1979) argues that organizations have progressively colonized certain spheres of control vis-à-vis the individual member. Originally, simple hierarchical control was adequate when firms were relatively small and unsophisticated. Workers were told what to do. As firms grew and became more complex, however, coordination and control problems increased, leading to the institutionalization of both technical control (in the form of machinery and work procedures) and bureaucratic control (in the form of policies, job descriptions, and rules). Instructions were complemented by impersonal, system-driven imperatives. As depicted in Figure 5.1, all three forms of control— hierarchical, technical, and bureaucratic—can be characterized as *external control* in that the individual is not required to believe in or internalize them as necessary and appropriate but merely to conform to them. Simply stated, the hands matter, but the head and heart do not.

A potentially more invasive form of control has gained recent recognition from both academics and practitioners: Normative or cultural control. Kunda (1992, pp. 11-12) defines normative control as "the attempt to elicit and direct the required efforts of members by controlling the underlying experiences, thoughts, and feelings that guide their actions . . . a sort of creeping annexation of the workers' selves." The well-known practices of symbolic management (e.g., mission statements, stories, rituals, physical setting) and substantive management (e.g., strategy formulation, reward systems, budgets, information sys-

Figure 5.1. Organizations as Systems of Domination
Note: The arrow signifies the growing use of internal control.

tems) are used to impart the organization's identity, seminal goals and values, prevailing beliefs and assumptions, and behavioral norms (Ashforth & Mael, 1996; Pfeffer, 1981). Thus, symbolic and substantive management is used to shape not only experience but also the meaning that is extracted from experience. Through these practices, normative control defines reality, virtue, and the means for navigating between the two. Members are thereby induced to internalize the organization's ideological and normative stance, to bind their self-conceptions to the organization's identity, and to become emotionally attached to the organization. In other words, members are induced to remake themselves in the image of the desired member.

What makes normative control potentially insidious is that, when complete, it is experienced not as externally imposed but as internalized and freely chosen. This is why it is classified as an *internal control* in Figure 5.1. Moreover, normative control can effectively substitute for external control (Kunda, 1992). It insinuates itself into one's workplace identity such that to resist it is to be at war with oneself. As Barker (1993, p. 427) said of self-managing teams that had developed their own work rules, "They had invested their human dignity in the system of their own control." It is this potential fusion of self and organization that makes normative control so appealing to organizations. Furthermore, as organizations continue to gravitate from mechanistic to organic structures to cope with growing environmental dynamism and complexity, normative control becomes increasingly attractive. Accordingly, Knights and Vurdubakis (1994, p. 173) can safely conclude that "attempts to shape the wills, desires, interests and identities of subjects are far more typical and routine than coercive domination."

Finally, regardless of the forms of control that are used, the *process* or means by which they are applied may also threaten the individual. Research on social justice indicates that perceptions of fairness and legitimacy depend on both the content of organizational decisions and the process by which they are determined and implemented. For example, Folger (1993) argues that respect for an individual is symbolized by outcomes such as pay and job latitude and by the use of due process (e.g., considerateness, timeliness, participation) to allocate the outcomes. In fact, individuals are often willing to accept negative outcomes such as a salary reduction if they are determined through a process that implicitly affirms the individual's dignity and value: Procedural justice can offset distributive *in*justice. Conversely, even a relatively benign form of control can be perceived as threatening if it is applied in a heavy-handed manner.

In summary, organizations function by regulating the actions—and increasingly, the thoughts and feelings—of their members. Insofar as the forms and process of control are thus viewed as invasive and threatening, they create the potential for resistance.

Tension Between Self and System

We like to think of ourselves as individuals, as more or less unique persons. To that end, we have little difficulty enumerating traits, attitudes, skills, and other characteristics that describe and differentiate us from others whom we know and with whom we associate. At the same time, we like to think of ourselves as members and possibly exemplars of various social groupings, such as family, community, occupation, church, sports team, and gender. To this end, we may list characteristics that we share with other members.

Whether as individuals or as members of groups, the characteristics we assume to be ours are abstracted from specific experiences that are necessarily situated in specific contexts at specific times. Furthermore, the very characteristics we "choose" are typically a product of the context. If one is a high steel ironworker, the traits of fearlessness and peer loyalty will likely become a salient part of one's occupational identity and, to the extent that that identity is valued, a salient part of one's generalized sense of self. To close the loop, these abstracted characteristics are then replayed in context and validated by others, thereby being experienced as essential aspects of self (Schlenker, 1986).

Identities, in short, are negotiated and sustained—are *embedded* in concrete settings.

Thus, the self is not an autonomous, closed, unified, and fixed entity—an unassailable and isolated fortress. The self is socially constructed, enacted, and validated in specific settings and in the larger cultural and historical context, and it is thus negotiable, multifaceted, open, and changeable (Kondo, 1990). It is precisely because of this quality of *porousness* that one may try very hard to assert and defend a favored conception of self.

This is the crux of the tension between self and system: Both our abstract sense of self, our uniqueness, and our "apartness" from others and our abstract sense of membership, our commonalities, and our togetherness are necessarily dependent on concrete comparisons within concrete contexts. The characteristics we choose to label, the referents we compare against, and the validation we seek are all tethered to particular times and places. As Kondo (1990, p. 257) states, " 'Self' and 'society' are not mutually exclusive." We simultaneously plumb our social worlds for signs of difference and signs of sameness.

With regard to organizations, the ascendance of normative control—with its internalized claims on thought and feeling—makes it particularly difficult to differentiate self from system. The resulting tension gives rise to a sense of *ambivalence* toward the organization—of being simultaneously attracted and repulsed.

Ambivalence

There are at least three avenues to ambivalence: (a) fear of loss of self, (b) conflicts among multiple identities, and (c) protection of dualistic values. First, because many organizations are inherently greedy, and because identities are constituted and maintained largely through social interaction, one's organizational self can come to dominate one's identity. Commitment to and identification with an organization represent a slippery slope—particularly for individuals with open-ended membership obligations—in that the more one gives, the more that is asked and the more difficult it is to hold back. Research on workaholism attests to the seductive and possibly addictive nature of work and its ready-made social identity (Porter, 1996). Thus, Smith and Berg (1987) describe the "paradox of identity," in which individuals struggle with the desires to meld with a group and to preserve a unique sense of self. As such, resistance becomes a means of establishing a bulwark or buffer against the encroachment of the organization.

Moreover, as a kind of social corollary to Newton's third law, the stronger the attraction to the organization, the stronger the potential *reaction*. This reaction acts as a counterpoint to the organization's identity; it declares an independent and autonomous self precisely because attraction threatens to erase such a self. Indeed, resistance may establish not only a bulwark but also a sharp, counternormative or deviant identity (e.g., rebel, gadfly, iconoclast). Just as adolescents often define themselves partly in terms of how they differ from their parents, the organization may serve as a foil for the individual: "It is thus *against something* that the self can emerge" (Goffman, 1961a, p. 320). In short, strong cultures may simultaneously provoke strong attraction and strong resistance.

A second avenue to ambivalence is identity conflict. Although identities are abstracted from contexts, identities and contexts are often only loosely coupled. Frequently, a given identity can be manifested in multiple contexts, and a given context can be the site for multiple identities. In a given context, identities are arrayed in a salience hierarchy, in which the most salient are the most likely to be activated. Identities are activated by an interaction of external (situational) and internal (psychological) cues, such that certain identities are most salient for certain people in certain settings and at certain times. A New Year's party may be seen by one person as an occasion to relax among friends, whereas another may see it as a chance to sell life insurance. Identities, however, are typically not mutually exclusive (e.g., colleague, friend, female, aggressive), such that multiple and possibly conflicting identities may be more or less salient at a given time. Broadhead (1980, p. 178) describes how female medical students feared that the professional ideal of emotional detachment might, symbolically, "turn them into men." Ambivalence occurs, then, because identities are not easily separable; to privilege one in terms of attention and action means that others may be slighted or even thwarted. Thus, resistance may be aimed at preserving a relative balance between valued selves.

A third cause of ambivalence is the protection of dualisms. Erikson (1976) argues that cultures consist not simply of core values but also of *axes* of values where the endpoints are anchored by dualities. A specific culture tends to award primacy to one endpoint of a given axis versus the other but nonetheless contains the capacity for the opposite. These dualities are experienced as ambivalence—the temptation to do both *A* and not-*A*. Thus, the reason that selflessness and duty are lauded in organizations is precisely because their counterparts—self-centeredness and sloth—are inherently tempting.[1] Organizational cultures, in awarding primacy to one side of a series of dualities, spawn counterdesires to express that which is denied. By declaring value preferences, organizations provoke ambivalence and the desire for resistance.

We contend that organizational members are often fundamentally ambivalent about their organizations, and that this ambivalence is normal and to a certain extent healthy. Unfortunately, survey measures of organizational commitment and identification, including our own (Mael & Ashforth, 1992), mask ambivalence by soliciting only generalized perceptions. For example, Cheney (1983) reports that an individual who had a moderate identification score described his or her relationship with the organization as "just a job" and yet expressed a yearning to identify with the company. Such ambivalence may leak out in acts that imply strong attachment to the organization and in other acts that imply precisely the opposite. In Collinson's (1994, p. 29) words, "Resistance frequently contains elements of consent and consent often incorporates aspects of resistance." Indeed, individuals may not even be aware of their resistant tendencies.

Identity Motives

Resistance is often used to forge or sustain valued conceptions of self in the face of situational pressures to do otherwise. At one extreme, resistance may be used to defend a relatively complete social identity. These practices are often discussed under the rubric of collective or group-based resistance. For example, Dalton (1968) reports that foremen resisted punching a time clock so that they would not be confused with rank-and-file workers, even though their resistance cost them overtime pay, and Kondo (1990) describes how the owner of a Japanese candy factory offered broken tarts to his employees at a greatly reduced price, but the employees refused the offer to avoid the implicit identity of children who are grateful for the benevolence of the father. Indeed, much of the rich literature on labor-management conflict can be interpreted as an identity struggle, in which workers resist perceived threats to their status and dignity (Burawoy, 1979; Collinson, 1992; Hodson, 1995).

At the other extreme, resistance may be used to defend idiosyncratic aspects of one's personal identity. These practices are discussed under a variety of labels, including reactance, defensive behavior, work adjustment, withdrawal, workplace deviance, and whistle-blowing. Our reading of the literature suggests that recurring identity motives for resistance include perceived threats to social regard (respect), self-regard (self-esteem), individuality, autonomy and self-efficacy, moral principles, and a welter of individual differences (e.g., extroversion, masculinity). For instance, Bies and Tripp (1996) found that public criticism, wrong or unfair accusations, and insults directed at organizational members precipitated desires for revenge, and some studies of total institutions, such as prisons, hospitals, and nursing homes, report that individuals who resist the institution's preferred definition of self as dependent and compliant tend to have greater life satisfaction, better health, and, where applicable, smoother adjustment outside of the institution (Coser, 1956; Goodstein, 1979). Generally, the less intrinsically fulfilling the role and the more oppressive the organization is perceived to be, the more likely one is to define the self *via* resistance: As noted, a deviant identity, such as gadfly or rebel, can help salvage some sense of an "honorable" workplace self.

Three key points must be underscored. First, both identity and threat are in the eye of the beholder: An assault on a cherished self exists when it is *perceived* to exist. Kramer (1996) argues that individuals who are self-conscious, under intense scrutiny, and insecure about their status may develop "paranoid cognitions" and become hypersensitive to real or imagined slights. In contrast to these thin-skinned individuals, those with thick skins may display great tolerance or indifference. This subjectivity suggests that there is wide variance across individuals and their groups in perceptions of threat.

Second, individuals generally seek to affirm their sense of themselves, even if their identities are socially undesirable: Consistency tends to be valued over enhancement (Swann, 1990). This desire for affirmation may induce one to resist opportunities that appear to others to be patently advantageous. For example, a person who believes that he or she is helpless and dependent may resist empowerment or a promotion.

Third, the form of resistance itself must not contradict a valued identity. Hodson (1991) found that individuals in various occupations resist undesirable work by delaying it rather than doing it poorly because the latter contravenes their identity of professionalism. Linn (1988) describes the moral quandary experienced by physicians who refused to provide medical care during a strike: The refusal was antithetical to their identity as caregivers. Ironically, the same identity that compels one to resist may also severely constrain *how* one resists.

In summary, workplace resistance is often about the struggle for meaning. Individuals are embedded in a rich organizational context that more or less imposes definitions of self, although organizations differ widely in the degree to which the imposition is deliberate and the definitions are complete. Individuals, however, have multiple social and personal identities and so must limit the breadth and depth of any given identity. Thus, because the individual is not a tabula rasa onto which the organization can simply inscribe an identity, ambivalence and resistance tend to result. In the following section, we examine the forms that resistance takes.

Nature of Resistance

Dimensions

We defined resistance as deliberate acts of defiance. There are *many* forms of resistance, including sabotage, insubordination, tardiness, and avoiding tasks. To provide a framework for discussing the various forms of resistance, we offer the following three bipolar dimensions.

Targeted Versus Diffuse Resistance

Resistance is targeted when it is focused directly on the perceived source of threat. Prasad (1993) describes how employees of a health maintenance organization resisted the computerization of administrative operations by challenging the wisdom of the change during training sessions, refusing to comply with trainers' instructions, disseminating literature that was critical of computerization, and sabotaging the new computers. Resistance is diffuse when it is not focused directly on the perceived threat but is displaced onto other aspects of the workplace. Diffuse resistance is thus compensatory. Gottfried (1994) reports how clerical workers attempted to compensate for their lack of autonomy by wearing inappropriate attire, working to rule, taking extra time in the bathroom, and misfiling.

As the examples suggest, targeted resistance is more likely to be overt and proactive than is diffuse resistance, whereas the latter is more likely to be covert and reactive or passive. Targeted resistance is also more likely to be employed when the source of threat is clear and there is a reasonable likelihood of thwarting the threat (the threat is remediable and the resister has sufficient power). Whereas targeted resistance is more likely to produce substantive change, diffuse resistance is valued for its symbolic rewards. As such, diffuse resistance facilitates "secondary adjustment" (Goffman, 1961a)—that is, accommodation to an otherwise objectionable status quo; the irony, of course, is that an act of resistance may actually facilitate that which is resisted.

One reason for the historical conversion of hierarchical control into technical, bureaucratic, and normative controls is that the conversion effectively *depersonalizes* the control and thereby veils the use of power (Barker, 1993). Control is embedded in "the system" and thus becomes more or less taken for granted. Ashforth (1989) found that production workers were more likely to complain, criticize, argue, break rules, and so on if hierarchical rather than technical or bureaucratic controls were perceived to be illegitimate. In the face of depersonalized controls, resistance is apt to be more muted, sporadic, and diffuse.

Facilitative Versus Oppositional Resistance

Brower and Abolafia (1995) define facilitative resistance as acts that further organizational or public interest goals, and they define oppositional resistance as acts that serve narrow self-interests, typically at the expense of such goals. Although our definition of resistance as defiance seems to imply oppositional resistance, one may believe that others are corrupt, misguided, or incompetent, and that resistance is ultimately in the best interests of the organization or public. Hodson (1991, p. 62) quotes a worker in a metal molding shop: "When they give me specific instructions, I just nod my head and say 'yea, sure.' Deep

down I'm still gonna do it the way I want because I know it's better."
Instances of whistle-blowing, rule breaking, playing dumb, and pro-
crastination are often impelled by similar motives. Indeed, part of the
utility of formal empowerment initiatives is that they legitimate and
harness what may have been facilitative resistance.

Authorized Versus Unauthorized Resistance

Following Prasad and Caproni's (1993) notion of "counterplay,"
authorized resistance includes acts that are within the normative limits
set by the organization itself, such as complaining to one's boss and
filing grievances. Following Prasad and Caproni's notion of "fundamental resistance," unauthorized resistance includes acts beyond the
bounds set by the organization, such as insubordination and violence.
Thus, if facilitative or oppositional resistance pertains to the *ends* to
which resistance is aimed, then authorized or unauthorized resistance
pertains to the *means* by which the ends are pursued. This distinction
is important because ends and means are conceptually orthogonal:
Authorized means can be used toward oppositional ends, and unauthorized means can be used toward facilitative ends.

Crossing these three dimensions yields the model in Figure 5.2.
Note that the entries in each cell are merely illustrative: Many forms
of resistance are amenable to multiple cells (depending on the intent
of the resister and the ends and normative structure of the organization), and no single cell is necessarily associated with certain forms. To
the extent that forms do cluster in cells for a given person, organization, or event, then the forms may serve as crude substitutes. For
example, Paules (1991) describes how waitresses dealt with poor tip-
pers by confronting them directly, refusing to serve them the next time
they came, or providing poor service (targeted, oppositional, and unauthorized resistance).

Symbolic Value of Resistance

As suggested by the examples in Figure 5.2, acts of resistance are
often small, if not trivial—in part because systems of domination are
designed to preclude resistance. Nevertheless, small acts often have
immense symbolic importance because they can express the oppositional side of one's ambivalence and thereby preserve the integrity of

	Targeted		Diffuse	
	Facilitative	**Oppositional**	**Facilitative**	**Oppositional**
Authorized	-dissent -attempt to disprove a negative label ("unreliable") -use a suggestion box/hotline	-strike -grievance -refuse to work over time	-joke about incompetent superiors -apologize to clients for red tape -bend rules	-perfunctory compliance with directives -frivolous grievances -hide behind rules
Unauthor-ized	-whistle-blowing -disobey an ill-conceived order -break a rule that impairs task achievement	-sabotage -play dumb -ignore a directive	-criticize incompetent superiors -feign compliance with dysfunctional directives	-theft -absenteeism -tardiness

Figure 5.2. Dimensions of Resistance
Note: The entries are illustrative: Many forms of resistance are amenable to multiple cells and no single cell is necessarily associated with certain forms.

those valued social and personal identities that do not align with the prescribed organizational identity (Hodson, 1995; Prasad, 1993). As such, the process of resistance—the *fact* that one resists—often matters more than any substantive change or outcomes. As illustrated by the quotes at the beginning of the chapter, many acts are performed primarily or exclusively for their symbolic value. Thus, resistance per se can be salutary to identity.

Typically, there are several prime audiences for the symbolism of resistance: Oneself, one's peers, and those in positions of authority. Acts of resistance are critical incidents that declare to oneself and others that one rejects at least portions of the normative order. Following Salancik (1977), acts that are perceived to be explicit, irrevocable, public, and volitional have the greatest symbolic value because they tend to be attributed to the person, thus defining him or her as a resister. These perceptions are more likely if resistance is targeted (because it is typically overt and explicit), oppositional, and unauthorized (because it is counternormative, implying volition and perhaps irrevocability).

Kunda (1992) recounts how members of a high-tech firm immersed themselves and participated actively in top management presentations, as signaled by laughing, applauding, nodding, and note taking. Before and after the presentations, however, members would assume a more cynical stance, as signaled by parodying conventions, criticizing management views, and qualifying their own involvement. This rapid alteration between what Goffman (1961b) terms "role embracement" and "role distancing" symbolized the ambivalence of members. Indeed, one could argue that it was precisely *because* members "subtly, playfully, or humorously" (Kunda, 1992, p. 107) dramatized their resistance—thereby distancing themselves from the prescribed organizational identity—that they felt sufficiently comfortable to temporarily submerge themselves in the identity.[2] Symbolic resistance allows one to walk the fine line between the identity of management's dupe and that of management's adversary.

Collective Resistance

Resistance often occurs in collusion with others or with their tacit support. First, many of the pressures that prompt resistance are often focused on specific groups (e.g., work group, occupation, rank, seniority level, demographic) rather than at individuals, thus fostering an in-the-same-boat sense of shared fate and identity. For example, groups that perform tasks that are widely perceived as physically, socially, or morally tainted (e.g., funeral directors, prison guards) are often able to create and sustain a positive identity by transforming the very features that are stigmatized into badges of honor and distinction (Ashforth & Humphrey, 1995). Subcultures often evolve around groups that feel threatened, providing a fertile seedbed for collusive activities (Trice, 1993). To the extent that a shared identity and cohesion emerge, the group's interests gain salience relative to individual and organizational interests, and members watch out for one another's interests as if they were their own. Ultimately, a threat to any one member may be perceived as a threat to all. Indeed, one incident against a single member has the potential to radicalize an entire group. Furthermore, collective resistance against an outside force is a potent means of externalizing group tensions and thereby cementing group identity and solidarity.

Second, task interdependencies and interpersonal proximity often implicate others in acts of resistance. Mars (1994) documents how various "wolfpacks" (i.e., work groups such as longshoremen and garbage disposal workers) actively cooperate in everyday "fiddles"

(scams). Task interdependencies necessitate and facilitate such cooperation. Finally, because groups are social entities, they can develop
and sustain countervailing views of what is just and appropriate behavior. The popularity of occupational stories (often apocryphal)
about resistance attests to the deep and common chord they strike with
many employees (Hodson, 1995). Thus, groups can legitimate resistance by articulating and sharing rationalizations that an individual
acting alone may find more difficult to accept.

Resistance at the group level, however, is sometimes as laced with
ambivalence as resistance at the individual level. Wells (1988) describes
how the staff at a Girl Scout camp distanced themselves from the
cloying wholesomeness of the Girl Scout identity by ridiculing the
identity, defacing the camp uniform, parodying camp songs, and playing pranks that mocked authority. The staff, however, regarded "the
initiation of campers into the traditions and values of Scouting as a
sacred trust" (p. 114) and were careful to support the image of the
organization in any dealings with the public. Ambivalence toward the
organization, however, tends to be less prevalent in collective resistance than in individual because, as we will argue, groups help individuals justify and thereby normalize their defiance.

Resisting the Collective

Whereas ambivalence toward the organization may be reduced,
ambivalence toward the group itself may be high because the latter
necessarily overlays a group identity on one's other identities. Groups
gain their moral authority and power from having members that are
able and willing to pursue group interests. This pursuit is typically
predicated on a strong group identity, cohesion, and norms that support group efforts and by rituals and symbolic expressions that maintain the salience and coherence of the group. Groups are inherently
fragile, however, because they are composed of individuals with various idiosyncratic identities and thus potentially contradictory goals,
values, beliefs, perceptions, and so on (Deaux, Reid, Mizrahi, & Ethier,
1995). Thus, groups must *work* to maintain their viability and cohesion—and the more precarious the group, the more likely that individuals who resist the group's norms and do not participate in its
rituals will be seen as rejecting the group itself. The implication is that

groups can become quite tyrannical in demanding ritualistic conformity, thereby exacerbating ambivalence toward the group.

Consequently, just as groups may be motivated to resist the organization, individuals may be motivated to resist the group. Barker (1993) describes how self-managing teams in a manufacturing firm distilled abstract values (e.g., take ownership for success, emphasize quality) into concrete decisions and norms (e.g., learn all jobs required by the team, come to work on time). These decisions and norms became progressively formalized as rules that team members policed (e.g., dock a day's pay for lateness), such that team meetings began to have a confrontational tone. The rules, although backed with the moral authority of team consensus, were perceived by many—particularly newcomers—as an "iron cage" in which conformity was expected and nonconformity was punished, precipitating stress and resentment.

Ironically, management practitioners and scholars have increasingly touted self-managing teams and empowerment as antidotes to the claustrophobia and inertia often induced by conventional control systems; the normative control exerted by such teams, however, may be experienced as *more* constraining than the externally imposed controls they were said to have replaced (Barker, 1993; Collinson, 1992).

Justifying Resistance

To understand acts of control and resistance, one must understand the *meanings* that the actors attribute to their behavior. Those in power tend to be somewhat insulated from the potential fallout of their actions by values, ideologies, norms, and traditions that legitimate the distribution of power and the means by which it is exercised. For instance, Sunar (1978) argues that powerful actors such as slave owners often rely on pejorative stereotypes of the powerless to justify the status quo. Moreover, as the values and ideologies of powerholders become embedded in the organization—as hierarchical control is transformed into technical, bureaucratic, and normative control—they become institutionalized and taken for granted, conferring a sense of legitimacy and permanence and thus discouraging resistance (Ashforth & Humphrey, 1995).

The upshot, then, is that an act of resistance requires one to reject the "definition of the situation" (Hodson, 1995, p. 84) provided by the powerholders. Judging by the sheer prevalence of resistance in contemporary organizations, most individuals appear able to reject at least portions of the organizational orthodoxy and blunt some of its demands. There are several reasons why this might be so. First, life in industrialized societies requires that one wear many hats across situations and over time: Parent, coworker, spouse, community member, and so on. In response to the need to juggle the often competing demands among these social identities, one develops a facility for compartmentalizing identities and donning and doffing the appropriate hat(s) as each situation requires. The self, in short, is multifaceted, and the search for balance leads one to bracket the demands of any single identity (Broadhead, 1980). Furthermore, a multifaceted self has more internal resources for resisting external demands. Whistleblowers, for instance, often have a strong moral orientation derived from external social identities (e.g., family, church) (Near & Miceli, 1987).

Second, regarding the organizational self in particular, the much-publicized erosion of job security and the growing contingency workforce have severely affected the willingness of individuals to trust in organizational orthodoxies. As loyalty gives way to cynicism and detachment, the popular press proclaims the death of the "organization man" and urges individuals to protect themselves by maintaining their options and managing their own careers ("Managing Your Career," 1996). Thus, a 1987 survey by Ashforth and Lee (1989) reported that the perceived legitimacy of managerial influence over employees had greatly eroded since a comparable study in 1962.

Third, research on various self-serving biases indicates that individuals tend to focus on aspects of a given situation that are most consistent with their own interests, to interpret ambiguous situations in a manner consistent with those interests, and to use various cognitive defense mechanisms to ward off threats to self- and social esteem (Cramer, 1991; McClure, 1991). Thus, individuals are adept at constructing self-serving interpretations of organizational events and edicts and to conclude that they are being treated unfairly. It is a small step to rationalize acts that are detrimental to the organization as justified acts of resistance. Following Sykes and Matza's (1957) typology of "techniques of neutralization," common justifications for sabotage, theft, tardiness, and sloppy work include denial of victim (the organization deserved it), denial of injury (it can afford the loss), condemnation of condemners (it does worse things), defense of necessity (e.g., refusing to be cowed by a tyrannical boss), and, for collective resistance, higher loyalties (Giacalone & Rosenfeld, 1987; Hodson, 1991; Hollinger, 1991). A common thread running through these justifications is *identity maintenance:* The resister seeks rationales that preserve an image of rectitude.

Finally, as noted, subcultures often emerge around collections of individuals that feel threatened. Such subcultures are characterized by shared myths that provide self-serving explanations for the threat, positively differentiate the group from others, and provide justifications for actions against other groups and wider organizational interests (Tajfel, 1984). In short, threatened groups develop a local cosmology that acts as a countervailing force to the dominant culture. Sitkin and Stickel (1996) describe how scientists in a corporate research laboratory feared that a new total quality management program would demystify the research process and undermine their claims to professionalism. Consequently, they focused selectively on aspects of the program that clashed with their values and practices, while ignoring those that did not, and they developed self-serving rationales for their subsequent opposition. A precursor of such resistance, and a recurring theme in studies of rank-and-file resistance, is the balkanization of the organization into "us versus them" (Collinson, 1992; Thompson, 1983).

Thus, the involvement of peers in the social construction and enactment of resistance tends to *normalize* the practice, a normality that is reinforced with each iteration. Mars (1994, pp. 17-18) describes how workers came to regard fiddles as "an everyday part of work-life" such that "it was often abnormal *not* to fiddle." Indeed, acts of resistance often take on moral overtones as the rationales invoked by the subculture cloak resistance in noble pursuits, such as justice and dignity ("righteous indignation," "moral outrage," "objecting on principle") (Folger, 1993). Bies and Tripp (1996, p. 259) found that attributions for negative organizational events often occurred in settings "with others who would help construct and support the victim's view of the event" and thus stoke their desire for retribution.

Given the relative ease with which acts of resistance can be justified, there is a real danger of romanticizing resistance. Labor process and radical or critical theorists often paint a portrait of the noble but downtrodden worker fighting valiantly against a system of oppression governed by greedy capitalists or impersonal bureaucracies

(Braverman, 1974; Nichols & Beynon, 1977). There are undoubtedly many cases in which this is an apt description. It must be remembered, however, that the legitimacy of resistance is in the eye of the beholder, and the cultures—whether dominant or otherwise—that provide the legitimating ideologies are constructed through the prism of members' self-interests. One of the enduring truths about control and resistance is that people in each camp tend to believe *they* are on the side of the angels.

In summary, although resistance can be displayed in countless forms, all forms can be arrayed on at least three underlying dimensions: Targeted versus diffuse, facilitative versus oppositional, and authorized versus unauthorized. Many acts of resistance are intended, consciously or not, to provoke substantive change, to make a symbolic declaration of one's views and identity (if only to oneself), or both. Where the primary or sole motive is symbolic, resistance may appear quite quixotic to observers. Groups can greatly amplify the power of resistance by legitimating self-interested behavior and by lending raw clout. Groups, however, tend to impose their own values, beliefs, and norms on members and may therefore become an object of resistance in their own right. Finally, although acts of resistance require at least tacit justification in the eyes of the resister, people tend to be incredibly versatile at rationalizing even acts that are patently self-serving.

The Resistance Cycle

Control → Resistance

Research on role transitions suggests that newcomers settle into new work roles by simultaneously adapting the self to suit the situation and adapting the situation to suit the self (Brett, 1984). One outcome is a "psychological contract," a more or less tacit understanding of the terms of exchange between the newcomer and the organization (Rousseau, 1995). Any unilateral change to these terms is apt to be perceived as a breach of contract and therefore a threat to face, inciting anger and a desire to retaliate (Morrison & Robinson, 1997). Moreover, reactance theory suggests that the terms in question will become more valued precisely because they are under attack (Brehm,

1993); ironically, aspects of identity may not be valued or even salient until they are threatened.

The implication is that resistance is most likely when an instance of control is first imposed or is changed in an undesired way. This is particularly true if norms of procedural justice are not observed (e.g., lack of warning or justification), the threat is perceived to be severe, and one mistrusts the organization because these conditions exacerbate the threat to one's identity as a self-determining person deserving of status and due process. Furthermore, because people need to believe that bad things do not happen accidentally—they require a causal agent—the greater the threat to face, the more likely one is to believe that the threat was deliberate and to personalize blame (Rousseau, 1995). Nonetheless, because of the ambivalence of even the most committed members, the ubiquity of self-serving biases, and the ease with which self-interested acts can be rationalized, resistance is frequently lodged against organization-backed changes both big and small.[3]

If one chooses *not* to resist a salient threat when it first becomes apparent, however, then resistance will become progressively less likely. Compliance creates strong normative expectations of continued compliance, bolstered by a revised psychological contract, emergent behavioral scripts, and an identity of nonresister (e.g., "loyal," "wimp"). Individuals may not resist because, in a real sense, they do not know how to break their emerging normative constraints. Miller (1986) suggests that such constraints largely account for the failure of many subjects in the famous Milgram obedience experiments to defy the authority figure.

Power and Resistance

Power is correlated with the willingness to engage in targeted resistance because it affects the likelihood that resistance will thwart the threat and it helps insulate one from any repercussions. For example, Tucker (1993) found that temporary employees tended to avoid confronting management directly with their complaints for fear of being reprimanded or fired and instead resorted to gossip, theft, and noncooperation or simply tolerated the issues. Nonetheless, a recurring theme in studies of seemingly powerless people, such as slaves and concentration camp inmates, is the variety of ingenious avenues for resistance—although covert and unauthorized—that they often discover (Mellon, 1990). Power, therefore, has a stronger impact on the form of resistance than on its frequency.

Resistance → Countercontrol

There are countless cases in which resistance has proved effective in provoking substantive change. Acts that are targeted, facilitative, and authorized tend to be the most effective because they focus attention directly on organizationally sanctioned issues using organizationally sanctioned means. Conversely, the more diffuse the act, the more readily the cause can be ignored or the less likely that the cause will be apparent; and the more oppositional and unauthorized the act, the more likely that it will be perceived as a threat to the organization's hegemony and provoke countercontrol.

Thus, just as the imposition of organizational control may threaten the identity of the individual, certain acts of resistance may threaten the organization's identity as self-determining. The greater the perceived threat to the organization, the swifter and more severe the countercontrol. For example, Near and Miceli (1987) conclude that the more dependent an organization is on a given wrongdoing, the more likely it is to retaliate against a whistle-blower: What matters most is the degree of threat, not the veracity of the whistle-blower's claim. Indeed, if resistance is not anticipated, management may be panicked into a reflexive and heavy-handed response.

Sometimes, the purpose of resistance is to *incite* countercontrol—to bait or goad management into reacting harshly. Again, this is particularly true of targeted, oppositional, or unauthorized acts. Inciting harsh countercontrol accomplishes two purposes: It tarnishes the reputation of management as rational and fair, and it may enhance the subcultural reputation of the resister. In yet another irony of resistance dynamics, it is management's reaction that sanctifies the resister's identity as that of a "martyr," "leader," "troublemaker," or whatever designation is valued by the subculture: Ignoring the act is tantamount to ignoring the actor, leaving him or her to appear impotent. Kunda (1992, p. 105) describes how an engineer strongly challenged a vice president during a presentation. Rather than take the bait, the vice president simply smiled, effectively reframing the attack "as a playful, humorous incident, an affirmation . . . rather than a rejection of [his] point of view."

Countercontrol → Resistance

As a reaffirmation if not an escalation of organizational control, countercontrol may well provoke further resistance. Countercontrol not only denies the legitimacy of the individual's reasons for resistance but also may brand the resister with a self-fulfilling label: If the label is perceived by the resister (and his or her subculture) as desirable, he or she may become motivated to live up to the label; if the label is instead perceived as undesirable, he or she may become motivated to seek vindication and continue to resist (Ashforth & Humphrey, 1995). Thus, a further irony of the resistance cycle is that "manager reprisals, intended to quiet the [resister], may actually serve to transform and politicize the individual" (Rothschild & Miethe, 1994, p. 252).

The resistance cycle, then, is potentially a vicious circle (Collinson, 1994). As in other models of interpersonal and intergroup conflict, the circle is sustained by self-serving biases, stereotypes, and strong emotions (Smith, 1982). Goodwill and trust may erode to the point where both sides are predisposed to read evil in the acts of the other, and the original grievances become lost amid recriminations and counterclaims. The conflict per se becomes the focus.

Resistance Over the Long Run

Because escalating resistance is difficult to endure, organizations often institutionalize means for processing complaints (e.g., grievance committees, ombudspersons, hotlines), thereby redirecting defiance into authorized channels. Many of the issues that trigger identity concerns, however, do not constitute admissible grounds for the machinery of dispute resolution.

In such cases, a range of outcomes is possible. At one extreme, as noted, resistance may produce substantive change in organizational practices. At the other extreme, resistance that produces little change or insufficient symbolic value may taper off. What was once unthinkable may become normal and expected. Indeed, if one comes to internalize a more negative identity consistent with the imposed control, resistance may cease altogether.[4] Shield (1988) chronicles how nursing home residents were inadvertently made to feel dependent and useless, and how this undermined their identity as efficacious adults and thus their willingness to assert themselves. Furthermore, resisters may be coopted, intimidated, or punished or—following Hirschman's (1970) exit-voice-loyalty model—may leave the organization. It is very unlikely, however, that resistance can be totally eradicated. As Hodson (1995, p. 94) states, "In the face of repression, it is easy for workers to temporarily discontinue resistance, to increase the subterfuge involved, or to substitute less observable forms of resistance."

Short of either extreme, resisters and their organizations are apt to muddle toward a revised psychological contract. According to negotiated order theory, organizations are composed of "tacit agreements and unofficial arrangements" (Day & Day, 1977, p. 130) that enable members to work more or less cooperatively in the face of conflict and ambiguity. Seemingly fixed and formal structures and procedures are often interpreted and applied in fluid ways that reflect the needs of the moment and of interested parties. Although the theory emerged largely from studies of health professionals in hospitals, the central notion of a negotiated order—of *mutual accommodation*—is applicable even to seemingly powerless individuals in highly formalized settings. Studies of factory life are replete with examples of routine rule violations that are tacitly condoned by management as long as the violations are not flagrant and do not seriously impair productivity (Balzer, 1976; Collinson, 1992).

The negotiated order of routinized resistance often assumes a ritualistic cast: Certain rules are chronically violated, and management periodically enforces them to remind employees of its authority. Morgan (1975, p. 214) described how factory workers habitually broke rules regarding the use of radios, provoking crackdowns: " 'You occasionally get witch hunts here. . . . Things are hot for a week or so and then everyone forgets about it.' " The dance of resistance-countercontrol is mutually acceptable because it allows employees to exercise their preferred identities, but it does not seriously challenge the hegemony of management (Burawoy, 1979; Collinson, 1994). To an outsider, the dance may appear childish; to an insider, given ambivalence and the symbolic value of resistance, it is laden with meaning.

In summary, resistance over the long run tends to resemble a punctuated equilibrium model (Gersick, 1991). An imposition or change of control that is perceived to threaten a valued facet of one's identity is likely to be resisted. Resistance may assume a variety of forms—targeted or diffuse, oppositional or facilitative, and authorized or unauthorized—depending on the nature and severity of the threat and the relative power of the players. This resistance may trigger iterations of countercontrol and further resistance. Typically, the outcome is a mutual accommodation that, perhaps grudgingly, becomes encoded in a revised psychological contract and is more or less taken for granted. As this occurs, resistance that may initially have been targeted is likely to give way to more diffuse and sporadic acts. The outcome is a more or less stable and ritualistic dance of mutually tolerable acts of resistance and countercontrol. Emerging issues may prompt new impositions of control, however, punctuating the equilibrium and triggering new iterations of resistance and countercontrol. As Morgan (1975, p. 224) states, "Order is actively maintained and at the same time continually open to question."

Conclusion

To function effectively, organizations must regulate the activities of their members in the service of organizational goals. Increasingly, controls that regulate behaviors are being complemented or supplanted by normative controls that regulate the very thoughts and feelings of members. Part of the normative freight conveyed by such controls includes organizationally endorsed values, beliefs, modes of sense-making, and definitions of the organizational self. Because individuals have existing and emerging self-conceptions abstracted from experiences and roles beyond their organizational involvement, the imposition of definitions may be perceived as threatening and trigger ambivalence toward the organization. In this light, resistance can be seen as a contest for meaning, a way of asserting or preserving a valued sense of identity independent of—or antagonistic to—the organization's definition.

Acts of resistance can be arrayed along at least three dimensions: As targeted to the perceived source of threat (vs. diffuse), as facilitative of organizational or public interest goals (vs. oppositional), and as consistent with organizational norms for expressing dissent (as authorized vs. unauthorized). Regardless of their form, acts of resistance have tremendous symbolic value in the contest for meaning, even if they go unwitnessed. Resistance, however, often occurs in collusion with others, particularly work group peers. The involvement of others lends weight to the substantive and symbolic impact of resistance and can help foster supportive views of what resistance signifies. As unions grasped long ago, there is power in numbers. Groups, however, typically impose their own prescriptions for identity and may therefore also come to be a target of resistance. Whether in response to the organization's definition of self or the group's, acts of resistance tend to be easily justified: Individuals routinely construct their world through a self-serving lens. Finally, acts of resistance are often embedded in an iterative cycle of control → resistance → counter-control, eventually leading to a mutual and more or less stable accommodation. This equilibrium, however, tends to be periodically punctuated by emergent or recurrent issues, provoking new iterations of the cycle.

The overarching theme of this chapter is that resistance often concerns the negotiation of meaning. Organizations, largely through normative control, foster images of not only how one should act but also of what one should value and believe and how one should think. Organizations, in short, at least tacitly foster images of *who* one should be. The pernicious aspect of normative control is that it can overwhelm or undermine one's existing sense of self. As Kunda (1992, p. 221) concluded from his study of a high-tech firm, normative control can provoke an "ambivalent, fluctuating, ironic self, at war with itself and with its internalized images" of the prescribed organizational member. Acts of resistance can help foster and sustain a countervailing sense of organizational self that is more consistent with one's own sense of self, as grounded in valued social and personal identities.

The negotiation of meaning is readily apparent in how administrators tend to construct employees' resistance. There is a pervasive tendency to *personalize* it—to view acts that defy authority as driven by the personal failings of the individual and his or her peers. The power of administrators to regulate action, thought, and feeling is institutionalized in systems of control that veil the use of power and confer a patina of legitimacy, thus making resistance appear unwarranted and ultimately pointless. Thus, resisters "are depicted as disgruntled workers opposing the change efforts or control systems of rational managers" (Brower & Abolafia, 1995, p. 150). It becomes easy to think of the resister as a hysterical reactionary—a misguided neoLuddite. At the risk of romanticizing resistance, we view many acts of resistance (but by no means all) as a response to such institutionalized or systemic forces. Resistance is often about one's willingness and ability to negotiate identity in the face of pressures to simply accept a prefabricated definition of organizational self. Indeed, it may well be the more committed organizational members that care most deeply about meaning and react most strongly to definitions they regard as inappropriate.

In conclusion, a certain ambivalence toward the organization and its definitions of self appears to be natural and healthy and fuels resistance. As such, resistance has the potential power to challenge the normative order. In addition, if hierarchical, technical, and bureaucratic controls are indeed being supplanted by normative control—whether at the organization or group level—then such challenges may become increasingly common.

Notes

1. Similarly, some identities derive their appeal from contrasts with other identities and the tension between them. For example, play on the job is enjoyed precisely because it represents a time-out from work; continuous play would be self-defeating because it would deprive play of its meaning.

2. This functionalist view of resistance is reminiscent of the functionalist view of deviance in groups: It demarcates the bounds of acceptable resistance, it shows that a group is tolerant within these bounds, and, if a member exceeds them, it allows the group to close ranks and affirm their identity and legitimacy (Dentler & Erikson, 1959).

3. Of course, there is not a necessary one-to-one correspondence between threats and acts of resistance. A "tipping effect" may occur in which, as minor grievances accumulate, trust and goodwill erode to the point where even a trivial issue may incite resistance ("the last straw").

4. Many fictional works on the future, such as George Orwell's *1984* and Margaret Atwood's *Handmaid's Tale*, portray a society that extrapolates and exaggerates insidious elements of our own, creating a sharp contrast. What makes these works so frightening is not the contrast per se but the depiction of the exaggerated elements as normal and accepted.

References

Ashforth, B. E. (1989). The experience of powerlessness in organizations. *Organizational Behavior and Human Decision Processes, 43*, 207-242.

Ashforth, B. E., & Humphrey, R. H. (1995). Labeling processes in the organization: Constructing the individual. In L. L. Cummings & B. M. Staw (Eds.), *Research in organizational behavior* (Vol. 17, pp. 413-461). Greenwich, CT: JAI.

Ashforth, B. E., & Lee, R. T. (1989). The perceived legitimacy of managerial influence: A twenty-five year comparison. *Journal of Business Ethics, 8*, 231-242.

Ashforth, B. E., & Mael, F. A. (1996). Organizational identity and strategy as a context for the individual. In J. A. C. Baum & J. E. Dutton (Eds.), *Advances in strategic management* (Vol. 13, pp. 19-64). Greenwich, CT: JAI.

Balzer, R. (1976). *Clockwork: Life in and outside an American factory.* Garden City, NY: Doubleday.

Barker, J. R. (1993). Tightening the iron cage: Concertive control in self-managing teams. *Administrative Science Quarterly, 38,* 408-437.

Bies, R. J., & Tripp, T. M. (1996). Beyond distrust: "Getting even" and the need for revenge. In R. M. Kramer & T. R. Tyler (Eds.), *Trust in organizations: Frontiers of theory and research* (pp. 246-260). Thousand Oaks, CA: Sage.

Braverman, H. (1974). *Labor and monopoly capital: The degradation of work in the twentieth century.* New York: Monthly Review Press.

Brehm, J. W. (1993). Control, its loss, and psychological reactance. In G. Weary, F. Gleicher, & K. L. Marsh (Eds.), *Control motivation and social cognition* (pp. 3-30). New York: Springer-Verlag.

Brett, J. M. (1984). Job transitions and personal and role development. In K. M. Rowland & G. R. Ferris (Eds.), *Research in personnel and human resources management* (Vol. 2, pp. 155-185). Greenwich, CT: JAI.

Broadhead, R. S. (1980). Multiple identities and the process of their articulation: The case of medical students and their private lives. In N. K. Denzin (Ed.), *Studies in symbolic interaction* (Vol. 3, pp. 171-191). Greenwich, CT: JAI.

Brower, R. S., & Abolafia, M. Y. (1995). The structural embeddedness of resistance among public managers. *Group & Organization Management, 20,* 149-166.

Burawoy, M. (1979). *Manufacturing consent: Changes in the labor process under monopoly capitalism.* Chicago: University of Chicago Press.

Cheney, G. (1983). On the various and changing meanings of organizational membership: A field study of organizational identification. *Communication Monographs, 50,* 342-362.

Collinson, D. (1994). Strategies of resistance: Power, knowledge and subjectivity in the workplace. In J. M. Jermier, D. Knights, & W. R. Nord (Eds.), *Resistance and power in organizations* (pp. 25-68). London: Routledge.

Collinson, D. L. (1992). *Managing the shopfloor: Subjectivity, masculinity and workplace culture.* Berlin: de Gruyter.

Coser, L. A. (1974). *Greedy institutions: Patterns of undivided commitment.* New York: Free Press.

Coser, R. L. (1956). A home away from home. *Social Problems, 4,* 3-17.

Cramer, P. (1991). *The development of defense mechanisms: Theory, research, and assessment.* New York: Springer-Verlag.

Dalton, M. (1968). Reorganization and accommodation: A case in industry. In H. S. Becker, B. Geer, D. Riesman, & R. S. Weiss (Eds.), *Institutions and the person* (pp. 14-24). Chicago: Aldine.

Day, R., & Day, J. V. (1977). A review of the current state of negotiated order theory: An appreciation and a critique. *Sociological Quarterly, 18,* 126-142.

Deaux, K., Reid, A., Mizrahi, K., & Ethier, K. A. (1995). Parameters of social identity. *Journal of Personality and Social Psychology, 68,* 280-291.

Dentler, R. A., & Erikson, K. T. (1959). The functions of deviance in groups. *Social Problems, 7,* 98-107.

Edwards, R. (1979). *Contested terrain: The transformation of the workplace in the twentieth century.* New York: Basic Books.

Erikson, K. T. (1976). *Everything in its path: Destruction of community in the Buffalo Creek flood.* New York: Touchstone.

Folger, R. (1993). Reactions to mistreatment at work. In J. K. Murnighan (Ed.), *Social psychology in organizations: Advances in theory and research* (pp. 161-183). Englewood Cliffs, NJ: Prentice Hall.

Gersick, C. J. G. (1991). Revolutionary change theories: A multilevel exploration of the punctuated equilibrium paradigm. *Academy of Management Review, 16,* 10-36.

Giacalone, R. A., & Rosenfeld, P. (1987). Reasons for employee sabotage in the workplace. *Journal of Business and Psychology, 1,* 367-378.

Goffman, E. (1961a). *Asylums: Essays on the social situation of mental patients and other inmates.* Garden City, NY: Doubleday.

Goffman, E. (1961b). *Encounters: Two studies in the sociology of interaction.* Indianapolis, IN: Bobbs-Merrill.

Goodstein, L. (1979). Inmate adjustment to prison and the transition to community life. *Journal of Research in Crime and Delinquency, 16,* 246-272.

Gottfried, H. (1994). Learning the score: The duality of control and everyday resistance in the temporary-help service industry. In J. M. Jermier, D. Knights, & W. R. Nord (Eds.), *Resistance and power in organizations* (pp. 102-127). London: Routledge.

Hirschman, A. O. (1970). *Exit, voice, and loyalty: Responses to decline in firms, organizations, and states.* Cambridge, MA: Harvard University Press.

Hodson, R. (1991). The active worker: Compliance and autonomy at the workplace. *Journal of Contemporary Ethnography, 20,* 47-78.

Hodson, R. (1995). Worker resistance: An underdeveloped concept in the sociology of work. *Economic and Industrial Democracy, 16,* 79-110.

Hollinger, R. C. (1991). Neutralizing in the workplace: An empirical analysis of property theft and production deviance. *Deviant Behavior, 12,* 169-202.

Jackall, R. (1988). *Moral mazes: The world of corporate managers.* New York: Oxford University Press.

Knights, D., & Vurdubakis, T. (1994). Foucault, power, resistance and all that. In J. M. Jermier, D. Knights, & W. R. Nord (Eds.), *Resistance and power in organizations* (pp. 167-198). London: Routledge.

Kondo, D. K. (1990). *Crafting selves: Power, gender, and discourses of identity in a Japanese workplace.* Chicago: University of Chicago Press.

Kramer, R. M. (1996). Divergent realities and convergent disappointments in the hierarchic relation: Trust and the intuitive auditor at work. In R. M. Kramer & T. R. Tyler (Eds.), *Trust in organizations: Frontiers of theory and research* (pp. 216-245). Thousand Oaks, CA: Sage.

Kunda, G. (1992). *Engineering culture: Control and commitment in a high-tech corporation.* Philadelphia: Temple University Press.

Linn, R. (1988). Moral judgment in extreme social contexts: Soldiers who refuse to fight and physicians who strike. *Journal of Applied Social Psychology, 18,* 1149-1170.

Mael, F., & Ashforth, B. E. (1992). Alumni and their alma mater: A partial test of the reformulated model of organizational identification. *Journal of Organizational Behavior, 13,* 103-123.

Managing your career. (1996, January 15). *Fortune,* 33-78.

Mars, G. (1994). *Cheats at work: An anthropology of workplace crime* (rev. ed.). Aldershot, UK: Dartmouth.

McClure, J. (1991). *Explanations, accounts, and illusions: A critical analysis.* Cambridge, UK: Cambridge University Press.

Mellon, J. (Ed.). (1990). *Bullwhip days: The slaves remember: An oral history.* New York: Avon.

Miller, D. (1986). Milgram redux: Obedience and disobedience in authority relations. In
    N. K. Denzin (Ed.), *Studies in symbolic interaction* (Vol. 7A, pp. 77-105). Greenwich,
    CT: JAI.

Mintzberg, H. (1979). *The structuring of organizations: A synthesis of the research*. Englewood
    Cliffs, NJ: Prentice Hall.

Morgan, D. H. J. (1975). Autonomy and negotiation in an industrial setting. *Sociology of
    Work and Occupations, 2*, 203-226.

Morrison, E. W., & Robinson, S. L. (1997). When employees feel betrayed: A model of how
    psychological contract violation develops. *Academy of Management Review, 22*,
    226-256.

Near, J. P., & Miceli, M. P. (1987). Whistle-blowers in organizations: Dissidents or reform-
    ers? In L. L. Cummings & B. M. Staw (Eds.), *Research in organizational behavior*
    (Vol. 9, pp. 321-368). Greenwich, CT: JAI.

Nichols, T., & Beynon, H. (1977). *Living with capitalism: Class relations and the modern factory*.
    London: Routledge & Kegan Paul.

Paules, G. F. (1991). *Dishing it out: Power and resistance among waitresses in a New Jersey
    restaurant*. Philadelphia: Temple University Press.

Pfeffer, J. (1981). Management as symbolic action: The creation and maintenance of orga-
    nizational paradigms. In L. L. Cummings & B. M. Staw (Eds.), *Research in orga-
    nizational behavior* (Vol. 3, pp. 1-52). Greenwich, CT: JAI.

Porter, G. (1996). Organizational impact of workaholism: Suggestions for researching the
    negative outcomes of excessive work. *Journal of Occupational Health Psychology,
    1*, 70-84.

Prasad, A., & Caproni, P. (1993, August). *Combatting the ideology of work place aggression:
    Towards a typological understanding of resistance*. Paper presented at the annual
    meeting of the Academy of Management, Atlanta.

Prasad, P. (1993, August). *Opposition and disengagement as resistance: Symbolic affirmation
    and the creation of personal space*. Paper presented at the annual meeting of the
    Academy of Management, Atlanta.

Rothschild, J., & Miethe, T. D. (1994). Whistleblowing as resistance in modern work or-
    ganizations: The politics of revealing organizational deception and abuse. In J. M.
    Jermier, D. Knights, & W. R. Nord (Eds.), *Resistance and power in organizations*
    (pp. 252-273). London: Routledge.

Rousseau, D. M. (1995). *Psychological contracts in organizations: Understanding written and
    unwritten agreements*. Thousand Oaks, CA: Sage.

Salancik, G. R. (1977). Commitment and the control of organizational behavior and belief.
    In B. M. Staw & G. R. Salancik (Eds.), *New directions in organizational behavior*
    (pp. 1-54). Chicago: St. Clair Press.

Schlenker, B. R. (1986). Self-identification: Toward an integration of the private and public
    self. In R. F. Baumeister (Ed.), *Public self and private self* (pp. 21-62). New York:
    Springer-Verlag.

Shield, R. R. (1988). *Uneasy endings: Daily life in an American nursing home*. Ithaca, NY:
    Cornell University Press.

Sitkin, S. B., & Stickel, D. (1996). The road to hell: The dynamics of distrust in an era of
    quality. In R. M. Kramer & T. R. Tyler (Eds.), *Trust in organizations: Frontiers of
    theory and research* (pp. 196-215). Thousand Oaks, CA: Sage.

Smith, K. K. (1982). *Groups in conflict: Prisons in disguise*. Dubuque, IA: Kendall/Hunt.

Smith, K. K., & Berg, D. N. (1987). *Paradoxes of group life: Understanding conflict, paralysis,
    and movement in group dynamics*. San Francisco: Jossey-Bass.

Sunar, D. G. (1978). Stereotypes of the powerless: A social psychological analysis. *Psychological Reports, 43,* 511-528.

Swann, W. B., Jr. (1990). To be adored or to be known? The interplay of self-enhancement and self-verification. In E. T. Higgins & R. M. Sorrentino (Eds.), *Handbook of motivation and cognition* (Vol. 2, pp. 408-448). New York: Guilford.

Sykes, G., & Matza, D. (1957). Techniques of neutralization: A theory of delinquency. *American Sociological Review, 22,* 664-670.

Tajfel, H. (1984). Intergroup relations, social myths and social justice in social psychology. In H. Tajfel (Ed.), *The social dimension: European developments in social psychology* (Vol. 2, pp. 695-715). Cambridge, UK: Cambridge University Press.

Terkel, S. (1975). *Working.* New York: Avon.

Thompson, W. E. (1983). Hanging tongues: A sociological encounter with the assembly line. *Qualitative Sociology, 6,* 215-237.

Trice, H. M. (1993). *Occupational subcultures in the workplace.* Ithaca, NY: ILR.

Tucker, J. (1993). Everyday forms of employee resistance. *Sociological Forum, 8,* 25-45.

Wells, P. A. (1988). The paradox of functional dysfunction in a Girl Scout camp: Implications of cultural diversity for achieving organizational goals. In M. O. Jones, M. D. Moore, & R. C. Snyder (Eds.), *Inside organizations: Understanding the human dimension* (pp. 109-117). Newbury Park, CA: Sage.

6

Losing Our Religion

On the Precariousness of Precise Normative Standards in Complex Accountability Systems

PHILIP E. TETLOCK

In *Paradise Lost*, John Milton (1643/1975) declared that his task was to explain the ways of God to man, not the ways of man to God. Modern decision theorists, devoutly secular almost to the last man or woman, do not anchor their prescriptive rules of judgment and choice in any divine mandate, but they arguably do do the functional equivalent. They make strong ontological assumptions from which follow stern normative principles of sound judgment and rational choice. Some posit, for example, that people are intuitive economists who try to maximize expected utility in competitive markets (Becker, 1996). People err when they fall short of this standard by ignoring opportu-

AUTHOR'S NOTE: I appreciate Rod Kramer's helpful comments. This work was supported by NSF Grant SBR 732396 and by the Mershon Center at The Ohio State University.

nity costs, struggling to recoup sunk costs, or failing to confront difficult value trade-offs (Kagel & Roth, 1995; Thaler, 1991). Other contemporary theorists assume that people are intuitive scientists who aspire
to cognitive mastery of the causal structure of their environment
(Kelley, 1967). People err when they fail to use rules of causal or
probabilistic inference that the scientific community considers normatively defensible (Fiske & Taylor, 1991). Examples of judgmental shortcomings within this framework include the fundamental attribution
error (the tendency for people to be too quick to jump to conclusions
about the personalities of others even when plausible situational explanations for others' conduct exist), belief perseverance (the tendency
for people to be too slow to adjust their prior impressions in response
to new evidence), and overconfidence (the tendency to think that one
knows more than one does).

   In this chapter, I do not argue that the search for stable normative
benchmarks against which to assess human performance is inherently
misguided. I do argue, however, that the conceptual problems that
arise in making such judgments are often sorely underestimated. I
sketch an approach to judgment and choice that rests on ontological
commitments that highlight the controversial character of claims about
human rationality. The guiding assumption is that, for many purposes,
it is useful to think of people as intuitive politicians whose primary
goal is to protect their social identities in the eyes of the key constituencies to whom they feel accountable. The core function of thought
becomes assessing the justifiability of response options. Consciously
or unconsciously, people often engage in internalized dialogues such
as, "If I did this, what would others say? What could I say in response?
What conclusions should reasonable observers then draw about my
competence or character?" Within this intuitive-politician framework,
we lose the precise standards for judging rationality that flow so
readily from the intuitive economist and scientist research programs.
Judgments of the rationality or morality of opinions and decisions now
become inherently contestable. What looks like an error from one
ideological perspective will often look eminently reasonable from
other perspectives.

   Of course, metaphors are not explanations. It clarifies little to say
that people are intuitive politicians. Some politicians are renowned for
their flexibility (or opportunism)—their chameleon-like ability to take
on different personas in front of different audiences (Snyder, 1979).

Others are renowned for their rigidity (or faithfulness to principle)—their unwillingness to compromise even if it costs them their offices or lives. Whereas there is a voluminous body of research that unpacks the exact meaning of the scientist or economist metaphors by clarifying the various senses in which people are skilled or bumbling intuitive scientists or economists, there is a relative paucity of studies that shed light on the various senses in which people might be said to be good or bad intuitive politicians. It is, accordingly, necessary to descend from the ethereal realm of metaphorical meta-theory and to advance testable middle-range theories of how people function as intuitive politicians.

This chapter is organized into two sections. The first section takes up the challenge of specifying a testable middle-range theory of the intuitive politician. I discuss four foundational assumptions of accountability theory, sketch predictions concerning when various cognitive, emotional, and behavioral strategies of coping with accountability are likely to be activated, and note some pockets of relevant evidence.

In the second section, the focus shifts away from the descriptive and explanatory adequacy of accountability theory and toward the normative implications of the framework. Here, a wistful autobiographical digression may be justified. I began experimental work on the impact of accountability on judgment and choice approximately 17 years ago with a simple-minded mission: to document when people can be induced to think in more complex, self-critical ways than the emerging cognitive-miser paradigm seemed to permit (Kahneman, Slovic, & Tversky, 1982; Nisbett & Ross, 1980). I viewed accountability as a "debiasing manipulation," but my data quickly taught me to circumscribe sharply the types of debiasing claims I could make for accountability manipulations (Tetlock, 1983b, 1985a, 1985b, 1992). Only certain types of accountability motivate complex, self-critical thought. Much hinges on what people are asked to justify, on when they learn of the need to do so, and on the perceived attributes of the audience to whom accounts must be given. Moreover, even when I succeeded in motivating complex self-critical thought, doing so was useful in attenuating only certain judgmental biases, such as primacy, overattribution, and overconfidence. There are large categories of biases on which motivating self-critical thought has no effect (e.g., the conjunction fallacy, insensitivity to base rates and sample sizes, and preference reversals) and still other biases that are actually amplified by encouraging self-critical thought (e.g., the dilution effect, ambiguity aversion, compromise and attraction effects, and loss aversion). Delineating the social boundary conditions on judgmental biases proved a far more complex undertaking than I initially supposed (Simonson & Nye, 1992; Tetlock, 1992; Tetlock & Lerner, in press).

Approximately 5 years ago I began to investigate more complex forms of accountability that prevail in real-life organizational and political settings but are difficult to "stage" in the laboratory. It became clear that accountability is not just a set of "empirical boundary conditions" on the bias-and-error portrait of the human decision maker: It highlights "normative boundary conditions" as well. An empirical boundary condition stipulates when a given response tendency (assumed to be an error or bias) is attenuated or amplified by some form of accountability. Tetlock and Kim (1987), for example, found that accountability to a well-informed audience with unknown views sharply reduced overconfidence in the predictions that subjects made of the future behavior of others—an effect at least partly mediated by the tendency of accountable subjects to form more complex impressions of the personalities of others that allowed for situational exceptions and characterological inconsistencies to broad-brush trait attributions such as "he's dominant" or "she is friendly." In the jargon of accountability theory, "preexposure-to-evidence accountability to a well-informed audience of unknown views" defines an empirical boundary condition on the well-replicated overconfidence bias. A normative boundary condition stipulates when judgments of "error or bias" depend on both the accountability matrix within which the decision maker is embedded and on the theoretical or ideological orientation of the observers who are passing judgment on the decision process. Tetlock, Lerner, and Boettger (1996) offer a simple, apolitical example of a normative boundary condition that foreshadows the more complex, politically charged cases to be examined later. They noted that some scholars view the dilution effect—a form of underconfidence—as a rational response to conversational norms that direct us to look for relevant information in others' utterances (Schwarz, 1994), whereas other scholars view it as a cognitive bias rooted in overreliance on the representativeness heuristic (Nisbett, Zuckier, & Lemley, 1981). Consistent with a conversational-norm interpretation, Tetlock et al. (1996) found the strongest dilution effect when people expected to justify their judgments to their putative conversational partner and thought the norm of relevance held; consistent with a cognitive bias interpretation, however, the dilution effect persisted even when people believed that conversational norms did not hold and that all judgments were anonymous. The dilution effect can apparently be broken down into normatively defensible and indefensible components.

In this chapter, I focus on the unjustly neglected problem of documenting normative boundary conditions. Drawing on results from surveys of both public- and private-sector managers, I present findings on managers' views of the rationality of cognitive tendencies often hypothesized to be errors or biases, their views of the adaptiveness of coping strategies often hypothesized to be triggered by various types of accountability, and their views of the efficacy and even morality of accountability ground rules on which institutions often rely to correct cognitive or motivational shortcomings of individual human beings. Here, we discover an intriguingly lawful pattern of individual differences, with liberals and conservatives often in deep disagreement at all three levels of analysis: on what counts as a bias at the individual level, on what counts as a laudable or at least defensible response to accountability at the meso level, and on what counts as a just or unjust accountability regime at the macro level.

Here, there is an anti-Miltonian moral for social psychology and organizational behavior. Rather than judging decision processes against supposedly eternal normative truths, we need to recognize the conflicting functionalist and normative criteria that different camps invoke to judge the rationality of individual judgment and of the accountability regimes designed to correct human imperfections.

Accountability Theory

Earlier versions of the theory have been presented elsewhere (Tetlock, 1985b, 1992). The basic assumptions of the framework can therefore be summarized simply.

Accountability as a Universal
Feature of Decision Environments

Accountability is a ubiquitous feature of judgment and choice outside the psychological laboratory. It links individual decision makers to the institutions within which they live and work by reminding them of the need to (a) act in accord with prevailing norms and (b) advance compelling justifications or excuses for conduct that deviates from those norms. No social system can function for long without accountability checks on group members (Axelrod, 1984; Edgerton, 1985). Of course, social systems also cannot rely exclusively on external modes of social control for maintaining order (Kramer & Tyler, 1996). The transaction costs of monitoring everybody all the time would be staggering. Accordingly, accountability theory stipulates that trust and self-accountability are necessary for the smooth functioning of institutions but hardly sufficient.

Audience-Approval Motive

People seek approval for both intrinsic and extrinsic reasons. Evidence for an intrinsic motivation comes from laboratory studies that point to a propensity—that appears remarkably early in human development—to respond automatically and viscerally to frowns, angry looks, and other signs of censure. We can interpret this robust finding (Baumeister & Leary, 1995) in either a social-learning framework (in the course of life, other people become incredibly potent secondary reinforcers via their association with primary drive reduction) or in an evolutionary framework (people have been naturally and sexually selected to be sensitive to signs of disapproval because the survival of our ancestors hinged on maintaining the goodwill of their fellow hominids). Evidence for extrinsic motivation comes largely from the exchange theory tradition (Rusbult, Farrell, Rogers, & Mainous, 1988) in which we seek the approval primarily of the powerful, who control what we want to a greater degree than we control what they want ("asymmetric resource dependency").

Motive Competition

Although social approval is a major motivator, it is not the simple and sovereign regulator of all conduct. The model identifies four additional motives that may conflict with or transform the expression of the approval motive, including (a) achieving cognitive mastery of causal structure (emphasized by classic attribution theory [Kelley, 1967]), (b) minimizing mental effort and achieving quick closure (emphasized by recent theories of social cognition [Fiske & Taylor,

1991; Kruglanski & Webster, 1996]), (c) maximizing benefits and minimizing the costs of relationships (emphasized by exchange theories [Blau, 1964]), and (d) holding true to one's principles and convictions (emphasized by theories of ego and moral development as well as by theories of cognitive consistency [Festinger, 1964; Loevinger, 1976]).

Linking Motives to Coping Strategies

The final component of the model links broad motivational orientations to particular coping strategies by specifying how each core motive can be amplified or attenuated by the interpersonal and institutional context. The conceptual formula for generating predictions is to identify situational or dispositional variables that either increase or decrease the perceived importance of a core motive or the perceived feasibility of achieving a motivational objective in a given context. For example, well-known individual difference scales, such as social anxiety, public self-consciousness, self-monitoring, and need for affiliation, should moderate the approval motive; scales such as need for cognition, need for closure, and tolerance for ambiguity should moderate willingness to invest cognitive effort in solving accountability predicaments; scales such as Machiavellianism should predict a calculating exchange-theoretic approach to social life; and measures of moral and ego development should predict resistance to social pressure to violate internalized values. Situational manipulations, such as the importance of the audience or the size of the material incentive to act opportunistically, should respectively alter the perceived importance of social approval or the temptation to "defect"; manipulations such as the perceived ability of the audience to detect sloppy or self-serving thinking should motivate complex self-critical thought; and manipulations of cognitive load should affect decision makers' ability to engage in complex, self-critical thought.

Accountability theory maintains that every request for justification raises the question of how one will "define oneself" in the eyes of either external constituencies (that one sees as separate from one's "self") or internalized constituencies (familiar voices "inside one's head" that one accepts as integral parts of one's self). In each case, diverse facets of one's social identity may be at stake: Will others view me as cooperative or confrontational, sycophantic or candid, flexible or rigid, principled or opportunistic, compassionate or efficient, a can-do implementer or a chronic complainer, a supine yes person or a courageous whistle-blower? I consider five identity-defining choices that frequently arise in accountability predicaments, how people might deal with them, and how observers might react to the various strategies people might deploy.

To Accommodate the Audience or to Be True to One's Self

Perhaps the most fundamental choice in any accountability predicament is the balancing of internal convictions ("I believe X") and external pressures ("They want me to endorse Y"). Accountability theory posits that the widely observed phenomenon of attitude shifting (Cialdini, Levy, Herman, Kozlowski, & Petty, 1976; Jones & Wortman, 1973; Tetlock, 1983a) is likely to the degree that the social approval motive is strong: The audience should be powerful (it should control resources that the decision maker values but the decision maker should control little that the audience values), and the audience should be firmly committed to its position and intolerant of other positions (a further incentive for accommodating it rather than arguing or reasoning with it). Strategic attitude shifting is, however, a feasible strategy only to the degree that one knows the views of the anticipated audience, and attitude shifting becomes a psychologically costly strategy to the degree that it requires compromising basic convictions and principles (triggering dissonance) and it becomes socially costly to the degree that shifting one's attitude requires backtracking on past commitments (making one look duplicitous, hypocritical, or sycophantic to others). When the optimal preconditions have been satisfied, however, attitude shifting represents a cognitively efficient, politically expedient strategy that does not undermine one's concept as a principled being or one's reputation for integrity in the wider social arena.

Accountability theory also warns to expect controversy over how to evaluate coping strategies. Some audiences (especially those with individualistic values) will deplore attitude shifting as duplicitous or sycophantic and applaud expressing one's true attitudes as candid and courageous; other audiences (especially those that value collectivist interdependence) will react in the opposite fashion—applauding attitude shifters as diplomatic team players and denouncing those who say what is on their minds as tactless boors.

Self-Criticism Versus Self-Justification

People can respond to demands for accountability in a preemptively self-critical fashion (anticipating reasonable objections that critics might raise to one's position [Tetlock, Skitka, & Boettger, 1989]), or they can respond in a self-justifying fashion (directing mental effort toward generating as many plausible reasons as they can to bolster past positions taken [Staw, 1980]). In each case, accountability motivates thought, but in the former the thoughts take a dialectically complex form ("on the one hand, . . . on the other hand . . .") and in the latter the thoughts all run in one evaluative direction.

Accountability theory identifies certain conditions as most conducive to preemptive self-criticism: (a) decision makers are accountable either to an audience with unknown views (there is good reason to anticipate objections from both ends of the political spectrum) or to two audiences with conflicting views that recognize the legitimacy of the other point of view (there is hope of finding a viable compromise), (b) decision makers perceive the audience to be powerful (and equally powerful if more than one audience), (c) decision makers perceive the audience or audiences to be cognitively sophisticated (and equally sophisticated if more than one audience), and (d) decision makers do not hold strong private views and are unconstrained by public commitments. Defensive bolstering, the cognitive mirror image of preemptive self-criticism, is most likely to be activated when decision makers (a) are accountable to powerful audiences that are not believed to be knowledgeable about the topic, (b) are accountable for past actions that cast some doubt on their competence or morality and that cannot be retracted or reversed, and (c) recognize that it is impossible to deny responsibility for the conduct in question.

Again, accountability theory predicts political controversy over the "value spin" to be placed on coping strategies. Audiences that are tolerant of ambiguity and dissonance will view preemptive self-criticism as a sign of cognitive maturity (pointing to its effectiveness in attenuating biases such as overattribution, overconfidence, and belief perseverance [Tetlock, 1992]) and defensive bolstering as a sign of self-righteous rigidity (pointing to its role in escalating commitment to sunk costs [Staw, 1980]). Audiences of a more authoritarian bent will take the opposite perspective—viewing self-criticizers as confused or weak-kneed vacillators (pointing to their increased susceptibility to the dilution effect and loss aversion [Tetlock & Boettger, 1989, 1994]) and viewing the bolsterers as principled souls who take courageous stands (in politics, consistency often connotes strength [Suedfeld, 1992; Tetlock, McGuire, & Mitchell, 1991]).

To Duck, to Take a Stand, or to Mediate

People are often accountable not just to a single audience but also to two or more audiences that may be in deep disagreement. Account-ability theory posits that people cope with these contradictory de-mands in one of three distinct ways: (a) by decision-evasion tactics, such as buck-passing (transferring responsibility to others), procrasti-nation (delaying the decision until the controversy subsides), and obfuscation (shrouding one's position in opaque bureaucratic and technical language). These tactics are especially likely when the con-flicting constituencies are approximately equally powerful, each con-stituency denies the legitimacy of the other's point of view (an apparently irreconcilable conflict), there are institutional precedents for evading taking a stand, and decision makers' own views are rela-tively weak; (b) by plunging into controversy and aligning oneself with one or another constituency. This tactic is tempting when the conflict-ing constituencies deny each other's legitimacy, there are no institu-tional precedents for decision avoidance, one audience is more powerful than the other and favors a position similar to one's own personal preference, and the decision makers themselves are publicly committed to strongly held personal opinions; and (c) by mediating the dispute between the conflicting constituencies. This strategy is likely when the disputants are both equally powerful, they acknowl-edge each other's legitimacy (so the conflict appears, in principle, to be resolvable), and there are no institutional precedents for decision evasion.

Again, only a modicum of political imagination is required to envision the positive and negative value spins that might be attached to these strategies: Is decision evasion cowardly or shrewd? Is plunging into controversy brave or reckless? Is trying to mediate a dispute public spirited or naive meddling?

To Implement or Resist the Collective Mission?

Thus far, the focus has been on contexts in which people feel accountable for expressing opinions or decisions but not for actual work performance (be it assembling more widgets, increasing billable hours for the firm, or generating more publications). In many work settings, doing what the evaluative audience wants may require long days of grueling labor and emotionally wrenching trade-offs involving family and friends. The identity-defining choice is now between "good organizational citizenship" and resisting the new accountability regime.

Accountability theory predicts internalization of demanding performance-appraisal standards when people perceive the standards to be high but attainable, perceive that the standards were set through fair procedures, and perceive the standards to be necessary for organizational survival (Kelman, 1958). Accountability theory also identifies predictors of covert or overt forms of resistance to standards. Resistance is especially likely when people perceive the standards (a) to be unreasonably high (employees see no method of achieving them that does not involve either unethical conduct or superhuman effort), (b) to have been set in a procedurally unjust manner (employees' perspectives were ignored), and (c) to be unnecessary for organizational survival (the standards "privilege" some small group, such as top management, that may reap "windfall profits"). The preferred first line of resistance is some variant of the voice option. Drawing on the arguments of Hirschman (1970) and the evidence of Tyler (1990), accountability theory predicts not only that people will seize opportunities to protest, to offer accounts, and to appeal to higher authorities but also that the institutional availability of such opportunities will both enhance the legitimacy of the accountability regime and reduce the anger triggered by the imposition of "unfair" performance standards. The mere existence of the voice option can thus reinforce loyalty to the system. Depriving people of the voice option triggers a second, more destructive form of resistance that undermines both organizational loyalty and efficiency. People may now express their resentment by exploiting loopholes in the performance appraisal standards or by doing the bare minimum necessary to avoid dismissal. Corner-cutting is the preferred coping response when people are alienated from the accountability regime, perceive exploitable ambiguities or inconsistencies in performance appraisal standards, and regard dismissal as unlikely and exit as unattractive. Finally, there is a third line of resistance: exercising the exit option—an option likely to be triggered when people are alienated from the accountability regime, see no loopholes to be exploited in performance appraisal standards, and regard dismissal for nonperformance as likely and exit as more attractive than the status quo (Rusbult et al., 1988; Withey & Cooper, 1989).

It is relatively easy to attach a negative, positive, or neutral value spin on each resistance strategy. "Protest" can be deplored as whining or praised as a willingness to stand up to authority (Ashforth, 1992). Excuses or justifications for performance shortfalls may be dismissed as transparently defensive efforts to escape responsibility for failure or heeded as valuable information that highlights the work unit's perspective on the difficulties it confronts and on other contributions it is making (Schlenker, 1985; Scott & Lyman, 1968). Strategic redirection of work effort may be condemned as immoral, even criminal, or it may be viewed (e.g., from a Marxist viewpoint) as a laudable effort to reclaim workers' right to control the terms of their employment (Jackall, 1988). Appeals to higher authority may appear to be litigious game-playing and bureaucratic obstructionism from the authority's standpoint, but they may appear to be courageous whistle-blowing and valiant efforts to protect important values under siege from the standpoint of workers and their activist allies outside the organization (Near & Miceli, 1987). Role disengagement may be viewed as apathetic, self-indulgent, and lazy or as a self-protective or affirmative response to an abusive work environment. Finally, exiting the accountability system may be disparaged as desertion and disloyalty or accepted as a rational response to a competitive labor market.

When all forms of resistance to "illegitimate" accountability demands have been blocked, the theory predicts "grudging compliance"—a prediction consistent with the portrait that Withey and Cooper (1989) offer of some loyalists as "entrapped persons" who have abandoned hope of successfully exercising either the voice or exit options. Grudging compliance, however, is much less attractive (from an organizational perspective) than voluntary internalization of the accountability mandate. Grudging compliance carries a high price tag in terms of demoralization of workforce (the feeling of being treated with contempt and intrusively monitored) as well as in terms of transaction costs (the agents of social control must continually guard against subordinates developing new ingenious strategy for identifying loopholes or disengaging from their roles or appealing to external authorities). Consistent with the advice of a long string of social theorists, including Weber, Parsons, and Hirschman, accountability theory affirms that effectively functioning social systems are populated by people trying to do the right thing even when no one is watching.

Diffusing Sacrifice Versus Concentrating Pain

A burdensome requirement of many managerial roles is the necessity of implementing budget cuts. One strategy is to spread the required sacrifice across many constituencies, thereby avoiding severe impact on any one; another strategy is to concentrate the pain of the budget cuts on a small subset of constituencies that might be chosen on efficiency grounds (the least productive) or on political grounds (the least connected). The former strategy is especially likely when decision makers confront small budget cuts (that can be easily diffused to the point of invisibility across many constituencies), it is difficult to identify distinctive pockets of inefficiency, and the groups singled out for deep budget cuts in the past have demonstrated a formidable ability to mobilize political protest. Here, many observers, especially those sympathetic to communitarian notions of corporate social responsibility, will approve of spreading the pain of the budget cuts widely (although others will be unconvinced, warning of demosclerotic degeneration [Rauch, 1994]). By contrast, decision makers will be inclined to concentrate cuts on a small number of constituencies to the degree that they confront large budget cuts, they can easily distinguish more from less efficient work units, and they know that groups previously singled out for deep cuts have little capacity to resist. Here, many observers, especially those who have internalized the efficiency value of neoclassical economics, should applaud the "bite-the-bullet" willingness of decision makers to do what is necessary to preserve the long-term viability of the organization (although others will be unconvinced, warning of the damage to "social capital" from ruthless "downsizing" [Etzioni, 1996]).

Normative Boundary Conditions

The foregoing discussion underscores the ease of putting flattering or unflattering "spins" on each coping strategy identified by accountability theory. Which interpretation prevails often hinges on a political struggle in which ideological proponents and detractors do their utmost to convince moderates that decision makers have responded prudently or imprudently to accountability demands.

This political dimension to judgments of irrationality is strangely missing from both laboratory studies of individual judgment and many field studies of organizational decision making. In a series of questionnaire studies of private- and public-sector managers, I tried to correct this omission by systematically probing the implicit normative theories that managers possess concerning the (ir)rationality of widely discussed cognitive biases (such as overconfidence and the fundamental attribution error), the (mal)adaptiveness of coping strategies for dealing with accountability demands (including attitude shifting, preemptive self-criticism, protesting, and corner-cutting), and the (in)appropriateness of alternative accountability systems for achieving organizational or societal goals (e.g., shareholder vs. stakeholder models of corporate governance and hierarchical vs. multiple advocacy methods of structuring decision-making systems). The Appendix presents some illustrative scenarios to which an ad hoc sample of private- and public-sector managers ($N = 259$) was asked to respond—by judging either the character of the central actor or the soundness of the institutional configuration of accountability ground rules.

Although the results will not startle students of political ideology, they merit serious consideration from students of decision making. Systematic individual differences emerge in the evaluations offered of both coping strategies and institutional ground rules (for more detailed presentation, see Tetlock, 1998). The most reliable predictor of evaluations was a six-item political-ideology scale that measured confidence that free-market solutions were superior to government intervention in solving societal problems, concern about the income inequality that "unregulated free enterprise" creates, skepticism toward government bureaucracy, belief that high taxes impede economic growth, and ideological self-identification. A useful supplementary predictor proved to be an ad hoc cognitive-style scale that was created by sampling items from Kruglanski's need-for-closure scale. The following sections discuss the key findings.

Ideology and Cognitive Bias

Liberal managers regarded overattribution and overconfidence as more serious errors than did conservatives, who, in turn, were more concerned with the dangers of underconfidence and of failing to hold people responsible for outcomes they could have controlled. Overconfidence connoted arrogance for many liberals but a can-do enthusiasm for many conservatives; insensitivity to situational explanations struck many liberals as harsh, uncaring, and punitive but struck many conservatives as a useful check on unbridled discretion and as a powerful means of focusing employee attention on "what matters." From this conservative perspective, insensitivity to situational explanations was not a sign that managers were defective intuitive scientists guilty of the fundamental attribution error; rather, it was a sign that they were shrewd intuitive prosecutors who knew how to pressure people to perform.

Ideology and Coping Strategies

Liberal managers often praised "preemptively self-critical thought" as a sign of an open-minded willingness to consider plausible objections to one's point of view, whereas conservatives often viewed the same coping strategy as evidence of an irresolute, wishy-washy, and confused style of thinking (echoing Truman's famous complaint that he needed a one-handed economist from whom he could extract some unequivocal advice). These ideological disagreements carried over to other coping strategies as well. Conservatives gave more positive evaluations than did liberals to "bolsterers," who downplayed trade-offs and made as strong a case as they could for a specific policy recommendation (bolsterers were seen as clear and decisive vs. simplistic and rigid). Also, liberals were more sympathetic than conservatives to "underdogs" in accountability regimes who tried to escape responsibility to conflicting audiences by buck-passing (sensible and not cowardly), who exercised the "voice option" to protest unfair new performance standards (justifiable complaint and not whiny), or who exploited loopholes in performance standards when all the voice options of expressing discontent had been systematically foreclosed (understandable frustration, not just "cheats and liars"). Liberals were also likely to defend managers who diffused the pain of budget costs across a wide range of constituencies (fair and compassionate), whereas conservatives were more inclined to defend managers who "bit the bullet" and concentrated budget cuts on the least efficient sectors of the organization.

Ideology and Accountability Regimes

The dependent variable shifts from judgments of actors to those of organizational and social systems. Regarding evaluations of hierarchical versus multiple advocacy methods of structuring internal decision making, liberals were more negative toward the top executive team in which tightly constraining norms limited the arguments that could be raised but kept meetings moving along quickly. By contrast, liberals were more positive toward the team that displayed tolerance for dissent, even though this resulted in prolonged meetings. Relative to conservatives, liberals stressed the dangers of incestuous in-group accountability (sometimes mentioning groupthink). By contrast, conservatives stressed the advantages of like-minded people working together smoothly and making decisions efficiently.

An even more pronounced pattern of ideological polarization emerged when managers judged the merits of the shareholder versus the stakeholder models of corporate governance. Conservatives favored the monistic regime of accountability solely to shareholders ("It is hard enough to do one thing well, less still have a dozen"), whereas liberals embraced the value of accountability to a host of constituencies whose interests would often have to be combined in different ways in different situations ("Corporations can't be allowed just to focus on making money" and "There is more to running a society than just efficiency").

Although many respondents were aware of normative counterarguments, awareness should not be confused with acceptance. Some conservatives feared that liberal efforts to promote the stakeholder model of corporate governance reflected a fundamental misunderstanding of capitalism and would impair long-term economic growth by encumbering corporate executives and boards with ever more elaborate communitarian regulations ("You can't do anything until the local politicians, labor unions, environmentalists, minority-rights activists, and other assorted opportunists have all had their palms crossed with silver") and by creating an open-ended source of excuses for poorly performing managers to put off long-suffering shareholders ("The stakeholder model aggravates the principal-agent problem at the heart of corporate capitalism—It gives agents too much wiggle room to evade their responsibility to promote the principal's interest"). Some liberals returned the compliment ("People who like the shareholder model are just out for number one and they really don't give a damn what happens to anybody else" or "Society created corporations and it has the right to define the ground rules under which they operate").

Concluding Remarks

The current results affirm a key implication of the intuitive politician metaphor for thinking about judgment and choice: Cognitive biases and institutional correctives are in the eye of the ideological beholder. The politician metaphor reminds us not only of when people can be induced to become more thoughtful or vigilant but also of the inherent contestability of the standards we use for labeling individuals or institutions as irrational or flawed. There is no divine mandate for current classifications of errors and biases. People make normative judgments and these judgments are deeply colored by their intellectual and ideological preconceptions.

It is still certainly reasonable, however, to ask for a more precise understanding of the cognitive and motivational mechanisms underlying conflicting evaluations of both social systems and human responses to those systems. Attributing these individual differences to "political ideology" or, for that matter, to "cognitive style" leaves much unexplained. We need a more nuanced understanding of observers' intuitive theories about how society works and about when investing cognitive effort in complex decision rules does or does not pay off in particular environments. We also need to tease apart the relative importance of factual versus value disagreements in driving ideological controversies over both accountability regimes and individual rationality. Liberals and conservatives sometimes agree that there is an efficiency cost, for example, to adopting the stakeholder model of corporate governance, but the liberals may feel that the price is worth paying because of what we gain in promoting other societal values, whereas conservatives may view the price as too steep.

Another caveat is in order. The mere existence of ideological disagreement does not mean that all existing classifications of error and bias are misconceived. Liberals and conservatives sometimes agree that certain response tendencies (e.g., breakdowns in transitivity in choice tasks, conservatism in Bayesian belief-adjustment tasks) are indeed irrational. Also, when liberals and conservatives do disagree on what constitutes a bias—the fundamental attribution error or overconfidence—or on what constitutes a prudent accountability regime for checking imperfections of human nature, it may still be possible to sort out the various respects in which one camp is right or wrong. The ideologically charged character of the evaluations does, however, suggest a serious potential for bias within the overwhelmingly liberal research community within the behavioral and social sciences (Lipset & Rabb, 1978). Insofar as judgments of judgmental bias and of how to correct it hinge on the observer's assessment of human nature, of the political world, and of the worthiness of competing values, there is a nontrivial risk that the disciplines of social psychology, behavioral decision theory, and organizational behavior may be offering an ideologically skewed portrait of both our cognitive ills and accountability correctives.

Finally, I return to Milton, who has personified high-handed prescriptivism in this chapter. It is worth noting, however, that William Blake, an unlikely defender, insisted that the author of *Paradise Lost* was really of the "devil's party" without knowing it. Milton, notwithstanding his protestations, was every bit as interested in explaining the ways of man to God as those of God to man. In this spirit, I might also be suspected of membership in the devil's party. The intuitive politician metaphor encourages insolence; it gives us license to talk back to the secular deities of rationality that exert as much influence on the postindustrial world of the late 20th century as interpretations of God's will once exerted on the agrarian theocracy of mid-17th-century England.

Appendix

Illustrative Scenarios for Assessing Evaluations of
Cognitive Biases, Coping Strategies, and
Accountability Regimes

Cognitive Biases

Insensitivity/hypersensitivity to situational explanations (fundamental attribution/situational error)

> a. "J. M. is a manager who adopts a 'no-excuses' approach to
> evaluating the people who report to him. He feels that most
> people are just far too inventive at concocting stories for failing
> to achieve organizational goals. He therefore holds people
> strictly accountable for objective performance indicators, tak-
> ing into account only extreme extenuating circumstances."

> b. "J. M. is a manager who thinks it is a bad idea to base evalu-
> ations of the people reporting to him on 'so-called objective per-
> formance indicators.' He needs to hear the employees'
> perspectives on why they failed or succeeded in achieving key
> organizational goals and always bases his evaluations primar-
> ily on the accounts that employees provide on what is actually
> going on in both the business and their personal lives.

Over- and underconfidence

> (a) and (b) "L. B. is a manager who believes that it is possible
> to make one of two basic mistakes in decision making: to be
> underconfident (to think one does not have useful information
> in hand when one really does) or to be overconfident (to think
> one has useful information in hand when one really does not).
> [L. B. believes, however, that underconfidence or overconfi-
> dence is a much more serious threat to high-quality decision
> making.]"

Strategies of Coping With Accountability

Attitude shifting versus candor

> (a) and (b) "A. F. has been asked by his boss to write an analysis of a controversial problem that he has never seen before. His boss, however, has already taken a strong and difficult to reverse stand. He knows what the boss wants to see in the analysis. [He responds by putting his own views to the side and slanting the report strongly in the direction of his boss's views.] [He responds by offering the most accurate analysis he knows how to offer, even though some conclusions may run contrary to his boss's views.]"

Preemptive self-criticism versus bolstering

> (a) and (b) "K. M. has been asked by senior management for his views on which research and development projects should be put on the 'fast track.' The 'favorites' of senior management are at this point impossible even to guess. Also, K. M. is not on record as having taken any prior stands on the issue. He responds by [offering a complex and balanced appraisal of the pros and cons of each project, anticipating the key criticisms that can be leveled at each, and specifying the trade-offs that management confronts] [identifying the projects he considers most promising and making as powerful and compelling a case as he can for those options]."

Coping with conflicting audiences

> (a)-(d) "V. S. is caught between the conflicting demands of two senior managers who are in bitter disagreement. One wants V. S. to endorse a particular proposal; the other insists that V. S. should reject it. V. S. [finds a way of shifting responsibility for making the final decision to a committee] [tries to come up with a complex compromise solution that might be satisfactory to both senior managers] [makes a political judgment as to which senior manager is likely to prevail in the struggle for power and endorses the course of action preferred by the manager] [makes

a personal judgment as to which course of action is the best on its merits and endorses it]."

Coping with rising performance standards

(a) and (b) "P. T. learns that the work unit he manages will be expected in the coming year to achieve an increase in productivity he considers unreasonably and unfairly large. His unit was not consulted at all during the process of setting the new productivity standard, and the firm is doing well and is in no danger of insolvency. P. T. [protests by providing a detailed set of reasons why he considers the new standards to be both unreasonable and unfair to his work unit] [keeps his objections to himself and does the best he can do to achieve the new performance standards]."

Coping with loss of voice option

(a)-(c) "P. T. learns that the work unit he manages will be expected in the coming year to achieve an increase in productivity he considers unreasonably and unfairly large. His unit was not consulted at all during the process of setting the new productivity standard, and the firm is doing well and is in no danger of insolvency. P. T. also learns that senior management is absolutely committed to implementing the new performance standards and wants to hear 'no protests, no excuses, no appeals.' P. T. [starts looking for another job] [starts looking for ways to play the performance-evaluation game in a more strategic way, finding ways to boost the numbers that senior management cares about and cut back on responsibilities and functions that are important to the organization but not rewarded] [does his best to implement the new standards down to the last detail]."

Accountability Regimes

Shareholder versus stakeholder models of corporate governance

(a) and (b) "Corporation X is founded on the philosophy that it exists [for one overriding purpose: to maximize return to shareholders, and that, if all corporations were faithful to the same mission, the net result would be a vibrant economy that would yield the greatest prosperity for the greatest number] [to achieve a variety of sometimes conflicting goals, including providing competitive returns to shareholders; ensuring all employees of good livelihoods and respectful treatment; maintaining good relations with customers, suppliers, and local communities; and pursuing sound social and environmental policies. In this view, if all corporations were faithful to the same mission, the net result would be a fundamentally more decent and just society]."

Hierarchical versus multiple advocacy models of internal decision making

(a) and (b) "Top management in this organization has worked together a long time and know each other well. [They think it most important to make decisions efficiently, minimizing unnecessary discussion and getting to the key points quickly. Accordingly, they have streamlined the decision process, requiring top managers to justify important decisions to the group but rarely going outside the group to solicit critical suggestions.] [They think it critical that important decisions be subjected to thorough, critical analysis from a variety of viewpoints inside and outside the organization, even if it is time-consuming. Accordingly, top managers can never be sure of the types of objections that might be raised to their proposals in decision-making meetings.]"

References

Ashforth, B. E. (1992). The perceived inequity of systems. *Administration and Society, 24,* 375-408.

Axelrod, R. (1984). *The evolution of cooperation.* New York: Basic Books.

Baumeister, R. F., & Leary, M. F. (1995). The need to belong: Desire for interpersonal attachments as a fundamental human motive. *Psychological Bulletin, 117,* 497-529.

Becker, G. (1996). *The economic way of looking at behavior: The Nobel lecture.* Stanford, CA: Stanford University, Hoover Institution on War, Revolution, and Peace.

Blau, P. (1964). *Exchange and power in social life.* New York: John Wiley.

Cialdini, R. B., Levy, A., Herman, C. P., Kozlowski, I. T., & Petty, R. E. (1976). Elastic shifts of opinion: Determinants of direction and durability. *Journal of Personality and Social Psychology, 34,* 663-672.

Edgerton, R. B. (1985). *Rules, exceptions, and social order.* Berkeley: University of California Press.

Etzioni, A. (1996). *The new golden rule: Community and morality in a democratic society.* New York: Basic Books.

Festinger, L. (Ed.). (1964). *Conflicts, decision, and dissonance.* Stanford, CA: Stanford University Press.

Fiske, S., & Taylor, S. (1991). *Social cognition.* New York: McGraw-Hill.

Hirschman, A. O. (1970). *Exit, voice, and loyalty: Responses to decline in firms, organizations, and states.* Cambridge, MA: Harvard University Press.

Jackall, R. (1988). *Moral mazes: The world of corporate managers.* New York: Oxford University Press.

Jones, E. E., & Wortman, C. (1973). *Ingratiation: An attributional approach.* Morristown, NJ: General Learning Press.

Kagel, J. H., & Roth, A. E. (Eds.). (1995). *The handbook of experimental economics.* Princeton, NJ: Princeton University Press.

Kahneman, D., Slovic, P., & Tversky, A. (Eds.). (1982). *Judgment under uncertainty: Heuristics and biases.* New York: Cambridge University Press.

Kelley, H. H. (1967). Attribution theory in social psychology. In D. Levine (Ed.), *Nebraska symposium on motivation* (Vol. 15, pp. 192-240). Lincoln: University of Nebraska Press.

Kelman, H. C. (1958). Compliance, identification, and internalization: Three processes of attitude change. *Journal of Conflict Resolution, 2,* 51-60.

Kramer, R. M., & Tyler, T. R. (Eds.). (1996). *Trust in organizations: Frontiers of theory and research.* Thousand Oaks, CA: Sage.

Kruglanski, A. W., & Webster, D. M. (1996). Motivated closing of the mind: "Seizing" and "freezing." *Psychological Review, 103,* 263-268.

Lipset, S., & Raab, E. (1978). *The politics of unreason.* Stanford, CA: Stanford University Press.

Loevinger, J. (1976). *Ego development—Conceptions and theories.* San Francisco: Jossey-Bass.

Milton, J. (1975). *Paradise lost* (S. Elledge, Ed.). New York: Norton. (Original publication 1643)

Near, J. P., & Miceli, M. P. (1987). Whistle-blowers in organizations: Dissidents or reformers? In L. L. Cummings & B. M. Staw (Eds.), *Research in organizational behavior* (Vol. 9, pp. 321-368). Greenwich, CT: JAI.

Nisbett, R. E., & Ross, L. (1980). *Human inference: Strategies and shortcomings of social judgment.* New York: Appleton-Century-Crofts.

Nisbett, R. E., Zukier, H., & Lemley, R. (1981). The dilution effect: Nondiagnostic information. *Cognitive Psychology, 13,* 248-277.

Rauch, J. (1994). *Demosclerosis: The silent killer of American government.* New York: Times Books.

Rusbult, C. E., Farrell, D., Rogers, G., & Mainous, A. G. (1988). Impact of exchange variables on exit, voice, loyalty, and neglect: An integrative model of responses to declining job satisfaction. *Academy of Management Journal, 31,* 599-627.

Schlenker, B. R. (Ed.). (1985). *The self and social life.* New York: McGraw-Hill.

Schwarz, N. (1994). Judgment in a social context: Biases, shortcomings, and the logic of conversation. In M. P. Zanna (Ed.), *Advances in experimental social psychology* (pp. 123-162). San Diego: Academic Press.

Scott, M., & Lyman, S. (1968). Accounts. *American Sociological Review, 33,* 46-62.

Simonson, I., & Nye, P. (1992). The effect of accountability on susceptibility to decision errors. *Organizational Behavior and Decision Processes, 51,* 416-446.

Snyder, M. (1979). Self monitoring processes. In L. Berkowitz (Ed.), *Advances in experimental social psychology* (Vol. 12, pp. 86-128). New York: Academic Press.

Staw, B. (1980). Rationality and justification in organizational life. In B. Staw & L. Cummings (Eds.), *Research in organizational behavior* (Vol. 2). Greenwich, CT: JAI.

Suedfeld, P. (1992). Cognitive managers and their critics. *Political Psychology, 13,* 435-453.

Tetlock, P. E. (1983a). Accountability and complexity of thought. *Journal of Personality and Social Psychology, 45,* 74-83.

Tetlock, P. E. (1983b). Accountability and the perseverance of first impressions. *Social Psychology Quarterly, 46,* 285-292.

Tetlock, P. E. (1985a). Accountability: A social check on the fundamental attribution error. *Social Psychology Quarterly, 48,* 227-236.

Tetlock, P. E. (1985b). Accountability: The neglected social context of judgment and choice. In B. Staw & L. Cummings (Eds.), *Research in organizational behavior* (Vol. 7, pp. 297-332). Greenwich, CT: JAI.

Tetlock, P. E. (1992). The impact of accountability on judgment and choice: Toward a social contingency model. *Advances in Experimental Social Psychology, 25,* 331-376.

Tetlock, P. E. (1998). *Cognitive biases and organizational correctives: Do both disease and cure lie in the eye of the ideological beholder?* Unpublished manuscript, The Ohio State University, Columbus.

Tetlock, P. E., & Boettger, R. (1989). Accountability: A social magnifier of the dilution effect. *Journal of Personality and Social Psychology, 57,* 388-398.

Tetlock, P. E., & Boettger, R. (1994). Accountability amplifies the status quo effect when change creates victims. *Journal of Behavioral Decision Making, 7,* 1-23.

Tetlock, P. E., & Kim, J. I. (1987). Accountability and judgment processes in a personality prediction task. *Journal of Personality and Social Psychology, 52,* 700-709.

Tetlock, P. E., & Lerner, J. S. (in press). The social contingency model of judgment and choice: Multifunctional but still dual-process? In S. Chaiken & Y. Trope (Eds.), *Dual process theories in social psychology.* New York: Guilford.

Tetlock, P. E., Lerner, J. S., & Boettger, R. (1996). The dilution effect: Judgmental bias, conversational convention, or a bit of both? *European Journal of Social Psychology, 26,* 915-935.

Tetlock, P. E., McGuire, C., & Mitchell, P. G. (1991). Psychological perspectives on nuclear deterrence. In *Annual review of psychology.* Palo Alto, CA: Annual Reviews.

Tetlock, P. E., Skitka, L., & Boettger, R. (1989). Social and cognitive strategies for coping with accountability: Conformity, complexity, and bolstering. *Journal of Personality and Social Psychology, 57,* 632-640.

Thaler, R. H. (1991). *Quasi rational economics.* New York: Russell Sage.

Tyler, T. R. (1990). *Why people obey the law.* New Haven, CT: Yale University Press.

Withey, M., & Cooper, W. (1989). Predicting exit, voice, loyalty, and neglect. *Administrative Science Quarterly, 34,* 521-539.

Under the Influence?

Organizational Paranoia and the Misperception of Others' Influence Behavior

RODERICK M. KRAMER
BENJAMIN A. HANNA

LBJ:	You better check with the Teleprompters. They went wild on us last night. . . . What was wrong with it?
Reedy:	It was a short circuit.
LBJ:	What caused it?
Reedy:	A short-circuit, sir, is when a wire gets overheated . . . and the wire snaps. . . . They're hard as hell to locate.
LBJ:	*I thought that it was almost sabotage, George.* [italics added]

—President Lyndon Johnson to aide George Reedy (as quoted in Beschloss, 1997, p. 361) during a secretly recorded exchange in the White House following a nationally broadcast speech

AUTHORS' NOTE: Earlier versions of this research were presented at conferences at the Harvard Law School Program on Negotiation, the University of Michigan Graduate School of Business Administration, the UCLA Anderson School of Management, the Stanford Center for Conflict and Negotiation, and the Russell Sage Foundation Conference on Trust in Organizations. We are grateful for comments from participants at these conferences and especially to Kenneth Arrow, Robert Cialdini, Russell Hardin, Jeff Pfeffer, Lee Ross, Bob Sutton, and Robert Wilson for their thoughtful suggestions.

M ost people recognize that success in organizational life depends, in no small measure, on the skillful use of social influence. People use social influence to obtain valuable organizational resources, to accomplish important goals they have set for themselves, and to more effectively manage their relationships with other people with whom they work. Along these lines, organizational theorists have long argued that the effective use of social influence is critical to obtaining and maintaining power in organizations (Cialdini, 1988; Gardner, 1990; George, 1980; Pfeffer, 1992). As Pfeffer noted, "The fact that we live in a social world and that organizations are interdependent social systems means that we can get things done only with the help of other people" (p. 225).

When people act as agents of influence, they are likely to consult their intuitions and beliefs about which influence strategies, of all those available to them, are likely to be effective against a given person in a given situation. Thus, for example, an employee may engage in acts of "strategic" ingratiation before asking for a raise because he or she believes the path to promotions is paved with flattery. Similarly, a manager may attempt to put a subordinate in a good mood before making an onerous request because he or she believes that people in good moods are more conciliatory. Yet another person may intentionally juxtapose intimidation and cajolery when dealing with a recalcitrant opponent in a negotiation because he or she believes a mixture of "good cop-bad cop" will be more effective than either good cop or bad cop alone.

Although people are often agents of influence, they recognize also that they are sometimes the targets of others' influence attempts, and the evidence suggests that perceptions and beliefs matter in these situations as well (Cialdini, 1988). Thus, a young faculty member may believe that his department chair has given him a particularly burdensome load of committee assignments to thwart his prospects for tenure, or a female physician may believe a senior male colleague is trying to undermine her confidence by continually questioning her surgical technique while in the operating room.

Such perceptions, of course, may be veridical. Sometimes people do attempt to exert influence over our perceptions and behavior, and sometimes our construal of the intentions and motives behind their actions are completely accurate. Just as obvious, however, is that our perceptions regarding their influence behavior can be in error. For example, the department chair in the first example may believe his junior colleague has tremendous potential and has given him useful committee assignments to bolster his visibility and raise his prospects for tenure. In the second example, the senior surgeon may simply be trying to develop the surgical talents of the young female resident in exactly the same way that he does with all those under his supervision.

As these examples suggest, people in organizations sometimes draw strikingly "sinister" inferences from even benign influence attempts by others—attributing overly personalistic and malevolent motives to what are, in fact, innocent or well-intentioned actions by others. Unfortunately, our understanding of this process of mistaken or flawed inference about others' influence attempts remains far from complete. Although there is a considerable literature on the social influence process (Cialdini, 1988), the sources of misperception in the influence process are less perfectly articulated. In what circumstances, for example, are people likely to make mistaken attributions about others' influence attempts? When and why are suspicions regarding others' influence behaviors exaggerated or misplaced?

These are the central questions we engage in this chapter. To do so, we take an exploratory approach to investigating some of the antecedents and consequences of misperception of influence attempts in organizations. In particular, we explore the role organizational paranoia plays in the misperception of others' influence attempts. Using as a point of departure Colby's (1981) conceptual model of clinical paranoia, we define organizational paranoia as an individual's exaggerated perceptions and beliefs that he or she is being harassed, threatened, harmed, persecuted, tormented, and thwarted by other individuals or groups in the organization. We argue that psychological and situational factors that increase organizational paranoia lead, in turn, to an exaggerated perception of others' influence behaviors.

To develop this general thesis, the current research uses as a point of departure a number of recent accounts that have suggested that former United States President Lyndon Baines Johnson began to display patterns of perception and behavior that bear striking similarities to clinical accounts of paranoia during the final years of his administration. According to these accounts, as opposition to his Vietnam policy increased in the late 1960s, President Johnson became convinced powerful enemies, both inside and outside the corridors of power in Washington, were out to get him and block attainment of his goals.

Extrapolating from these accounts, we derive a conceptual framework that explicates some of the antecedents and consequences of exaggerated suspicions about others' influence behavior in organizations.

We note at the outset that this model is based on a large volume of historical data on the Johnson presidency, including transcripts of recently released presidential tapes, oral histories, memoirs, journalistic accounts, and political biographies, including the following primary sources:[1] Anderson (1993), Barber (1972), Barrett (1993), Berman (1982, 1989), Beschloss (1997), Burke and Greenstein (1989), Califano (1991), Caro (1982), Clifford (1991), Dallek (1991), Goodwin (1988), Gruber (1991), Halberstam (1972), Heath (1975), Herring (1993), Johnson (1971), Kearns-Goodwin (1976), Miller (1980), Van DeMark (1991), and Wicker (1991).

Conceptualizing Organizational Paranoia

Before discussing the historical evidence, it is helpful first to provide a brief overview of theory and research on organizational paranoia, indicating how this concept and related concepts have been treated in prior work. Paranoia is a diagnostic psychiatric category that includes individuals suffering from a mental disorder that encompasses primarily delusions of reference (American Psychological Association [APA], 1987). Among the most conspicuous symptoms of this disorder is the paranoid person's insistence that he or she is the focus or target of other's behavior or actions (Cameron, 1943). As Colby (1981) noted,

> Around the central core of persecutory delusions [that preoccupy the paranoid person] there exists a number of attendent properties such as suspiciousness, hypersensitivity, hostility, fearfulness, and self-reference that lead the paranoid individual to interpret events that have nothing to do with him [sic] as bearing on him personally. (p. 518)

For example, Cameron (1943) and Fenigstein and Vanable (1992) recount the case of a woman who was so preoccupied with her own appearance that she became convinced other people were constantly noticing her looks as well, causing them to making disparaging remarks about her appearance behind her back.

Central to the concept of paranoia is the notion of paranoid cognitions, which have been defined by Colby (1981) as "persecutory delusions and false beliefs whose propositional content clusters around ideas of being harassed, threatened, harmed, subjugated, persecuted, accused, mistreated, wronged, tormented, disparaged, vilified, and so on, by malevolent others, either specific individuals or groups" (p. 518).

In clinical psychology, paranoid cognitions have usually been regarded as symptomatic of a psychiatric disorder (APA, 1987; Cameron, 1943) and have been presumed to be caused by abnormal personality factors that presumably give rise to such cognitions (Siegel, 1994). Recent social cognitive research, however, has advanced a very different conception of paranoid cognitions—one that affords considerably more attention to their social and situational determinants (Fenigstein & Vanable, 1992; Kramer, 1995b; Zimbardo, Andersen, & Kabat, 1986). This latter conception proceeds from the intuition that, in milder form, paranoid cognitions appear to be rather prevalent and can be observed even among "normal" individuals, especially when individuals find themselves in certain social situations. As Fenigstein and Vanable have cogently observed in this regard, ordinary people

> in their everyday behavior often manifest characteristics—such as self-centered thought, suspiciousness, assumptions of ill will or hostility, and even notions of conspiratorial intent—that are reminiscent of paranoia. . . . On various occasions, one may think one is being talked about or feel as if everything is going against one, resulting in suspicion and mistrust of others, as though they were taking advantage of one or were to blame for one's difficulties. (pp. 130-133)

In addition to suggesting that paranoid cognitions are fairly common, this research has also shed considerable light on their antecedents and determinants. Of particular relevance to the current analysis is evidence that paranoid cognitions are likely to occur in situations in which individuals (a) experience a heightened sense of self-consciousness, (b) feel under intense evaluative scrutiny, (c) feel that their identity or self-esteem is threatened, or all three.

As we argue in the next section, many of these conditions came together for Lyndon Johnson in the late 1960s as he confronted the most serious political crisis in his long and tumultuous rise to political power.

Organizational Paranoia in the Johnson White House: An Overview of the Evidence

During the late 1960s, President Lyndon Johnson found himself engaged in an increasingly difficult and all-consuming political struggle to convince members of Congress, the press, and the American people of the wisdom of his Vietnam policy. Unwilling to become the first American president to lose a major ground war, he remained reluctant to change the course of American policy in Southeast Asia. Although holding true to his course, he felt under enormous political pressure and experienced considerable physical and psychological stress over his Vietnam policy (Berman, 1989; Janis, 1983). A number of writers, including some who were quite close to Johnson and enjoyed intimate access to his personal views, have suggested that Johnson's behavior during this period bore striking similarities to clinical accounts of paranoia.

The most detailed and compelling of these descriptions have been provided by Johnson's aide, confidante, and eventual biographer, Doris Kearns-Goodwin. In describing Johnson's thought processes concerning opposition to Vietnam, Kearns-Goodwin (1976) stated,

> Members of the White House staff who had listened to the President's violent name-calling were frightened by what seemed to them signs of paranoia. Suddenly, in the middle of a conversation, his voice would become intense and low-keyed. He would laugh inappropriately and his thoughts would assume a random, almost incoherent quality, as he began to spin a vast web of accusations. (p. 316)

Equally dramatic incidents are recounted by Johnson's former speechwriter and adviser Richard Goodwin (1988). In assessing Johnson's paranoia, Goodwin noted that it was not so much what he said or did, but rather the

> disjointed, erratic flow of thought, unrelated events strung together, yet seemingly linked by some incomprehensible web of

connections within Johnson's mind. . . . It was a giant, if always partial, leap into unreason, an outward sign that the barriers separating rational thought and knowledge from delusive belief were becoming weaker, and more easily crossed. (pp. 401-402)

Commenting on the evolution of Johnson's paranoia, Kearns-Goodwin (1976) noted,

Sometimes it seemed as if Johnson himself did not believe what he was saying. . . . At other times [his] voice carried so much conviction that his words produced an almost hypnotic effect. . . . The worse the situation in Vietnam became, the more Johnson intruded his suspicions and his fears into every aspect of his daily work. (p. 317)

As the attacks on his policy and character continued, Johnson became suspicious even of his closest aides and advisers. He complained bitterly to Goodwin (1988), "I can't trust anybody anymore" (p. 392). In response, he began to withdraw socially, drawing the political wagons in an ever tighter circle around the White House. By the end of his administration, he had become convinced that he was engaged in a life-or-death struggle in which not only his foreign policy but also his presidency and, ultimately, even his legacy in history were at stake.

As he tried to make sense of his difficulties persuading people of the wisdom of his policies, Johnson began to articulate the belief that a conspiracy of enormous proportions existed. Goodwin (1988) stated,

No longer satisfied with impugning the motives of his critics . . . or attributing his difficulties to "those Kennedys" or "those Harvards" or to the traitorous citizens who lived in seeming innocence along the banks of Boston's Charles River, Johnson began to hint privately . . . that he was the target of a gigantic Communist conspiracy in which his domestic adversaries were only players—not conscious participants perhaps, but unwitting dupes. (p. 402).

He later confided the following to Kearns-Goodwin (1976):

Two or three intellectuals started it all, you know. They produced all the doubt, they and the columnists in the *Washington
Post,* the *New York Times, Newsweek,* and *Life.* And it spread and
spread. . . . Bobby began taking it up as his cause and, with
Martin Luther King on his payroll, he went around stirring up
the Negroes. . . . Then the Communists stepped in. They control
the three networks, you know, and the forty major outlets of
communication. It's all in the FBI reports. They prove everything. Not just about the reporters, but about the professors too.
(p. 316)

Johnson was so convinced of the veridicality of his perceptions
regarding this conspiracy that he berated CIA Director Richard Helms
for his inability to find evidence of the "money trail" linking American
opposition to the war to its Communist origins. Johnson complained in
exasperation, "I simply don't understand why it is that you can't find
out about that foreign money" (as quoted in Miller, 1980, p. 626).

Johnson's belief in this conspiracy persisted long after he left the
White House. Even years later, when trying to write his memoirs, he
remained fatalistic about his ability to overcome those who were
against him. Johnson stated (as quoted in Kearns-Goodwin, 1976),

They'll get me anyhow, no matter how hard I try. . . . No matter
what I say in this book, the critics will tear it apart. . . . The
reviews are in the hands of my enemies—the *New York Times*
and the Eastern magazines—so I don't have a chance. (p. 357)

Antecedents of Organizational Paranoia:
An Inductive Analysis

In trying to explain the origins of Lyndon Johnson's paranoia about
opposition to the Vietnam War, it is useful to understand first how
Johnson initially construed that conflict. The political predicament that
most absorbed Johnson's attention during his second term in office was
clearly Vietnam. It was not, however, only the matter of what to do
about Vietnam that preoccupied Johnson: He was haunted and consumed as well about how to manage what he perceived as the ferocious
and malevolent opposition to that war. Johnson simply could not

understand why he, of all presidents, should be absorbing so much hatred and disdain, given all he had given of himself and all he had accomplished for the American people on so many fronts, including poverty, civil rights, and education.

Overly Personalistic Construal of Political Conflict

It is noteworthy that, in the early phase of developing his policy toward Vietnam, Johnson believed that the conflict in Southeast Asia would be merely a "sideshow" in his administration. It was, he thought, a manageable political issue that would not divert either his attention or the attention of the American people away from his more ambitious—and more important—plans for the "Great Society" (Caro, 1982; Dallek, 1991; Goodwin, 1988; Kearns-Goodwin, 1976). Even as late as 1967, he was convinced that "with a bit of financial tinkering and a dash of vigorous campaigning, both [his] foreign and domestic needs could be met" (Turner, 1985, p. 171). Equally important, Johnson was confident that he possessed the personal skills and political power needed to overcome whatever opposition he might encounter, just as he had so many times before in his career (Johnson, 1971). When the first rumblings reached Johnson that the road to political consensus might be rocky, he derisively dismissed these critics as "nervous nellies," "knee-jerk liberals," and "half-brights" (a pun he used to refer to the Fulbrights and other intellectuals who opposed him) (Berman, 1989; Goodwin, 1988; Kearns-Goodwin, 1976).

As his attempts to win over his critics failed, however, Johnson began to believe that the adversaries lined up against him were more powerful and sinister than any he had encountered before. Moreover, the scope of the conspiracy that he imagined marshalled against him grew, seemingly in perverse proportion to the extent to which he felt besieged. It was almost as if, to explain to himself why his enormous personal skills and institutional advantages as president were not enough, he had to conjure up enemies of comparable stature, cunning, and power.

From a psychological perspective, several features of the way in which Johnson construed political opposition to his policy seemed particularly central to the development of his paranoid cognitions. First, Johnson believed he was under unrelenting scrutiny by a variety of hostile audiences. With respect to Vietnam, he felt as if every presidential gesture and deed were being severely and unfairly condemned. He began to view himself as surrounded by a mob of hostile critics that included not only his all-too-familiar political enemies in Washington but also a national press whose approval he had assiduously courted and a vast citizenry whose love and affection he had long sought.

He could not understand how someone whose intentions were obviously so noble, and whose legislative accomplishments so grand, could suddenly be so universally disdained (Goodwin, 1988; Gruber, 1991; Kearns-Goodwin, 1976). The sense of betrayal was particularly acute with respect to the public because Johnson felt he had done so much for the disadvantaged in society: the blacks, the college students, and the poor who, he believed, now repaid him by turning against him when he most needed their support (Henggeler, 1991; Wicker, 1981). As Berman (1989) noted, "It pained him that those he believed had been helped the most by his presidency [e.g., educators, students, blacks, and liberals] were leading the opposition to the war" (p. 183).

Johnson's perception that he was under hostile scrutiny was no doubt exacerbated by the way in which he had acquired his presidency. With the death of President Kennedy, Johnson had at long last achieved his ultimate political goal (indeed, when asked by a colleague in 1960 why he had accepted Kennedy's offer of the vice presidency, against the advice of so many close aides, Johnson confided, "I'll be a heartbeat away from the presidency"). The dubious circumstances surrounding his ascendancy, however, made the victory pyhrric: Johnson regarded himself, at best, as an accidental president, especially during his first term. He was, in his eyes, the undeserving beneficiary of a tragic turn of fate. More important, he feared that others regarded him as a mere pretender to the throne—the illegitimate heir to Camelot (Gruber, 1991).

There is a revealing irony here. On the one hand, Johnson felt as if he were under relentless scrutiny—trapped in the harsh and lugubrious limelight of public attention. On the other hand, he was consumed by doubts as to whether or not he would even be remembered after his presidency had expired. Laing (1961) provided a perceptive observation about this complex and somewhat paradoxical phenomenology of paranoid cognitions:

> In typical paranoid ideas of reference, the [paranoid] person feels that the murmurings and mutterings he [sic] hears as he

walks past a crowd are all about him. . . . When one gets to know such a person more than superficially, however, one often discovers that what tortures him is not so much his delusions of reference, but his harrowing suspicion that he is of no importance to anyone, that no one is referring to him at all. . . . He is persecuted by being the center of everyone else's world, yet he is preoccupied with the thought that he never occupies first place in anyone's affection. (pp. 136-137)

Organizational leaders, of course, live under the continual scrutiny of multiple audiences and constituencies to whom they feel accountable and on whom their power depends (Ginzel, Kramer, & Sutton, 1992; Tetlock, 1992). As Pfeffer (1992) observed, "To be in power is to be watched more closely, and this surveillance affords one the luxury of few mistakes" (p. 302). In this respect, being in the limelight was hardly a new or unique experience for Johnson. What was unique was the extent to which Johnson personalized this scrutiny—every expression of doubt and criticism, even from close friends and even when intended as constructive, was transformed in Johnson's mind into a personal assault on his character or his claim on the nation's leadership.

Also unique was the diffuse and heightened sense of accountability that Johnson felt: He felt assaulted from all directions; any attempt at persuasion or reconciliation that satisfied one constituency seemed to further alienate the others. As Johnson himself lamented to Kearns-Goodwin (1976) when recalling this period,

I felt that I was being chased on all sides by a giant stampede coming at me from all directions. . . . I was forced over the edge by rioting blacks, demonstrating students, marching welfare mothers, squawking professors, and hysterical reporters. And then the final straw. The thing I feared from the first day of my presidency was actually coming true. Robert Kennedy had openly announced his decision to reclaim the throne in the memory of his brother. And the American people, swayed by the magic of the name, were dancing in the streets. The whole situation was unbearable. (p. 329)

Construing the threat in such personalistic terms seemed to bring to the surface, and with renewed intensity, the long-standing doubts and insecurities described earlier that seemed to plague Johnson throughout his presidency. As Berman (1989) noted, "As his political maneuverings failed to achieve their anticipated goals, Johnson's great personal insecurities manifested themselves. All president's feel ill-treated by the press, but with Johnson it became an obsession" (p. 183).

Social psychological research has shown that when individuals experience events that threaten their self-esteem, security, or identity, they are likely to engage in a variety of cognitive coping strategies—some effective and some self-defeating—to reduce or eliminate those threats (Janoff-Bulman, 1992; Lazarus & Folkman, 1984; Steele, Spencer, & Lynch, 1993). For Johnson, many of these strategies seemed to fail: Each new attempt to cope with the threats he confronted only entrapped him further in a painful avoidance-avoidance conflict, with no attractive alternatives and no discernible "win-win" solutions.

Another important psychological consequence of the way Johnson construed political opposition to the war is that it appeared to threaten his perceived control over events. Throughout his career, Johnson labored to control every facet of his political career, trying to leave as little as possible to chance. In his rise to power, for example, he had demonstrated a remarkable ability to orchestrate myriad social and political forces around him as he saw fit to achieve his ends (Caro, 1982; Dallek, 1991; Gruber, 1991). With Vietnam, however, Johnson found himself, "for almost the first time, encompassed by men and events that he could not control: Vietnam and the Kennedys, and, later, the press, Congress, and even the public whose approval was essential to his own esteem" (Goodwin, 1988, p. 399).

Johnson also, largely as a consequence of his own actions, found himself increasingly isolated and removed from critical sources of political and social support. In the past, he had often relied on the counsel and solace of a circle of close colleagues and advisers when dealing with a political crisis. Now, Johnson cut off access to many of these same people because he felt they were no longer trustworthy. He felt they were pulling back or jumping ship either to cover their own political assets or because they lacked the resolve needed to stay the course. Rather than the unconditional support he had so often enjoyed in the past and sought now, these same friends seemed to be publicly questioning or denouncing his policy and leadership.

In blaming others for his difficulties, Johnson failed to appreciate how his own brutal behavior and irrational persistence were driving away some of the best and brightest of his advisers, including John Gardner, Robert McNamara, Clark Clifford, and Hubert Humphrey. Although he felt they had deserted him, he had in fact largely driven and pushed them away.

Dysphoric Self-Consciousness

As a result of feeling under such intense accountability and scrutiny, Johnson became increasingly self-conscious not only about his role in the war's escalation but also about his responsibility for the economic and social costs it was inflicting on the country. The Great Society, which he had once graphically described as like a beautiful and desirable lady, now seemed to him like an old and withered woman. Johnson stated (as quoted in Kearns-Goodwin, 1976),

> She's getting thinner and thinner and uglier and uglier all the time. . . . Soon she'll be so ugly the American people will refuse to look at her; they'll stick her in a closet to hide her away and there she'll die. And when she dies, I, too, will die. (pp. 286-287)

Johnson's dysphoric self-consciousness reflected as well his fear that the unfulfilled promise of the Kennedy administration would continue to cast a pall over his own efforts to sculpt this Great Society. As Goodwin (1988) commented,

> The enduring shadow of Camelot —glamorous, popular, intellectual, enshrined in steadily growing myth—seemed to him to obscure the achievements of his own presidency, preventing others from seeing how much more he was accomplishing than had his predecessor. (p. 396)

Even within the cloistered recesses of the White House, Johnson found little respite from these painful feelings of self-consciousness. As Barber (1983) noted,

> Johnson felt a stranger among his inherited advisers, extraordinarily sensitive to the slurs by all the "overbred smart alecks who live in Georgetown and think in Harvard." And he

wondered continually about his adequacy to be what he so desperately wanted to be, a Great President. (p. 79)

He imagined that those around him, especially the carryovers from the Kennedy administration, were continually making invidious comparisons between him and his predecessor (Henggeler, 1991). As a result, he felt trapped: unable to relax with them but reluctant to remove them, fearing the public would view any change in his cabinet as an act of disrespect toward its recently slain leader (Gruber, 1991).

Hypervigilance

As a result of his heightened self-consciousness, Johnson became extremely vigilant about the conflict over Vietnam. It was, however, a vigilance that differed in form and intensity from the kind of adaptive vigilance that Johnson had displayed so often in the past. As observers of Johnson's rise to power frequently commented, Johnson's intense political preoccupations had often played an important role in his early triumphs. Heath (1975) noted that Johnson

> studied, analyzed, catalogued, and remembered the strengths and weaknesses, the likes and the dislikes, of fellow politicians as some men do stock prices, batting averages, and musical compositions. He knew who drank Scotch and who bourbon, whose wife was sick, who needed new post offices . . . who was in trouble with organized labor . . . and who owed him for a past favor. (p. 179)

Such vigilance increased Johnson's effectiveness as a bargainer by helping him recognize subtle opportunities that were strewn across the political landscape—opportunities that others missed (Caro, 1982; Dallek, 1991; Pfeffer, 1992). It also helped inform him as how best to tailor his influence approach to the specific person with whom he was dealing. "To gain a senator's vote on a bill, Johnson would spend hours studying every conceivable motivation. . . . The fellow never knew what hit him" (Matthews, 1988, p. 30). In discussing the functional role such vigilance played in Johnson's effectiveness, Matthews observed,

It may seem all the more surprising that a man with [Johnson's] towering ego should have climbed to such heights by studying the inner as well as the outer needs of others. Yet it was his willingness to focus on other people and their concerns, no matter how small, that contributed to the near total communication or at least access that Johnson achieved with those he sought to influence. (p. 27)

As Johnson himself noted (as quoted in Goodwin, 1988), to successfully influence someone,

You've got to understand the beliefs and values common to them all as politicians, the desire for fame and the thirst for honor, [but] then you've got to understand the emotion most controlling that particular senator when he thinks about this particular issue. (p. 261)

Along these lines, Pfeffer (1992) has argued that the ability to take the perspective of the other party is crucial to success in acquiring power:

One has to be able, at least for the moment, to stop thinking about oneself and one's own needs and beliefs. Somewhat ironically, *it is this capacity to identify with others that is actually critical in obtaining things for oneself* [italics added]. (p. 173)

Johnson's vigilance was translated into a voracious appetite—an almost insatiable demand—for whatever information he thought would help him make more effective decisions. As Valenti (1975) once noted,

LBJ for all his days enjoyed and appreciated the spacious dimension of intelligence coupled with a resolution capable of enduring (indeed, savoring) tedium and detail, knowing to the tiniest jot of accuracy, all that was possible to know of the problem or the issue involved. (p. 258)

In sharp contrast with such adaptive vigilance, the data suggest that Johnson began to experience a much less functional form of hypervigilance during the late 1960s. Herring (1993) commented,

> If Ronald Reagan was the Teflon president, to whom nothing stuck, Johnson was the flypaper president, to whom everything clung. A compulsive reader, viewer, and listener who took every criticism personally and to heart, he was at first intent on, and then obsessed with, answering every accusation, responding to every charge. (p. 95)

Johnson began to scrutinize his interactions—not only those involving his obvious enemies but also those involving his once trusted aides and advisers—seeking out evidence of defection or disloyalty.

From Johnson's perspective, of course, such extreme vigilance was justified. As Kearns-Goodwin (1976) noted,

> When every situation is translated into one of power lost or gained, all relationships, including friendships, are reduced to a series of shifting and undependable alliances. In such a world it is easy to succumb to the belief that even one's closest friends must be watched for signs of treason. (p. 388)

Rumination

Another psychological dimension of Johnson's behavior during this period was his intense and seemingly uninterrupted rumination not only about his role in the escalating political crisis over Vietnam but also in the role that he thought his opponents were playing in his difficulties. According to Kearns-Goodwin (1976), Johnson often

> consciously and deliberately decided not to think another thought about Vietnam. Nonetheless, discussions that started on poverty or education invariably ended up on Vietnam. If Johnson was unhappy thinking about Vietnam, he was even less happy not thinking about it. . . . He found himself unwilling, and soon unable, to break loose from what had become an obsession. (p. 299)

Johnson also ruminated at length about his deteriorating image as a leader. Social psychological research on the consequences of dysphoric rumination has shown that one of the effects of prolonged rumination on social judgment is that individuals tend to formulate unrealistic and overly personalistic construals of others' behavior (see Kramer, 1994; Kramer, in press for reviews). In Johnson's case, these tendencies were exacerbated by his propensity to make invidious comparisons between his own popularity and that of the late President Kennedy. Kennedy once had quipped that the worse he did, the more popular he became. Johnson found that he, however, was not accorded such generous treatment by either the public or the press. The sudden erosion of public affection, from the same people who, in his eyes, only months before had granted him one of the strongest mandates in U.S. history, perplexed him. "Why don't people like me?," he once asked Dean Acheson. To which Acheson reportedly replied, "Because, Mr. President, you are not a very likable man" (Barber, 1992, p. 77).

In searching for answers to such questions, Johnson directed his attention outward toward others, scrutinizing his relationships and pondering the concealed motives and intentions of those he felt had betrayed him. Kearns-Goodwin (1976) noted, "Discussions on legislation would be interrupted by diatribes against the 'critics.' Private luncheons and dinners would be dominated by complaints about 'the traitors' " (p. 317). Even close aides and long-trusted advisers were not immune to such scrutiny.

In tracing the origins of Lyndon Johnson's paranoia, it is important to note that it did not emerge suddenly or full blown. Instead, its development can be viewed in terms of a gradual process that reflected a confluence of situational and dispositional factors that produced an exaggerated distrust and suspicion of others.

Dispositional Factors

Throughout his long political career, Lyndon Johnson had often displayed a remarkable perceptiveness about other people, especially when it came to detecting their hidden political motives and agendas. He also displayed a pervasive and profound distrust and suspicion of other individuals, especially those he considered political rivals or threats. Johnson tended to construe others' motives and intentions largely in calculative, political terms. Thus, he often believed that, lurking behind the public behavior of a politician, lay a concealed motive or agenda. Few of his friends or allies were spared Johnson's probing scrutiny of their presumed hidden aims and ambitions. Thus, as opposition to the war mounted, Johnson was convinced that the only reason former friends and political supporters could be opposed to his policy must be because their own presidential ambitions or desire for publicity drove them to seek the limelight, even if that meant demonstrating their disloyalty to the president.

Such concerns prompted Johnson to be extraordinarily vigilant about political threats that such individuals posed to his aspirations. He remained poised to detect such threats, ever ready to construe even the slightest and most benign interaction in sinister terms. For example, close friend and adviser Clark Clifford (1991) once noted that Johnson

> saw real or imagined slights everywhere. He told me that on one occasion, while he was sitting in the small room outside the Oval Office waiting to see President Kennedy, Bobby Kennedy walked rapidly through the room and entered the Oval Office without even acknowledging or greeting him. Whatever the facts of this story, it rankled the proud Lyndon Johnson enormously. (p. 390)

In trying to explain why these seemingly slight threats could assume such significance in Johnson's mind, it is important to note that Johnson's political identity was central to his sense of self: Indeed, politics were by all accounts his whole life. As John Connally (as quoted in Gruber, 1991) once observed,

> He had no interest really except politics. That was his whole life. He was totally committed to it. He never read anything except politics. He didn't care about any sports. He didn't read any books. I don't know of one book he read in all of the years I've known him.

Self-affirmation theorists (Steele et al., 1993) have argued that, when a threat to one aspect of an individual's self-identity occurs, he or she can attenuate the impact of that threat and repair damage to the self by affirming other positive personal or social identities. In Johnson's case, there was no other identity to affirm: His personal and political identities were so heavily intertwined that this coping strategy was unavailable. Thus, it is perhaps not altogether surprising that Johnson construed the attacks on his political leadership and policy in such personalistic terms.

These intense reactions also seemed to be fueled by a variety of long-standing personal doubts and insecurities. Many of Johnson's insecurities were centered around doubts regarding not only his ability to lead but also whether he was admired and loved by those he led. For example, Johnson frequently expressed concerns about the waning of public affection toward him: He wanted to be loved and admired for all he had done. As Jack Valenti stated, "He had one goal: to be the greatest president doing the greatest good in the history of the nation" (p. 24). At the same time, however, he felt enormously inadequate about his talents and insecure about the extent to which people even liked him.

In most circumstances, people's knowledge regarding their own influence behavior helps them make sense of others' influence attempts. As Friestad and Wright (1994) argued in this regard,

> In everyday life, people often move rapidly and fluently between the roles of target and agent. Their persuasion knowledge supports this flexibility by providing them with the resources necessary to do the basic tasks of persuasion coping and persuasion production. (p. 3)

In the case of the extremely Machiavellian social actors, however, their own behavior provides a skewed source of data for estimating the base rate behavior of other people. They are prone to overestimate others' Machiavellianistic tendencies.

Gilovich (1991) has provided a thoughtful analysis of reasons why people may be able to sustain beliefs in such questionable interpersonal strategies. Because a given strategy is intiially thought to be effective, he notes, only that strategy is likely to ever be employed. As a consequence, a person never learns what would have happended had a different approach been taken. As a result, he or she cannot assess the true effectiveness of the strategy. He observes, "Because no single failure serves to disconfirm the strategy's effectiveness (after all, nothing works all the time), the only way it can be shown to be ineffective is by discovering that the rate of success is lower with this strategy than with others" (p. 164). Given that the alternative strategies are not employed or not systematically evaluated, however, the person never discovers the strategy (and theory behind it) are wrong or ineffective. This can be aided and abetted, Gilovich goes on to note, by a self-fulfilling prophecy. Like someone who believes the only way to get ahead is to be competitive or come on strong, such a person will consistently push for what he wants. The occasional success will "prove" the wisdom of the rule.

At best, of course, such psychological factors constitute merely a "perceptual readiness" to detect emerging political threats and dangers. To fully understand the development of Johnson's paranoia, it is important to consider the impact of situational factors that influenced how those threats were ultimately construed.

Having identified some of the antecedents of organizational paranoia, we now describe consequences of such paranoia, especially as they influence how people perceive others' influence attempts.

Organizational Paranoia and the Misperception of Others' Influence Attempts

As noted earlier, there are different ways in which people can misperceive others' influence attempts. These include thinking an influence attempt is occurring when, in fact, it is not and also misattributing the intention or motive behind an influence attempt. Three forms of misperception are evident in the data.

Sinister Attribution Error

The sinister attribution error reflects a tendency for individuals to overattribute hostile intentions and malevolent motives to other's actions (Kramer, 1995b). Research on the sinister attribution error has shown that when individuals find themselves in situations that make them feel a heightened sense of self-consciousness and/or feel under intense evaluative scrutiny, they are more likely to overestimate the extent to which others are paying attention to them and critically evaluating them (Fenigstein & Vanable, 1995; Kramer, 1994; Kramer, in press; Zimbardo, Andersen, & Kabat, 1981). In Johnson's case, the continued presence of Robert Kennedy, one of the political rivals he despised and feared most above all others, and also a constant reminder of the late President's legacy, contributed to this lingering feeling of being under intense scrutiny. This perception of being under scrutiny prompted, in turn, an intense scrutiny of Robert Kennedy by Johnson himself.

Along similar lines, Henggeler (1991) noted that,

> [Then Vice President] Johnson's concern about Robert [Kennedy] was so prevalent, and his behavior so peculiar, that those closest to him thought he was "paranoid." He was convinced that Robert not only poisoned [President Kennedy's] opinions against him but also the judgments of reporters; together they were engineering his removal from the 1964 ticket. According to Reedy, this possibility became "an obsession with Johnson— a conviction that peopled the world with agents of the President's brother all seeking to do him in." (p. 62)

Even the seemingly most benign events could take on sinister import in Johnson's mind. For example, when relatives of the Kennedy family accompanied him on one world tour, he was convinced they were acting as spies for Robert Kennedy (Henggeler, 1991, p. 62).

With respect to Vietnam, these suspicions intensified dramatically. Johnson believed that many of the actions of his political enemies, especially those of Robert F. Kennedy, were intended not only as challenges to his foreign policy but also to mock and humiliate him. (Later, a bemused Bobby Kennedy [as quoted in Goodwin, 1988, p. 396], perhaps underestimating the threat he posed to Johnson, asked Goodwin, "Why does he keep worrying about me? I don't like him, but there's nothing I can do to him. Hell, he's the president and I'm only a junior senator.")

Biased Punctuations of Influence Situations

Biased punctuation of influence situations refers to a tendency for individuals to construe the history of interaction with others in a self-serving fashion. Because of biased punctuation, a decision maker A is likely to construe the course of an interaction with another decision maker, B, as a sequence B-A, B-A, B-A, in which the initial hostile or aggressive move was made by B. Actor B, however, punctuates the same history of interaction as A-B, A-B, A-B, in which the roles of aggressor and defender are reversed. At the heart of this bias is a divergence between actors in their basic causal structuration of the same episode.

General evidence for the biased punctuation of social interaction comes from several sources. First, social cognition research has shown that when individuals view ongoing social events, they typically do not perceive them as continuous; rather, they tend to perceive them in terms of a "punctuated" sequence of discrete "chunks" of causally interdependent activity (Swann, Pelham, & Roberts, 1987). This tendency has been observed in both historical case studies and experimental simulations of social and organizational conflicts (Jervis, 1976; Kahn & Kramer, 1990; Kramer, 1989).

Paranoid cognitions contribute to the biased punctuation of influence because the paranoid social perceiver tends to draw sinister linkages between even distant and seemingly unrelated events—events that a more neutral observer would construe as clearly disconnected. Johnson manifested this tendency in one of many rambling accounts of his troubles to Kearns-Goodwin (1976) when he stated,

> Isn't it funny that I *always* [italics added] received a piece of advice from my top advisers *right after* [italics added] each of them had been in contact with someone in the Communist world? And isn't it funny that you could *always* [italics added] find Dobrynin's car in front of Reston's house the *night before* [italics added] Reston delivered a blast on Vietnam? (pp. 315-317)

Later, Johnson noted,

> Look what happened *whenever* [italics added] I went to make a speech about the war. The week before my speech, the St. Louis *Post-Dispatch* or the *Boston Globe* or CBS News would get on me over and over, talking about what a terrible speaker I was . . . and pretty soon the people began to wonder, they began to think that I really must be uninspiring if the papers and the TV said so. . . . You see the way it worked: The opponents of the war went on jags which pretty much originated in the Communist world and eventually found their way to the American critics. (Kearns-Goodwin, 1976, pp. 315-317)

The biased punctuation of influence reflects the operation of both cognitive and motivational processes. Gilovich (1991) provides an illustration of how cognitive processes can influence the inferences an individual draws from negative events:

> [As I stand impatiently waiting for a bus] I can become convinced that all of the buses are headed in the wrong direction by observing quite a number headed the wrong way before I encounter one going in my direction. Note that the opposite cannot happen: Unless I have difficulty boarding, I never observe several going my way before I discover one headed in the opposite direction. If a bus is going in my direction, I take it. Because of this asymmetry, we can experience a certain kind of "bad streak," but not a complementary streak of good fortune. (p. 68)

The effects of such differential availability of information during encoding are amplified by motivational processes that influence retrievability of information from memory as well (Kunda, 1987).

Exaggerated Perceptions of Conspiracy

The third form of misperception that Johnson displayed is the exaggerated perception of conspiracy. This refers to the paranoid perceiver's tendency to view the actions of his or her enemies as more tightly coupled and more connected then they actually are; in other words, it reflects a tendency to overattribute coherence and coordination to others' influence attempts (Kramer, 1994; Pruitt, 1987; Stein, 1988). It is not enough to think that a single or even a few individuals are privately plotting against one; instead, all are joined in a concerted effort to bring one down. Just as biased punctuation entails the overperception of causal linkages among disparate events, so the exaggerated perception of conspiracy entails the exaggerated perception of social linkages.

Johnson believed that the political conspiracy marshalled against him assumed enormous proportions. What had started out as a domestic political conflict involving Robert Kennedy and anti-Vietnam voters came gradually, and insidiously, linked together in Johnson's mind in a broader and more sinister worldwide Communist conspiracy.

In Johnson's case, the belief that a conspiracy of powerful political forces was aligned against him helped explain (to him at least) why a man of his enormous political talents and who possessed such great institutional power could be so successfully thwarted in his legitimate pursuit of victory in Vietnam. In this respect, exaggerated perceptions of conspiracy serve two critical functions for the organizational leader who feels beseiged. First, they provide a rational explanation for what they construe as uncharacteristic and inexplicable impotence at solving their difficulties and the frustration to which such impotence gives rise. Second, they serve an important motivational function, reassuring the leader that his problems are legitimate and require the sort of extreme responses he has been using to meet them. In Johnson's case, this included decisions to vigorously investigate political rivals and engage in illegal wiretaps of their private conversations.

There is some evidence that perceptions of conspiracy may be buttressed by cognitive heuristics such as the representative bias (Stein, 1988) and motivated recruitment of memory about previous social interactions (Kramer, 1994). Perceptions of conspiracy also may be reinforced by the sinister attribution error and biased punctuation of past conflicts. For example, in piecing together the elements of what he perceived to be a monolithic Communist conspiracy, Johnson perceived connections everywhere. He once observed (as quoted in Kearns-Goodwin, pp. 315-317), "McGeorge Bundy had lunch with Dobrynin and *suddenly* [italics added] he became an ardent advocate for peace."

Influencing the Influencers:
Self-Defeating Behavioral Consequences of
Organizational Paranoia

One of the primary reasons researchers have emphasized the importance of accurate perception in influence situations is that such perceptions are presumably linked to the efficacy of an actor's influence attempts. In this respect, we argue that exaggerated perceptions of conspiracy undermine an individual's effectiveness in organizations because they promote adoption of ineffectual or counterproductive influence strategies. Consideration of the links between Johnson's beliefs about the conspirators lined up against him and the actions he should take in dealing with them is instructive in this regard.

As noted earlier, Johnson enjoyed a reputation throughout his life as a highly skilled influence agent. Accounts of the famous "Johnson treatment" are legendary in Washington. At the top of his form, Johnson's influence behavior represented a bewildering, beguiling, and ultimately overwhelming mixture of positive and negative influence strategies. As longtime Johnson associate George Reedy (as quoted in Gruber, 1991) recalled, the Johnson treatment was an

> incredible blend of badgering, cajolery, reminders of past favors, promises of future favors, predictions of gloom if something didn't happen. . . . When that man started to work on you, all of a sudden you just felt as if you were standing under a waterfall and the stuff was just pouring on you.

Johnson was, in short, a kind of one man good cop-bad cop. Moreover, and significantly, each administration of the treatment was uniquely tailored to fit its intended target.

When dealing with critics of his Vietnam policy, however, Johnson displayed none of his usual flexibility in deciding how to influence others: gone was his willingness to engage in ingratiation, as was his willingness to use conciliation or creative bargaining. Instead, as opposition to that policy grew, Johnson turned increasingly to the use of coercive influence tactics, such as threats and ultimatums, to silence his critics. For example, he told Goodwin (1988), "I'm going to get rid of everybody who doesn't agree with my policies. . . . I'll take a tough line" (p. 392). Also, when one democratic senator (Frank Church) tried to defend himself by telling Johnson that he had, after all, not gone any further in his criticism of Johnson than had Walter Lippmann, Johnson put his arm around the senator's shoulder, looked him in the eye, and said (as quoted in Turner, 1985), "Well, Frank . . . the next time you need money to build a dam in your state, you'd better go see Mr. Lippmann" (pp. 184-185).

Moreover, Johnson uncharacteristically abandoned many of his own intuitions about how to effectively exert influence—well-honed intuitions that had served him well in the past. For example, Kearns-Goodwin (1976) noted,

> The more defensive Johnson became about the war, the more
> he demanded sole credit for the laws Congress passed. [In so
> doing] he violated his own principle of sharing publicity and
> credit in order to create a base of good will for the future.
> (p. 300)

Other close associates were similarly struck by the extent to which
Johnson increasingly pursued ineffectual and self-defeating strategies
when trying to influence others (Goodwin, 1988; Kearns-Goodwin,
1976; Skowronek, 1993).

To be sure, the use of such "hardball" influence strategies was
certainly not new or unique to this situation: Johnson was always
tough, especially when the going got rough, as Wicker (1981) once
observed. He had been known to reduce grown men, including Vice
President Humphrey, literally to tears (Goodwin, 1988). What was
distinctive in the late 1960s is the extent to which Johnson relied on
such tactics to the exclusion of other approaches that had also charac-
teristically been a part of the Johnson treatment. Thus, rather than
eliciting the concessions he desired or sought from the other party,
Johnson's rigid bullying behavior merely escalated his difficulties by
intensifying reactance and resistance.

In assessing the full extent to which Johnson's influence attempts
became increasingly self-defeating, it is important to note that his
influence attempts were ineffective with respect to changing the attitudes or behavior of not only those specific individuals at whom they
were targeted but also those who were the observers of his bizarre
behavior, especially his supporters and advisers. Without intending to
do so, Johnson's actions disrupted and eroded a number of important
social and political relationships on which he depended. For example,
Johnson's increasingly irrational and harsh actions drove away many
of the "best and brightest" in his administration, including such talented policymakers and loyal advisers as Clark Clifford, John Gardner,
and Robert McNamara. His behavior also alarmed potential allies
whose causes he had often championed and whose respect he had
earned through his efforts with respect to civil rights, the war on
poverty, education, and other important domestic issues. Thus, without intending to do so, Johnson estranged himself from those whose
counsel and reassurance might otherwise have been enormously helpful in trying to manage the predicament of Vietnam.

In thinking about the origins of these misperceptions of others' influence attempts, it is interesting to note that the tendency to see the world as populated with untrustworthy and plotting political rivals may have reflected as well the projection of Johnson's own political proclivities onto others. Johnson possessed an extremely strategic and calculative view of political life. He regularly engaged in campaigns of political deception and disinformation, often concealing his true aims and ambitions from even close advisers and friends. Moreover, he often resorted to complex Machiavellian machinations to achieve his political ends. As Kearns-Goodwin (as quoted in Gruber, 1991) perceptively noted in this regard, Johnson

> was so used to using words as a means of persuasion, to get somebody to do something, so used to talking to seven different people telling them seven different things, so that they would all come together to do what he wanted, that lying and persuasion were all part of the same thing for him, and I don't think he even knew the truth. I'm sure there was truth for him. . . . Truth was the action, the product, the means didn't matter.

Research in social psychology on the false consensus bias has shown that individuals often overestimate the extent to which other people share their values and worldviews. Extrapolating from this research, it seems plausible to argue that Johnson may have found himself entrapped in a Piradellian prison of his own making: "seeing" sinister machinations where none were present and chronically overestimating the extent to which other political actors were engaging in behavior like his own, necessitating the need for them to be watched and doubted.

In this respect, imagined, exaggerated, and misattributed influence attempts constitute a very interesting class of organizational cognitions at several levels. First, they tell us something about our intuitive beliefs about the social influence process: They reveal what we think about the kinds of things influential people are using "against" us and others, and they are informative about our beliefs about the kinds of people "out there" with whom we are dealing (e.g., whether or not they are trustworthy and their behavior honorable). They can exert powerful influences on our behavior as well. If, for example, employees believe subliminal influence techniques "work" and that management is using such techniques to manipulate their productivity at work, they may be especially vigilant of even seemingly innocent changes in the organization, such as piping in music. People who believe that others are always well intentioned and their behavior above board, however, may tend to underestimate the extent to which more Machivellian or manipulative strategies and tactics are being used against them.

A Functionalist Perspective on Organizational Paranoia

So far, the analysis has emphasized largely the dysfunctional consequences of organizational paranoia. The paranoid perceiver has been portrayed largely as a social misperceiver who exaggerates the intensity of others' influence efforts and who misconstrues the sources of social influence attempts in his or her environment. In certain respects, this emphasis is appropriate. After all, to the extent paranoid cognitions contribute to misperception and self-defeating behavior in organizations, they are obviously maladaptive. It is important to consider, however, the possible adaptive roles such cognitions play in organizational life.

There are several observations that prompt consideration of such roles. First, suspicion is not always irrational. In highly political organizations, an individual may have quite legitimate cause for suspicion and concern. As Frank (1987) noted, "In their rise to power, leaders are almost certain to encounter superiors who wish to hold them back, rivals who seek to displace them, and subordinates seeking to curry favor" (p. 339). In such environments, the cost of misplaced trust may be substantial. Thus, even though the fears and suspicions of paranoid individuals may seem exaggerated or inappropriate to others, this does not mean that their distrust is entirely misplaced or unwarranted. As Intel President and Chief Executive Officer Andrew Grove (1996) frequently argues, "Only the paranoid survive" (p. 3). In expounding further, he reasoned,

> I believe in the value of paranoia [italics added]. Business success contains the seeds of its own destruction. The more successful you are, the more people want a chunk of your business and then another chunk and then another until there is nothing left. I believe that the prime responsibility of a manager is to guard con-

stantly against other people's attacks and to inculcate this guardian attitude in the people under his or her management [italics added].
(p. 3)

Thus, those in positions of power may intuit better than more trusting observers that prudence and caution are better than regret. Relatedly, the increased vigilance of others' behavior and the propensity to ruminate about their motives may be quite functional in such environments. As Goodwin (1988) noted in his discussion of Lyndon Johnson's paranoia, presidents have very real adversaries. Thus, the predisposition to view others "as a potential source of opposition or even danger" can help them remain "on the alert—observing and listening—to discern the hidden intentions of others, thus sharpening skills that can give them a remarkable intuitive understanding of others—their concealed ambitions, weaknesses, greeds, and lusts" (p. 398). Texas Governor John Connolly, a lifelong friend of Lyndon Johnson, stated (as quoted in Goodwin, 1988),

We often hear that someone worries too much. But in some fields [like politics], you *can't* worry too much. If worrying means recognizing that things may go wrong and planning how to deal with these inevitable setbacks. Those blissful souls who speed so self-confidently along life's straight, smooth highways are often the ones who end up in the ditch when the road suddenly veers. (p. 199)

In terms of the efficacy of one's own influence attempts, there also may be a number of strategic advantages associated with cultivation and diffusion of the belief that one is a beleaguered victim engulfed and thwarted by a vast conspiracy. First, when viewed as an influence strategy, the reputation for being paranoid, coupled with a few carefully timed displays of paranoid behavior, may confer considerable bargaining leverage, especially when interacting with individuals whose taste for confrontation and willingness to bear the costs of conflict are low. Such individuals may decide, at the margin, to defer or avoid conflict (Hersh, 1983). Thus, a carefully nurtured reputation for being an irrational, unpredictable, and explosive paranoid leader may serve a useful deterrent role. In this sense, strategic displays of paranoia may function much like strategic displays of anger and other forms of negative affect (see Smith's [1988] discussion of "porcupine power").

Along related lines, by strategically framing their organizational problems in terms of powerful enemies, leaders may be able to recruit other individuals to come to their assistance. In this fashion, a leader may foster a sense of collective paranoia to build cohesiveness and mobilize support by suggesting the existence of a common enemy against which a group can unite. As Frank (1987) perceptively noted in this regard, "Perhaps the most common justification for the power drive today is the claimed necessity to defend against a powerful and evil enemy, *thereby shifting responsibility for one's own aggressive actions to the opponent* [italics added]" (p. 340). More subtly, a leader can use such claims to force others to take sides and declare where their loyalties lie. Along these lines, Johnson frequently used the technique of sharing an intimate revelation about his suspicions to assess the reaction of the person to whom he was speaking, thereby gauging the person's loyalty and commitment to him (Goodwin, 1988).

Paranoid cognitions may also play an important role in the maintenance of a leader's motivation and persistence. In much the same way that defensive pessimism enhances individuals' motivation to engage in effective preemptive failure avoidant behavior (Norem & Cantor, 1986), paranoid cognitions might help individuals maintain their motivation to overcome perceived dangers and obstacles, even in situations in which those dangers and obstacles, from the perspective of a more neutral observer, seem grossly exaggerated. In fact, precisely because they are so willing to expend considerable cognitive resources, including a willingness to maintain vigilance and to ruminate at length about other's intentions, motives, and plans, such individuals might actually be more likely to detect patterns of threat that others fail to see.

A functionalist account of organizational paranoia, therefore, emphasizes the role paranoid cognitions play in a leader's attempt at making sense of the chaotic and perilous environments in which the leaders' political actions are embedded. In the best of circumstances, sensemaking in organizations is a problematic enterprise, fraught with ambiguity and risk (Cohen & March, 1974; Weick, 1993a, 1993b). Leaders attempt to reduce this ambiguity and complexity using a variety of satisficing heuristics (George, 1980). By maintaining a heightened, even exaggerated, sensitivity to the interpersonal dangers that surround them, leaders maintain their alertness and focus their attention. As Lewis and Weigert (1985) have noted, distrust and suspicion help reduce complexity and uncertainty in organizational life by "dictating a course of action based on suspicion, monitoring, and activation of institutional safeguards" (p. 969).

As the fall of Lyndon Johnson shows, however, this argument raises the prospect of ironic and potentially tragic errors in sensemaking. In this regard, it is interesting to view the final months in Ernest Hemingway's life as a cautionary tale of the sensemaking dilemmas and perceptual errors the paranoid actor confronts. Late in his life, Hemingway began to display signs of paranoia. For example, much to the dismay of his wife and friends, he would often point out various men in dark suits who, he asserted, were FBI agents sent by J. Edgar Hoover to follow his movements and harass him. Moreover, he claimed, the FBI was intercepting his mail and tapping his phone lines. He confided to friend A. E. Hotchner (1996, p. 144), "It's the worst hell. They've bugged everything. . . . Can't use the phone . . . mail intercepted."

At the time, these claims—and the confidence and vehemence with which they were asserted—were viewed as evidence of Hemingway's clinical paranoia. To be sure, Hemingway was suffering from a variety of mental difficulties linked to painful physical ailments, depression, chronic alcohol abuse, and difficulties in writing. Several decades later, however, we know now that at least some of Hemingway's perceptions were veridical. Documents released under the Freedom of Information Act have revealed that, in fact, Hemingway was under FBI surveillance and that, at J. Edgar Hoover's instigation, the FBI was engaged in an intense program of surveillance and harassment, in part because Hoover suspected Hemingway's Communist ties and leanings.

Ironically and revealingly, Johnson's suspicions that some conspiring had taken place in turning his advisers against him were also not entirely misplaced. When Clark Clifford became Johnson's secretary of defense following Robert McNamara's dismissal, Clifford became convinced there was no way the war could be won in the current circumstances. He also recognized that a lone voice of dissent would, as had so many others, be dismissed. Johnson would view him as just another nervous nellie or traitor. Accordingly, Clifford decided to turn to the so-called "wise men"—the very counselors who had given their approval only months before to the president's policy. As Clifford (as cited in Gruber, 1991) recounted,

> Although it might sound somewhat conspiratorial, I thought it wise to contact a good many of [the wise men] first. So I did. I knew them all. . . . They all came back, went through the same process (reading cables, getting briefed). . . . I got a feeling from them. I made 4, 5, or 6 contacts. And found that in each instance, Tet had changed their mind. . . . They'd all turned around. The impact was profound—so profound [Johnson] thought something had gone wrong and he used the expression, "I think someone has poisoned the well."

In a very real sense, of course, someone had poisoned the well, and Lyndon Johnson, the ever-vigilant and ruminative sensemaker, had intuited something had gone wrong to thwart his ambitions and plans. This possibility, of course, is the other edge of the sword of suspicion. As Shapiro (1965) aptly notes,

> Suspicious thinking is unrealistic only in some ways, while, in others, it may be sharply perceptive. . . . Suspicious people are not simply people who are apprehensive and "imagine things." They are, in fact, extremely keen and often penetrating observers. They not only imagine, but also *search* [italics added]. (pp. 55-58)

As the old adage reminds us—or alerts us—"Just because you are paranoid doesn't mean they aren't out to get you" often contains more than a kernel of truth.

Note

1. This chapter reflects an extension and integration of several previously developed frameworks on the origins and dynamics of organizational and political paranoia (Kramer, 1995a, 1995b, 1997). This new version incorporates insights from a number of recent theoretical advances (Pipes, 1997; Robins & Post, 1997–1997; Siegel, 1994) and also incorporates recently available empirical data, including transcripts and audiotape recordings, as well as other previously classified materials (Beschloss, 1997; Sheshol, 1997; Van Diver, 1997).

References

American Psychological Association. (1987). *Diagnostic and statistical manual of mental disorders*. Washington, DC: Author.

Anderson, D. L. (1993). *Shadow on the white house: Presidents and the Vietnam war*. Lawrence: University of Kansas Press.

Barber, B. (1983). *The logic and limits of trust*. New Brunswick, NJ: Rutgers University Press.

Barber, J. D. (1972). *The presidential character: Predicting performance in the White House*. Englewood Cliffs, NJ: Prentice Hall.

Barrett, D. M. (1993) *Uncertain warriors: Lyndon Johnson and his Vietnam advisors*. Lawrence: Kansas University Press.

Berman, L. (1982). *Planning a tragedy: The Americanization of the war in Vietnam*. New York: Norton.

Berman, L. (1988). Lyndon B. Johnson: Paths chosen and opportunities lost. In F. I. Greenstein (Ed.), *Leadership in the modern presidency*. Cambridge, MA: Harvard University Press.

Berman, L. (1989). *Lyndon Johnson's war*. New York: Norton.

Beschloss, M. R. (1997). *Taking charge: The Johnson White House tapes, 1963-1964*. New York: Simon & Schuster.

Bullock, A. (1993). *Hitler and Stalin: Parallel lives*. New York: Vintage/Random House.

Burke, J. P., & Greenstein, F. I. (1989). *How presidents test reality: Decisions on Vietnam, 1954 and 1965*. New York: Russell Sage.

Califano, J. A. (1991). *The triumph and tragedy of Lyndon Johnson*. New York: Simon & Schuster.

Cameron, N. (1943). The development of paranoic thinking. *Psychological Review, 50*, 219-233.

Caro, R. A. (1982). *The path to power: The years of Lyndon Johnson*. New York. Vintage.

Cialdini, R. (1988). *Influence: Science and practice* (2nd ed.). Glenview, IL: Scott, Foresman.

Clifford, C. (1991). *Counsel to the president*. New York: Random House.

Cohen, M. D., & March, J. G. (1974). *Leadership and ambiguity* (2nd ed.). Cambridge, MA: Harvard Business School Press.

Colby, K. M. (1981). Modeling a paranoid mind. *Behavioral and Brain Sciences, 4*, 515-560.

Dallek, R. (1991). *Lone star rising: Lyndon Baines Johnson*. New York: Oxford University Press.

Fenigstein, A., & Vanable, P. A. (1992). Paranoia and self-consciousness. *Journal of Personality and Social Psychology, 62*, 129-138.

Frank, J. D. (1987). The drive for power and the nuclear arms race. *American Psychologist, 42*, 337-344.

Friestad, M., & Wright, P. (1994). The persuasion knowledge model: How people cope with persuasion attempts. *Journal of Consumer Research, 21*, 1-31.

Gardner, J. W. (1990). *On leadership*. New York: Free Press.

George, A. (1980). *Presidential decisionmaking in foreign policy: The effective use of information and advice*. Boulder, CO: Westview.

Gilovich, T. (1991). *How we know what isn't so: The fallibility of human reasoning in everyday life*. New York: Free Press.

Ginzel, L. E., Kramer, R. M., & Sutton, R. (1992). Organizational impression management as a reciprocal influence process. In L. L. Cummings & B. M. Staw (eds.), *Research in organizational behavior* (vol. 15, pp. 227-266). Greenwich, CT: JAI Press.

Goodwin, R. N. (1988). *Remembering America: A voice from the sixties*. New York: Harper & Row.

Grove, A. S. (1996). *Only the paranoid survive.* New York: Doubleday.

Gruber, D. (1991). *LBJ: A biography* [Video]. Dallas: North Texas Public Broadcasting.

Halberstam, D. (1972). *The best and the brightest.* New York: Random House.

Heath, J. (1975). *Decade of disillusionment: The Kennedy-Johnson years.* Bloomington: Indiana University Press.

Henggeler, P. R. (1991). *In this steps: Lyndon Johnson and the Kennedy mystique.* Chicago: Dee.

Herring, G. C. (1993). The reluctant warrior: Lyndon Johnson as Commander in Chief. In D. L. Anderson (Ed.), *Shadow on the White House: Presidents and the Vietnam War, 1945-1975* (pp. 87-112). Lawrence: University of Kansas Press.

Hersh, S. M. (1983). *The price of power: Kissinger in the Nixon White House.* New York: Summit.

Hotchner, A. E. (1996). *Papa Hemingway.* New York: Random House.

Janis, I. L. (1983). *Groupthink* (2nd ed.). Boston: Houghton Mifflin.

Janoff-Bulman, R. (1992). *Shattered assumptions: Towards a new psychology of trauma.* New York: Free Press.

Jervis, R. (1976). *Perception and misperception in international politics.* Princeton, NJ: Princeton University Press.

Johnson, L. B. (1971). *The vantage point: Perspectives on the presidency, 1963-1969.* New York: Holt, Rinehart & Winston.

Kahn, R. L., & Kramer, R. M. (1990). Untying the knot: De-escalatory processes in international conflict. In R. L. Kahn & M. N. Zald (Eds.), *Organizations and nation-states: New perspectives on conflict and cooperation.* San Francisco: Jossey-Bass.

Kearns-Goodwin, D. (1976). *Lyndon Johnson and the American dream.* New York: New American Library.

Kramer, R. M. (1989). Windows of vulnerability or cognitive illusions? Cognitive processes and the nuclear arms race. *Journal of Experimental Social Psychology, 25,* 79-100.

Kramer, R. M. (1994). The sinister attribution error: Origins and consequences of collective paranoia. *Motivation and Emotion, 18,* 199-230.

Kramer, R. M. (1995a). In dubious battle: Heightened accountability, dysphoric cognition and self-defeating bargaining behavior. In R. M. Kramer & D. M. Messick (Eds.), *Negotiation as a social process.* Thousand Oaks, CA: Sage.

Kramer, R. M. (1995b). The distorted view from the top: Power, paranoia, and distrust in organizations. In R. Bies, R. Lewicki, & B. Sheppard (Eds.), *Research on negotiations* (Vol. 5). Greenwich, CT: JAI.

Kramer, R. M. (in press). Paranoid cognition in social systems: Thinking and acting in the shadow of doubt. *Personality and Social Psychology Review.*

Kunda, Z. (1987). Motivated inference: Self-serving generation and evaluation of causal theories. *Journal of Personality and Social Psychology, 53,* 636-647.

Laing, R. D. (1961). *Self and others.* New York: Penguin.

Lazarus, R. S., & Folkman, S. (1984). *Stress, appraisal, and coping.* New York: Springer.

Lewis, J. D., & Weigert, A. (1985). Trust as a social reality. *Social Forces, 63,* 967-985.

Matthews, C. (1988). *Hardball.* New York: Summit.

Miller, M. (1980). *Lyndon: An oral biography.* New York: Ballantine.

Norem, J. K., & Cantor, N. (1986). Defensive pessimism: Harnessing anxiety as motivation. *Journal of Personality and Social Psychology, 51,* 1208-1217.

Pfeffer, J. (1992). *Managing with power.* Cambridge, MA: Harvard Business School Press.

Pipes, D. (1997). *Conspiracy: How the paranoid style flourishes and where it comes from.* New York: Free Press.

Pruitt, D. (1987). Conspiracy theory in conflict escalation. In S. Moscovici & C. F. Graumann (Eds.), *Changing conceptions of conspiracy.* New York: Springer-Verlag.

Robins, R. S., & Post, J. M. (1997). *Political paranoia: The psychopolitics of hatred.* New Haven, CT: Yale University Press.

Shapiro, D. (1965). *Neurotic styles.* New York: Basic Books.

Shesol, J. (1997). Mutual contempt: Lyndon Johnson, Robert Kennedy, and the feud that defined a decade. New York: Norton.

Siegel, R. K. (1994). *Whispers: The voices of paranoia.* New York: Crown.

Skowronek, S. (1993). *The politics presidents make.* Cambridge, MA: Belknap/Harvard University Press.

Smith, H. (1988). *The power game.* New York: Random House.

Steele, C. M., Spencer, S. J., & Lynch, M. (1993). Self-image resilience and dissonance: The role of affirmational resources. *Journal of Personality and Social Psychology, 64,* 885-896.

Stein, J. G. (1988). Building politics into psychology: The misperception of threat. *Political Psychology, 9,* 245-271.

Swann, W. B., Pelham, B. W., & Roberts, D. C. (1987). Causal chunking: Memory and inference in ongoing interaction. *Journal of Personality and Social Psychology, 53,* 858-865.

Tetlock, P. E., Skitka, L., & Boettger, R. (1989). Social and cognitive strategies for coping with accountability: Conformity, complexity, and bolstering. *Journal of Personality and Social Psychology, 57,* 632-640.

Turner, K. J. (1985). *Lyndon Johnson's dual war: Vietnam and the press.* Chicago: University of Chicago Press.

Valenti, J. (1975). *A very human president.* New York: Norton

Van DeMark, B. (1991). *Into the quagmire: Lyndon ohnson and the escalation of the Vietnam War.* New York: Oxford University Press.

Van Diver, F. F. (1997). *Shadows of Vietnam: Lyndon Johnson's wars.* College Station: Texas A&M University Press.

Weick, K. E. (1993a). Sensemaking in organizations. In J. K. Murnighan (Ed.), *Social psychology in organizations: Advances in theory and practice.* Englewood Cliffs, NJ: Prentice Hall.

Weick, K. E. (1993b). The collapse of sensemaking in organizations: The Mann Gulch disaster. *Administrative Science Quarterly, 38,* 628-652.

Wicker, T. (1981). *JFK and LBJ: The influence of personality upon politics.* Chicago: Dee.

Wicker, T. (1991). *One of us: Richard Nixon and the American dream.* New York: Random House.

Zimbardo, P. G., Andersen, S. M., & Kabat, L. G. (1981). Induced hearing deficit generates experimental paranoia. *Science, 212,* 1529-1531.

Some Ethical Aspects of the Social Psychology of Social Influence

DAVID M. MESSICK
RAFAL K. OHME

Much of social psychology, historically, has focused on the under-standing of social influence. One of the fundamental facts of social life is that people influence each other, for better or worse. Education is about influence. Communication is about influence. Organization, child rearing, coercion, and advertising are all about influence. As social psychologists study variables that affect behavior, they are studying variables that influence or have a causal connection to behavior, and in this uninteresting sense one can claim that all of social psychology is about influence.

The more interesting sense is the explicit emphasis on social influence. Social impact theory (Latané, 1981), theories of persuasion and attitude change (Eagly & Chaiken, 1993), social power (French & Raven, 1959), social conformity (Crutchfield, 1955), and the explicit analysis of the strategies that people use to influence each other (Cialdini, 1993) all focus on the processes that are involved when people change the beliefs or behavior of others or both.

Intentional influence represents the subfield of social psychology that we focus on in this chapter. The prototypical situation that we have in mind contains a minimum of two elements: an agent of influence, the influencer, and a target of influence, the influenced. As Latané (1981) noted in his social impact theory, the agent or the target or both can be either single or multiple persons. What further characterizes this prototypical situation is that the agent wishes, prefers, or desires some outcome that the target can bring about. The influence episode(s) consists of the efforts made by the agent to achieve a desired outcome by having the target perform some action or actions. Examples of intentional influence that fit this prototype include parents urging their children to brush their teeth, professors requiring students to rewrite a paper to improve its clarity, drugs being administered to calm an aroused student, or supervisors telling their employees to falsify quality testing reports.

Intentional influence can be exerted by acts of omission. Foreseeable and predictable things happen that are intentionally permitted to occur, and we do not exclude such events from consideration. An intentional decision not to urge children to brush their teeth is a type of influence as is the decision to conceal the dangers of a product, process, or policy. One difference between influence attempts that consist of acts of omission and acts of commission is the potential difference in one's ability to infer the intention of the agent. The inference of intention is crucial in judgments of the ethicality of many influence attempts, and acts of omission often obscure the intent of the agent. There are usually more reasons for nonaction than for action, making the identification of the reasons for nonaction less clear.

Social psychologists have drawn many useful distinctions in their study of social influence. Kelman's (1958) famous distinction of the three responses to social influence provides insights into the psychological consequences of influence processes. He differentiates among what he calls compliance, identification, and internalization. These responses vary, in a sense, in terms of the "depth" of the psychological changes that are presumed to occur. Compliance occurs when an individual submits to an influence attempt in the hopes of achieving a favorable reaction or of avoiding an unfavorable reaction. Compliance is shallow and does not imply belief change. For example, an employee goes to church because it makes a good impression on the boss and not because of religious conviction. Identification occurs when an individual adopts behavior associated with a role or imitates role models. When a new employee of a firm expresses contempt for a competing firm for which he or she nearly went to work, he or she may be reflecting the organizational "culture," adopting the local beliefs, attitudes, and habits that characterize employees of the firm. The process of identification may not be intentionally manipulative or even conscious, and it represents a deeper commitment to the behavior patterns than mere compliance. Finally, according to Kelman (1958), internalization occurs when an individual accepts influence because the induced behavior is congruent with his or her value system. The behavior seems like the right thing to do. One could falsify a report because one was ordered to and feared the repercussions of refusing (compliance), because one thought that such falsifications were the way things were done in the organization (identification), or because one believed that falsification in the circumstances was the appropriate action to take (internalization). Kelman posits that these three responses are not necessarily mutually exclusive.

Other research on social influence is based on French and Raven's (1959) well-known analysis of the bases of social power. This classic book identifies five psychological bases of social power. Reward power derives from the influencer's ability to mediate rewards for the target; coercive power stems from the influencer's ability to mediate punishments. Reward and coercive power often reside in the same person, but it is useful to distinguish them. With reward power, for instance, it is in the target's interest to demonstrate compliance so that surveillance processes are unnecessary. With coercive power, targets may try to conceal noncompliance, requiring the establishment of mechanisms to validate compliance. Legitimate power derives from a role relationship in which the influencer has a legitimate right to prescribe behavior, such as when a supervisor instructs a subordinate to perform a duty, and expert power (also called informational power) comes from an information asymmetry in which the influencer has some special knowledge, expertise, or ability that the target needs. Finally, referent power results when the target of an influence attempt identifies strongly with the influencer.

The social psychological foundation that we find the most useful, however, was proposed by Deutsch and Gerard (1958). These authors proposed that interpersonal influence has two conceptually independent components that they called normative and informational influence. Informational influence involves accepting information from another as "evidence about reality" (p. 629). Normative influence has to do with trying to please another, where the "other" can be another person, a group, or one's self. Informational influence is involved when a broker persuades a client that, because of the broker's information, the client will become rich if he or she invests in a particular mutual fund; normative influence is involved when the broker tells the client that the broker will like the client more if he or she buys the fund. Insko, Sedlak, and Lipsitz (1982) restated this distinction as the concern for being right (informational) and the concern for being liked (normative). The concern for being right focuses on the ways in which people use the social world to learn about reality, and the concern for being liked deals with the maintenance of positive social relationships.

The distinction between informational and normative sources of influence is derived from the study of conformity. The question must be answered whether this distinction is useful in examining other forms of influence. We believe that it is, and we offer evidence to support this belief. First, Skinner (1957) makes a similar distinction in his classification of verbal behavior. He describes two classes of verbal acts, "tacts" and "mands." Tacts are statements such as "That dress is red," "It is going to get cold tonight," or "Seventy six percent of the people surveyed preferred candidate A to candidate B." Such statements are presumed to be descriptions of reality, at least reality as the speaker knows it. Presumably, such statements represent contact with reality and transmit information about it to the audience. Such statements, implicitly or explicitly, are instruments of informational influence.

Mands are statements that are intended to elicit action on the part of the audience. "Sit down," "Please close the door," or "I don't care how you do it, reduce your costs by 12%" are statements that attempt to influence the behavior of the listener rather than describe reality. The neologism *mand* is derived from the words "com*mand*" and "de*mand*." Mands are words that direct action, usually with the connotation that the speaker will be displeased if the command is not followed. Thus, mands seem to correspond to normative sources of influence. To the extent that language is the medium through which the influence attempt occurs, Skinner's (1957) distinction approximately parallels that of Deutsch and Gerard (1958). As Skinner notes, however, these categories of speech acts may functionally overlap each other. When one says, "It is cold in here," one may actually be saying to the listener, "Close the window." Likewise, when one's boss says, "Don't show this document to Charlie," he or she is revealing something about his or her perception of the (social) reality of the organization.

A second synthesis that we offer comes from a consideration of the six methods of influence that Cialdini (1993) analyzes in his important book on techniques of influence. The point is that if the distinction that Deutsch and Gerard (1958) offer is indeed general, it should be applicable to the principles that Cialdini induces. A quick examination of these principles reveals that the informational-normative distinction makes good sense with all but one of Cialdini's rules. Three of Cialdini's principles—reciprocation, friendship/liking, and commitment/consistency—clearly deal with normative means of influencing behavior. Reciprocation refers to the felt need to return a favor, such as sending in a contribution to a charity after receiving return address labels with the solicitation attempt. Friendship and liking are nearly the definition of normative pressures—we want to be liked and do things that are instrumental to achieving this outcome. Commitment/consistency refers to the tendency for people to continue to do something that they have done previously. For example, people are more likely to agree to a more costly request if they previously agreed to a smaller related request. The psychological processes that are involved in this phenomenon seem likely to be normative in that people do not want to appear inconsistent either to others or to themselves. Neither principle refers to changes in what one believes about the world. They have to do with seeking approval or fulfilling obligations or both.

Two of the principles, social validation and scarcity, clearly deal with informational influence. Social validation refers to the reliance on others' statements about what is or is not true in the world. When we are told that most people prefer brand A over brand B (social validation), we infer that brand A is better than brand B. If we are told that brand A is scarce whereas brand B is commonplace, we may infer that brand A is more valuable than brand B (and hence more worth purchasing). These mechanisms for making us feel positive about brand A rely on inferential processes that have nothing to do with our desire to be liked by another or others.

Cialdini's remaining principle, authority, is slightly more subtle. Authority, the tendency to be more influenced by an authority figure than by a mere peer, probably involves both normative and informational influences. It is important to be liked by persons in authority because such people have control of resources that we want and need. We are more likely to comply with a request from the boss than a request from a peer not only because of the legitimate power the boss has (French & Raven, 1959) but also because the consequences of refusing the boss are more severe than those of refusing the peer. At the same time, we also believe that authority figures have better access to sources of knowledge and expertise that peers lack. They are better able to tell us about reality than peers. Physicians are effective at selling health care products because we assume that they are experts. Athletes are good at selling breakfast cereals because we want to emulate them or earn their approval. Authority works both ways.

In this chapter, we explore some issues dealing with informational influence, some issues concerning the aspect of normative influence that pertains to authority, and one additional mode of social influence—biological influence. We mention this last mode of influence not because much is known about it by psychologists but because it promises to be a source of ethical controversy in the near future.

Biological Influence

Biological influence refers to the use of biological interventions to alter behavior. We include influence efforts that involve the prescription of drugs, the use of surgery, or, more vexingly, the alteration of a genotype to influence behavior. Both surgery and drugs can be used explicitly as influence strategies to alter the behavior of specific targets who may or may not want to have their behavior altered.

The use of biological influence has a long history within medicine and the treatment of mental disorders. Frontal lobotomy and electroshock therapy, used to "cure" mental illness, were controversial treatments, as is the use of castration and sterilization to control sexual misbehavior. Objections to these treatments are based only in part on the fact that they may be involuntary and partly on the potential for harm that they may cause. A different level of objection is that the treatments somehow render the recipient of the treatment less than a complete human.

The classic film *The Stepford Wives* is an excellent illustration of the malaise that is created by surgically manipulated people. In this film, women in the town of Stepford were turned into compliant and dutiful robots by surgical means. The Stepford wives were neither dangerous nor threatening. The distress that they created was due at least in part to the fact that they appeared to be normal persons; they almost mimicked a normal wife.

More common but no less controversial is the use of drug therapies for behavior control. Drugs to control hyperactivity (Ritalin), sexual impulses (saltpeter), depression (Prozac), or anxiety (Valium) have all been controversial not only because they are suspected of causing harm to their users but also because they reduce the user to a less than fully human condition.

Genetic manipulation is a more complex form of influence because it purports to alter the behavior of persons as yet unborn. If there are genes that cause aggressive behavior, criminal acts, or sexually violent acts against others, and if it is within the capacity of modern science to alter those genes, are we not doing a social good by "fixing" the problematic genes to reduce their frequency?

The use of genetic engineering to create new species is extremely controversial, even when the genetic manipulation has nothing to do with human genetics. The creation of genetically engineered foods, called Frankenfood by critics of the industry, creates opposition because such foods are not considered "natural" and because the risks that are associated with genetically novel products are hard to assess, especially in the short run.

Some of the ethical controversy that surrounds biological interventions concerns genetic manipulation and the creation of new forms of life. For instance, can a new life form be patented (Cole-Turner, 1995)? If one views all life forms as sacred, filing a patent for a new life form represents an immense conceit. Humans may be seen as attempting to usurp powers that they have no claim on. Supporters of biotechnology claim that there is little difference between new compounds that are "alive" and compounds that are made from new molecules that are not alive. The very meaning of life is challenged by biotechnology.

The ethical values that seem to be involved with biological forms of influence and control have to do with autonomy, integrity, and personhood. A person whose behavior is under the control of a drug or whose conduct has been affected by surgical means is seen as less than fully human. Such a person is not a fully moral actor with the volition and intention that we ascribe to "normal" people. There is something lacking—something that is disturbing, even if the person is not perceived as dangerous.

The use of biological means to change people is not only ethically controversial in the domain of influencing people's behavior but also ethically questionable. Although we admire people who improve their appearance through diet or physical activity, we do not admire people whose strength is increased through the use of performance-enhancing drugs such as anabolic steroids or whose youthful demeanor is maintained (or restored) through cosmetic surgery. The fact that most uses of performance-enhancing drugs are voluntary suggests that the ethical objection to drug-induced behavior control is not based solely on the fact that the target of such control does not desire to be controlled. At least part of the ethical objection seems to be based on the notion that drugs bypass the normal route to peak performance, that they are an inappropriate short-cut, and that they are therefore "artificial" and deceitful.

Similarly, a youthful appearance that derives from a good diet and a healthy lifestyle (not to mention good genes) is admired, whereas a similar appearance that emerges from cosmetic surgery is suspect. Kalick (1988) reports that photographs of cosmetic surgery patients were rated more negatively by an experimental group of subjects who were told of the patients' surgery than by a control group that was uninformed. The knowledge that cosmetic surgery was performed on a person renders that person's appearance less attractive than the same appearance without surgery. Kalick also mentions that plastic surgeons are among the least prestigious class of physicians.

What we have recorded here are our impressions that people harbor deep concerns about biological means of altering behavior or appearance. What the origins of these concerns are we can only guess. We know of little direct research on the question. Some of the concern seems to reflect the falseness of an appearance or performance that is biologically enhanced. That one would resort to such means to achieve better looks or performance may also signal undue vanity. Some of the concern may reflect the assumption that biological enhancement of performance or appearance is counterfeit in that it represents a cheap and bogus means of attaining recognition that should be more costly. Physical attractiveness or fitness is admired when achieved through careful diet, exercise, and denial of excess. They are admired, in part, because they signal virtuous behavior. Finally, we suspect that there is a prevalent belief that although biological interventions are acceptable to prevent death, to cure disease, or to restore normal behavioral or psychological functions, they are wrong to make a person something different from normal, even if that difference is an "improvement."

These speculations about people's ethical concerns regarding bio-logical forms of social influence are somewhat digressive from the two topics that are the main foci of this chapter, informational influence and the use and misuse of authority.

Informational Influence

Informational social influence works when people accept "infor-mation obtained from another as *evidence* about reality" (Deutsch & Gerard, 1958, p. 629). Informational social influence works by influenc-ing what people believe about the world. We take informational influ-ence to include the vast terrain that covers issues of truth-telling, honesty, deceit, lying, concealment, and disclosure. These are concerns that deal with a prototypical situation in which truth is known by one or more parties and either is or is not accurately communicated to one or more other parties. The intent of the agent is obviously an important element in any ethical analysis, as is the knowledge that the agent has about what the target knows about the issue.

There are a secondary set of issues that we also include in this category. These are issues that arise when truth is not known. Whereas the first set of questions engage the ethical issues of honesty and truth-telling, the issues surrounding the second category deal with the responsibility to discover truth. At the heart of this issue is the fact that there are circumstances in which it is beneficial for an agent to be ignorant of some condition. Maintaining that ignorance is of strategic importance because knowledge of the condition may require expen-sive or embarrassing action. As long as one does not know that one's product causes harm to its users, one is not obliged to either prevent the harm or to warn of it. Such ignorance may also shield one from legal and moral liability.

As noted earlier, the ethical issues that are involved are those of honesty and truth-telling. Generally, the ethical prohibition against lying is part of our moral common sense (Goodpaster, 1982). Bok (1978) has written what may be the definitive book on the issue of lying, arguing that it is hard to imagine circumstances in which lying is morally acceptable. She defines a lie as "any intentionally deceptive message which is stated" (p. 13). Bok's definition is important in that it stresses the intent to deceive, and it defines a lie as an act of commission, a stated message. One cannot accidentally lie, nor can one lie by refusing to make a statement. One can deceive through silence, as when one declines to correct an erroneous belief of another, and one can deceive accidentally, if one communicates an erroneous fact. Lying, according to Bok, however, requires both intent and action.

Bok argues that there may be times when one feels compelled to lie to serve a higher moral purpose, such as when one may lie to protect an innocent person against unjustified harm, but the fact that there is a good reason to lie does not make lying moral. It only provides an excuse for the lie. One should ask to be forgiven for having lied and not to be praised.

What is at the heart of the ethics of honesty is the need to be able to place confidence and credence in normal sources of information and communication. Human communication, whether it is written or verbal, provides one of the greatest cognitive efficiencies humans possess. Communication allows for the sharing of experience and the coordination that are required for life in complex social organizations. It is important that the messages that we receive be trustworthy—that is, that they be presumed to be accurate and well-intended. By this we mean that the messages are not randomly generated (making them uncorrelated with reality), and that they are not intended to purposefully mislead the recipient. The presuppositions of accuracy and honesty are the bedrock assumptions that are required for communication to work.

Imagine a world in which it was not assumed that communication was accurate and honest, in which messages were as likely to be false as true, or in which people told the truth when and only when it was convenient for them to do so and in which they would lie if there was an advantage to doing so, or all of these. How would messages be processed in this world? It is easy to see that communications would have diminished, if any, value. The ability to infer reality from communications would be vitiated. Messages would lose their meanings because there would be no confident attachment of significance to symbols. In short, the value of human communication would be debased in the absence of accuracy and honesty. The ethical prohibitions against inaccuracy and dishonesty reflect our collective recognition of the dependence of the value of communication on accuracy and honesty.

Honesty has a social dilemma quality. Collectively, we understand that communication has value only to the extent that we can trust the content of communications. There are many occasions, however, in which it may be in our personal interests to distort the content of our own communications for one reason or another, but we also know that if everyone did this we could trust nothing that we heard or read. Therefore, just as we may value a clean environment and yet litter, or may enjoy public television and radio and yet not support them financially, we may also proclaim the virtue of honesty while dissembling now and then.

Although there may not be much dispute about the ethics of lying—we point out that there is some disagreement about Bok's position (Nyberg, 1993)—other cases are more controversial, for example, the (possibly) best-selling book, *The Discipline of Market Leaders* (Treacy & Wiersema, 1995). According to an article by Stern (1995), the authors of this book, consultants Michael Treacy and Fred Wiersema, systematically placed small orders for the book from a wide selection of retail bookshops across the country. The purchases were made in the names of office staff and other employees of CSC Index and not those of the authors or of the consulting firm for whom they worked, CSC Index. Some purchases were made on the credit cards of these employees, who were than reimbursed by the firm for their purchases. The books that were bought were sent to a warehouse for storage until they could be used in the consulting practice. In most cases, CSC Index paid full retail price for the books, whereas they were qualified to buy them directly from the publisher for a sizable discount. What purpose could have been served by this needlessly expensive and time-consuming method of buying the book?

Stern (1995) suggests that the scheme was to place orders in such a way as to place the book on the *New York Times* best-seller list, guaranteeing enhanced publicity, sales, and higher speaking fees for the authors. Because the best-seller list methodology discounts bulk sales of business books, it was essential to disguise the actual purchaser and to make it appear as if the books were being bought by many small purchasers across the country. In other words, the strategy was, according to Stern (1995), to trick the *New York Times* into thinking that the book was more broadly popular than it actually was in an effort to make more money for the authors. For this strategy to work, deceit was essential.

The authors of this deception, according to Stern (1995), claim that they did nothing unethical. They were aggressively marketing their book, they claim, and did not step over the ethical line. Such a claim raises the question of how to find this ethical line. It is clearly the case that complete disclosure of the details of a marketing strategy is not required of an ethical approach, so what differentiates an ethical from an unethical strategy? The *Discipline* case poses an interesting challenge.

There are two ways to approach the question of the ethics of the previously discussed and related deceptions. The first is to question the universalizability of the practice (Velasquez, 1992). Universilizability asks what would happen if all participants behaved in a similar way. What if all authors tried to simulate patterns of sales so that best-seller lists would be led to exaggerate the demand for and sales of their books? If this were the case, and everyone knew it, best-seller lists would record those books whose authors were the most clever at gaming the lists. Such lists would cease to have the meaning that we now attribute to them, namely, that they estimate popularity as measured by sales. Popularity is an indication of social validation in Cialdini's (1993) scheme, and it provides a useful, although imperfect, cue of the value of a book. The *Discipline* strategy can only succeed if people still believe in the cue value of a best-seller list. If the list is assumed to list those that are the best simulators of popularity, the social validation cue is destroyed and there will be no reason to try to be on the list. From this perspective, the deception is not universalizable and fails to meet the test of ethicality.

There is a far simpler test, however. The American Marketing Association has published a code of ethics that defines the professional standards for marketing. If the strategy violates one or more of these standards, then one can conclude that the strategy has crossed the line, and one can do so without having to resort to Kantian logic. One of the duties described in this code (as published in Smith & Quelch, 1993, pp. 799-801) pertaining to promotions is "avoidance of sales promotions that use deception or manipulation." There can be little doubt that the *Discipline* sales promotion used both deception and manipulation to market the book. There can also be little doubt that it violated the ethical standards promulgated by their professional association. Hence, with respect to professional marketing ethics, the *Discipline* strategy clearly crossed the line into unethical territory.

As shall be shown, there are a host of organizational issues that we could discuss about the misrepresentation of what we know to be true. Before we mention these, we discuss the second major concern about informational social influence—the problem of knowing what is true. There are circumstances in which ignorance of a problem is a moral defense. In such circumstances, there is an incentive for people to remain strategically ignorant.

Two organizational examples illustrate this phenomenon. First, there is the case of whistle-blowers (Miceli & Near, 1992). Many whistle-blowers report that they took their knowledge of wrongdoing in their organizations to superiors and were told, in effect, that their bosses did not want to hear about the infractions. To receive and acknowledge the allegations of wrongdoing would commit the bosses to costly efforts to confirm or disconfirm the allegations, and if the charges proved to have merit, the bosses would be obliged to do something to stop the practice and to punish the guilty persons. It may be far easier merely to avert one's glance and remain ignorant of the problem. If one is convincingly ignorant of a corrupt practice, one cannot be accused of condoning it. Thus, whistle-blowers threaten the tranquillity of their bosses and create problems that the bosses would prefer to ignore. Once told about a problem, however, the bosses are placed in jeopardy if they fail to take some investigatory or remedial action, which is why it is important for them to shield themselves from the evidence in the first place. Nowhere was this reluctance to hear and act on reports of wrongdoing more dramatic than in Frank Serpico's widely popular account of corruption in the New York Police Department (Lardner, 1993a, 1993b; Maas, 1973).

A second and somewhat more subtle form of strategic ignorance arises with the introduction of new products, especially those that may influence people biologically, such as pharmaceutical products, foods and additives and other substances that could be ingested or inhaled (such as cigarette smoke or asbestos fibers), or products that may remain in the body for extended periods of time (such as breast or penal implants, medical devices, or tattoo inks). With new products, there are powerful incentives for firms to undertake research to discover useful applications, benefits, and ways in which the product can be sold. There are few incentives for firms to study the potentially harmful effects of their products.

It is precisely because the incentives discourage research on harmful or problematic aspects of drugs that the Food and Drug Administration (FDA) requires applications for approval of new drugs to document that the product is effective and that it is not harmful. In other words, to win FDA approval for a new drug, the manufacturer must document the research that has probed potential risks of the drug.

Not all potentially dangerous products are regulated by the FDA, however, and cigarettes are a good example of products that are unregulated and harmful. Cigarette manufacturers have nothing to gain from the knowledge that cigarettes cause disease and kill smokers. Not only is there no reason for them to conduct such research but also there is good reason for them to deny that they have such knowledge if they did do the research. Knowingly and willfully selling a dangerous product while concealing the knowledge of the dangers would be grounds for punitive damages in civil litigation. It is bad enough to unwittingly sell a product that is dangerous; it is far worse to do so with full knowledge of the danger.

A well-publicized tactic of plausible deniability comes into play. Plausible deniability refers to the creation of conditions that allow one to argue that one was ignorant of the possible harm or, in the case of whistle-blowing, of the wrongdoing. Since knowledge of the truth requires some action, ignorance of the truth must be at least plausible as a shield against blame. There are at least two strategies available for creating plausible deniability. The first is to claim that although some people knew the truth, the defendant, who typically would be a high-ranking officer in an organization, did not know. This is a commonly used defense in politics, having been employed by Presidents Nixon, Reagan, and Clinton, and it is common in the corporate world, having been claimed, for instance, by officers of Johns Manville Corporation with regard to health risks of asbestos and by officers of A. H. Robins corporation with regard to health risks of the Dalkon Shield.

The second strategy is to deny the risk itself. This has been the strategy of the cigarette industry. The strategy is simply to deny that the product is harmful. To question the accuracy of the research that purports to show a relationship between smoking and disease is to cast doubt on the truth. Plausible deniability in this form denies the truth rather than denying prior knowledge of it.

This strategy involves very different tactics from the first form of plausible deniability. First, it involves a reluctance or unwillingness to conduct research that would be definitive. If research must be conducted, it should be done later rather than sooner. The worst outcome would be the discovery of a clear link between a product (or practice) and disease (or harm), so research that could produce such findings should be avoided. An obvious incentive is created to conduct poor research that would be unlikely to find a connection even if the relationship is present.

Part of this mode of denial is to deny that the burden of proof lies with the manufacturer. Who should shoulder the responsibility to determine if a product (or practice) creates harm for others? Should it be the company, government agencies, consumer groups, or regulatory institutions? In some cases, this burden is clearly determined, as it is with pharmaceutical firms wishing to introduce a new product. In other cases, the burden is far less clear. Imagine the case of a pesticide maker that sells the product to a foreign firm for use in a different country. Evidence trickles in that workers in that country are displaying symptoms of conditions that could be caused by overexposure to the pesticide. Is it the duty of the firm to investigate? Is it the duty of the health service, if there is one, of the nation in which the product is being used? Is it the responsibility of the corporation, which may or may not be a U.S. company, on whose crops the pesticide is being used? It is not always clear where the burden of proof lies or who should pay to search for that proof. Prolonging the debate about who has the burden of proof naturally works to the advantage of the party that is creating deniability.

Others may conduct the research, however, and this second strategy requires that negative findings be impugned. There are many ways of doing this, depending on the circumstances. One common way is to question the adequacy of the methodology that was used and to claim that the methods were flawed. Valid knowledge cannot be born of improper methods. Another is to direct attention to other research that leads to contradictory conclusions. This strategy can be used when the research problem is a complex one in which there are numerous hurdles that can derail valid research. Another effective mode of denial is to insist on a standard of proof that will be difficult to meet. To claim, as some tobacco executives have, that the evidence that smoking causes lung cancer is weak because it is "statistical" is to imply that most proof of medical facts is "nonstatistical," whatever that might be. A different form of this type of denial is to claim that there is not a consensus among experts, a claim that is relatively easy to make if "experts" can be purchased to testify to whatever the client pays them to say (Clossen, 1994). A final tactic used in denying truth is to attack the motives, ability, or both of the persons presenting it. This entails characterizing critics of smoking, for instance, as incompetent or biased. Whistle-blowers are typically attacked by those whom they accuse as being malcontents, liars, thieves, or all three. Evidence given by such persons does not require rebuttal. The wells have been poisoned.

There are many areas of organizational behavior that raise ethical issues about the management of other's perceptions of reality. There is not enough space here to do more than mention a few of these areas. One important area deals with the honesty requirements during negotiation (Dees & Cramton, 1991). Negotiating parties are not required to divulge information that would be harmful to their negotiation positions, but are they permitted to deceive the other? Is there a difference between misrepresenting one's internal states, such as one's reservation price, and misrepresenting an alternative offer? Is one "entitled" to be dishonest if one suspects that one's negotiation partner is dishonest? If so, how do we know that our beliefs about the partner's dishonesty are not the result of our wish to be deceitful rather than its cause (Tenbrunsel, 1995)?

Authority Influence

Authority, status differences, and hierarchies are essential for the efficient functioning of organizations. Authority may be used to encourage others to work effectively, to introduce new ideas, or to promote new work procedures. The formation of hierarchically organized groups creates advantages in coping with external threats as well as internal frictions (Milgram, 1974). Social hierarchies stabilize and coordinate the relations among group members, and by clearly defining the status of each member they reduce competition and conflict among members.

Hierarchies, however, because they allocate power, resources, and status unequally, create the opportunity for abuse of power by those at the top of the hierarchy. The very efficiencies that allow organizations to create value can be used to pursue selfish or evil ends. Authority requires enlightened leadership from those at higher levels of the organization and, just as important, dedicated "followership" from those at the lower levels. When the ideal characteristics exist at the lower levels but not at the higher levels, organizations are vulnerable to corruption and the production of evil. Stanley Milgram (1974), the first social psychologist to study obedience to authority experimentally as a social phenomenon, recognized this paradox when he wrote, "It is ironic that the virtues of loyalty, discipline, and self-sacrifice that we value so highly in the individual are the very properties that create destructive organizational engines of war and bind men to malevolent systems of authority" (p. 188). This paradox makes authority and its flip side, obedience, problematic.

Authority is a role relationship between two actors within a social unit in which one actor is entitled to make certain demands, whereas the other actor is obligated to accede to those demands (Kelman & Hamilton, 1989). French and Raven (1959) conceptualize legitimacy of authority as the power that stems from internalized values in a target that dictate that the influencer has a legitimate right to influence the target, and that the target has an obligation to accept this influence. Legitimate authority, therefore, differs from sheer power in that obedience to legitimate authority is not merely following orders or compliance in Kelman's (1958) scheme but also identification or internalization that results from the acceptance of either the role relationships or the influencer's values.

Reactions or responses to legitimate authority are often automatic, thoughtless, fast, and shallow, with very little processing or analysis. Recent theories have emphasized that people tend to react "mindlessly" to social stimuli (Langer & Piper, 1987), to enact routine scripts (Schank & Abelson, 1977), or to process information shallowly and heuristically (Eagly & Chaiken, 1993), often independently of their attitudes and preferences (Abelson, 1982). Barnard (1971) writes about a "zone of indifference" within an individual within which orders are accepted without conscious questioning of their authority. A painful example of blind obedience is recounted by Cohen and Davis (1981); they write about a doctor who instructed the duty nurse to administer eardrops to the patient's right ear by leaving the written direction "place in R ear." The nurse placed them in the patient's rectum, and neither she nor the patient questioned the treatment.

The legitimacy of authority is the main determinant of its social power according to Kelman and Hamilton (1989). The greater the perceived legitimacy of the authority, the higher the probability that organization members will obey orders. Kelman and Hamilton propose that there are three structural elements of legitimate authority situations that are necessary conditions for predictable obedience: the social context in which authority is used, the character of the authority holders, and the nature of the specific demands they make. Consequently, three sources of information must be conveyed to induce compliance. First, the situational definition is usually available from the physical structure of the setting in which the two parties interact (e.g., in a courtroom, police situation, classroom, and research laboratory). Second, presentation of the agent refers to information about the influencer's credentials as an authority who has the right to speak for the system and make demands on its behalf. The role of the influencer is important, as is his or her physical attractiveness, persuasiveness, and expertise. The third kind of information, specification of response, specifies the particular response demanded and reasons why that response is the only way for the target to meet his or her obligation in the present situation.

We illustrate this scheme with two examples, one that we believe to be perfectly acceptable and one that we deem completely inappropriate. A person thinks nothing of being told by a nurse in a physician's office to "Take a seat." In that setting (doctor's office), with a legitimate person of authority (the nurse), the person does not object to or even think twice about performing the innocuous and banal act of sitting down. If a colleague enters a person's university office and asks him or her to give a passing grade to a student doing failing work, however, that person's reaction is very different. The setting (the person's office) is not one in which he or she normally relinquishes control to others. The influencer (a colleague) is not someone who has an organizational role that would require compliance, and the response requested (passing a failing student) is considered wrong. Compliance would be very unlikely in this scenario.

In Milgram's (1974) celebrated and controversial experiments, the psychiatrists who incorrectly predicted that most subjects would refuse to administer painful and possibly dangerous shocks to another person placed too much weight on the response and not enough on the situation and the person. They judged that people would refuse to possibly harm another regardless of the situation and the nature of the person making the request. The force of the situation, an experiment, in which people may tacitly agree to relinquish control to an experimenter, and the force of the experimenter, wearing a lab coat and clad in the garb of medical and scientific authority, were underestimated, even by so-called experts in predicting behavior.

There are many aspects of influence by authority that merit attention. Kipnis (1972) has written about the effects of power on the powerholders, and he suggests that more powerful managers are likely to employ more assertive tactics than less powerful ones. Fiske (1993) has written about the tendency of more powerful people in organizational hierarchies to pay less attention to less powerful people than vice versa, a point that is echoed by Jackall (1988).

Focusing on the agents of influence, Lifton (1986) interviewed the German physicians who were stationed at Auschwitz during the World War II and who were responsible for selecting the prisoners who were to be executed in the gas chambers. The doctors found complying with their work obligations extremely stressful. They often did them drunk or got drunk after them. They nevertheless had to fit into the situation, and they created rationalizations for their actions. Similarly, Milgram's (1974) subjects reported being in a state of great conflict about whether or not to obey the orders to shock the other. Their response was anything but unemotional.

Examining the target of influence, Kelman and Hamilton (1989) propose three social processes that weaken the usual moral inhibitions against wrongdoing. Authorization, the ordering of illegal or unethical acts by legitimate authority, tends to override moral considerations when an unethical act is explicitly ordered, implicitly encouraged, or tacitly approved. At least part of this effect stems from the targets' sense that they are not responsible for their actions, that they are not free agents but extensions of the authority. Routinization, the transformation of an immoral job into a "routine, mechanical, highly programmed operation" (p. 18), reduces moral resistance to the job in several ways. First, it permits habitual, mindless, mechanical action, minimizing the need for moral analysis. Second, people can focus on the details of the job rather than on its meaning or ethical significance. Routinization is facilitated by the use of euphemisms to describe the action(s), further reducing objections to it. For example, "final solutions" are less outrageous than "mass murders," "downsizing" evokes fewer moral associations than "layoffs" or "firings," and "pacification" is more acceptable than "razing villages." The list of euphemisms created to disguise immoral, unpleasant, or illegal actions is very long.

Dehumanization, the act of depriving victims of human status so as to exempt them from inclusion in the moral community, is the final process that Kelman and Hamilton (1989) describe. Victims are deprived of identity, of independence, of volition to make their own choices, and of their rights to legal and moral protection. Although Kelman and Hamilton are concerned mainly with homicide, the willing killing of other humans, dehumanization makes many actions that will cause harm to others more palatable.

Loewenstein (1996), for instance, differentiates statistical victims from identifiable victims. Statistical victims are numbers, those 1, 2, or 40,000 people who will be laid off or who were killed in rioting or by floods. They are pallid statistics. Identifiable victims are individuals with pasts, families, faces, and stories. They are people, whereas statistical victims are numbers, barely human. Loewenstein hypothesizes that people are far less concerned with the fate of statistical victims than with identifiable ones, making it easier to harm or ignore the suffering of statistical rather than identifiable victims.

People in authority can easily use these processes of authorization, routinization, and dehumanization to induce compliance, identification, and even internalization among the targets of influence. In complex organizations, the techniques for inducing obedience are not easily traced to a single person, making it difficult to place responsibility for the wrongdoing that occurs. Thus, organizations such as corporations can not only foster wrongdoing, if individuals in authority wish it, but also shield those in authority from blame and culpability.

Summary

The goal of this chapter was to describe some elementary ideas about the ethical dimensions of power and influence that derive from social psychological research. We have not attempted to put forward a comprehensive, integrated, and coherent theory. Rather, we have described some of this research and its supporting theoretical scaffolding and speculated about the ethical implications thereof. Much of the research that is done by social psychologists, on the topic of influence or on other topics, involves inquiries into empirical issues that have clear moral dimensions. Social psychologists also care about improving things in the business world and in other contexts. Stanley Milgram's pioneering work and the early work on conformity, which constitute the wellspring for many of the ideas outlined in this chapter, focused on explaining how a civilized country such as Germany could have become an evil empire such as the Third Reich. The ideal was not merely to comprehend but also to use the understanding to arrange affairs so that such a thing could not happen again. In the process of studying these issues, moral decisions were made about how to investigate the psychological processes hypothesized to be involved, decisions dealing with the deception of human subjects and the possibility of inflicting psychological harm on them. Thus, social psychologists are relatively naive moralists and relatively sophisticated empiricists whose insights help illuminate the relationship between psychology and morality.

References

Abelson, R. P. (1982). Three modes of attitude-behavior consistency. In M. P. Zanna, E. T. Higgins, & C. P. Herman (Eds.), *Consistency in social behavior.* Hillsdale, NJ: Lawrence Erlbaum.

Barnard, C. I. (1971). The theory of authority. In S. A. Yelaya (Ed.), *Authority and social work: Concept and use.* Toronto: University of Toronto Press.

Bok, S. (1978). *Lying.* New York: Vintage.

Cialdini, R. B. (1993). *Influence: Science and practice* (3rd ed.). New York: HarperCollins.

Clossen, C. (1994). *Tainted truth.* New York: Simon & Shuster.

Cohen, M., & Davis, N. (1981). *Medication errors: Causes and prevention.* Philadelphia: Stickley.

Cole-Turner, R. (1995, October 6). Religion and gene patenting. *Science, 270,* 52-53.

Crutchfield, R. A. (1955). Conformity and character. *American Psychologist, 10,* 191-198.

Dees, J. G., & Cramton, P. C. (1991). Shrewd bargaining on the moral frontier. *Business Ethics Quarterly, 1,* 135-167.

Deutsch, M., & Gerard, H. B. (1958). A study of normative and informational social influence upon individual judgment. *Journal of Abnormal and Social Psychology, 51,* 629-636.

Eagly, A. H., & Chaiken, S. (1993). *The psychology of attitudes.* Fort Worth, TX: Harcourt, Brace, Jovanovich.

Fiske, S. T. (1993). Controlling other people: The impact of power on stereotyping. *American Psychologist, 48,* 621-628.

French, J. R. P., & Raven, B. (1959). The bases of social power. In D. Cartwright (Ed.), *Studies in social power.* Ann Arbor: University of Michigan Press.

Goodpaster, K. E. (1982). *Some general avenues for ethical analysis in general management* (Case No. 383-007). Cambridge, MA: Harvard Business School Press.

Insko, C. A., Sedlak, A. J., & Lipsitz, A. (1982). A two-valued logic or two-valued balance resolution of the challenge of agreement and attraction effects in p-o-x triads, and a theoretical perspective on conformity and hedonism. *European Journal of Social Psychology, 13,* 143-167.

Jackall, R. (1988). *Moral mazes.* Oxford, UK: Oxford University Press.

Kalick, S. M. (1988). Physical attractiveness as a status cue. *Journal of Experimental Social Psychology, 24,* 469-489.

Kelman, H. C. (1958). Compliance, identification, and internalization: Three processes of attitude change. *Journal of Conflict Resolution, 2,* 51-60.

Kelman, H. C., & Hamilton, V. L. (1989). *Crimes of obedience.* New Haven, CT: Yale University Press.

Kipnis, D. (1972). Does power corrupt? *Journal of Personality and Social Psychology, 24*(1), 33-41.

Langer, E., & Piper, A. (1987). The prevention of mindlessness. *Journal of Personality and Social Psychology, 53,* 280-287.

Lardner, J. (1993a, July 5). The whistle-blower—Part 1. *New Yorker,* p. 53.

Lardner, J. (1993b, July 12). The whistle-blower—Part 2. *New Yorker,* p. 39.

Latané, B. (1981). The psychology of social impact. *American Psychologist, 36,* 343-365.

Lifton, R. J. (1986). *The Nazi doctors: Medical killing and the psychology of genocide.* New York: Basic Press.

Loewenstein, G. (1996). Behavioral decision theory and business ethics: Skewed trade-offs between self and other. In D. M. Messick & A. E. Tenbrunsel (Eds.), *Codes of conduct* (pp. 214-227). New York: Russell Sage.

Maas, P. (1973). *Serpico.* New York: Viking.

Miceli, M. P., & Near, J. P. (1992). *Blowing the whistle.* New York: Lexington.

Milgram, S. (1974). *Obedience to authority: An experimental view.* New York: Harper & Row.

Nyberg, D. (1993). *The varnished truth.* Chicago: University of Chicago Press.

Schank, R. C., & Abelson, R. P. (1977). *Scripts, plans, goals, and understanding.* Hillsdale, NJ: Lawrence Erlbaum.

Skinner, B. F. (1957). *Verbal behavior.* New York: Appleton-Century-Crofts.

Smith, N. C., & Quelch, J. A. (1993). *Ethics in marketing.* Boston: Irwin.

Stern, W. (1995, August 7). Did dirty tricks create a best-seller? *Business Week,* p. 22.

Tenbrunsel, A. E. (1995). *Justifying unethical behavior.* Unpublished doctoral dissertation, Northwestern University, Kellogg Graduate School of Management, Evanston, IL.

Treacy, M., & Wiersma, F. (1995). *The discipline of market leaders.* Reading, MA: Addison-Wesley.

Velasquez, M. G. (1992). *Business ethics.* Englewood Cliffs, NJ: Prentice Hall.

Two Faces of the Powerless

Coping With Tyranny in Organizations

ROBERT J. BIES

THOMAS M. TRIPP

I dread each day coming to work. Once inside the door, I feel "chained" to my desk like a prisoner. My boss is the "prison warden" who delights in "torturing" me with a daily barrage of public criticism and ridicule. I feel so powerless, like a "pawn" being played in one of his power games. My friends ask me why I just don't quit? . . . Why do I stay and take that abuse? I don't know why . . . I guess I hope things will change, even though they don't. So I stay . . . hating him, and hating myself.
      —Manager, global telecommunication company

I do not try to justify [Fletcher Christian's] crime, his mutiny, but I condemn the tyranny that drove him to it.
      —Roger Byam (from the movie *Mutiny on the Bounty*, 1935)

T he words persecution, oppression, and tyranny conjure up terrifying images of evil dictators, such as Hitler and Stalin, who employed brutal and ruthless methods to dominate nations and people. Indeed, these words bring to mind the frightening vision of a totalitarian world in which those in power are obsessed with controlling the hearts and minds of people through fear and intimidation (Orwell, 1949).

Although political scientists and sociologists study the dynamics of tyranny (Gilliom, 1997; Scott, 1990), there is little, if any, mention of tyranny in the dominant models of leadership and power (Pfeffer, 1992). As the introductory quotation to this chapter suggests, however, people can and do describe their work experiences in those exact terms (see Shorris, 1981, for additional examples). Moreover, the popular press has provided ample anecdotal evidence of tyranny in organizations in articles on the "intolerable boss" (Lombardo & McCall, 1984), the "unbearable boss" (Goleman, 1986), and the "psycho boss from hell" (Dumaine, 1993). Ironically, these types of bosses, which are celebrated on business magazine covers, are deeply resented and scorned by their employees, who nickname them "Captain Bligh" (Nordhoff & Hall, 1932) and "Captain Queeg" (Wouk, 1951)—names that have become synonymous with tyranny in the workplace.

Although contemporary academics have been silent on tyranny by leaders and those in power, the most important and influential organizational theorist, Max Weber, was not. Weber (1946) worried about the potential for tyranny when he wrote about the concentration of power in the hands of a few masters in bureaucracy, which would imprison humanity in an "iron cage"[1] (p. 228). Although our paradigms of leadership and power have ignored a discussion and analysis of tyranny (Treviño & Bies, 1997), there has been episodic scholarly interest in the phenomenon—for example, the sociological analysis by Miller, Weiland, and Couch (1978) and Ashforth's (1994) social psychological analysis of "petty tyranny." In addition, Hornstein (1996) provides some empirical evidence of the dynamics and consequences of tyranny in his analysis of the "brutal boss."

In acknowledging the existence of tyranny in the workplace, the important theoretical (and practical) question is raised as to how people cope with tyranny (Bies, in press). History is filled with inspiring examples of people under the oppression of tyranny who, through creativity and the sheer will to live, have invented coping strategies to maintain their dignity (Scott, 1990) and sustain them in their pursuit of freedom (Havel, 1985). Although recent research in organizational settings provides some illustrative findings of how people cope with tyranny (Bies & Tripp, 1996; Tripp & Bies, 1997), there is clearly a large gap in our knowledge of how people cope with tyranny in the workplace.

The purpose of this chapter is threefold. First, we present the results of an empirical study of tyranny in the workplace, thus adding to a much needed empirical foundation for analyzing this phenomenon. In our study, we chose to focus on tyranny as manifested in the "abusive boss." The abusive boss is one whose primary objective is the control of others, and such control is achieved through methods that create fear and intimidation (Hornstein, 1996).

Second, we present data on how people cope with the tyranny of an abusive boss in the workplace. Our study finds evidence of a variety of coping responses, ranging from resignation to resistance. Finally, we explore implications of our findings and conclude with reflections on the academic silence—if not suppression—with respect to the study of tyranny in organizations.

The Abusive Boss: Profiles in Tyranny

In this study, we surveyed working managers about their experiences with the tyranny of abusive bosses. The respondents were participants in an Executive MBA program, a group that included 30 men and 17 women that had an average of 12 years of work experience. In the survey, we asked respondents to think of a specific boss for whom they had worked whom they would label as an abusive boss or a boss from hell. They were asked to describe the boss in as much detail as possible and then to identify how they coped with that boss.

The unit of analysis was the profile or description of the particular boss for whom the respondent had once worked. Respondents described the behaviors and characteristics of the abusive boss and how they coped with the abuse. The analysis strategy followed the grounded theory approach outlined by Glaser and Strauss (1967). In general, the method entails continually comparing theory and data until adequate conceptual categories are developed. To ensure accuracy and reliability of the coding process, the same data were coded independently by two raters.

The data suggest that the abusive boss engages in specific behaviors that comprise tyranny.[2] Specifically, the abusive boss displays one or more of the following behaviors: acts as a "micromanager," provides inexplicit direction with decisive delivery, exhibits "mercurial" mood swings, demonstrates an obsession with loyalty and obedience, derogates the status of employees, is capricious, exercises raw power for personal gain, obsesses on gathering personal information about employees, and at times uses coercion to corrupt employees. A more detailed discussion of each of these aspects of the abusive boss is presented.

Micromanager

In describing the abusive boss as a micromanager, respondents agreed on two key characteristics of a micromanager: an obsession with details and an obsession with perfection.

Obsession With Details

One of the signature features of abusive bosses is that they must have "their hands in everything." One respondent described her boss as follows: "He had to attend every meeting, and then he had to review and sign off on *every* piece of paper produced by the group." Indeed, as another respondent reported, "No detail was too small for his [boss's] concern or inspection." The obsession with details also causes abusive bosses to want to know every movement and action of employees. For example, one respondent described his boss as "demanding knowledge of everybody's calendars 2 months in advance." Another respondent described her boss as "wanting to know my whereabouts *to the minute,* even when I was in the bathroom."

Obsession With Perfection

In almost "Queeg-like" fashion, our respondents reported the abusive boss has an obsession with perfection. This obsession manifests itself in the setting of unreasonably high performance expectations and, at the same time, being impatient with, and unforgiving of, any mistakes. Also, not surprisingly, it was never the boss's fault for performance failures; blame was always assigned to the subordinates. As one respondent described her boss, "No excuses was his motto." The obsession with perfection was also manifest in the "second-guessing" of employees' actions and decisions. One respondent reported, "No matter what I did, he second-guessed me. He was so pathological that he was even 'second-guessing' his second guesses!"

Inexplicit Direction With Decisive Delivery

The abusive boss created a "double bind" for many respondents because, although they were asked to provide high-quality performance, the abusive boss would never define what "quality" meant. One respondent described his boss as one who demanded quality "with precision in his commands, but precisely what he meant by quality was never clear. What it meant, ultimately, was what we did not do to his satisfaction." In a similar fashion, abusive bosses usually articulate no priorities because "everything is a priority," as one respondent described her boss's motto. As a result, many respondents felt they received "inexplicit direction with decisive delivery."

What further heightened the vagueness of directions was when the boss would send conflicting signals and messages. One method of sending conflicting signals was playing a question "cat-and-mouse" game. In this game, one respondent described her difficulty in reading "my boss's mind and anticipating his every need" because she typically had no clue about the boss's intentions.

Mercurial Mood Swings

Several respondents reported that the abusive boss exhibited volatile mood swings, which were mercurial in nature and often for no apparent reason. One manager reported that his boss had a "Dr. Jeckyll and Mr. Hyde" personality. This meant that in one moment the boss could be very calm, peaceful, and satisfied; then, without any warning, the boss would erupt into a loud, angry, temper tantrum, a public tirade directed at one or all employees. Moreover, the intensity of the mood swings did not vary as a function of the seriousness of the triggering event—that is, the tirades were always loud and emotional.

Tirades were not limited to emotional outbursts. Respondents reported tirades that included the destruction of physical property (e.g., throwing telephones at the wall) or threatening, and occasionally even using, physical violence (e.g., shoving an employee). One respondent stated that when "he [the boss] went ballistic, we went for cover."

Obsession With Loyalty and Obedience

Much like a dictator, the abusive boss exhibits an obsession with loyalty and obedience. This obsession manifests itself in punishing those employees who dissented with the boss's viewpoint or position. For example, one manager, who challenged her boss' decision on technical and ethical grounds, received a strong negative performance appraisal, even though her record heretofore had been exemplary.

In another form of punishment, the abusive boss would often stigmatize any dissenter with pejorative labels (e.g., "traitor" and "troublemaker"). As loyal "subjects," employees were expected to humbly submit to and endure the public tirades and other punishments meted out by the boss.

Finally, abusive bosses may also test the loyalty of employees in an almost *1984*-like (Orwell, 1949) fashion by demanding that employees bring gossip and rumors about other employees. Respondents reported of bosses who would use their secretaries as "spies" to ferret out the "disloyal."

Status Derogation

Another signature feature of the abusive boss was the boss's willingness and ability to derogate employees in public. An example, shared by several respondents, is the boss who publicly criticizes the performance and character of an employee, even to the point of ridiculing him or her. Also, on more than one occasion, such actions would "bring men and women to tears," reported one respondent. Another respondent described his boss as the "master of sarcasm" who delighted in "putting people down" in public.

Capricious Actions

The abusive boss is also noted for arbitrariness and hypocrisy. For example, one respondent described how, when the sales group was just about to reach their target for the year (a record level), the boss raised the sales target, without any justification, causing the group to lose their bonus. Indeed, making arbitrary decisions, with no justification, was a common behavior of abusive bosses.

Hypocrisy took the form of employing double standards in dealing with employees. One example of hypocrisy was the boss "who left work early to run personal errands, but chastised me for attempting to do the same," as reported by one respondent. When she brought the hypocrisy to the boss's attention, she was told by the boss to "do as I say not as I do."

Exercises Raw Power for Personal Gain

For several respondents, it was in the use of "raw power" that defined the essence of tyranny. One example of raw power was the boss who "held up my approved job transfer because he wanted me to stay to serve his interests," reported one respondent. Another respondent reported an example of the boss who kept employees waiting for 3 hours into the early morning after their job was completed satisfactorily just because the boss had not finished his job. Raw power also took the form of blatantly stealing credit for a subordinate's idea.

In some cases, raw power took the form of coercion. Two stories illustrate this coercion. First, an employee was told that he had to fire one of his own subordinates, even though that subordinate was a good performer. The boss, however, did not personally like that subordinate and implied that if the employee did not fire his subordinate, it may reflect adversely on his managerial capabilities and limit his future at this company. This employee, being young and recently married with a newborn, submitted and terminated the employee, even though he knew it was wrong.

Second, one boss forced an employee to add a fourth vendor to a competitive bidding process, even though the vendor had failed to meet the requirements. Then, after one of the original three vendors technically won the competition, the employee was told to give it to the fourth vendor, with whom the boss had connections.

The Social Toxins of Tyranny: Poisoning the Mind, Body, and Spirit

There can be no darker or more devastating tragedy than the death of man's faith in himself and in his power to direct his future.
—Alinsky (1971, p. xxvi)

In describing abusive bosses, respondents provided us with some insight on how they "experienced" the effects of tyranny. Specifically, they outlined some effects of tyranny in cognitive, affective, and physiological terms. Often, these effects were lingering and interrelated. Furthermore, the effects went beyond mere issues of dissatisfaction and lower productivity; indeed, tyranny was viewed by many of our respondents as a "social toxin," poisoning their professional and personal lives.

Common responses to tyranny were the thoughts and feelings of betrayal, distrust, resentment, frustration, and mental exhaustion. In addition, several respondents reported a variety of physiological reactions to tyranny, including uncontrollable crying, "knots in the stomach," and physical exhaustion.

According to the respondents in our study, the bosses' actions were oriented toward one primary goal—control. Control was achieved through creating fear and intimidation and creating confusion and disorientation. Indeed, several respondents reported feeling "paranoid," and a few reported feeling "terror-stricken" and, at times, "paralyzed." One person reported that "I would stay at my desk and not even go to the bathroom, for the fear, if I was away from my desk, my boss would 'hammer' me in public." Not surprisingly, such people reported feeling vulnerable and powerless because the boss's tyranny had "broken the spirit and willingness to fight back," as described by one respondent.

Responses to Tyranny:
Coping Strategies

Society is a very mysterious animal with many faces and hidden personalities, and . . . it's extremely shortsighted to believe that the face of society that happens to be presenting to you at a given moment is its only true face. None of us knows all the potentialities that slumber in the spirit of the population.
—V. Havel (May 31, 1990)

Our analysis of the data suggests that responses to tyranny can be fruitfully explored in a framework that has two dimensions. The first dimension is the persona or face that we project to the public. The sec-

TABLE 9.1 Responses to Tyranny

	Public Face	
Private Face	*Consent*	*Dissent*
Consent	Surrender	Disguise
Dissent	Disguise	Confrontation

ond dimension is the persona or face that we keep private or hidden to ourselves—one that reflects our true beliefs and attitudes.

With respect to the tyrant boss, people can present two faces—one that consents to or agrees with the boss and the other that dissents from or disagrees with the boss. In this framework, then, the public persona may or may not be consistent with the private face, resulting in a two-by-two framework for analysis. Table 9.1 presents this framework, and in the following sections we describe the more specific coping strategies as reflected in this framework.

Public Consent, Private Consent: Surrender

For some of our respondents, coping with their tyrant bosses was made "easy" by changing their own private beliefs to be consistent with those of the boss. A few respondents coped by realigning their private beliefs with their boss's beliefs and policies. Such realignment, they reported, resolved the conflict they had with their bosses. In other words, they "surrendered" and "gave up" completely.

Similarly, other respondents reported coping by loyally following orders or by simply accepting the tyranny as social reality. By accepting their "fate," it made the tyranny less oppressive. One respondent described her position as follows: "Once I gave in, and stopped trying to fight it, it became easier."

Public Consent, Private Dissent: Disguise

> When the great lord passes, the wise peasant bows deeply and silently farts.
> —Ethiopian proverb (as cited in Scott, 1990, p. v)

Several respondents reported that they coped with their tyrannical bosses by only appearing to change their own private beliefs. That is, respondents would publicly espouse their bosses' beliefs and support the bosses' policies but privately vehemently disagree with their bosses' beliefs and policies. In other words, our respondents reported disguising their true feelings by presenting a public face that was quite different than their private beliefs.

The acts of disguise can take a variety of forms, according to our respondents. One common form of disguise is in how people "manage" their bosses. For many respondents, efforts to better manage their bosses included keeping their bosses informed of all details, better preparing for meetings with their bosses, and better determining their bosses' needs and goals. Respondents also reported that they mirrored their bosses' working styles to avoid criticisms of their own work styles.

Managing the boss also included the strategic use of information. For example, one respondent reported how he "told the boss just enough information to avoid trouble, and reported successes, not failures." Most respondents noted that they managed their relationships with their bosses not because they liked their bosses but because they viewed it as "a personally effective survival strategy," as one respondent reported. They did not believe it was in their own best interests to make their bosses aware of the depth of their disaffection, so they hid their true feelings and tried to work with their bosses.

A second form of disguise involved keeping a "low profile." This meant "offering no challenges or criticisms," in the words of one respondent. Other respondents kept a low profile by minimizing contact with their bosses—an "evade and avoid" strategy. While keeping a low profile, respondents also secretly documented their bosses mistakes and transgressions, predicting that such documentation might become beneficial in the future.

A third form of disguise occurred in one's head. For example, many respondents highlighted the value of "revenge fantasies" in which they dreamed of getting even with their bosses but they projected the public face of "getting along" with the bosses. Relying on revenge fantasies was viewed by one respondent as a "mental survival" strategy. Another respondent described his perspective as follows: "While he plays his mind games with me, I play my own mind games."

As another enactment of disguise, some respondents acted out their revenge fantasies, but in ways that could not be recognized as getting even or as any kind of challenge. For example, some respondents reported withholding support from their bosses at critical times, resulting in failures for the bosses. Others reported following all orders, no matter how stupid some orders might be. Also, with those bosses who were obsessed with details and information, some respondents would deliberately feed their bosses so much information as to overload them while appearing as "dutiful subordinates keeping the boss informed," as one respondent stated.

A fifth form of disguise was "carnival" techniques. By carnival, respondents meant a festive gathering held at the boss's expense but without the boss knowing. For example, in small private gatherings, employees would demonize their bosses—that is, vent their frustrations, assign blame, call the bosses names (e.g., "Beelzebub"), and generally bad-mouth their bosses. In one case, subordinates used humor to ridicule their boss by holding an initiation ceremony for a new employee who had just had his first abusive encounter with the boss.

Finally, some respondents reported creating "refuges" from the boss for other subordinates. These people acted as buffers between the boss and the other subordinates. The buffer worked in two directions: It shielded the subordinates from the boss's tantrums and confusing edicts and shielded the boss from the subordinates' dissent.

Public Dissent, Private Dissent: Confrontation

Progressive forces need trumpets, not farts.
—Handler (1992, p. 727)

More than a few respondents reported engaging in confrontation in which they openly challenged their bosses. Some would directly confront their bosses, challenging them on their decisions in an open, public forum. Others would take the public challenge even further by openly ridiculing the boss. In a few cases, public challenges involved acts of insubordination, such as making decisions without the boss's knowledge or approval.

Confrontation also took the form of going around the boss to deal with the boss. Examples of such an "end-runs" around the boss included talking to the boss's boss, involving a third party such as a representative from human resources or legal departments, and consulting a lawyer. As part of these strategies, any private documentation of the boss's actions was brought to public light.

A final act of confrontation involved exiting the situation. Exit took the form of quitting or leaving the organization but with "a little panache" in the words of one respondent. For example, one respondent stated that her exit was done with a "blaze of glory, distributing e-mail and hard copy documentation with a list of her boss's crimes."

Public Dissent, Private Consent: Disguise

Our data did not reveal any direct evidence of this form of disguised behavior. Indirect evidence, however, was provided by a few respondents in their examples of secretaries and other employees acting as spies for the boss. In this role of the "mole" for the boss, secretaries would express their public disaffection with the boss as a means of disarming other employees to become more forthcoming about their true negative feelings about the boss. This intelligence gathered by the spies was then fed back to the boss. In other words, the secretaries hid or disguised their true loyalty to the boss by pretending to be dissatisfied with the boss.

Beyond the Data:
Impressions and Implications

In interpreting these data, some interesting, albeit preliminary, conclusions emerge. First, even though our sample is small, leading us to be reasonably tentative, the findings are strikingly similar to descriptions made by other researchers, such as Hornstein (1996) and Ashforth (1994). They identified dimensions to describe tyranny in organizations similar to those found in our study (e.g., micromanagers, obsession with protection, and exercise of raw power). This convergence with the findings of other researchers suggests that we are capturing the essence and dynamics of tyranny in organizations, particularly in the form of the abusive boss.

Second, our data shed additional light on the dark side of power and politics in organizations. Indeed, it is very clear that in the use of power there can be the abuse of power (Bies & Tripp, 1995). Also, abuse does not take its toll in only economic terms; it also has a toxic effect and impact on the human lives of people who work in organizations. Any complete analysis of power can not only focus on its functional rationality in achieving organizational goals and objectives but also must account for the dysfunctional and irrational consequences of its use.

What distinguishes our research from the work of Hornstein (1996) and Ashforth (1994) is the identification of a broader range of coping strategies, and particularly how individuals manage and even manipulate their public persona as central to coping with tyranny. The most intriguing finding to us was people's rather extensive use of disguise and, in particular, the use of carnival techniques.

Although this "two-faced" approach can be difficult because employees are "living within a lie" (Havel, 1985), our respondents reported that the use of disguise can, in fact, be a rational and functional coping strategy. It is functional because it protects them to some extent from the unbridled wrath of a tyrant bent on harming those who disagree or dislike the tyrant. In addition, it is functional because it provides the employee with some measure of control and efficacy with respect to his or her environment (Bies & Tripp, 1996, in press; Tripp & Bies, 1997).

In particular, two aspects of the use of disguise proved especially interesting to us. First, respondents reported that through their acts of disguise they led the tyrant bosses to believe that they have a more supportive and submissive group of employees than was actually true. In other words, bosses, based on their observations of the employees' loyal and obedient behavior, made inferences that led to a false consciousness and a false consensus as to the level of affection or disaffection with their leadership (Nord & Doherty, 1994). In that sense, duplicity was central to managing conflict.

Indeed, in our data, there is clear evidence of a rich "underground" in organizations. In this underground world, people share common experiences and provide social support in a rich, liturgical fashion. They often engage in party-like social gatherings with initiation rites and storytelling. The evidence of this underground is strikingly similar to that found in research on how citizens cope with repressive political regimes (Scott, 1990) and quite consistent with evidence of the "everyday resistance" by those under the scrutiny of surveillance and regulation (Gilliom, 1997).

Beyond the Sounds of Silence:
The Study of Tyranny in Organizations

An emerging body of research on tyranny and its consequences leads us to ask the following question: Why are our organization and management theories so silent on the abuse of power by leaders? One answer could be that researchers are simply unaware of the existence of the social phenomenon of tyranny in organizations. Given a growing body of empirical evidence of tyranny and its consequences, however, this answer is not persuasive.

A more likely answer to the question is found in the prevailing ideological assumptions of organization and management theory—the organizational imperative (Scott & Hart, 1979). The organizational imperative is based on a primary and absolute proposition, "Whatever is good for the individual can only come from the modern organiza- tion" (p. 43), and the related secondary proposition, "Therefore, *all behavior must enhance the health of such organizations* (italics added)" (p. 43). Indeed, as Scott and Hart conclude, "The organizational im- perative is the sine qua non of management theory and practice . . . the metaphysic of management: absolute and immutable" (p. 46).

The ideology of the organizational imperative has important im- plications for the study of tyranny because, as is known, ideological assumptions shape theory building and empirical research (Barley & Kunda, 1992; Hatch, 1997; Scott & Hart, 1971). The ideology of the organizational imperative has resulted in "blinding" people from "see- ing" tyranny and its consequences (Bies & Tripp, in press; Treviño & Bies, 1997). As the empirical evidence continues to grow, however, ignoring or failing to see tyranny will become harder to do. Thus, the "defenders" of the ideology will be faced with the task of inventing new responses to legitimate the ideology.

One likely response will be "reframing" the methods and conse- quences of tyranny. That is, while acknowledging tyranny, it will be argued that although such methods may be harsh or even cruel, they are absolutely necessary and essential for creating high-performance organizations. In other words, the survival of the organization de- mands tyranny!

A second possible response will be to shift the focus away from the tyrant and the agents of tyranny and to highlight—and "condemn"— the actions of those who fight back against oppression in the workplace. No longer will the initial harmdoer be wrong because it will be the initial victim who is wrong! In other words, in an Orwellian twist, the harmdoer becomes the victim, and the victim becomes the harm-doer.

This move to "blaming the victim" also results in a biased punctuation of the research problem because the focus will not be on the situational events or organizational practices that can precipitate, or even justify, a victim's response to harm and wrongdoing (Bies & Tripp, 1996, in press; McLean Parks, 1997; Tripp & Bies, 1997). This biased punctuation of the problem should not be surprising because it follows from the ideology of the organizational imperative that any response to tyranny that attacks the interest of the organization—as articulated by its leaders—is by definition "wrong," "bad," and "deviant" (Robinson & Bennett, 1995).

To counteract the ideological bias of the organizational imperative, Treviño and Bies (1997) "nailed" a normative manifesto to the doors of the academy in an open challenge to the defenders of the ideology of the organizational imperative. In this manifesto, they argue that many organizational theorists and researchers assumed the roles of apologists and excuse-makers for management and its interests. As a result, theory and research have excluded the voices of a large group of people in organizations—those who are relatively powerless. Moreover, the efforts of many researchers may have contributed to perpetuating the use of dehumanizing or exploitative management practices (Scott & Hart, 1979).

For those theorists and researchers who have the courage to study tyranny—let alone speak out against it—your role will be that of a social critic: on the margin, not in the mainstream, motivated by what Beaney (1966) calls "a never-ending quest to increase the respect of all . . . for the essential values of human life" (p. 271). The choice to join this quest is yours. It always has been.

Notes

1. We thank Mayer Zald for this reference.
2. We do not suggest that abusive bosses do not possess other qualities that assist them in accomplishing tasks. Just because an abusive boss may be "effective" on some performance indicators, however, it does not follow that his or her behavior is any less abusive nor does the boss's success mitigate judgments about his or her abusive behavior.

References

Alinsky, S. D. (1971). *Rules for radicals: A pragmatic primer for realistic radicals.* New York: Random House.

Ashforth, B. (1994). Petty tyranny in organizations. *Human Relations, 47,* 755-778.

Barley, S. R., & Kunda, G. (1992). Design and devotion: Surges of rational and normative ideologies of control in managerial discourse. *Administrative Science Quarterly, 37,* 363-399.

Beaney, W. M. (1966). The right to privacy and American law. *Law and Contemporary Problems, 31,* 253-271.

Bies, R. J. (in press). Interactional (in)justice: The sacred and the profane. In J. Greenberg & R. Cropanzano (Eds.), *Advances in organizational behavior.* San Francisco: New Lexington.

Bies, R. J., & Tripp, T. M. (1995). The use and abuse of power: Justice as social control. In R. Cropanzano & M. Kacmar (Eds.), *Organizational politics, justice, and support: Managing social climate at work* (pp. 131-145). New York: Quorum.

Bies, R. J., & Tripp, T. M. (1996). Beyond distrust: "Getting even" and the need for revenge. In R. M. Kramer & T. Tyler (Eds.), *Trust in organizations* (pp. 246-260). Thousand Oaks, CA: Sage.

Bies, R. J., & Tripp, T. M. (in press). Revenge in organizations: The good, the bad, and the ugly. In R. W. Griffin, A. O'Leary Kelly, & J. Collins (Eds.), *Dysfunctional behavior in organizations, Vol. 1: Violent behaviors in organizations.* Greenwich, CT: JAI.

Dumaine, B. (1993, October 18). America's toughest bosses. *Fortune,* 39-50.

Gilliom, J. (1997). Everyday surveillance, everyday resistance: Computer monitoring in the lives of the Appalachian poor. In A. Sarat & S. S. Silbey (Eds.), *Studies in law, politics, and society* (Vol. 16, pp. 275-297). Greenwich, CT: JAI.

Glaser, B. G., & Strauss, A. L. (1967). *The discovery of grounded theory: Strategies for qualitative research.* New York: Aldine.

Goleman, D. (1986, December 28). When the boss is unbearable. *New York Times,* Section 3, pp. 1, 29.

Handler, J. F. (1992). Postmodernism, protest, and the new social movements. *Law and Society Review, 26,* 697-732.

Hatch, M. J. (1997). *Organization theory: Modern, symbolic, and postmodern perspectives.* Oxford, UK: Oxford University Press.

Havel, V. (1985). The power of the power less. In J. Keane (Ed.), *The power of the power less: Citizens against the state in central-eastern Europe.* Armonk, NY: M. E. Sharpe.

Hornstein, H. A. (1996). *Brutal bosses and their prey.* New York: Riverhead Books.

Lombardo, M. M., & McCall, M. W., Jr. (1984, January). The intolerable boss. *Psychology Today,* 44-48.

McLean Parks, J. (1997). The fourth arm of justice: The art and science of revenge. In R. J. Lewicki, R. J. Bies, & B. H. Sheppard (Eds.), *Research on negotiation in organizations* (Vol. 6, pp. 113-144). Greenwich, CT: JAI.

Miller, D. E., Weiland, M. W., & Couch, C. J. (1978). Tyranny. In N. Denzin (Ed.), *Studies in symbolic interaction* (Vol. 1, pp. 267-288). Greenwich, CT: JAI.

Nord, W. R., & Doherty, E. M. (1994). Toward an improved framework for conceptualizing the conflict process. In R. J. Lewicki, B. H. Sheppard, & R. J. Bies (Eds.), *Research on negotiation in organizations* (pp. 173-240). Greenwich, CT: JAI.

Nordhoff, C., & Hall, J. N. (1932). *Mutiny on the bounty.* Boston: Little, Brown.

Orwell, G. (1949). *1984.* New York: Harcourt Brace.

Pfeffer, J. (1992). *Managing with power.* Cambridge, MA: Harvard Business School Press.

Robinson, S. L., & Bennett, R. J. (1995). A typology of deviant work place behaviors: A multidimensional scaling study. *Academy of Management Journal, 38,* 555-572.

Scott, J. C. (1990). *Domination and the arts of resistance.* New Haven, CT: Yale University Press.

Scott, W. G., & Hart, D. K. (1971). The moral nature of man in organizations: A comparative analysis. *Academy of Management Journal, 14,* 255.

Scott, W. G., & Hart, D. K. (1979). *Organizational America: Can individual freedom survive within the security it promises?* Boston: Houghton Mifflin.

Shorris, E. (1981). *The oppressed middle: Politics of middle management (scenes from corporate life).* Garden City, NY: Anchor/Doubleday.

Treviño, L. K., & Bies, R. J. (1997). Through the looking glass: A normative manifest of organizational behavior. In C. L. Cooper & S. E. Jackson (Eds.), *Creating tomorrow's organizations: A handbook for future research in organizational behavior* (pp. 439-452). London: Wiley.

Tripp, T. M., & Bies, R. J. (1997). What's good about revenge? The avenger's perspective. In R. J. Lewicki, R. J. Bies, & B. H. Sheppard (Eds.), *Research on negotiation in organizations* (Vol. 6, pp. 145-160). Greenwich, CT: JAI.

Weber, M. (1946). *From Max Weber: Essays in sociology* (H. H. Gerth & C. W. Mills, Eds.). New York: Oxford University Press.

Wouk, H. (1951). *The Caine mutiny.* Garden City, NY: Doubleday.

10

Personality Correlates of Structural Holes

RONALD S. BURT

How much of the association between network structure and manager performance is due to manager personality? I have been
troubled by contemporary emphasis on manager networks over personality (Kilduff & Krackhardt, 1994, offer a compelling discussion of
the concern). It is not that personality is put aside as irrelevant so much
as personality is uninterestingly complex in comparison to the consequential and tractable complexity of network structure. There is reason
to boldly assume that individuals have personality as a function of the
history of network positions they have occupied, which frees scholars
to ignore personality as emergent and focus theory on the underlying
action and belief implications of network structure.[1]

In this chapter, I use survey network and personality profile data
to explore the idea that personality varies systematically with struc-

AUTHOR'S NOTE: I am grateful to the University of Chicago students who participated
in this study and to David Krackhardt, Holly J. Raider, and David Willer for their
comments on the manuscript. Portions of this chapter are reprinted from Burt (1997)
and Burt, Jannotta, and Mahoney (1998).

tural holes, a theoretically significant element of network structure associated with manager performance. I begin with an introduction to the association between structural holes and manager performance. I then explore personality data on several students to look for systematic association with structural holes in the student networks. I find a strong association consistent with the structural hole argument. Structural holes are associated with the personality of an entrepreneurial outsider (vs. conforming and obedient insider), in search of authority (vs. security), thriving on advocacy and change (vs. stability). I summarize with a network entrepreneur personality index that defines a surprisingly accurate probability of the respondent having an entrepreneurial network. I conclude with cautionary evidence from a survey of corporate staff in a large financial organization. Where the personality index is associated with entrepreneurial networks (lower ranks), neither the index nor the networks are associated with manager performance. Where manager performance is significantly linked with entrepreneurial networks (more senior ranks), the personality index is not associated with network structure, and performance is not higher for managers with more entrepreneurial personalities. In summary, the personality data are an interesting correlate, but no substitute, for network data.

Structural Holes and Performance

Structural hole theory gives concrete meaning to the social capital metaphor by describing how social capital is a function of the brokerage opportunities in a network. The following is a brief synopsis (see Burt, 1992, for detailed discussion).

The structural hole argument draws on several lines of network theorizing that emerged in sociology during the 1970s, most notably Granovetter (1973) on the strength of weak ties, Freeman (1977) on betweenness centrality, Cook and Emerson (1978) on the power of having exclusive exchange partners, and Burt (1980) on the structural autonomy created by network complexity. More generally, sociological ideas elaborated by Simmel (1922/1955) and Merton (1957/1968) on the autonomy generated by conflicting affiliations are mixed in the hole argument with traditional economic ideas of monopoly power and oligopoly to produce network models of competitive advantage. In a perfect market, one price clears the market. In an imperfect market, there can be multiple prices because disconnections between individuals, holes in the structure of the market, leave some people unaware of the benefits they offer one another. Certain people are connected to certain others, trust certain others, obligated to support certain others, and dependent on exchange with certain others. Assets get locked into suboptimal exchanges. How an individual is positioned in the structure of these exchanges can be an asset in its own right. That asset is social capital, in essence a story about location effects in differentiated markets. The structural hole argument defines social capital in terms of the information and control advantages of being the broker in relations between people otherwise disconnected in social structure. The disconnected people stand on opposite sides of a hole in social structure. The structural hole is an opportunity to broker the flow of information between people and control the form of projects that bring together people from opposite sides of the hole.

Information Benefits

The information benefits are access, timing, and referrals. A manager's network provides access to information well beyond what he or she could process alone. It provides that information early, which is an advantage to the manager acting on the information. The network that filters information coming to a manager also directs, concentrates, and legitimates information received by others about the manager. Referrals get the manager's interests represented in a positive light, at the right time, in the right places.

The structure of a network indicates the redundancy of its information benefits. Redundancy is indicated by either of two conditions. The first is cohesion. Cohesive contacts (contacts strongly connected to each other) are likely to have similar information and therefore provide redundant information benefits. Structural equivalence is the second indicator. Equivalent contacts (contacts who link a manager to the same third parties) have the same sources of information and therefore provide redundant information benefits.

Nonredundant contacts offer information benefits that are additive rather than redundant. Structural holes are the gaps between nonredundant contacts. The hole is a buffer, like an insulator in an electric circuit. A structural hole between two clusters in a network need not mean that people in the two clusters are unaware of one another. It simply means that they are so focused on their own activities that they have little time to attend to the activities of people in the other cluster. A structural hole indicates that the people on either side of the hole circulate in different flows of information. A manager who spans the structural hole, by which I mean a manager who has strong relations with contacts on both sides of the hole, has access to both information flows. The more holes spanned, the richer the information benefits of the network.

Figure 10.1 provides an example. James had a network that spanned one structural hole. The hole is the relatively weak connection between the cluster reached through contacts 1, 2, and 3 and the cluster reached through contacts 4 and 5. Robert took over James's job and expanded the social capital associated with the job. He preserved connection with both clusters in James's network but expanded the network to a more diverse set of contacts. Robert's network, with the addition of three new clusters of people, spans 10 structural holes.

Information benefits in this example are enhanced in several ways. The volume is higher in Robert's network simply because he reaches more people indirectly. Also, the diversity of his contacts means that the quality of his information benefits is higher. Each cluster of contacts is a single source of information because people connected to one another tend to know the same things at about the same time. Nonredundant clusters provide Robert with a broader information screen and therefore greater assurance that he will be informed of opportunities and impending disasters (access benefits). Furthermore, since Robert's contacts are only linked through him at the center of the network, he is the first to see new opportunities created by needs in one group that could be served by skills in other group (timing benefits). He stands at the crossroads of social organization. He has the option of bringing together otherwise disconnected individuals where in the network it would be rewarding. And because Robert's contacts are more diverse, he is more likely to be a candidate for inclusion in new opportunities (referral benefits). These benefits are compounded by the fact that having a network that yields such benefits makes Robert more attractive to other people as a contact in their own networks.

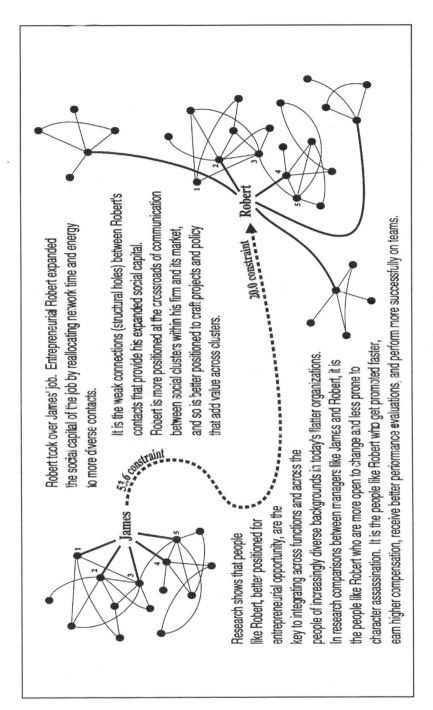

Figure 10.1. Structural Holes and Performance

Control Benefits

The manager who creates a bridge between otherwise discon-nected contacts has a say in whose interests are served by the bridge. The disconnected contacts communicate through the manager, giving the manager an opportunity to adjust his or her image with each contact (the structural foundation for managerial robust action; Padgett & Ansell, 1993). More, the sociological theories of Simmel and Merton describe the role of people who derive control benefits from structural holes (see Burt, 1992, pp. 30-32, for review). It is the *tertius gaudens* (literally "the third who benefits"), a person who benefits from brokering the connection between others. As the broker between two otherwise disconnected contacts, a manager is an entrepreneur in the literal sense of the word—a person who adds value by standing be-tween others (Burt, 1992, pp. 34-36; see Martinelli, 1994, for historical review of the term in economic sociology). There is a tension here but not the hostility of combatants. It is merely uncertainty. In the swirling mix of preferences characteristic of social networks, where no demands have absolute authority, the tertius negotiates for favorable terms. Structural holes are the setting for tertius strategies, and information is the substance. Accurate, ambiguous, or distorted information is strategically moved between contacts by the tertius. The information and control benefits reinforce one another at any moment in time and cumulate together over time.

Networks rich in structural holes present opportunities for en-trepreneurial behavior. The behaviors by which managers develop these opportunities are many and varied, but the opportunity itself is at all times defined by a hole in the social structure around the man-ager. In terms of the structural hole argument, networks rich in the entrepreneurial opportunities of structural holes are entrepreneurial networks, and entrepreneurs are people skilled in building the inter-personal bridges that span structural holes.

Predicted Effect on Manager Performance

Managers with contact networks rich in structural holes know about, have a hand in, and exercise control over the more rewarding opportunities. They monitor information more effectively than it can be monitored bureaucratically. They move information faster, and to more people, than memos. These entrepreneurial managers know the parameters of organization problems early. They are highly mobile relative to people working through a bureaucracy, easily shifting network time and energy from one solution to another. More in control of their immediate surroundings, entrepreneurial managers tailor solutions to the specific individuals being coordinated, replacing the boilerplate solutions of formal bureaucracy. There is also the issue of costs; entrepreneurial managers offer inexpensive coordination relative to the bureaucratic alternative. In sum, managers with networks rich in structural holes operate somewhere between the force of corporate authority and the dexterity of markets, building bridges between disconnected parts of the firm where it is valuable to do so. They have more opportunity to add value, are expected to do so, and are accordingly expected to enjoy higher returns to their efforts. The prediction is that in comparisons between otherwise similar people like James and Robert in Figure 10.1, it is people like Robert who should be more successful.

The social capital difference between James and Robert can be measured by the relative extent to which their contact networks are constrained. Network constraint is an index, computed from the structure of relations around a person, that varies from 0 toward 100 with the extent to which the person's relations are directly or indirectly concentrated in a single contact (see Network Data). Constraint is lower in large networks. It is higher in dense or hierarchical networks. The range of network constraint scores across the people to be discussed is illustrated by the 20 to 54 difference between Robert and James respectively in Figure 10.1.

Empirical research comparing managers like Robert and James shows that the competitive advantage lies with Robert. The summary sentence at this point is that high levels of constraint in manager's networks are associated with poor team performance, poor job evaluations, low compensation, and late promotion (see Burt, 1997, 1998, for review and illustrative results).

The Motivation Issue

Motivation is an issue. Network structure can be measured for its entrepreneurial opportunities, and evidence can be presented of manager achievement correlated with opportunity. However, opportunities do not by themselves turn into achievement, and some people are not comfortable pursuing the information and control benefits of structural holes. Thus the motivation issue: To what extent is the connection between success and brokerage contingent on having a personality suited to working with structural holes? The motivation issue can be assumed away,[2] dismissed as correlate of network structure,[3] or addressed directly.[4]

The preliminary question is whether personalities differ across the structural hole continuum, changing in some systematic way from the cliques that provide little social capital to the large, sparse entrepreneurial networks rich in the social capital of structural holes. The only empirical evidence bearing directly on the question is Janicik's (1997) experiments with subjects learning social structures. He shows that learning a new social structure that contains structural holes is much easier for people whose current network contains structural holes. Whatever the explanation for Janicik's results—holes enhance the ability to learn, people see more clearly network structures with which they have experience, or more intelligent people better report the holes in the social structure around them—there is a clear association between structural holes and individual differences in learning. It is a short step to broader individual differences in personality.

Searching for Personality Correlates

My data are questionnaire responses from University of Chicago MBA students in two sections of a required course in organization behavior. Although students, these are toward the mature end of the distribution of student populations. They are typically in their late twenties, on average have several years of full-time work experience, and many were employed in a full-time job. Although the students are not a probability sample, they are informatively heterogeneous. They work in diverse industries. They span stages of the degree program (41% are in their second year). A third are women (35%). A fifth are racial minorities (18%).

Network Data

More important to this analysis, the students have diverse kinds of networks. I have network data from a survey network instrument completed at the beginning of the course to better tie the course content to each student's personal experience. The student's contact network is computer analyzed for structure and composition. Students can compare their network to the networks of the sample managers discussed in class. The questionnaire is analogous to the survey network instruments in Burt's (1992, 1997) and Podolny and Baron's (1997) studies with probability samples of managers. Students were asked, with respect to their current or most recent job, to name their most important contacts for personal discussion (the 1985 General Social Survey name generator), socializing, supervision, political support, and career advice, as well as competitors, and especially difficult co-workers. The students were then asked to describe the relative strength of their relationship with each contact and between each pair of contacts. These data define a contact network around each student. Measuring the lack of structural holes in a network, network constraint decreases with the number of contacts in the network (network size), increases with the average strength of relations between contacts (network density), and increases with the extent to which relations among contacts are concentrated in a single contact (network hierarchy).[5] The student networks are as diverse in size, density, and hierarchy as networks I have observed around junior managers more generally.[6]

Personality Profile

Personality data on the students are from a self-administered instrument widely used in human resource consulting. The instrument was developed by a commercial consulting firm, Management Research Group (MRG), to help respondents better identify features of their organizational personalities that were strong, or that needed development, or that were perceived differently by colleagues above, below, and around the respondent in the organization (see Mahoney & Mahoney, 1990, for reliability and benchmark results). Any of several alternative personality instruments could be used for this study. I use the MRG instrument for three reasons: (a) It includes a diverse array of personality items, which improves the odds of finding personality correlates of network structure if there are any; (b) the firm gave me permission to use the instrument for the exploratory purposes of this study; and (c) I have confidence in the instrument's reliability because

		MOST		NEXT	
1. When evaluating opportunities, I am likely to look					
a. to use my specialized skills		5	4	3	2
b. for a chance to be in a position of authority		5	4	3	2
c. for the long-run implications		5	4	3	2
2. My strength lies in the fact that I have a knack for					
a. getting a point across clearly		5	4	3	2
b. being easygoing		5	4	3	2
c. never breaking a promise		5	4	3	2

Figure 10.2. Example of MRG Personality Item Clusters

it has been refined over more than a decade of successful commercial use.

The MRG instrument is a sequence of 252 statements that the respondent rates for the extent to which each describes the respondent. The 252 items are organized into 84 clusters of three items as illustrated in Figure 10.2. Each item cluster begins with a header phrase (e.g., "When evaluating opportunities, I am likely to look . . .") followed by three alternative endings. The respondent's task is to rate the alternative endings for the extent to which each is characteristic of the respondent. The "most" descriptive ending is given a 5 or 4 (5 for especially descriptive). The "next" most descriptive ending is given a 3 or 2 (2 for less descriptive). The least descriptive is left blank (for an implicit rating of 1).

The personality data are thus 252 items on a 1 to 5 scale indicating the extent to which each of 252 sentences describes the respondent.[7] With 252 personality items and 51 respondents, a few items are sure to be associated with almost any variable, network or other. It will be important to see that the content of personality items associated with network structure is consistent with network theory.

Tests for Selection Bias

The network questionnaire was part of the course curriculum, but the MRG questionnaire was optional. Students were invited to participate in this study at the end of the course. The relative importance of personality versus structure was an issue in class discussion from time to time, so this was a chance for interested students to see empirical evidence on the issue. Students who completed the questionnaire received $10 as a token of appreciation for their time and had the option of receiving a copy of the analysis. We have MRG questionnaires from 51 of 122 students (42%). All but 4 students returning a questionnaire asked to receive the analysis. Selection bias seems not to be an issue in the sense that the students who returned the MRG questionnaire were no different from the students not responding (with respect to degree program, first-year vs. second-year of program, final grade in course, class participation, gender, race, and network; Burt et al., 1998; Figure 10.2).

Results

The first task is to see if any item clusters vary with network structure. Most correlations are negligible between the 252 personality items and variables measuring the lack of structural holes in a respondent's network, less than .2 in magnitude. A few exceed .3 in magnitude. Taking .3 as an arbitrary initial cutoff (corresponds to a t test of 2.2), 26 of the 252 items are network relevant in the sense of having a correlation of magnitude .3 or more with one of the three network variables. These 26 network-relevant items cannot be analyzed independent of the other items in their clusters. The 26 network-relevant items come from 20 of the 84 item clusters.

Aggregate Correlation With Network Structure

Item clusters are listed in Table 10.1 in descending order of their aggregate correlation with network density, hierarchy, and constraint. The header phrase for each item cluster is listed to display the diversity of organization behaviors described by the items. Aggregate correlation is measured by canonical correlations—the first two of which are listed in Table 10.1 with a summary chi-square statistic for the hypothesis of no association between the three network variables and the three items in the row cluster. The null hypothesis is clearly rejected only for the four clusters at the top of the table.

TABLE 10.1 Item-Cluster Correlations With Network Structure

	Canonical Correlations		
First	Second	χ^2	Header Phrase for Item Cluster
.51	.43	23.7	1. When evaluating opportunities, I am likely to look
.55	.33	23.4	2. My strength lies in the fact that I have a knack for
.56	.21	20.1	3. In discussions among peers, I am likely to be regarded as
.55	.13	18.3	4. In evaluating my aims in my career, I emphasize
.48	.30	17.1	5. I think people get into more trouble by
.48	.26	16.7	6. In a leadership role, my strength lies in the fact that I
.43	.34	15.1	7. If I were a member of a project team, I would
.45	.31	15.0	8. Others are more likely to notice that I
.46	.24	13.9	9. In an emergency, I
.47	.16	12.7	10. I look to the future with
.41	.27	12.3	11. If I had to admit it, people would probably see me as
.38	.28	12.2	12. Others are likely to notice that I
.44	.18	11.8	13. My associates are likely to notice the fact that I
.43	.19	11.6	14. In my area, I insure that
.38	.21	9.8	15. An organization in which I am a member can count on me to
.35	.26	9.3	16. As a member of my group, my contribution comes from
.34	.27	9.3	17. I believe that the best way to get things done is to
.40	.15	9.0	18. People who meet me are likely to be impressed by my
.37	.17	8.3	19. Organization problems would be less if people were more
.32	.22	7.7	20. When I set goals, I

NOTE: These are the personality item clusters most associated with network structure. Each row is a canonical correlation model between the three items in the row cluster and three network variables (density, hierarchy, and constraint). Correlations are computed across the 51 respondents. The chi-square statistic has nine degrees of freedom and tests the hypothesis of no correlation between the items and the network variables. A chi-square statistic larger than 17 gives the null hypothesis less than a .05 probability.

Although concentrated in a small number of items, the association is strong (see Burt et al., 1998, for data displays of the association). The canonical correlations at the top of Table 10.1 show strong association. More specifically, (a) a large proportion of the variance in network constraint is associated with respondent differences on the personality items. Three-fourths of the variance in network constraint is described by the top 10 item clusters in Table 10.1. Gender, race, and the other respondent differences tested for selection bias have no effect on this association; (b) most of the strong association between network constraint and the personality items is concentrated in the first 4 item clusters (61% with only the first 4 item clusters predicting constraint, 76% with all 10 item clusters); (c) dichotomous personality items are

slightly more accurate than continuous items in capturing the association with network constraint. I had reason to look at dichotomous
items (equal to 1 if the respondent picks an item as "most" descriptive
of himself or herself, 0 otherwise).[8] The dichotomous items for the top
10 item clusters in Table 10.1 describe 85% of the variance in network
constraint (68% from the first 4 item clusters).

Content of the Personality Distinctions

The content of the personality items associated with network structure is consistent with the structural hole argument. The argument is
that people who broker connections across structural holes can add
value through the information and control benefits that reside in the
holes. The motivation question asks whether people are equally likely
to pursue the benefits. Individuals who pursue the benefits of structural holes—entrepreneurs in the language of the argument—are more
the authors of their own social world. Establishing relations with
otherwise disconnected people means negotiating ambiguity and conflicting demands; it means being an outsider. Remove the entrepreneur's ties to otherwise disconnected groups, and the groups drift
apart. At the other end of the structural hole continuum, cliques and
hierarchical structures of constrained networks are more stable, more
secure, because interdependent ties sustain the network. Remove one
person and the network is still held together by ties among the other
people in the network.

Compare the items at the top of Figure 10.3 with the items at the
bottom to get a sense of the personality distinctions most associated
with structural holes.[9] People like Robert in Figure 10.1 are at the top
of Figure 10.3. They see themselves as players, people responsible for
coordination and change. The two personality items most often
claimed by respondents with low-constraint networks are their desire
"for a chance to be in a position of authority" and their belief that
success will come because of their "ability to create an aura of excitement." These are independent people (looking for "position of authority," "won't let anyone make decisions for me," and "go it alone")
concerned with the accuracy of their information on colleagues ("seek
the advice of my colleagues," "trouble when people don't say what
they really think," and "let people know what I think of them"),
experienced with resistance ("trouble when people won't listen to

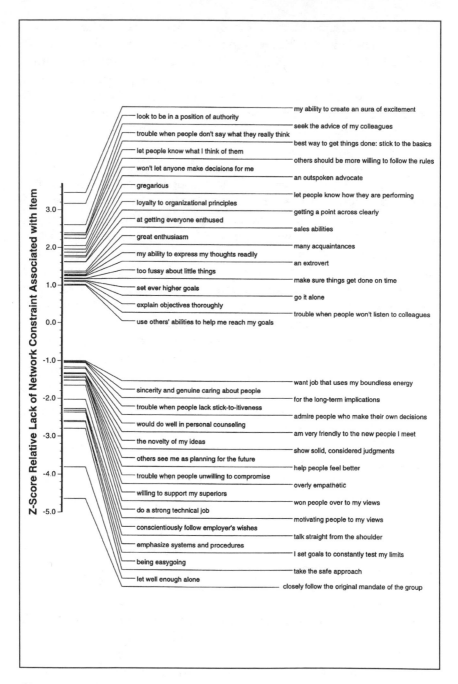

Figure 10.3. Personality Distinctions Associated With Structural Holes

colleagues" and "others should be more willing to follow the rules"), who enjoy convincing others ("ability to create an aura of excitement," "outspoken advocate," "getting a point across clearly," "my ability to express my thoughts readily," "sales abilities," and "an extrovert").

People like James in Figure 10.1 are at the bottom of Figure 10.3. They see themselves as the stalwarts of their organization, adding value through the infrastructure and stability they provide. At the bottom of Figure 10.3, two items stand apart as characteristic of the most constrained respondents; their desire to "let well enough alone" and their preference for project teams to "closely follow the original mandate of the group." In contrast to the entrepreneur's independence, respondents in the most constrained networks emphasize conformity and obedience ("conscientiously follow employer's wishes," "willing to support my superiors," and "trouble when people are unwilling to compromise") and thrive on the social support of close colleagues ("being easygoing," "overly empathetic," "help people feel better," and "would do well in personal counseling"). In contrast to the entrepreneur's emphasis on change, these are risk-averse people ("let well enough alone" and "take the safe approach"), focused on the technical details of their assignment ("do a strong technical job") and drawn to stability ("follow the original mandate of the group," "emphasize systems and procedures," "show solid, considered judgments," and "trouble when people lack stick-to-itiveness").

In sum, the personality distinctions associated with network structure are multiple but of a theme: Respondents in the least constrained networks claim the personality items of independent outsiders (vs. conforming and obedient insiders), in search of authority (vs. security), thriving on advocacy and change (vs. stability). The summary contrast, consistent with the structural hole argument, is between proactive and reactive. Respondents in entrepreneurial networks claim the personalities of people who are the authors of their own world. Respondents in constrained networks claim the personalities of people living in a world created by others.

Network Entrepreneur Personality Index

My closing evidence of association between student personality and network structure is an index of personality items that defines a surprisingly accurate probability of having an entrepreneurial network, a network rich in structural holes.

Items

The paired comparison items in Figure 10.4 correspond to the 10 MRG item clusters most associated with network structure (first 10 rows of Table 10.1). The items are simplified in two ways: The five-point MRG ratings are simplified to dichotomous ratings, and the three-item MRG clusters are simplified to paired comparisons. The three items in each MRG cluster are now one item.

Each question in Figure 10.4 contains a positive and a negative personal quality. For example, the first question asks whether the respondent evaluates opportunities in terms of "a chance to be in a position of authority" or "long-run implications." These are the two items within their MRG cluster most associated with network constraint. Respondents looking for "a chance to be in a position of authority" more than the "long-run implications" of opportunities tend to have low network constraint. This is a "positive" quality in the sense that it is associated with networks richer in structural holes. Respondents focusing instead on the "long-run implications" of opportunities tend to have constrained networks. This is a "negative" quality in the sense that it is associated with more constrained networks. Pairs of positive and negative qualities were identified in the same way for the other nine items.

The items in Figure 10.4 serve two purposes: The response task is simplified without eroding the association with network structure (judging from the results with dichotomous items in the preceding section and results to be presented), and the paired comparison items conceal the three items that jointly constitute the MRG item cluster and so protect the copyright on the commercial MRG instrument.

Index Scores

A respondent completes the instrument by circling the response from each pair that better describes the respondent (see instructions at the top of Figure 10.4). The index score is the number of positive personal qualities chosen. The positive choices are 1A, 2B, 3A, 4A, 5B, 6B, 7A, 8B, 9B, and 10A. The personal qualities in these choices span

Select the phrase under each item that better describes you (circle A or B). Select only one phrase per item. If you disagree with both phrases, select the one with which you disagree less. With so few questions, it is important to select phrases that describe how you actually operate, rather than how you feel you should or would like to operate. There are no right or wrong answers. When you are finished, you should have a total of 10 phrases circled.

1. When evaluating opportunities, I am likely to look . . .
  A. for a chance to be in a position of authority
  B. for the long-run implications

2. My strength lies in the fact that I have a knack for . . .
  A. being easygoing
  B. getting a point across clearly

3. In discussions among peers, I am probably seen as . . .
  A. an outspoken advocate
  B. motivating people to my views

4. In evaluating my aims in my career, I probably put more emphasis on . . .
  A. my ability to create an aura of excitement
  B. being in control of my own destiny

5. I believe that people get into more trouble by . . .
  A. being unwilling to compromise
  B. not letting others know what they really think

6. In a leadership role, I think my strength would lie in the fact that I . . .
  A. won people over to my views
  B. kept everyone informed

7. As a member of a project team, I . . .
  A. seek the advice of colleagues
  B. closely follow the original mandate of the group

8. Others are likely to notice that I . . .
  A. let well enough alone
  B. let people know what I think of them

9. In an emergency, I . . .
  A. take the safe approach
  B. am quite willing to help

10. I look to the future with . . .
  A. unshakable resolve
  B. a willingness to let others give me a hand

Figure 10.4. Index Items

the themes at the top of Figure 10.3 to describe an independent outsider, in search of authority, thriving on advocacy and change. A number of positive choices close to 10 indicates a personality associated with low-constraint networks, presumably a person comfortable with the entrepreneurial opportunities of structural holes. At the other extreme, the personal qualities in the negative choices in Figure 10.4 span the themes at the bottom of Figure 10.3 to describe a conforming and obedient insider in search of security and stability. A number of positive choices close to 0 indicates a personality associated with constrained networks, presumably a person uncomfortable with the information and control ambiguity of structural holes.[10]

From the student MRG responses, I counted the number of Figure 10.4 positive choices for each student. The response data are for MRG items in clusters of three as in Figure 10.2 and not in clusters of two as in Figure 10.4. I coded a student's response as positive if his or her rating of the positive quality within a paired comparison in Figure 10.4 is higher than his or her rating of the alternative negative quality. The average respondent made 3.9 positive choices. Scores range from 0 to 9, with a 2.1 standard deviation.

Association With Network Structure

The key question is how reliably this simple index distinguishes respondents in different network structures. Figure 10.5 shows a strong association with network constraint. The index predicts about half of the variance in network constraint (52%). Respondents are nicely clustered around the regression line in the graph. Gender, race, and other respondent differences tested for selection bias do not affect the association.

The correlations in the table below the graph in Figure 10.5 show the reliability of the association with network constraint. The −.74 index correlation with network constraint is −.75 if the index is computed only from the first four items in Figure 10.4, −.64 if the index is computed from only the odd-number items in Figure 10.4 (1, 3, etc.), and −.66 if the index is computed from only the even-number items (2, 4, etc.).[11]

Turning to aggregate network structure, I sorted respondents into three categories of networks significantly different in social capital arguments; entrepreneurial networks, cliques, and hierarchical net-

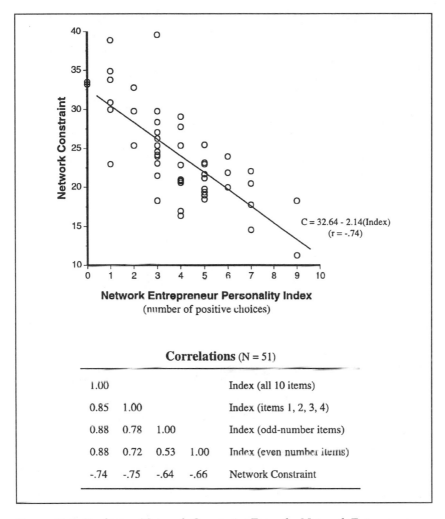

Figure 10.5. Predicting Network Constraint From the Network Entrepreneur Personality Index

works (Burt, 1992, 1998). The first cut is between respondents with flat versus hierarchical structures (a center-periphery structure in which relations among contacts are concentrated in a minority of contacts). Respondents with above-average Coleman-Theil hierarchy scores have hierarchical networks (see Note 5). The second cut is between dense and sparse flat structures. A respondent with a dense flat struc-

TABLE 10.2 Network Structure and the Network Entrepreneur Personality Index

Network Entrepreneur Personality Index	Probability That Respondent Has an Entrepreneurial Network	Respondents With Clique Networks	Respondents With Hierarchical Networks	Respondents With Entrepreneurial Networks
0	.01	2	—	—
1	.03	2	4	—
2	.08	2	1	—
3	.17	2	7	3
4	.32	1	6	3
5	.52	—	5	4
6	.72	—	—	3
7	.86	—	1	3
8	.94	—	—	—
9	.97	—	—	2
10	.99	—	—	—

NOTE: The probability of an entrepreneurial network is based on a logit function of the index predicting an entrepreneurial network versus a clique or hierarchical network (see Note 12).

ture has a clique network (hierarchy below average, constraint average or higher). A respondent with a sparse flat structure has an entrepreneurial network (hierarchy below average, constraint below average).

Respondents are ordered across the columns of Table 10.2 by network structure and down the rows by their index scores. The most reliable discrimination is between cliques and entrepreneurial networks. Entrepreneurial networks are of special interest because they contain the respondents most directly involved in structural holes. Respondents at the top of Table 10.2 made few positive choices. They tend to have a clique network. Their probabilities of having an entrepreneurial network are near 0. Respondents at the bottom of the table made primarily positive choices. Their probabilities of having an entrepreneurial network are close to 1. Almost every respondent making more than five positive choices from the 10 paired comparisons in Figure 10.4 has an entrepreneurial network. The null hypothesis of no association is easily rejected, the probability of an entrepreneurial network is independent of respondent gender and seven other respondent differences, and discriminant functions of the index items correctly predict the network category of most respondents.[12]

Cautionary Evidence From the Field

There are four interpretations of the evidence to be cautioned against. First, there is no implied causal order. This is a story about personality correlates of structural holes. People put into a position spanning structural holes could develop the personality characteristics of a network entrepreneur or having such a personality could lead people to build networks rich in structural holes.

Second, the analysis is an exploration of personality correlates. We are not equally informed about the two sides of the link between network and personality. I studied structural holes in terms of network constraint because constraint has the construct validity of accumulated evidence showing the expected negative association between constraint and manager performance. Taking a more open-ended view of personality, I studied 252 personality items in 84 clusters for association with network constraint. I already mentioned that such a large number of items means some items can be expected by random chance to be significant. Specifically, one could expect at a .05 level of confidence that 4.2 of the 84 item clusters will be associated by random chance with network constraint ($.05 \times 84 = 4.2$). Four clusters of items in Table 10.1 are the core of the association with network structure, and the broader set of items selected for the personality index in Figure 10.4 are held together more by covariation with network structure than by covariation among the items (see Note 11). Concern for the obvious risk of statistical artifact was my reason for focusing in the text on two results: (a) The strength of the association with network constraint— we can expect four item clusters to have nonrandom association with network constraint, but the observed association is much stronger than would be sufficient to reject random chance; and (b) the substance of the personality items associated with constraint—it is reassuring to see personality qualities one might expect of entrepreneurs who span structural holes.

Third, the respondents are a convenience sample of MBA students. The students are more mature than the usual MBA student, many were employed full-time during the study, and they are a heterogeneous set of people (in terms of percentage women, minorities, and diversity of the industries in which they work). Regardless, it is unreliable to offer conclusions about managers from a convenience sample of students.

The results in Figure 10.6 provide a more reliable foundation. I included the personality index items in a network survey of corporate staff in a large financial organization. The study population is several hundred employees in staff positions responsible for employment services, information services, training services, and so on. Respondents completed a survey instrument containing the items in Figure 10.4 and a survey network booklet similar to the one that the students completed. The 217 respondents are representative of employee backgrounds, gender, and job performance but disproportionately senior people (middle and senior managers are 40% of the study population and 53% of the respondents). I used the survey network data to measure the network constraint on each respondent and distinguish respondents with entrepreneurial networks (as in Note 5 and Table 10.2, respectively). I used the personality items to define a network entrepreneur personality index score for each respondent (as in Figure 10.5).

Figure 10.6 shows an association between network structure and the personality index but not for all employees. The association is strong for people in clerical and technical jobs and for junior managers (the MBA respondents would be at the high end of these ranks). The correlation between network constraint and the personality index is strong (.43, 3.6 t test, $p < .001$), and the bold line in Figure 10.6 shows a strong tendency for employees with high scores on the entrepreneur personality index to have entrepreneurial networks (2.5 logit t test, $p < .01$). The association disappears among middle and senior managers. The dashed line in Figure 10.6 shows that the personality index has no association with the tendency for a middle or senior manager to have an entrepreneurial network.

The implication of the results from students, combined with the Figure 10.6 results from the field, is that personality and network structure are more closely associated with one another in the lower ranks of an organization. The contingent value of social capital offers a plausible explanation. Networks rich in structural holes are more valuable to people who have more control over the substance of their work and so have to spend more time getting others to accept the way they chose to define their work (Burt, 1997). One consequence is that

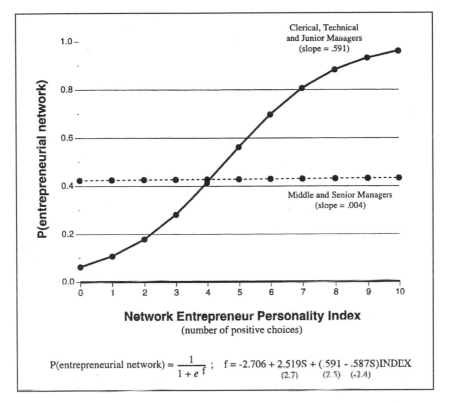

Figure 10.6. Identifying Employees Who Have Entrepreneurial Networks (S in Logit Equation Is a Dummy Variable for Middle and Senior Managers)

networks rich in structural holes are more valuable for more senior managers, which means that the networks around more senior managers are less discretionary—their networks are an integral part of their work. Informal relations between people low in the organization are more discretionary in the sense that work is more defined by the boss than by negotiation with peers. Personality and network structure are therefore more free to covary in the lower ranks of organizations.

The contingent association between personality and network structure is further illustrated with the fourth and final cautionary note. The caution is that the personality items are no substitute for network items in predicting manager performance. The association between personality and network structure could be interpreted as an

TABLE 10.3 Personality, Network Structure, and Job Evaluation

	Clerical and Technical Staff and Junior Managers (N = 102)		Middle Managers and Senior Managers (N = 115)	
Constant	−2.049	−2.176	−.140	.502
Network entrepreneur personality index	.050	.158	−.361	−.382
	(0.4)	(0.8)	(−2.6)	(−2.7)
Entrepreneurial network	.690	—	1.343	—
	(1.3)		(2.5)	
Network constraint	—	.009	—	−.090
		(0.3)		(−2.1)
Male	.146	−.722	.517	−.374
	(0.2)	(−0.5)	(0.8)	(−0.8)
Male × entrepreneurial net	−.076	—	−2.065	—
	(−0.1)		(−2.1)	
Male × network constraint	—	−.435	—	.197
		(−1.1)		(2.6)
χ^2	2.39	3.13	14.51	15.33
(4 df)				
Probability no effects	$p = .66$	$p = .54$	$p = .005$	$p = .004$

NOTE: These are logit results predicting which employees received the highest job evaluations in their last annual review (evaluation of A vs. B or C). Network entrepreneur personality index is the horizontal axis in Figure 10.6. Entrepreneurial network is a dummy variable (1 if employee has entrepreneurial network; Figure 10.6). Network constraint is measured relative to the average (C − mean C).

incentive to measure social capital with personality items, rather than the more costly strategy of using network items to measure social capital with sociometric data. The results in Figure 10.6 argue against such substitution because personality is not associated with network structure for all managers.

The results in Table 10.3 argue further against the substitution because personality is less associated with network structure where networks are more consequential. I have, from the firm's personnel records, background data on each employee including job evaluations. Employees are evaluated each year on an A, B, C scale with plus and minus used to distinguish higher from lower performances within grades. These job evaluations stay with the employee over time to determine compensation and promotion. In Table 10.3, I use the personality and network data to predict which employees receive the highest job evaluations (evaluation of A vs. B or C).

Three points are illustrated. First, neither the personality nor the network data are associated with job evaluations in the lower ranks. These are the ranks where personality is most associated with network structure (Figure 10.6). In other words, where personality is associated with network structure, performance covaries with neither.

Second, female middle and senior managers with entrepreneurial networks are more likely to receive the best job evaluations (2.5 *t* test for entrepreneurial network, −2.1 *t* test for network constraint). Men are hurt by having an entrepreneurial network. A man is better off with a constrained network of interconnected contacts (2.6 *t* test). This reverses the usual gender effect. Where men significantly outnumber women, it is the men who benefit more from entrepreneurial networks (Burt, 1998). This study population of corporate staff is predominantly women (men are 24% of all employees, 29% excluding clerical jobs), and it is the women who benefit more from entrepreneurial networks. Men and women are equally likely to receive the highest job evaluations (21 and 24%, respectively, .67 probability of no difference; this is not an instance of men being less able than women). What differs between them is returns to social capital. Having an entrepreneurial network increases a woman's, not a man's, odds of receiving the highest job evaluation.

It is a disadvantage to display an entrepreneurial personality. This is the third point illustrated in Table 10.3. In the second row of the table, high job evaluations are associated with low scores on the personality index (−2.6 and −2.7 *t* tests). Entrepreneurial networks are a competitive advantage; the personality is not. Women in this population do well if they build an entrepreneurial network while expressing the conformist team spirit of personalities associated with cohesive networks.

Summary

I used survey network and personality profile data to explore the idea that personality varies systematically with structural holes. I draw two conclusions from the analysis: (a) Personality does vary with structural holes. The association is concentrated in a few personality items (Table 10.1), but those few items describe three-fourths of the variance in network constraint; and (b) the association is consistent with the structural hole argument. Personality distinctions in Figure 10.3 and the contrast between positive and negative qualities in Figure 10.4 show that respondents in the least constrained networks claim the personality of an entrepreneurial outsider (vs. conforming and obedient insider), in search of authority (vs. security), thriving on advocacy and change (vs. stability). I summarized with a network entrepreneur personality index in Figure 10.4 that defines a surprisingly accurate probability of the respondent having an entrepreneurial network (Figure 10.5 and Table 10.2). I concluded with cautionary evidence from a survey of corporate staff in a large financial organization. The network entrepreneur personality index varies as expected with the structure of each employee's network, but the association is only significant for employees in lower ranks (clerical and technical people and junior managers; Figure 10.6). Moreover, where the personality index is associated with entrepreneurial networks (lower ranks), neither the index nor the network is associated with manager performance. Where manager performance is significantly linked with entrepreneurial networks (more senior ranks), personality is not associated with network structure, and performance is not higher for managers with more entrepreneurial personalities (Table 10.3). The personality data are an interesting correlate, but no substitute, for network data.

Notes

1. Personality was a key issue for the pioneers in sociometry who set the stage for contemporary network analysis, but network analysis in the 1970s was not as keyed to its sociometric roots as to anthropological cousins. Personality was not a focus of attention. A change in recent years significant for the network broker measures in this chapter is the strengthening presence of sociologists in business schools. Sociologists skilled in network analysis have mingled with the installed base of psychologists interested in organization behavior. Social context and groups broadly understood (e.g., in Leavitt, Pondy, & Boje's, 1989, widely used organization behavior reader) have become more specific and concrete with network theory and analysis (e.g., Nohria & Eccles', 1992, collection on networks and organizations; several chapters in Kramer and Tyler's, 1996, collection on trust in organizations). In return, there is new network interest in the cognitive, the personal (e.g., with respect to organization behavior, see Kilduf & Krackhardt, 1994, on bringing individuals back in). Personality as a concept seems to be no more popular with psychologists than sociologists, but the exchange between sociology and psychology in organization behavior focuses attention on individual differences above and beyond differences attributable to network structure.

2. If individuals are rationally self-interested in a microeconomic sense, they drop out of the equation. To know who succeeds, you only need to know who has the opportunity to succeed.

3. A more sophisticated dismissal is to assume that motivation is implicit in network structure (Burt, 1992, pp. 34-36). For reasons of a clear path to success (the average person is more likely to see entrepreneurial opportunities in a large, sparse network), or the personality of the person who constructed the network (people inclined toward entrepreneurial behavior build large, sparse networks), or the nature of the environmental factors responsible for the structure of the network (persons forced to live in large, sparse networks are more likely to learn entrepreneurial skills), large, sparse networks are more likely to surround a person motivated to be entrepreneurial.

4. Familiar examples are Weber's (1905/1930) argument that religion can encourage capitalism by making entrepreneurial behavior righteous, and McClelland's (1961) argument that the formation in childhood of a need to achieve is critical to later entrepreneurial behavior.

5. Described in Burt (1992, pp. 55-56, 125-126), network constraint C on person i is the sum of constraint c_{ij} in i's relation with each contact j; $C = \Sigma_j\, c_{ij}$, where c_{ij} equals $(p_{ij} + \Sigma_k p_{ik}p_{kj})^2$, $i \neq j \neq k$, where p_{ij} is the proportional strength of i's relationship with j (relation between i and i divided by the sum of i's relations in the network). I multiply C by 100 here and discuss points of constraint. Constraint c_{ij} increases with the extent to which (a) i allocates a high proportion of his or her network directly to the connection with j (p_{ij} is large) and (b) i has a large indirect allocation to the connection with j (the sum of $p_{ik}p_{kj}$ across k is large; the other people k with whom i has strong relations in turn have strong relations with j). If we regress C across size, density, and hierarchy for the 555 junior managers in the benchmark population (see Note 6), we see constraint decreasing with number of contacts (-.66 standardized regression coefficient), increasing with network density (.49), and increasing with network hierarchy (.23). The regression equation predicts 86% of the variance in C. The same three standardized coefficients for the student networks are -.58, .57, and .30 (predicting 87% of the variance in C).

6. I have accumulated from teaching and consulting projects benchmark contact network data on 1255 managers in diverse functions across three broad ranks; 555 junior managers, 552 middle managers (people who manage other managers), and 148 senior managers (president and chief executive officer down through the senior level of middle managers, e.g., the level above vice president in the usual financial firm or the level below vice president in the usual manufacturing firm). The student networks vary in size from 4 to 20 contacts around a 13.5 average. The average strength of relation between contacts (network density measured on a 0 to 100 scale) varies from 6 to 100 points around a 26.5 average. The concentration of connections in a single contact (network hierarchy measured on a 0 to 100 scale with the Coleman-Theil inequality index; Burt, 1992, pp. 70-71, 1998) varies from 0 to 24.6 points around a 9.1 average. Bartlett chi-square tests with one degree of freedom for differences between the variances in the student networks and the 555 junior manager networks in the benchmark population (which includes some employed MBA students from prior classes) are negligible: 2.24 for network size ($p = .13$), 1.96 for network density ($p = .16$), and 0.97 for network hierarchy ($p = .32$). All three network conditions are slightly less variable across the student networks, however, so combining them to measure network constraint yields less variable levels of constraint in the student networks (7.89 χ^2, 1 df, $p < .001$). The student networks vary from 12 to 46 points of constraint, with a mean of 25 and a standard deviation of 7.6 (vs. 11 to 67 across junior managers in the benchmark population with a mean of 28 and a 9.3 standard

deviation). In short, what is missing among the students are the extreme cases of junior managers dependent on a few strongly interconnected contacts (usually someone whose contacts are limited to their immediate workgroup). This could be a training effect (students complete the network questionnaire at the end of the first class on social capital) or it could be that junior managers who return for their MBA are in fact more entrepreneurial.

7. Given the many items, I tested for fatigue effects. Average ratings do not increase or decrease with item sequence. The variance of ratings decreases negligibly. The strength of correlation with network constraint does not increase or decrease across item sequence.

8. I include the dichotomous predictors for three reasons. (a) I do not want to overfit these data. Coding whether a respondent picks an item as "most" descriptive of himself or herself asks less precision of the data. (b) Associations with the network variables are not always linear across item ratings (Burt et al., 1998; Figure 10.4). I recomputed all 252 item correlations converting item ratings to a dummy variable (1 if the respondent rated the item as "most" descriptive of himself or herself, 0 otherwise). This added one item cluster to Table 10.1 that was below threshold when item correlations were computed with the full range of ratings. Otherwise, the same item clusters are identified as network-relevant though individual items vary in their correlations with the network variables. (c) The strong association with dichotomous items justifies replacing continuous ratings with simpler dichotomous paired comparisons for the network entrepreneur personality index.

9. For each of the 252 personality items, I computed the average network constraint on respondents who selected the item as "most" descriptive of themselves. The lower the average constraint on respondents selecting an item as "most" descriptive of themselves, the more the item is associated with structural holes. To highlight personality differences, I standardized the 252 constraint averages and present in Figure 10.3 the 51 items with z scores > 1 (201 items lie in the empty space between 1.0 and –1.0 in the figure). For the aesthetic of putting items associated with structural holes at the top of the list, items are listed in the figure by the relative lack of constraint with which they are associated (vertical axis is $-1 \times z$ score mean constraint).

10. Thus, the index is a variation on Thurstone scaling. The procedure is to (Thurstone & Chave, 1929) (a) have a panel of judges rate many items on the psychological continuum to be measured by the scale, (b) use average ratings of each item to select a set of items that span the continuum in equal intervals from low to high (avoiding items given widely different ratings by the judges), and (c) administer the scale by asking respondents to select the items with which they agree. A respondent's score on the scale is the average rating of the items with which the respondent agrees. I use network constraint scores as judge ratings. Items are sorted in Figure 10.3 by the relative network constraint on respondents selecting each item as "most" descriptive of themselves. Items are paired in Figure 10.4 for maximum difference in the mean network constraint on respondents selecting each as "most" descriptive and maximum difference in the correlation between network constraint and the five-point MRG ratings on each item. One way to score responses would be to sum the scale values of a respondent's choices from each paired comparison. Here are continuous weights for options A and B under each item in Figure 10.4, where weights are the z scores used to position items on the vertical axis in Figure 10.3: 2.3 and –1.0 for item 1, –2.6 and 1.6 for item 2, 2.0 and –2.0 for item 3, 3.2 and –.9 for item 4, –1.4 and 2.4 for item 5, –1.5 and .9 for item 6, 2.6 and –4.6 for item 7, –3.8 and 2.3 for item 8, –2.3 and .4 for item 9, and .3 and –.9 for item 10 (the item 10 pair differ on

hierarchy). For three reasons, I replace continuous weights with equal weights of 1 for positive choice and 0 for negative: (a) The respondents are not a probability sample of managers so I do not want to overfit these data; (b) equal weights are easier for respondents to score (instead of adding a sequence of continuous weights); and (c) equal-weight scoring in these data is strongly correlated with continuous-weight scoring (.97 correlation) and does about as well in predicting network structure.

11. The items do not covary as indicators of a single personality dimension so much as they covary in their association with network structure. The .53 split-half correlation in Figure 10.5 implies a modest .69 reliability for the whole 10-item index ($2r/[1 + r]$, where r is the split-half correlation)—less than the index correlation with network constraint. More to the point, there is no dominant factor in a principal component analysis of the personality items but strong canonical correlations between the personality items and network structure. The first factor (principal component) extracted from five-point ratings on the 20 items in the top-10 item clusters in Table 10.1 describes only 13.0% of item variance. The second and third factors describe almost as much (10.3 and 9.7%, respectively), and the subsequent handful of factors each describe about 1% less than the preceding factor. The items hold together in their association with network structure. In a Table 10.1 canonical correlation model predicting network structure from the 20 personality items in Figure 10.4, canonical correlations are near maximum (.91, .89, and .87). This is a setting for scaling methods that aggregate personality items based on covariance with network structure (e.g., canonical correlation) rather than aggregating on the basis of covariance among the items (e.g., factor analysis).

12. Consider three views of the association with network structure: (a) The probability of a respondent having an entrepreneurial network increases with index scores. Here is the logit function predicting entrepreneurial networks versus something else: $-4.20 + .86$ (index), which defines the probabilities in Table 10.2 and generates a 3.3 t test for the logit effect ($p = .001$); (b) index scores are significantly lower for respondents in clique networks and higher for respondents in entrepreneurial networks. Here is the analysis of variance predicting a respondent's index score from a dummy variable distinguishing cliques from other networks (CN) and a dummy variable distinguishing entrepreneurial from other networks (EN): $3.46 - 1.68$ CN $+ 1.99$ EN, in which the clique effect is significant (-2.6 t test, $p = .01$), the entrepreneurial network effect is significant (3.9 t test, $p < .001$), and so the index differs significantly across the three kinds of network structures [$F(2, 48) = 16.5$, $p < .001$]; and (c) the three categories of network structure are contingent on broad categories of index scores. Here is Table 10.2 reduced to the broad categories of low, moderate, and high index scores:

6	5	0
3	13	6
0	6	12

where low is 0, 1, or 2 positive choices (probability of an entrepreneurial network is less than 1 in 10), moderate is 3 or 4 positive choices (for which the probability increases to 1 in 3), and high is 5 or more positive choices (for which entrepreneurial networks are more likely than other networks). Rows and columns are not independent in the table (20.6 χ^2, 4 df, $p < .001$). Low index scores are associated with clique networks (2.9 log linear z score for cell 1,1; $p < .01$) and rare with entrepreneurial networks (-2.3 z score for cell 1,3; $p = .02$). High index scores are associated with entrepreneurial networks (2.9 z score for cell 3,3; $p < .01$) and rare with clique networks (-2.0 z score for cell 3,1; $p = .04$).

References

Burt, R. S. (1980). Autonomy in a social topology. *American Journal of Sociology, 85,* 892-925.
Burt, R. S. (1992). *Structural holes.* Cambridge, MA: Harvard University Press.
Burt, R. S. (1997). The contingent value of social capital. *Administrative Science Quarterly, 42,* 339-365.
Burt, R. S. (1998). The gender of social capital. *Rationality and Society, 10,* 5-46.
Burt, R. S., Jannotta, J. E., Jr., & Mahoney, J. T. (1998). Personality correlates of structural holes. *Social Networks, 20,* 63-87.
Cook, K. S., & Emerson, R. M. (1978). Power, equity and commitment in exchange networks. *American Sociological Review, 43,* 712-739.
Freeman, L. C. (1977). A set of measures of centrality based on betweenness. *Sociometry, 40,* 35-40.
Granovetter, M. S. (1973). The strength of weak ties. *American Journal of Sociology, 78,* 1360-1380.
Janicik, G. A. (1997). *The social cognition of social structure: Examining the learning of relations.* Doctoral dissertation, University of Chicago, Graduate School of Business, Chicago.
Kilduff, M., & Krackhardt, D. (1994). Bringing the individual back in: A structural analysis of the internal market for reputation in organizations. *Academy of Management Journal, 37,* 87-108.
Kramer, R. M., & Tyler, T. R. (Eds.). (1996). *Trust in organizations.* Thousand Oaks, CA: Sage.
Leavitt, H. J., Pondy, L. R., & Boje, D. M. (Eds.). (1989). *Readings in managerial psychology.* Chicago: University of Chicago Press.
Mahoney, J. T., & Mahoney, F. C. (1990). *Appraise Your World technical considerations* (Monograph No. 5). Portland, ME: Management Research Group.
Martinelli, A. (1994). Entrepreneurship and management. In N. J. Smelser & R. Swedberg (Eds.), *The handbook of economic sociology* (pp. 476-503). Princeton, NJ: Princeton University Press.
McClelland, D. C. (1961). *The achieving society.* Princeton, NJ: Van Nostrand.
Merton, R. K. (1968). Continuities in the theory of reference group behavior. In *Social theory and social structure* (pp. 335-440). New York: Free Press. (Original work published 1957)
Nohria, N., & Eccles, R. G. (Eds.). (1992). *Networks and organizations.* Cambridge, MA: Harvard Business School Press.
Padgett, J. F., & Ansell, C. K. (1993). Robust action and the rise of the Medici, 1400-1434. *American Journal of Sociology, 98,* 1259-1319.
Podolny, J. M., & Baron, J. N. (1997). Relationships and resources: Social networks and mobility in the workplace. *American Sociological Review, 62,* 673-693.
Simmel, G. (1955). *Conflict and the web of group affiliations* (K. H. Wolff & R. Bendix, Trans.). New York: Free Press. (Original work published 1922)
Thurstone, L. L., & Chave, E. J. (1929). *The measurement of attitude.* Chicago: University of Chicago Press.
Weber, M. (1930). *The Protestant ethic and the spirit of capitalism* (T. Parsons, Trans.). New York: Scribner's Sons. (Original work published 1905)

11

The Psychology of
Authority Relations

*A Relational Perspective on
Influence and Power in Groups*

TOM R. TYLER

In my recent work, I have been concerned with understanding why people comply with organizational rules. In particular, I have been interested in understanding why people often voluntarily defer to rules and to decisions made by organizational authorities, even when those rules and decisions are not in their self-interest.

One important reason that people defer to authorities is that they have internalized values that tell them that deference is the morally appropriate thing to do. One type of internalized value is the judgment that organizational authorities are legitimate and therefore entitled to be obeyed. In other words, people may respond to their feeling of obligation to defer to authorities without reference to the rewards or costs or both of such actions. I have been particularly interested in explaining why people adopt such values and, consequently, voluntarily defer to authorities.

Why do we care about the psychology of internalized values in organizational settings? We care because research suggests that it is very costly and inefficient for organizations to manage their members through control strategies based on rewards and threatened or actual punishments (Pfeffer, 1994). Such strategies are costly because they require organizations to expend resources to provide material rewards or pay the costs of surveillance to detect rule-breaking behavior. Furthermore, control strategies do not encourage self-regulation, motivate people to engage in voluntary helping behavior, or promote the development of new and creative ideas, all of which benefit the organization. On the contrary, they discourage intrinsic motivations. Hence, organizations are more efficient and effective when those within them have internalized values that lead them to want to behave in ways that benefit their organizations, without reference to rewards and punishments (Tyler, in press).

In my research, I have used interviews with the members of legal, political, and work organizations to try to understand why people within those organizations view as legitimate and defer to organizational authorities. One striking and consistent finding of these studies is that legitimacy and deference are related to judgments about the fairness of the procedures by which organizational authorities make decisions (Tyler, Boeckmann, Smith, & Huo, 1997; Tyler & Lind, 1992; Tyler & Smith, 1997). This procedural justice effect is robust, influencing the willingness to defer to decisions, evaluations of authorities, and subsequent willingness to follow organizational rules. It also shapes organizational commitment and future extra-role behavior.

These findings have important organizational implications because they suggest a mechanism through which organizational authorities can effectively bridge differences among the individuals and groups within an organization. They can do so by making decisions in ways that all parties to a dispute or conflict will regard as fair. This will lead everyone, both the "winner" and the "loser," to be more willing to defer to the decisions made by organizational authorities. Hence, procedural justice suggests a way for authorities to manage conflict within their organizations.

The finding that people respond to the fairness of decision-making procedures, rather than to the favorability of the outcomes they receive, goes against the social exchange models that have dominated past images of the basis of the relationship between organizations and the people within them. Social exchange theories suggest that people join and remain in organizations because those organizations provide them with desirable resources, such as high pay, and other benefits. If this is true, it suggests that people should gauge their loyalty and support for organizations in terms of the favorability of the resources that they receive from them. Procedural justice findings, however, suggest a different image of the relationship between people and organizations.

The question of concern is what image of the relationship between people and organizations is consistent with the findings of procedural justice studies? Drawing on social identity theory (Tajfel & Turner, 1979), I argue that people use the organizations to which they belong as an important input into the development of their social identities. These social identities influence their assessments of self-esteem and self-worth. From this perspective, the relationship between people and organizations is based on issues of status (Tyler & Smith, in press). If organizations communicate to their members that they have high status, people respond to the organizations, their rules, and their authorities with deference.

What evidence supports this identity-based argument? One type of evidence is the finding that people define the fairness of procedures in terms of "relational" criterion (Tyler, 1989; Tyler & Lind, 1992). These relational criterion include the neutrality of the decision-making process (neutrality), the degree to which authorities are judged to be acting out of benevolent or trustworthy motives (trustworthiness), and the extent to which people are treated with dignity and respect (status recognition).

Interestingly, these relational criteria, which reflect the quality of treatment received from authorities, are found to be more important in defining the fairness of procedures than are judgments about the favorability of outcomes or control over outcomes or both. In other words, people determine procedural fairness by evaluating the quality of their treatment by authorities and not the outcomes of their experiences.

My argument is that the quality of treatment by authorities is important because it reflects most directly on people's status within their organization. Hence, these findings support the argument that people are concerned about the messages they receive about their status from the organizations to which they belong. The findings that people react to the fairness of the procedures they experience and that they define the fairness of procedures by evaluating the quality of their treatment by authorities support an identity-based conception of authority relations in organizations. These findings suggest that people use their treatment by organizational authorities to provide them with information about their organizational status. If they are treated well, they view their status as high, and they both view as legitimate and defer to organizational authorities.

Although the findings I have outlined are consistent with an identity-based model of authority relations in organizations, it is important to consider what further types of evidence would support such a conception of authority. I outline four types of evidence that I think support the argument that people care about their treatment by organizational authorities because their treatment has implications for their social identities. This evidence includes social categorization effects, identity effects, the influence of treatment on self-esteem, and evidence of mediation of the treatment effect by status-relevant judgments.

The first type of evidence concerns when people care how they are treated by organizational authorities. According to the identity model I have outlined, people should care more about the quality of their treatment by authorities when that treatment has greater implications for their social identity. This suggestion is supported by research findings that indicate that people are more influenced by the quality of their treatment by authorities when they draw more of their social identity from their work organization and when they have a social relationship with authorities.

The argument that the importance that people place on treatment by authorities depends on the degree to which treatment has social identity implications also leads to a social categorization prediction: That people will be more influenced by the quality of their treatment by authorities when those authorities are members of their own group. When authorities are members of one's own group, they represent the group, and their actions communicate the judgments and feelings of the group. Hence, the actions of in-group authorities carry greater social meaning.

Tyler, Lind, Ohbuchi, Sugawara, and Huo (1998) tested this social categorization prediction in two studies of treatment by others during the resolution of a social conflict. In the first study, they compared conflicts occurring within a cultural group to conflicts across groups. In the second study, they compared employee-supervisor conflicts in situations in which the supervisor shared or did not share the ethnicity of the employee. The findings of both studies were the same: People cared more about how they are treated when the conflict occurred within a single group. When people were disputing within their own group, their willingness to accept conflict resolution decisions was strongly affected by how they were treated. When the dispute was with an outsider, however, people focused more strongly on the favorability of the decisions when deciding whether or not to accept them.

Smith, Tyler, Huo, Ortiz, and Lind (1997) tested the same idea experimentally. In one study, a graduate student experimenter treated subjects rudely. In some cases, the experimenter was from the student's own university, whereas in other cases the experimenter was from a rival university. They found that people reacted to how they were treated if the experimenter was from their own group but not if the experimenter was an outsider. If the experimenter was an outsider, people evaluated the outsider based on the favorability of the outcome they received from the outsider.

A second, similar argument is that people should be more influenced by their treatment by organizational authorities when they identify more strongly with the organization those authorities represent. The findings of several studies support this suggestion. Tyler and Degoey (1995) examined the willingness of citizens of San Francisco to defer to the decisions of a government regulatory board that set water-use policy during a drought. They found that people were more affected by their judgments about how that board treated citizens if they identified strongly with the city it represented. Smith and Tyler (1996) explored the willingness of white citizens in northern California to support congressional policies that reallocated resources to minorities. They found that those who identified more strongly with "America" evaluated congressional policies by assessing whether they felt that Congress treated citizens fairly, whereas those who identified with "whites" evaluated congressional policies by judging whether those policies benefited them and others in their racial group. Finally, Huo, Smith, Tyler, and Lind (1996) studied conflicts between employees and managers in a multicultural setting. They found that employees who identified more strongly with their work organization placed greater weight on the quality of their treatment by their supervisors when deciding whether to voluntarily accept supervisory decisions. Those who identified less strongly with their work organization placed greater weight on the favorability of those decisions when deciding whether or not to accept them.

The third aspect of treatment effects that supports an identity-based model of authority relations is the range of effects found. In particular, quality of treatment by authorities is found to directly influence people's self-esteem (Tyler, Degoey, & Smith, 1996). Strikingly, people's self-esteem was influenced by how they were treated by authorities but not by the favorability of the outcomes they received from them. If people's connection to authorities was based on resource exchange, it would be expected that they would feel good about themselves when they received favorable outcomes. This was not the case, however. Instead, people felt positively about themselves when they received high-quality treatment from organizational authorities.

Finally, there is evidence that treatment influences people's attitudes and behaviors because it changes their views about their status. Tyler et al. (1996) identified two aspects of status: the status of one's organization (pride) and one's status within that organization (respect). They showed that the impact of the quality of treatment received from group authorities on attitudes and behaviors was mediated by changes in these status judgments. In other words, the quality of the treatment a person received from group authorities changed his or her willingness to defer to group rules because it changed the person's views about his or her organizational status.

These findings suggest that people care about the quality of their treatment by authorities because they care about their organizational status. That status is important because people use it to create and maintain their social identities. Hence, these findings suggest that people's willingness to view as legitimate and defer to authorities is linked to their social relationship to the authorities with whom they deal.

As previously noted, authorities benefit when people defer to their decisions because those decisions are fairly made. The same logic suggests that authorities benefit when they are evaluated on relational criteria rather than in terms of the favorability of the outcomes they provide. Authorities are often in a position in which they cannot provide everyone all that they might want or feel they deserve. They can, however, behave neutrally, can treat everyone with whom they deal with respect, and can communicate that their motivations are to consider the needs and concerns of all parties to a dispute or conflict. Hence, authorities are more effectively able to manage conflicts if they are evaluated in terms of the quality of their treatment of those with whom they deal.

Because authorities benefit from being evaluated based on relational judgments, the findings outlined suggest several implications for ways to encourage such evaluations. First, the social categorization findings suggest the value of framing group boundaries in inclusive ways. For example, instead of thinking of a work organization as being composed of employees and managers—that is, two distinct groups—people should be encouraged to think of themselves as all members of a common group. Second, the identification findings suggest that organizations benefit by facilitating the development of identification with the organization. One important function of organizational cultures is to encourage such identification. Both these strategies will enhance the tendency to evaluate authorities based on relational judgments.

These studies all suggest that status issues influence the impact of treatment by authorities on views about their legitimacy and, through such views, the willingness to defer to their directives. There is also direct evidence to support the suggestion that rule-following is linked to status judgments. Smith and Tyler (1997) studied the influence of status judgments upon compliance with group rules in two samples: a group of college students and the members of university sororities. In both studies, they found that rule-following was directly linked to judgments of pride in the organization. Tyler (in press) conducted a similar analysis using two samples of employees. The first was a random sample of employees in Chicago and the second a multinational sample of employees in the United States, Germany, and Hong Kong. In both samples, he found that rule-following was influenced by both pride and respect. He also examined the influence of status judgments on legitimacy and found that status judgments influenced legitimacy (i.e., the perceived obligation to obey authorities).

These general-level findings focus not on particular experiences with authorities but on general evaluations of organizational status. They indicate a strong relationship between status judgments and compliance with organizational rules. Interestingly, this relationship is stronger than the connection between general judgments of the favor-ability of the resources one receives from the organization and compli-ance with organizational rules. In other words, people do not comply with rules because they feel that they receive excellent pay and other benefits from their organization. Furthermore, their feelings of obliga-tion to the organization are not primarily a response to judgments about general resource quality. Instead, judgments of status dominate behavioral and attitudinal reactions to organizations.

Smith and Tyler (1996) also demonstrate a direct link between judgments of status and social identity. They show that status judg-ments influence both personal and collective self-esteem. Collective self-esteem is particularly relevant because it reflects the status that people attach to the groups to which they belong. If people regard their organization as having higher status, view their own status within the organization as higher, or both, they indicate higher collective self-esteem. Interestingly, personal self-esteem is influenced by respect but not by pride. That is, personal self-esteem is more strongly linked to status within an organization than it is to the status of that orga-nization.

Taken together, the findings I have outlined suggest the value of reconceptualizing our view of the basis of authority relations in orga-nizations. Deference to authorities is linked more strongly to status within organizations than it is to the quality of the resources received from those organizations. These findings support the argument made by social identity theory that one important thing that organizations provide to those within them is identity-relevant information. This information is used to construct social identities and determine one's self-worth and self-esteem.

What is perhaps most striking about the findings outlined is not that people care about their social identities, but rather that the con-struction and maintenance of social identities dominates the psychol-ogy of authority relations. It has long been established that people are affected by evaluations of the justice of decision-making procedures (Lind & Tyler, 1988) as well as by the quality of their treatment by authorities (Tyler & Lind, 1992). These recent findings help us to under-stand why these justice effects occur. They occur because people use the fairness of procedures and the quality of treatment by authorities, two highly interrelated concepts, as a basis for making status evaluations. Such evaluations, in turn, shape feelings of obligation toward the group as well as rule-following behavior.

Perhaps what is most striking about these findings is the limited role of resource evaluations in shaping people's behaviors in organizations. Although it has been widely assumed, based on the predictions of social exchange approaches to organizations, that people's behavior in organizations is linked to the favorability of the resources received from those organizations, this perspective is not supported in the research. Certainly, resource favorability matters, but it does not dominate people's connections to organizations. Instead, the primary issues shaping authority relations involve questions of status (Tyler, in press; Tyler & Smith, in press).

References

Huo, Y. J., Smith, H. J., Tyler, T. R., & Lind, E. A. (1996). Superordinate identification, subgroup identification, and justice concerns: Is separatism the problem, is assimilation the answer? *Psychological Science, 7*, 40-45.

Lind, E. A., & Tyler, T. R. (1988). *The social psychology of procedural justice.* New York: Plenum.

Pfeffer, J. (1994). *Competitive advantage through people.* Cambridge, MA: Harvard University Press.

Smith, H. J., & Tyler, T. R. (1996). Justice and power. *European Journal of Social Psychology, 26*, 171-200.

Smith, H. J., & Tyler, T. R. (1997). Choosing the right pond: The influence of the status of one's group and one's status in that group on self-esteem and group-oriented behavior. *Journal of Experimental Social Psychology, 33*, 146-170.

Smith, H. J., Tyler, T. R., Huo, Y. J., Ortiz, D., & Lind, E. A. (1997). *The self-relevant implications of the group-value model: Group membership, self-worth, and procedural justice.* Unpublished manuscript.

Tajfel, H., & Turner, J. C. (1979). An integrative theory of intergroup conflict. In W. G. Austin & S. Worchel (Eds.), *The social psychology of intergroup relations.* Monterey, CA: Brooks/Cole.

Tyler, T. R. (1989). The psychology of procedural justice: A test of the group-value model. *Journal of Personality and Social Psychology, 57*, 830-838.

Tyler, T. R. (in press). Why people cooperate in organizational settings: An identity-based perspective. *Research in Organizational Behavior.*

Tyler, T. R., Boeckmann, R. J., Smith, H. J., & Huo, Y. J. (1997). *Social justice in a diverse society.* Boulder, CO: Westview.

Tyler, T. R., & Degoey, P. (1995). Collective restraint in a social dilemma situation: The influence of procedural justice and community identification on the empowerment and legitimacy of authority. *Journal of Personality and Social Psychology, 69*, 482-497.

Tyler, T. R., Degoey, P., & Smith, H. J. (1996). Understanding why the fairness of group procedures matters: A test of the psychological dynamics of the group-value model. *Journal of Personality and Social Psychology, 70,* 913-930.

Tyler, T. R., & Lind, E. A. (1992). A relational model of authority in groups. *Advances in Experimental Social Psychology, 25,* 151-191.

Tyler, T. R., Lind, E. A., Ohbuchi, K., Sugawara, I., & Huo, Y. J. (1998). Conflict with outsiders: Disputing within and across cultural boundaries. *Personality and Social Psychology Bulletin, 24,* 137-146.

Tyler, T. R., & Smith, H. J. (1997). Social justice and social movements. In D. Gilbert, S. T. Fiske, & G. Lindzey (Eds.), *Handbook of social psychology* (4th ed., Vol. 2, pp. 595-629). New York: McGraw-Hill.

Tyler, T. R., & Smith, H. J. (in press). Justice, social identity, and group processes. In T. R. Tyler, R. Kramer, & O. P. John (Eds.), *The psychology of the social self.* New York: Lawrence Erlbaum.

12

Uses and Misuses of Power in Task-Performing Teams

RUTH WAGEMAN
ELIZABETH A. MANNIX

As organizational researchers have struggled to understand and explain the causes of team effectiveness (or the lack of it), they have drawn on work in social psychology, sociology, and organizational behavior. From this work, several models have emerged on how group behavior influences group performance, and most models include task as well as relational and external functions (Goodman, Ravlin, & Schminke, 1987; Hackman, 1987). Task functions are directed toward the production or performance of a product or service, the end result of which can potentially be measured or evaluated. In addition, to achieve their common goals, teams must establish and maintain productive internal relationships (Levine & Moreland, 1990). Finally, externally directed activities are those that remind us that groups within organizations are not closed systems (Ancona, 1990; Goodman et al., 1987).

Research on team functions generally treats such behaviors as if they are enacted by the whole team. We pay closer attention to the issue

of who engages in these behaviors. Does it matter for team effectiveness whether particular behavioral functions are fulfilled by the group
as a whole or by particular individuals? This question bring us to the
focus of this chapter—the intersection of team effectiveness, team
member behavior, and power.

The Phenomenon

Teams in organizations are frequently composed of individuals
who vary in their hierarchical status, competency, resources, and other
characteristics that invest that person with power relative to other
group members. Thus, in most teams there exists broad potential for
particular individuals to exert more influence on team functioning than
the average member (Hollander, 1958). How powerful members use
their power and the influence on team effectiveness of their choices are
the central questions we address here. We limit our discussion to complex task-performing teams—that is, we treat only those teams that together produce a product or service and have the authority to determine
their work strategies and manage their internal processes. We thus exclude groups that exist primarily or solely for social purposes or those
groups that do routinized work and have little or no authority over their
process.

We define team effectiveness following Hackman (1990) as the
degree to which (a) the team's output meets the standards of quality
of the people who receive or review that output, (b) the process enhances the team's ability to work together interdependently and effectively in the future, and (c) the group experience contributes to the
personal well-being or satisfaction of the team members. The following
examples taken from some real teams illustrate the potential importance of the phenomenon.

During our time in the MBA classroom, we have had opportunity
to observe scores of project teams and to learn (via retrospective accounts by team members) about the dynamics in such teams, including
their power dynamics. These teams typically are asked to identify,
analyze, and make recommendations to solve a pressing management problem in a real-world organization. To that end, teams must
find a client organization. Most often, one member of the project group
acquires access to an organization of which he or she was a past

employee. Thus, at the launch of most of these teams, one team member has control of a critical resource—that is, the team project site and client. Because of this critical resource, this team member has the potential to exert influence over team functioning to a greater extent than those members who do not have any particular power source (Pfeffer, 1992).

How do these team members use this particular form of power? Our observations have uncovered at least three different patterns of power use by this team member—patterns that appear to have very different consequences for team outcomes. First is what we label the "overuse" pattern, in which the team member with the client contact uses his or her special status in the group to exert influence over most aspects of group functioning, including task processes (e.g., how the group will collect data), external relations (e.g., what questions the group should raise with the client), and interpersonal processes (e.g., the group operating norms). The individual uses his or her power to dominate team processes in ways that are in the powerholder's best interests or consistent with the powerholder's views of effective task strategies. Our observations suggest that many of these teams perform quite poorly. In addition, these teams are characterized by widespread member dissatisfaction and frustration with the group and with its final product.

The second pattern we label "abdication." In this pattern, we see the team member with client access behaving no differently from any other team member (generally to avoid taking on what is viewed as excessively difficult work), exerting no special influence over task, internal, or external relations processes—not even to the extent of managing the team's entry into the client organization. Our observations suggest that this, too, is a dysfunctional pattern. Such teams tend toward mediocre to poor performance (usually because of limited data from the client). By contrast to the first pattern, however, they tend to show relatively positive affective reactions to each other and to the team's work process.

The third pattern is referred to as "managing the resource." In this pattern, the powerful member influences other team members only in the specific domain of his or her special resource—that is, relations with the client. The powerful team member may influence the team in defining the client's problem, choosing whom in the organization would be good sources of information, and he or she may serve as the main contact who establishes meetings of the team with the client. On the basis of our data, this appears to be the most effective pattern; teams with this pattern of power use perform relatively well and show no particular tendency toward member dissatisfaction.

Thus, we argue that individual powerholders use their power for different ends, and that these different uses of power have differential consequences for team effectiveness—positively influencing some aspects of team effectiveness and negatively influencing others. Throughout this chapter, we define a "misuse of power" as an influence attempt by the powerholder that will undermine team effectiveness. We return to the example behaviors at the end of this chapter. We describe a functional view of team behavior in which it is argued that there are functions (task, internal, and external relations) that must be fulfilled for a team to perform effectively. We propose that all teams are better off when these functions are performed by someone; teams will perform best, however, when particular functions are performed by the team, whereas others are executed by a powerful individual. Through our discussion of team functions and power, we derive specific and testable propositions about the uses and misuses of individual power in task-performing teams. Finally, by identifying the critical similarities among functions that represent uses or misuses of individual power, we induce three general propositions that specify the kinds of functions that are best fulfilled by powerful individuals and those that are best fulfilled by the group as a whole. Our aim throughout this discussion is to develop researchable predictions about the consequences for group effectiveness of the arenas in which individual team members use their power.

Power and a Functional View of
Team Behavior

In the previous example, we focused on one particular type of power that might be available to individuals in project teams. Of course, individuals come to teams with a variety of backgrounds, experiences, and, often, different levels and sources of power. Power has been defined in several ways, but a simple definition is that with power one party can get the other to do what the latter normally would not do (Dahl, 1957; Kotter, 1979). Adding to this definition is the view of power as a function of the dependency of others on the focal individual (Emerson, 1964; Pfeffer & Salancik, 1977; Thibaut & Kelley, 1959). In their work on power, French and Raven (1959) identified five major bases of social power: reward power, coercive power, legitimate power, expert power, and referent power. Many contemporary discussions of power are grounded in this typology. Another prominent perspective is resource dependency theory, which defines power as the control over resources, including money, supplies, time, equipment, critical services, human capital, or all these (Pfeffer, 1992; Pfeffer & Salancik, 1974). Also important is network theory, which defines power by an individual's location in the organizational structure (Burt, 1992; Granovetter, 1973; Marsden, 1983; White, 1970). In the network view, issues of centrality, criticality, and weak and strong ties are important determinants of power.

Regardless of the power source, one of the important features of the theory of social power is the conceptual feature of "potentiality" (French & Raven, 1959). Power bases give individuals the potential to influence. How (and if) powerful individuals use their power to influence or lead the team can vary widely; they might shape task strategies, establish the teams' basic norms and values, allocate resources, coordinate group efforts, or negotiate with outsiders on behalf of the team. This chapter explores the appropriate uses and inappropriate misuses of power—regardless of its source—by team members. We define uses and misuses in terms of the consequences (positive or negative, respectively) for team effectiveness.

As outlined previously, we take a functional view of team behavior—that is, there are functions that must be fulfilled for a team to perform effectively. These team functions can be performed by particular individuals or by the team as a whole. In this view, all teams are better off when these functions are performed by someone; teams will perform best, however, when specific functions are performed by the team, whereas others are executed by a powerful individual. Although there are many functions that teams can perform, we use as examples those behaviors that we, as well as other theorists and researchers, have found to be important influences on team performance. In the following discussion, we break down team functions into two domains: task directed and relations directed.

The study of task functions has included developing task strategies and task-related values (Liang, Moreland, & Argote, 1995;

Wageman, 1995), setting team goals (Crowne & Rosse, 1995; Mitchell & Silver, 1990; Weingart, 1992), arriving at decision rules (Guzzo, 1982; Miller, 1989; Stasser, Kerr, & Davis, 1989), and role differentiation and the division of labor (Jackson & Schuler, 1985; Moreland & Levine, 1982; Turner & Colomy, 1988). Relational functions include both internally directed and externally directed behaviors. Internally directed behaviors include managing team boundaries and interpersonal relationships (Hackman, 1983, 1990; Mannix, Goins, & Carroll, 1996; Moreland, 1987), arriving at group values and norms of behavior (Argote, 1989; Bettenhausen & Murnighan, 1985; O'Reilly & Caldwell, 1985), and managing conflict (Ancona, Friedman, & Kolb, 1991; Bazerman, Mannix, & Thompson, 1988; Gladstein, 1984; Jehn, 1995). Externally directed behaviors include boundary-spanning and liaison with external parties (Alderfer & Smith, 1982; Ancona, 1987, 1990; Katz & Tushman, 1981; Tushman, 1977), follow-through on information and links to clients (Hackman, 1990), accessing external information or resources (Pfeffer, 1986; Pfeffer & Salancik, 1978), and the implementation, recommendation, and review of final team output (Nadler & Tushman, 1988).

Although we do not claim that all the previously discussed functional behaviors are essential to all teams at all times, we do argue that each of these functions is useful for the group to achieve a high-quality output and to enhance the satisfaction of group members. In the following sections, we draw on examples of particular behaviors within the two domains to make specific predictions about the connections between these functions, who performs them, and team outcomes.

Task Domain

As noted previously, research has identified a wide range of task-related behaviors that are observed to varying degrees in teams. Such behaviors include coordinating member activities, assigning specific task roles, and helping other team members. We focus on two particular task-related behaviors to illustrate our arguments: (a) active monitoring of the team's performance and (b) altering task strategies in response to performance decrements or changes in task demands (i.e., problem solving).

Both these basic task functions have been demonstrated to be important influences on team performance. Attending to feedback and actively seeking data about performance have often been identified as essential task functions that differentiate between superior and poor-performing teams (Hackman, 1987; Hare, 1976; Kolodny & Kiggundu, 1980; Nadler, 1979; Pearce & Ravlin, 1987). Druskat (1995) found, for example, that a tendency to focus attention on the team's strengths and weaknesses and to seek feedback directly from their work outcomes differentiated among superior- and average-performing teams. Similarly, McIntyre and Salas (1995) found that members of effective teams monitor performance and provide other team members with feedback.

By comparison, research is sparse on the devising of appropriate task strategies by teams. Many theorists do emphasize the importance of team strategies (Cohen, 1994; Goodman et al., 1987; Guzzo, 1986; Hackman, 1987; Schwarz, 1994; Steiner, 1972), and what little research has addressed the devising of task strategies has shown a positive relationship to team performance (Druskat, 1995; Wageman, 1996). Wageman, for example, showed that superb teams took time out from task execution to discuss different task strategies more often than did poor-performing teams.

Both monitoring performance and devising task strategies are functions that can be initiated and fulfilled by the team as a whole or by particular team members. In each case, we argue that teams that do engage in these behaviors will outperform those that do not. Nevertheless, our central question, unaddressed by any previous research, remains: Are groups better off if these functions are fulfilled by powerful individuals or by the team as a whole?

Previous studies of the effects of performance monitoring (or attention to feedback) have not differentiated between individual and group behavior. That is, the group is assumed to have attended to performance feedback if any individual in the group has done so. Some recent evidence suggests that for monitoring performance, this is a reasonable stance—that is, who does it matters less than whether it is done at all. A field study of 40 self-managing teams (Wageman, 1996) assessed via interview and observation the degree to which teams engaged in specific self-managing behaviors. In this study, teams that monitored their own performance regularly strongly outperformed those that did not on a variety of objective performance measures. In some cases, it was not the team as a whole that did the performance monitoring but rather a specific powerful individual (in this case, the "specialist," an individual who became an informal team leader on the basis of his or her technical expertise). This individual used his or her power to collect and interpret performance information and present these data to the team. In other teams, these actions were taken by various team members, and the data were reviewed by the team as a whole.

The data showed that there were no differences in the performance of teams whose specialist did the monitoring compared with teams who reviewed their performance together. Teams in which either the specialist or the team as a whole monitored performance, however, did outperform those teams that did not do it at all.

Thus, the basic function of collecting information and bringing it to the attention of the team can be done by anyone. Why does it not matter who does the monitoring? We suggest that monitoring of team performance requires only attention, a cognitive process that is more naturally an individual than a group process. To be sure, the process of making sense of data can draw effectively on multiple intelligences, but in the studies cited previously the researchers were concerned only with whether or not data were attended to and not how well those data were used. Attention by a single individual and the communication required to convey the data to the rest of the team are functions filled effectively by one person.

> *Proposition 1:* Performance monitoring—drawing performance feedback to the attention of the team—is an appropriate use of individual power.

In contrast to monitoring, strategy design is a creative task influenceable by collective knowledge and skills; moreover, task strategies require execution by the team as a whole. Consequently, the effects of task strategy on team performance depend to a great degree on the capabilities used to design it and the commitment of team members to execute it. Decades of group research attest to the notion that multiple perspectives and sources of expertise enhance group performance. Moreover, research has shown that as groups interact they add knowledge and creativity, increase the understanding and acceptance of ideas, and improve commitment and motivation (Levine & Moreland, 1990; Maier, 1970; McGrath, 1984; McGrath & Kravitz, 1982; Shaw, 1981;

Zander, 1979). Both capabilities brought to bear on a choice of task strategy and collective commitment to that strategy are likely to be lower
when strategy is determined by one individual.

Data from Wageman (1996) support the view that asserting task
strategies is a misuse of power by powerful individuals. First, teams
that frequently adapted their task strategies in response to data about
performance decrements strongly outperformed those that did not.
Groups in which the team as a whole determined strategy changes,
however, outperformed those in which the informal team leader did
so. Thus, for this team function, groups were better off when the team
as a whole determined performance strategies than when a powerful
individual used his or her influence to make such a decision for the
team.

> *Proposition 2:* Imposing a task strategy for the group is a misuse of
> individual power.

Before discussing relational functions, it is instructive to note the
similarities in the patterns of findings for the two task functions. For
both functions, the group performed more effectively when someone in
the group engaged in that function than when no one engaged in that
function. Although at one level this simply provides supportive evidence for our functional view of team behavior, it also provides a clue
about appropriate uses of power by individual team members. Some
teams fail to attend to important task-relevant feedback, or fail to adjust
their task strategies, to their ultimate detriment. When a group is avoiding a task-relevant issue, one appropriate use of power by an individual
member may be to influence the group to attend to that issue.

Relations Domain: Internal

The focus in this chapter is task-performing groups; thus, we are
most concerned with the effects of essential functions on task performance. As such, the internal relations in groups are relevant to the extent
that they affect the group interaction processes, and group interaction
is relevant to the extent that it influences performance. A group composed of individuals who agree on work values and norms, and who
are capable of handling conflict productively, should be better equipped

to enact task-relevant strategies and goals (Bar-Tal, 1989; Jehn, 1994; Jehn & Mannix, 1996; Schein, 1986). When the internal relations break down, the result can be motivation losses such as withdrawal or free riding (Maier, 1967; Steiner, 1972), opinion conformity (Janis, 1982), or destructive emotion-based conflict (Amason, 1996; Argyris, 1962; Jehn, 1995; Kelley, 1979). In the following sections, we focus on the internal relations issues of conflict, work values, and norms.

Conflict and Team Performance

Conflict is defined as an awareness by the parties involved of discrepancies, incompatible wishes, or irreconcilable desires (Boulding, 1963). Organizational researchers have recognized both the assets and the liabilities of conflict in group decisions. Some research has shown that conflict is detrimental to organizational functioning, decreases individual satisfaction, and lowers group productivity (Bourgeois, 1980; Evan, 1965; Gladstein, 1984; Schwenk & Crosier, 1993). Conversely, other findings show conflict to be beneficial, enhancing decision quality and planning, innovation, and productivity (Coser, 1970; Crosier & Rose, 1977; Eisenhardt & Bourgeois, 1988; Nemeth & Staw, 1989; Tjosvold, 1991).

It is apparent that the connection between conflict and performance remains less than well understood (Eisenhardt & Zbaracki, 1992). One key to unlocking this complex relationship lies in the differentiation of conflict as either relationship or task related (Crosier & Rose, 1977; Guetzkow & Gyr, 1954; Jehn, 1995; Pinkley, 1990; Wall & Nolan, 1986). Relationship conflict, also called affective conflict, is an awareness of interpersonal incompatibilities. It includes personal and affective components, such as friction, tension, and dislike among group members. Studies show that relationship conflict is detrimental to individual and group performance, member satisfaction, and the likelihood the group will work together in the future (Jehn, 1995; Jehn & Mannix, 1996; Shah & Jehn, 1993). When group members have interpersonal problems or feel friction with one another, they may be distracted from the task, work less cooperatively, and produce suboptimal products (Argyris, 1962; Kelley, 1979; Roseman, Wiest, & Swartz, 1994; Staw, Sandelands, & Dutton, 1981).

Task, or cognitive, conflict is an awareness of differences in viewpoints and opinions pertaining to the group's task. In contrast to relationship conflict, moderate levels of task conflict have been shown to be beneficial to group performance in various decision-making and group tasks. Teams performing complex cognitive tasks benefit from differences of opinion about the work being done (Bourgeois, 1985; Eisenhardt & Schoonhoven, 1990; Jehn, 1995; Jehn & Mannix, 1996; Shah & Jehn, 1993). Task conflict improves decision quality as groups drop old patterns of interaction and adopt new perspectives; the synthesis that emerges from the conflict is generally superior to the individual perspectives themselves (Mason & Mitroff, 1981; Schweiger & Sandberg, 1989; Schwenk, 1990).

The task conflict necessary to produce high-quality outcomes, however, may leave a feeling of negativity among team members (Amason, 1996; Schweiger, Sandberg, & Ragan, 1986; Schweiger, Sandberg, & Rechner, 1989). Critical evaluations, for example, seem to cause negative affective reactions regardless of the outcome (Baron, 1990). Negotiation researchers have consistently demonstrated the benefits of open conflict in reaching integrative solutions of high mutual gain in the dyad as well as the group (Ancona et al., 1991); a natural tendency of many negotiators, however, is to avoid the level of conflict necessary to reach optimal solutions (Lewicki & Litterer, 1994; Neale & Bazerman, 1991; Pruitt, 1981). In addition, some theorists have proposed that relationship, or affective, conflict can be the result of task conflict being misperceived as personal criticism (Amason, 1996; Brehmer, 1976; Deutsch, 1969). In other words, some groups develop a pattern of misinterpreting task conflict as relationship conflict—resulting in performance loss rather than gain. If this pattern is set, it is likely to continue (Bettenhausen & Murnighan, 1985), resulting in high overall levels of relationship conflict and reducing the performance of the group.

Thus, there are many complexities associated with the effective use of conflict within groups. What role might powerful individuals play in influencing the nature and handling of conflict to the team's benefit? Given research evidence that task conflict enhances whereas relational conflict undermines team performance, combined with the natural tendency in teams toward conflict avoidance, we argue that it is useful for individual group members with special influence to encourage task conflict and discourage relationship conflict. This function is especially critical if the group is unwilling or unable to manage its conflict collectively. A powerful individual (or subset of group members) may thus be able to control the timing and nature of conflict to the benefit of the group. Indeed, internal group members (rather than outside "supervisors") are uniquely suited to do so. Members of the team are more likely to have continuous access to the group's process as well as direct knowledge of the underlying causes of particular conflicts; they are thus able to intervene in a knowledgeable and well-timed fashion. A powerful team member also is likely to have the "idiosyncrasy credits" (Hollander, 1958) to both influence the group to open discussion of task approaches and to persuade the group to shelve interpersonal disagreements in team interaction.

> *Proposition 3:* Promoting well-timed task conflict is an appropriate use of individual power.

Work Values, Norms, and Group Performance

Norms are informal rules that groups adopt to regulate group members' behavior; they are among the least visible and most powerful forms of social control over human action (Hackman, 1976; Sherif, 1936). Although there has been a great deal of research on norms, most of it has focused on examining the impact norms have on other social phenomena (Feldman, 1984). There has been relatively little attention to how norms actually form and who is responsible for the norms we see operating in groups. The classic research on norm formation comes from Sherif (1936) and his work on the autokinetic effect. Sherif argued that his results demonstrated the basic psychological processes involved in the establishment of social norms; our experience is organized around or modified by collectively produced frames of reference. Feldman (1984) has presented a task-oriented alternative to this concept of emergent norms. He proposes that norms form in one or more of four ways: explicit statements by supervisors or coworkers—that is, by fiat; critical events in the group's history; primacy—that is, based on early behavior patterns that set up group expectations; and carryover behaviors from past situations. Norms generated by fiat are similar to rules, in which a powerful individual explicitly expresses values, norms, or prescribed behaviors. The remaining three forms might be categorized as variations of collectively emergent norms.

In a relatively recent study of how norms form, Bettenhausen and Murnighan (1985) examined the formation of norms using a multi-round negotiation exercise played over several weeks. They found that group norms regarding resource allocation emerged from the interaction between each group members' definition of the situation and the scripts or schemas that group members used to frame the situation. When group members had similar scripts, the group's interaction proceeded smoothly—each interaction confirmed the meaning that group members attached to the action. When the scripts were not similar, however, conflict resulted that was not always easy to resolve. At times, group members made overt persuasion attempts to pull the group toward their interpretation through challenges to the implied norm.

Thus, newly formed groups may or may not have a high level of agreement, or consensus, on important work-related norms and values. When group members have a high level of value consensus, members will tend to agree on norms regarding work, in turn promoting harmony and coordination (Nemeth & Staw, 1989). By contrast, when low-value consensus exists, members' core values and beliefs about their everyday work are challenged, causing friction and emotional upset (Bar-Tal, 1989; Schein, 1986). Differing values may cause group members to perceive situations and priorities differently, impeding the coordinated flow of work (Ravlin & Meglino, 1987). In addition, value differences between a leader and the rest of the group can be a continuous source of tension for the team (Gray, Bougon, & Donnellon, 1985).

Consensus, or the lack of it, on work-related norms has implications for the type and amount of conflict that a group experiences. Groups that agree too readily on work values and norms may be advantaged by low levels of relationship conflict but may be disadvantaged by similarly low levels of task conflict. Group members with divergent work values and norms may have the opposite problem— that is, high task conflict as well as high relationship conflict (Jehn, 1994). The first case may be dealt with by an intervention from a powerful group member or team leader, as described previously. The second case, however, is somewhat more difficult. It requires that the group come to a workable arrangement on a variety of important work-related norms. This might be done by fiat—that is, by a powerful individual—or it might be arrived at by the collective.

We argue that the definition of work-related values and norms should be left to the group as a whole. By allowing the group to negotiate their own work norms, they have the opportunity to discover the true underlying differences, fully understand one anothers' viewpoints, and struggle toward agreement. The conflict this generates is likely to increase acceptance, understanding, and commitment to the final outcome (Maier, 1967; Pruitt & Rubin, 1986). In fact, the discussion of norms should be clearly and openly addressed by all newly formed groups and periodically reexamined. Like conflict, explicit discussion of norms tends to be a function in groups that is avoided by most team members. The role for a powerful individual is in influencing the group to address its norms directly as well as redirecting relationship conflict back to the task.

> *Proposition 4a:* Influencing the group to address and evaluate its work values and norms is an appropriate use of individual power.
>
> *Proposition 4b:* Dictating work values or norms by fiat is a misuse of individual power.

Relations Domain: External

Although task behaviors and internal relations have a long history in theory and research about group effectiveness, group external activity has only recently come to the attention of groups researchers (Ancona, 1987). This oversight may in part be due to early focus on laboratory-based groups, which had no external clients nor an organizational context beyond the experiment itself. External relations may also have become more prominent because of recent changes in the kinds of organizational teams researchers have the opportunity to observe: As "empowerment" and self-directed work teams become more prevalent, many more teams have the authority to deal directly with clients, to manage resources, and to engage in other activities external to the team.

Evidence for the importance of external activities to team performance is mounting. For example, researchers have stressed that teams must match their information processing capability to the information processing demands of the task environment (Gresov, 1989; Nadler & Tushman, 1988). Those studying innovation have emphasized the importance of boundary-spanning activities (Katz & Tushman, 1979), whereas theorists interested in power have focused on the importance of external constituents for political action and influence (Pfeffer, 1992). Ancona and colleagues, however, truly developed this area of research by attempting to map out the full range of activities that groups use to cope with their environments (Ancona, 1987, 1990). This work begin with a study of 100 sales teams in the telecommunications industry (Gladstein, 1984). Ancona found that group members saw the process aspects of their work as divided into an internal and an external component. In her study, internal processes were associated with team member satisfaction and team-rated performance; external process, however, was associated with sales revenue. In subsequent work, she concluded that teams enact a distinct set of activities and strategies toward their external environment (Ancona, 1990; Ancona & Caldwell, 1992). We draw from this research to identify and focus on two particular external team functions: managing an outside authority and managing a client. We speculate as to the effects on team outcomes of a powerful individual team member fulfilling these functions alone versus the team as a whole fulfilling these functions.

It has been found that one of the important external relations that teams attempt to manage involves the perceptions and support of outside authority; Ancona and Caldwell (1992) labeled this "ambassadorial activity." This external-relations activity typically involves presenting the team capabilities and needs to managers in the larger organization to persuade authority that the team deserves and will use effectively additional resources. Although researchers have recognized that teams carry on this function, they have not addressed who in the team is likely to enact the behavior. It can, theoretically, be done by any or several team members or be a role shared at different times by different team members. We argue that a powerful team member is uniquely suited to fulfill this team function to the benefit of group performance.

As discussed earlier, individuals with greater power within the team may have that power for a variety of reasons, including higher status in the organizational hierarchy, special competence or expertise, a broad network of relations, or even extraordinary verbal ability. Just as these power sources allow the individual to have special influence over the actions of team members, they also can enhance the credibility of that individual with external authorities. Network relations, in addition, enhance the range of access that the individual has to organizational members with the authority to provide needed resources to the team. Thus, the capability of powerful individuals to fulfill this function to the benefit of the team is greater than that of other team members.

> *Proposition 5:* Managing the perceptions and support of outside authority is an effective use of individual power.

The second external activity we address is managing the relationship of the team with its client. Although not all teams have clients external to the organization, most teams do at least have a user of their product or service. Indeed, a definition of team effectiveness may include the degree to which the team product meets the standards of the people who receive or use the product (Hackman, 1990). In many organizational teams, direct client contact is maintained exclusively by one individual who has greater power in the organization than do other members. In consulting teams, for example, the project manager is usually a team member with greater status in the organizational hierarchy. This team leader meets with the client to outline the nature of the project and produce a prospectus, interprets client needs, and keeps the client informed throughout the project. Only at project completion do other team members typically meet with the client, often simply to present the team's conclusions. What effect does this pattern of behavior have on team performance? In our view, exclusive contact between a high-status team member and the client is likely to undermine team performance relative to contact between the client and the team as a whole. The pattern cited previously is defended typically on the basis of "efficiency"— that is, minimizing the time involved in meetings with a client while still satisfying their requirements. This means of managing client relations, however, can be detrimental to group performance for two reasons. First, direct contact with users of the team's product or service is known to be an important source of task-based motivation (Hackman & Oldham, 1980). Second, understanding the requirements of a client is an interpretive act, and determining the process of meeting those requirements is a creative one. Both activities can benefit from drawing on the unique perspectives and abilities of individual team members. When powerful individuals monopolize contact with the external client, both team-level motivation and the quality of work done for the client are compromised.

Proposition 6: Maintaining exclusive relations with the client is a misuse of individual power.

General Discussion

The arguments presented in the preceding section allow us to develop some general propositions about the uses and misuses of power by individual members of task-performing teams. We previously argued that groups were better off if the group as a whole (a) collectively established its operating norms and (b) participated in managing relations with external clients. In each case, the benefit of the group's involvement in these functions derives from their effect on team members' motivation or their commitment to team outcomes. Acceptance of the group norms that promote high standards is likely to be greater when those norms have been discussed and established by consensus rather than by fiat. Similarly, direct contact with the group's client influences the overall level of engagement members feel with their task. Consequently, when a powerful individual engages in these behaviors, only that individual's motivation is maximized, to the detriment of that of other team members.

General Proposition I: Fulfilling behavioral functions that influence the collective motivation of the team is a misuse of individual power.

We also argued that certain features of team effectiveness will suffer when powerful individuals (a) assert team task strategies rather than allowing them to be developed by the group as a whole or (b) exclusively manage relations with the client.

Team task performance will improve when the team as a whole fulfills these functions because task performance is influenced directly by the use made of collective knowledge and skills. When powerful individuals assert particular task strategies, or when they maintain exclusive contact with the client, only that individual's talents are brought to bear on the team's approach to its work. By contrast, when all team members are engaged in fulfilling these functions, the team has the opportunity to draw on the full range of capabilities within the team.

General Proposition II: Fulfilling behavioral functions that are influenced by the collective capabilities of the team is a misuse of
individual power.

An example of the negative consequences of General Propositions
I and II can be seen in our project team examples from the beginning of
this chapter. We labeled one pattern of individual power use as the overuse pattern. In this example, the powerful team member uses his or her
special status in the group to exert influence over most aspects of group
functioning. As we described, many of these teams perform quite
poorly and are characterized by widespread member dissatisfaction
and frustration. We suggest that the negative effects experienced by
these teams are the result of an individual team member that has taken
over group functions that are linked to team capabilities and motivation. By overusing power, that individual undermined the group's performance through reducing the level of talent that was brought to bear
on task strategy and the unity of execution that comes from collective
commitment. The widespread dissatisfaction may be a function of perceived poor performance, or it may be a result of team members feeling
their authority usurped and their contributions underutilized.

On the positive side, however, at least these groups have fulfilled
some of the important task and relationship functions. In contrast is
the second pattern we described, which we labeled abdication. In this
pattern, the powerful team member exerts no special influence over
task or relations processes—not even to the extent of managing the
team's entry into the client organization. Thus, a critical external function was inadequately addressed or addressed by members with less
likelihood of doing so effectively. These abdicating individuals also
missed important influence opportunities in other domains. By failing
to recognize their special influence, they may have been especially
complicit in allowing the group to avoid critical functions such as task
conflict; hence the smooth interpersonal relations of these groups—but
the subsequent poor performance.

Team performance is enhanced when appropriate performance
strategies are invented to deal with changing task demands. Thus, the
ability of the team to improve as a performing unit over time increases
when performance feedback is drawn to the attention of the team,
when the team needs are presented to higher authorities, and when its
interpersonal conflicts are dealt with. In addition, the commitment of

individual members within the team increases when values are articulated that appeal to team members and when its capabilities and successes are drawn to the attention of external entities. Those teams that fail to fulfill these functions do so to the detriment of team effectiveness. Measures to fill such gaps can be taken by a powerful individual team member with unique status in the group. Better still, if those missing functions are related to member motivation or collective capabilities, the powerful individual can influence the team to address issues that it has avoided or ignored.

> *General Proposition III:* Influencing the team to fulfill behavioral functions that the team has avoided or ignored is an effective use of individual power.

Thus, there is a role for a powerful team member to use his or her influence to the benefit of the group. Related to this notion is our third example of power use in project teams, labeled managing the resource. In this instance, the powerful member influences other team members only in the specific domain of his or her special resource—that is, smoothing and facilitating access to the client. Such individuals help the team interpret information and feedback from the client—although they do not assert strategies and interpretations without input from the group. On the basis of our observations, this appears to be a highly effective pattern of influence. In General Proposition III, we expand the range of this behavior to suggest that powerful team members also should encourage the team to address important task and relations functions, when and if they are being neglected or avoided.

In this chapter, we attempted to open and explore an area of research that has thus far been neglected—that of who enacts important task and relational functions within teams. Our purpose has been to raise the issue of the uses and misuses of individual power within groups, and how it might be related to team effectiveness and performance.

We close by raising two issues about power use in teams that we believe call for further exploration—one relevant to structural influences on power dynamics in teams and one about individual differences.

The first, more structural issue has to do with sources of power. We noted at the beginning of the chapter that certain team members may come to the team with greater power than others for a variety of reasons, including networks of relations outside the group, special skills, and access to critical resources. These structural influences on who holds power in groups may also have implications for the effects of power use on team outcomes. We note that the effectiveness of powerholders in managing the relations of the team to outside authority may be influenced by the individuals' source of power. For example, those who derive power in the team from having powerful external allies or from having extraordinary verbal skills are more likely to fulfill this function effectively than are those who derive their power from a special skill visible only to the team and not to outside authority.

The second issue is that individual powerholders vary in their political tactics and the skill with which they exert influence on team behavior. Individual differences in influence skills will surely affect the impact of power uses on team effectiveness. For example, the potential positive impact of a powerholder encouraging task-related conflict depends on that individual's skill in eliciting diverse opinions about task strategy and helping the group to determine the best course of action. It is at least conceivable that unskilled attempts to raise task conflict could foment relational conflict that undermines team effectiveness. We thus acknowledge the potential importance of considering power sources and skill differences in the relationships we have proposed. These issues, and the propositions we have presented, are meant to stimulate new directions for research and thinking about groups that might prove of interest to the theorist and of importance to the practitioner.

References

Alderfer, C. P., & Smith, K. K. (1982). Studying intergroup relations embedded in organizations. *Administrative Science Quarterly, 27,* 35-65.

Amason, A. (1996). Distinguishing effects of functional and dysfunctional conflict on strategic decision making: Resolving a paradox for top management teams. *Academy of Management Journal, 39,* 123-148.

Ancona, D. (1987). Groups in organizations: Extending laboratory models. In C. Hendrick (Ed.), *Group processes and intergroup relations.* Newbury Park, CA: Sage.

Ancona, D. (1990). Outward bound: Strategies for team survival in an organization. *Academy of Management Journal, 33,* 334-365.

Ancona, D., & Caldwell, D. (1992). Demography and design: Predictors of new product team performance. *Organization Science, 3*(3), 321-341.

Ancona, D., Friedman, R., & Kolb, D. (1991). The group and what happens on the way to "yes." *Negotiation Journal, 7*, 155-174.

Argote, L. (1989). Agreement about norms and work unit effectiveness: Evidence from the field. *Basic Applied Social Psychology, 10*, 131-140.

Argyris, C. (1962). *Interpersonal competence and organizational effectiveness.* Homewood, IL: Dorsey.

Baron, R. (1990). Countering the effects of destructive criticism: The relative efficacy of four interventions. *Journal of Applied Psychology, 75*, 235-245.

Bar-Tal, D. (1989). *Group beliefs: A conception for analyzing group structure, processes, and behavior.* New York: Springer-Verlag.

Bazerman, M. H., Mannix, E., & Thompson, L. (1988). Groups as mixed-motive negotiations. In E. J. Lawler & B. Markovsky (Eds.), *Advances in group processes: Theory and research, 5.* Greenwich CT: JAI.

Bettenhausen, K., & Murnighan, J. K. (1985). The emergence of norms in competitive decision-making groups. *Administrative Science Quarterly, 30*, 350-372.

Boulding, K. (1963). *Conflict and defense.* New York: Harper & Row.

Bourgeois, L. J. (1980). Performance and consensus. *Strategic Management Journal, 1*, 227-248.

Bourgeois, L. J. (1985). Strategic goals, environmental uncertainty, and economic performance in volatile environments. *Academy of Management Journal, 28*, 548-573.

Brehmer, B. (1976). Social judgement theory and the analysis of interpersonal conflict. *Psychological Bulletin, 83*, 985-1003.

Burt, R. (1992). *Structural holes: The social structure of competition.* Boston: Harvard University Press.

Cohen, S. G. (1994). Designing effective self-managing work teams. In M. Beyerlein & D. Johnson (Eds.), *Advances in interdisciplinary studies of work teams* (pp. 67-102). Greenwich, CT: JAI.

Coser, L. (1970). *Continuities in the study of social conflict.* New York: Free Press.

Crosier, R., & Rose, G. (1977). Cognitive conflict and goal conflict effects on task performance. *Organizational Behavior and Human Decision Processes, 19*, 378-391.

Crowne, D., & Rosse, J. (1995). Yours, mine, and ours: Facilitating group productivity through the integration of individual and group goals. *Organizational Behavior and Human Decision Processes, 64*, 138-150.

Dahl, R. (1957). The concept of power. *Behavioral Science, 2*, 201-218.

Deutsch, M. (1969). Conflicts: Productive and destructive. *Journal of Social Issues, 25*, 7-41.

Druskat, V. U. (1995). *A team competency study of self-managed manufacturing teams.* Unpublished doctoral dissertation, Boston University, Boston.

Eisenhardt, K., & Bourgeois, J. (1988). Politics of strategic decision making in high-velocity environments: Toward a midrange theory. *Academy of Management Journal, 31*, 737-770.

Eisenhardt, K., & Schoonhoven, C. (1990). Organizational growth: Linking founding team, strategy, environment, and growth among U.S. semiconductor ventures 1978-1988. *Administrative Science Quarterly, 35*, 504-529.

Eisenhardt, K., & Zbaracki, M. (1992). Strategic decision making. *Strategic Management Journal, 13*, 17-37.

Emerson, R. M. (1964). Power-dependence relations: Two experiments. *Sociometry, 27*, 282-298.

Evan, W. (1965). Conflict and performance in R & D organizations. *Industrial Management Review, 7,* 37-46.

Feldman, D. C. (1984). The development and enforcement of group norms. *Academy of Management Review, 9,* 47-53.

French, J. R. P., Jr., & Raven, B. (1959). The bases of social power. In D. Cartwright (Ed.), *Studies in social power.* Ann Arbor: University of Michigan Press.

Gladstein, D. (1984). A model of task group effectiveness. *Administrative Science Quarterly, 29,* 499-517.

Goodman, P., Ravlin, E., & Schminke, M. (1987). Understanding groups in organizations. In L. Cummings and B. Staw (Eds.), *Research in organizational behavior* (Vol. 9, pp. 121-173). Greenwich, CT: JAI.

Granovetter, M. (1973). The strength of weak ties. *American Journal of Sociology, 78,* 1360-1379.

Gray, B., Bougon, M. G., & Donnellon, A. (1985). Organizations as constructions and destructions of meaning. *Journal of Management, 11,* 83-98.

Gresov, C. (1989). Exploring fit and misfit with multiple contingencies. *Administrative Science Quarterly, 34,* 431-453.

Guetzkow, H., & Gyr, J. (1954). An analysis of conflict in decision making groups. *Human Relations, 7,* 367-381.

Guzzo, R. (Ed.). (1982). *Improving group decision making in organizations: Approaches from theory and research.* New York: Academic Press.

Hackman, J. R. (1976). Group influences on individuals. In M. Dunnette (Ed.), *Handbook of industrial and organizational psychology.* Chicago: Rand McNally.

Hackman, J. R. (1983). *A normative model of work team effectiveness* (Tech. Rep. No. 2, Group effectiveness research project). New Haven, CT: Yale University, School of Organization and Management.

Hackman, J. R. (1987). The design of work teams. In J. Lorsch (Ed.), *Handbook of organizational behavior* (pp. 315-342). Englewood Cliffs, NJ: Prentice Hall.

Hackman, J. R. (Ed.). (1990). *Groups that work (and those that don't): Creating conditions for effective teamwork.* San Francisco: Jossey-Bass.

Hackman, J. R., & Oldham, G. (1980). *Work redesign.* Reading, MA: Addison-Wesley.

Hare, A. P. (1976). *Handbook of small group research* (2nd ed.). New York: Free Press.

Hollander, E. (1958). Conformity, status and idiosyncrasy credit. *Psychological Bulletin, 65,* 117-127.

Jackson, S., & Schuler, R. (1985). A meta-analysis and conceptual critique of research on role ambiguity and role conflict in work settings. *Organizational Behavior, 36,* 16-78.

Janis, I. L. (1982). *Victims of groupthink* (2nd ed.). Boston: Houghton-Mifflin.

Jehn, K. (1994). Enhancing effectiveness: An investigation of advantages and disadvantages of value-based intragroup conflict. *International Journal of Conflict Management, 5,* 223-238.

Jehn, K. (1995). A multimethod examination of the benefits and detriments of intragroup conflict. *Administrative Science Quarterly, 40,* 256-282.

Jehn, K., & Mannix, E. A. (1996, December). *The dynamic nature of conflict: A longitudinal study of intragroup conflict and group performance* (Working paper).

Katz, R., & Tushman, M. (1979). Communication patterns, project performance, and task characteristics: An empirical evaluation and integration in an R&D setting. *Organizational Behavior and Human Performance, 23,* 139-162.

Katz, R., & Tushman, M. (1981). An investigation into the managerial roles and career paths of gatekeepers and project supervisors in a major R&D facility. *Administrative Science Quarterly, 27,* 103-110.

Kelley, H. H. (1979). *Personal relationships.* Hillsdale, NJ: Lawrence Erlbaum.

Kolodny, H. F., & Kiggundu, M. N. (1980). Towards the development of a sociotechnical systems model in woodlands mechanical harvesting. *Human Relations, 33,* 623-645.

Kotter, J. (1979). *Power in management.* New York: AMACOM.

Levine, J., & Moreland, R. (1990). Progress in small group research. *Annual Review of Psychology, 41,* 585-634.

Lewicki, R., & Litterer, J. A. (1994). *Negotiation* (2nd ed.). Homewood, IL: Irwin.

Liang, D. W., Moreland, R., & Argote, L. (1995). Group versus individual training and group performance: The mediating role of transactive memory. *Personality and Social Psychology Bulletin, 21*(4), 384-393.

Maier, N. R. F. (1967). Assets and liabilities in group problem-solving: The need for an integrative function. *Psychological Review, 74,* 239-249.

Maier, N. R. F. (1970). *Problem solving and creativity: In individuals and groups.* Monterey, CA: Brooks/Cole.

Mannix, E., Goins, S., & Carroll, S. (1996, June). *Starting at the beginning: Team formation, process and performance* (Working paper).

Marsden, P. (1983). Restricted access in networks and models of power. *American Journal of Sociology, 88,* 686-717.

Mason, R. O., & Mitroff, I. I. (1981). *Challenging strategic planning assumptions.* New York: John Wiley.

McGrath, J. (1984). *Groups: Interaction and performance.* Englewood Cliffs, NJ: Prentice Hall.

McGrath, J., & Kravitz, D. (1982). Group research. *Annual Review of Psychology, 33,* 195-230.

McIntyre, R. M., & Salas, E. (1995). Measuring and managing for team performance: Lessons from complex environments. In R. Guzzo & E. Salas (Eds.), *Team effectiveness and decision making in complex organizations.* San Francisco: Jossey-Bass.

Miller, C. (1989). The social psychological effects of group decision rules. In P. Paulus (Ed.), *Psychology of group influence* (2nd ed.). Hillsdale, NJ: Lawrence Erlbaum.

Mitchell, T. R., & Silver, W. (1990). Individual and group goals when workers are interdependent: Effects on task strategies and performance. *Journal of Applied Psychology, 75,* 185-193.

Moreland, R. (1987). The formation of small groups. In C. Hendrick (Ed.), *Group process* (pp. 80-110). Newbury Park, CA: Sage.

Moreland, R., & Levine, J. (1982). Socialization in small groups: Temporal changes in individual-group relations. In L. Berkowitz (Ed.), *Advances in experimental social psychology* (Vol. 15, pp. 137-192). New York: Academic Press.

Nadler, D. (1979). The effects of feedback on task group behavior: A review of the research. *Organizational Behavior and Human Decision Processes, 23,* 309-338.

Nadler, D. A., & Tushman, M. (1988). *Strategic organizational design: Concepts, tools, and processes.* Glenview, IL: Scott Foresman.

Neale, M. A., & Bazerman, M. H. (1991). *Cognition and rationality in negotiation.* New York: Free Press.

Nemeth, C. J., & Staw, B. (1989). The tradeoffs of social control in groups and organizations. *Advances in Experimental Social Psychology, 22,* 175-210.

O'Reilly, C., & Caldwell, D. (1985). The impact of normative social influence and cohesiveness on task perceptions and attitudes: A social information processing approach. *Journal of Occupational Psychology, 58,* 193-206.

Pearce, J. A., & Ravlin, E. C. (1987). The design and activation of self-regulating work groups. *Human Relations, 40,* 751-782.

Pfeffer, J. (1986). A resource dependence perspective on intercorporate relations. In M. S. Mizruchi & M. Schwartz (Eds.), *Structural analysis of business* (pp. 117-132). New York: Academic Press.

Pfeffer, J. (1992). *Managing with power: Politics and influence in organizations.* Cambridge, MA: Harvard University Press.

Pfeffer, J., & Salancik, G. (1974). Organizational decision making: The case of a university budget. *Administrative Science Quarterly, 19,* 135-151.

Pfeffer, J., & Salancik, G. (1977). Organizational design: The case for a coalitional model of organizations. *Organizational Dynamics, 6,* 15-29.

Pfeffer, J., & Salancik, G. (1978). *The external control of organizations: A resource dependence perspective.* New York: Harper & Row.

Pinkley, R. (1990). Dimensions of the conflict frame: Disputant interpretations of conflict. *Journal of Applied Psychology, 75,* 117-128.

Pruitt, D. G. (1981). *Negotiation behavior.* New York: Academic Press.

Pruitt, D. G., & Rubin, J. Z. (1986). *Social conflict.* Random House: New York.

Ravlin, E. C., & Meglino, B. M. (1987). Effects of values on perception and decision making: A study of alternative work value measures. *Journal of Applied Psychology, 72,* 666-673.

Roseman, I., Wiest, C., & Swartz, T. (1994). Phenomenology, behaviors and goals differentiate emotions. *Journal of Personality and Social Psychology, 67,* 206-221.

Schein, E. H. (1986). What you need to know about organizational culture. *Training and Development Journal, 8*(1), 30-33.

Schwarz, R. (1994). *Team facilitation.* Englewood Cliffs, NJ: Prentice Hall.

Schweiger, D., & Sandberg, W. (1989). The utilization of individual capabilities in group approaches to strategic decision making. *Strategic Management Journal, 10,* 31-43.

Schweiger, D., Sandberg, W., & Ragan, J. (1986). Group approaches for improving strategic decision making: A comparative analysis of dialectical inquiry, devil's advocacy, and consensus approaches to strategic decision making. *Academy of Management Journal, 29,* 51-71.

Schweiger, D., Sandberg, W., & Rechner, P. (1989). Experiential effects of dialectical inquiry, devil's advocacy, and consensus approaches to strategic decision making. *Academy of Management Journal, 32,* 745-772.

Schwenk, C. (1990). Conflict in organizational decision making: An exploratory study of its effects in for-profit and not-for-profit organizations. *Management Science, 36,* 436-448.

Schwenk, C., & Crosier, R. (1993). Effects of the expert, devil's advocate and dialectical inquiry methods on prediction performance. *Organizational Behavior and Human Decision Processes, 26,* 409-424.

Shah, P., & Jehn, K. (1993). Do friends perform better than acquaintances? The interaction of friendship, conflict and task. *Group Decision and Negotiation, 2,* 149-166.

Sherif, M. (1936). *The psychology of social norms.* New York: Harper.

Stasser, G., Kerr, N., & Davis, J. (1989). Influence processes and consensus models in decision-making groups. In P. Paulus (Ed.), *Psychology of group influence* (2nd ed.). Hillsdale, NJ: Lawrence Erlbaum.

Staw, B. M., Sandelands, L., & Dutton, J. (1981). Threat-rigidity effects in organizational performance. *Administrative Science Quarterly, 28,* 582-600.
Steiner, I. (1972). *Group process and productivity.* New York: Academic Press.
Thibaut, J. W., & Kelley, H. H. (1959). *The social psychology of groups.* New York: John Wiley.
Tjosvold, D. (1991). Rights and responsibilities of dissent: Cooperative conflict. *Employee Responsibilities and Rights Journal, 4,* 13-23.
Turner, R., & Colomy, P. (1988). Role differentiation: Orienting principles. In E. J. Lawler & B. Markovsky (Eds.), *Social psychology of groups: A reader.* Greenwich, CT: JAI.
Tushman, M. (1977). Special boundary roles in the innovation process. *Administrative Science Quarterly, 22,* 587-605.
Wageman, R. (1995). Interdependence and group effectiveness. *Administrative Science Quarterly, 40,* 145-180.
Wageman, R. (1996, June). *A field study of leadership of self-managing teams: The effects of team design and coaching* (Working paper).
Wall, V., & Nolan, L. (1986). Perceptions of inequity, satisfaction, and conflict in task oriented groups. *Human Relations, 39,* 1033-1052.
Weingart, L. R. (1992). Impact of group goals, task component complexity, effort, and planning on group performance. *Journal of Applied Psychology, 77,* 33-54.
White, H. C. (1970). *Chains of opportunity.* Cambridge, MA: Harvard University Press.
Zander, A. (1979). The psychology of group process. *Annual Review of Psychology, 30,* 417-451.

13

To Be or Not to Be (Self-Promoting)

The Consequences of Counterstereotypical Impression Management

LAURIE A. RUDMAN

I n Wendy Wasserstein's (1990, p. 171) award-winning drama, *The Heidi Chronicles and Other Plays,* the "boy-meets-girl" scene evolves as follows:

AUTHOR'S NOTE: This research was partially supported by a National Science Foundation (NSF) Graduate Fellowship and a University of Minnesota Doctoral Dissertation Fellowship awarded to the author. Preparation of this chapter was supported by National Research Service Award No. 1 F32 MH11632-01. Portions of this research were presented at the American Psychological Society in New York City, June 1995; the Joint Meeting of the European Association of Social Psychology and the Society for Experimental Social Psychology in Washington, D.C., September 1995; and the Stanford Graduate School of Business conference on power, politics, and influence in organizations in Palo Alto, California, May 1996. I thank Gene Borgida, Marti Hope Gonzales, Tony Greenwald, and Erika Peterson for their comments on an earlier version of the manuscript.

Scoop: I like you. You're prissy, but I like you a lot.
Heidi: Well, I don't know if I like you.
Scoop: Why should you like me? I'm arrogant and difficult.
          But I'm very smart. So you'll put up with me. What?
Heidi: What what?
Scoop: You're thinking something.
Heidi: Actually, I was wondering what mothers teach their sons
          that they never bother to tell their daughters.
Scoop: What do you mean?
Heidi: I mean, why the hell are you so confident?
          —Excerpt from "The Heidi Chronicles" in
          The Heidi Chronicles and Other Plays, copyright © 1990
          by Wendy Wasserstein, reprinted by permission of
          Harcourt Brace & Company.

Like many men, Scoop displays a flair for self-promotion, an impression management (IM) strategy that appears prominently in any taxonomy of social influence styles (Jones & Pittman, 1982). Designed to enhance one's status and worth, self-promotion includes highlighting one's best qualities, downplaying one's deficits, and calling attention to one's achievements. It is especially useful in situations in which the self-promoter is not well-known or is competing against others for scarce resources (e.g., while vying for a job, a promotion, or a date). It is therefore an important tactic for any competitor, male or female. As Heidi ruefully notes, however, self-promotion is more normative for men than for women. Traditionally, men have been socialized to speak well of themselves to compete for economic resources and romantic attention from women (Buss, 1988). In contrast, women have been socialized to speak well of others, to be modest about their own achievements, and to cooperate versus compete (Bakan, 1966; Eagly, 1987). As a result, self-promotion may come less "naturally" for women than it does for men (Riordan, Gross, & Maloney, 1994; Strutton, Pelton, & Lumpkin, 1995).

An Impression Management Dilemma

Self-promotion in performance settings may serve important functions for women. Laboratory and field research show a positive relationship between hiring and promotion decisions and self-promotional skills, perhaps because self-enhancement is associated with qualities considered to be prerequisites for many occupations (e.g., confidence, competence, and ambition; Jones & Pittman, 1982; Kacmar, Delery, & Ferris, 1992; Stevens & Kristof, 1995). These are precisely the qualities traditionally more associated with men than with women (Fiske & Stevens, 1993). Thus, self-promotion may potentially counteract gender stereotyping and sex discrimination in the workplace.

In fact, it may be incumbent upon women attempting to move into traditionally male-dominated occupations to manage a "high-powered" impression or risk losing to male rivals who will automatically be perceived as better qualified by virtue of their gender (Berger, Webster, Ridgeway, & Rosenholtz, 1986; Glick, Zion, & Nelson, 1988). Consistent with this view, a recent study of academic success found that women's explanations for why their male colleagues soared ahead to tenure and promotion while they lingered behind focused on gender differences in "political style" (Sonnert & Holton, 1996). In general, men were viewed as having more "entrepreneurial spunk." As Sonnert & Holton note, "Male scientists are . . . more aggressive, combative, and self-promoting in their pursuit of career success, and so they achieve higher visibility. In short, they are better at playing the political game of career advancement" (p. 67). Undoubtedly, this disparity cuts across a variety of occupations.

Despite their socioeconomic implications, IM theorists have largely overlooked gender differences in self-presentational tactics (Giacolone & Rosenfeld, 1998; Jones & Pittman, 1986; Tedeschi & Norman, 1985). It seems obvious (as it did to Heidi), however, that men and women are socialized to behave differently in this regard—in IM terms, to adopt self-focused (e.g., self-promotion) versus other-focused (e.g., ingratiation) strategies, respectively (Kacmar et al., 1992; Nelson, 1978). Unfortunately, recent efforts to address this "gender gap" have centered on intrapsychic mediators. Women, it is argued, are unable to self-promote due to low self-esteem (i.e., a belief that "they have nothing about which to brag" [Kacmar & Carlson, 1994, p. 690]). Alternatively, women may refrain from self-promotion for largely interpersonal reasons. Self-promoting women may be perceived as confident and competent, but they may also suffer a backlash effect in the form of social and economic repercussions. Because self-promotion is largely a male prerogative, behaviors viewed as assertive and indicative of leadership ability in men may be labeled bossy, domineering, and even neurotic in women (Costrich, Feinstein, Kidder, Marecek, &

Pascale, 1975; Eagly, Makhijani, & Klonsky, 1992). Given that social influence is a function of both respect and likability (Carli, LaFleur, & Loeber, 1995), women are caught in a double bind. If they adopt a "masculine" style, they may gain respect but suffer social reprisals. If they adopt a "feminine" style, they may be popular but not be perceived as particularly qualified or ambitious. In summary, women may be stuck in a Catch-22 in which they are damned if they do self-promote and damned if they do not.

Sociological work suggests the prevalence of what has been termed the "feminine modesty effect" (Gould & Slone, 1982; Heatherington et al., 1993). In this research, women are shown to be more prone toward modesty and self-effacement in public (vs. private) situations. The implication is that men and women do not differ intrinsically in their perceptions of self-worth (Kacmar & Carlson, 1994), but rather that women are responding to normative pressures to conform to gender stereotypes. In addition, Crittenden's cross-cultural work has shown that women react to interpersonal demands for modesty and self-effacement by adopting attributional styles that characterize them as more socially sensitive and likable but less competent (Crittenden, 1991; Wiley & Crittenden, 1992). Specifically, women show a tendency to attribute success to external forces (e.g., "luck") and failure to internal forces (e.g., ability), whereas men show the opposite pattern (Deaux, 1976; Deaux & Emswiller, 1974). This is directly pertinent to IM differences because self-promotion involves (in part) publicly making internal versus external attributions for one's achievements. Again, the argument is that sex differences in attributional styles may be derived more from interpersonal than from intrapsychic forces. The research presented in this chapter is also grounded in this perspective and was undertaken to investigate the interpersonal barriers that women face when they consider using self-promotion as a means to social influence (Rudman, in press).

The Current Research:
A Two-Step Model of Individuation

The previous discussion suggests that women who seek to gain entry into male-dominated fields may be caught between professional demands to counteract gender stereotypes (e.g., to self-promote) and interpersonal demands to conform to gender stereotypes (e.g., to self-efface). Thus, one issue addressed by the current research is whether self-promotion would enhance the likelihood that a qualified female job applicant would be individuated by evaluators (i.e., judged on her own merits) versus judged on the basis of sex stereotypes. A second issue concerned delineating factors that might alter the outcome of individuation for such a woman. That is, do women always risk social censure when they violate prescriptions to "be modest" or are there situations in which a woman will be more likely to benefit from "tooting her own horn"?

These questions imply a two-step model of individuation for women. The first step is to counter evaluators' tendencies to stereotype women as less competent, ambitious, and qualified than men (Heilman, 1995). Impression formation theory posits that two factors are important at this juncture: (a) actors (i.e., targets) who disconfirm the stereotype and (b) evaluators (i.e., perceivers) who are motivated to attend to the evidence and thereby form individuated versus category-based impressions (Fiske & Neuberg, 1990). For example, when perceivers are exhorted to "be accurate" (i.e., are accuracy motivated) or are given a vested interest in the target (i.e., are outcome dependent), their impressions are likely to be less stereotypic. This is because perceivers concerned with accurate social perception elicit diagnostic information from targets, allowing for stereotypic beliefs and expectations to be overturned (Hilton & Darley, 1991). For example, a motivated personnel director might ask job-relevant questions of a previously "mommy-tracked" candidate regarding her qualifications for a position, whereas a nonmotivated interviewer (e.g., one simply going through the motions) might concentrate on pictures of her children.

So far so good, provided the applicant provides information that disconfirms gender stereotypes (e.g., via self-promotion). As noted previously, however, counteracting stereotypes can "backfire" on women, causing them to be censured for deviating from feminine norms. Thus, the second step is to determine conditions that might mitigate the backlash effect for counterstereotypical behavior. Given that motivation influences detecting atypical targets (Fiske & Neuberg, 1990), a question under investigation was whether perceivers' goals might influence reactions to atypical targets as well. Specifically, it seemed likely that both accuracy-motivated and outcome-dependent evaluators would ask stereotype-relevant questions and thus "detect" an atypical woman during a job interview, but that they might have different reactions to her. Accuracy-motivated evaluators might view female self-promotion as "unfeminine" and exhibit the backlash effect (i.e., rate a self-promoting woman as more competent but less socially attractive and hirable than a self-effacing woman). In contrast, out-come-dependent participants might favor the self-promoter (i.e., rate her as more competent, socially attractive, and hirable than a self-effacing woman). After all, if individuals required a woman to be atypical and she assured them of her qualifications, she would have enabled them to form accurate, self-serving judgments. Under these conditions, participants might reward rather than censure a self-promoting woman. In summary, it was predicted that self-promotion would uniformly augment a woman's perceived competence, but that a self-promoting woman would subsequently be evaluated negatively or positively by accuracy-motivated and outcome-dependent perceivers, respectively. That is, the same behavior would be viewed as inappropriate or valuable, depending on perceivers' goal condition. Support for this hypothesis would underscore the need to consider evaluators' motivational differences not only when predicting factors likely to enhance target individuation but also when predicting the subsequent outcomes of individuated targets (e.g., the backlash effect). Although extensive research has addressed the first issue (Brewer, 1988; Fiske & Neuberg, 1990; Hilton & Darley, 1991), the second issue has been underinvestigated and was a primary focus of the current research (Rudman, 1998).

Experiment 1:
Will Perceivers' Goals Moderate the Backlash Effect?

To explore the possibility that perceivers' goals might moderate the backlash effect for female self-promotion, college student participants (40 women and 40 men) were asked to interview a female job candidate as a possible game partner for a computerized version of *Jeopardy*. Participants were told that the game required "a facility for facts and fig-ures, the ability to think fast under pressure, considerable computer game skill, and a competitive nature." The objective was to model a

real-life situation in which a woman might be overlooked for a job that required masculine skills unless she managed an atypical impression (Glick et al., 1988). The job candidate was, in fact, an accomplice of the researcher (hereafter referred to as the target). The target was instructed to either self-promote or self-efface during the interviews, depending on random assignment. Cross-cutting this manipulation, participants were assigned to either accuracy-motivated or outcome-dependent goal conditions. Accuracy-motivated interviewers were exhorted to "be accurate" in their target assessments to ensure the success of the project. Outcome-dependent interviewers were led to believe that they would compete for a cash prize with their game partner as part of an experiment-wide competition. Thus, if the target proved to be a suitable teammate, participants stood to gain $25.00.

The interviews were structured in that participants were given 16 possible questions to ask the target and were instructed to choose 8 prior to the interview. This allowed for the target's answers to be scripted and memorized in advance while preserving a semblance of choice from the interviewer's point of view. Half the questions were task-relevant (e.g., "Are you good at computer games?" and "Do you perform well under pressure?"). The other half were neutral questions (e.g., "Have you traveled much?"). To avoid "heavy-handed" presentations, the target was instructed to self-promote or self-efface only when asked task-relevant questions, whereas neutral questions elicited neutral responses. In all, participants asked an average of 4.58 task-relevant questions during the interviews.[1]

Following sociolinguistic research (Lakoff, 1990; Tannen, 1990), the self-effacing script was designed to be more feminine and less powerful than the self-promoting script. For example, it included disclaimers and hedges (e.g., "I'm no expert, but . . ."). In contrast, the self-promoter spoke directly and assertively (e.g., "I do my best work in pressure situations"). To illustrate, the self-promoter responded to the question, "Are you by nature a competitive person?" as follows: "Definitely. But I mean that in a healthy way, of course—I'm not obsessed by competition. But I do enjoy competing. To tell you the truth, I hate to lose at anything." In contrast, the self-effacer replied, "I would not say that I am by nature a competitive person. Of course, if competition is necessary, I will try and do my very best. Still, if it is all the same to everyone, I would like everyone to win—know what I mean?"

Following the interview, participants assessed the target's IM style, atypicality, task aptitude (e.g., competence), social attractiveness, and hirability on 8-point scales. After completion of the dependent measures, participants were debriefed and compensated.

Results

Manipulation Checks

A check on the target's IM manipulation revealed that participants viewed the self-promoter as more confident, assertive, and powerful (i.e., self-promoting) and more atypical than the self-effacer, $ps < .001$ (combined $Ms = 5.93$ vs. 4.02). A check on participants' goal condition revealed that accuracy-motivated and outcome-dependent participants were equally motivated to form accurate perceptions of the target. Outcome-dependent participants, however, were, not surprisingly, more concerned than accuracy-motivated participants with selecting the best game partner and with performing well at the task, $ps < .001$.

Task Aptitude Ratings

A task aptitude index was formed by averaging participants' ratings of the target's competence, intelligence, and effectiveness with assessments of her ability to perform under pressure and in a competitive situation. As expected, the self-promoter was rated as more qualified than the self-effacer irrespective of goal condition, $p < .001$ ($Ms = 6.64$ vs. 5.77).

Social Attraction Ratings

A social attraction index (composed of likability, popularity, and friendliness ratings, combined with participants' willingness to "get to know" the target) revealed an unexpected IM × Goal × Gender interaction, $p < .05$. As the top half of Figure 13.1 shows, male participants followed predictions exactly. That is, men rated the self-effacer as more socially attractive in the accuracy-motivated condition ($Ms = 6.48$ vs.

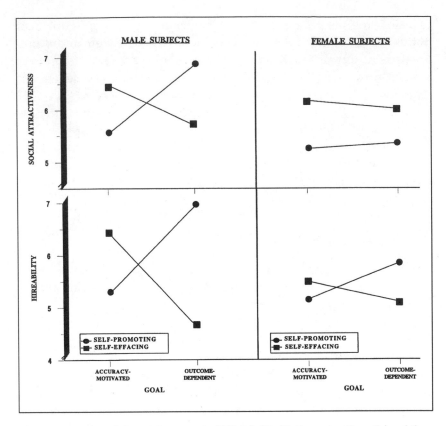

Figure 13.1. Social Attractiveness and Hireability Ratings as a Function of the Target's IM Strategy, Subject Goal, and Subject Gender (Experiment 1)

5.54) but switched their preference to the self-promoter in the outcome-dependent condition (Ms = 6.80 vs. 5.73), ps < .05. Women rated the self-promoter as less socially attractive than the self-effacer, however, irrespective of goal condition, p < .05 (Ms = 5.53 vs. 6.33).

Hirability Ratings

The hirability index was composed of three items: "If you could hire this person as a game partner, would you?"; "How likely would you be to choose this person as a partner for a computer game?"; and "How close is this person to your 'ideal' game partner?" Results

revealed an unexpected three-way interaction, $p < .05$ (Figure 13.1, bottom). Again, men followed predictions, whereas women did not. Specifically, accuracy-motivated men favored hiring the self-effacer over the self-promoter (Ms = 6.45 vs. 5.33), whereas outcome-dependent men favored hiring the self-promoter over the self-effacer (Ms = 7.00 vs. 4.65), $ps < .01$. For women, no effects emerged on this measure (Ms = 5.48 vs. 5.33 for the self-promoter and self-effacer, respectively). Thus, women did not reject the self-promoter in the accuracy-motivated condition, but neither did they prefer hiring her even when it would have benefited them to do so (i.e., increased their chances of winning a prize).

Summary and Implications

Across all conditions, the self-promoter was perceived as more confident, competent, and qualified for a job that required stereotypically masculine skills than the self-effacer. Thus, the hypothesis that female self-promotion would enhance perceptions of a woman's qualifications for a task linked to masculine attributes was supported. In this respect, female self-promotion may function as an important tool for counteracting gender stereotypes, given that it enhances women's status and competence (Jones & Pittman, 1982). What of the backlash effect, however (i,e., social and economic repercussions for counteracting gender stereotypes)? As predicted, accuracy-motivated participants showed the backlash effect by rating the self-promoter as less socially attractive (and for men, less hirable) than the self-effacer. The key prediction that outcome dependency would mitigate the backlash effect was also supported but with one important qualification: provided interviewers were male. Specifically, outcome-dependent men rewarded the self-promoter with higher social attraction and hirability ratings than the self-effacer, as expected. In contrast, women uniformly found the self-promoter less socially attractive than the self-effacer, irrespective of goal condition. Moreover, they failed to prefer hiring the self-promoter, even when they had a vested interest in her capabilities. In summary, perceivers were sufficiently motivated to ask diagnostic questions and thus to perceive differences in competence between the self-promoting and self-effacing targets, as expected (Fiske & Neuberg, 1990). The hypothesis that motivation

would also moderate the backlash effect for counterstereotypical behavior, however, was only supported by male (and not female) perceivers.

Although the gender differences that emerged in reactions to a self-promoting woman were intriguing, they were unexpected and thus required replication. This was one objective of Experiment 2. Moreover, although motivation may moderate reactions to atypical behavior (as the results of Experiment 1 suggested), social context is an equally important factor to consider. Specifically, given the double standard inherent in self-promotion (i.e., that it is largely a male pre-rogative), it was important to examine reactions to a self-promoting woman in a context that included a male competitor.

Experiment 2 was designed to address this issue. It was hypothe-sized that when a self-promoting woman directly competed against a self-promoting man, the latter might be favored despite objectively equal qualifications. In the first place, a man might automatically be perceived as a better "fit" for a stereotypically masculine job (Heilman, 1983). Thus, he might receive higher task aptitude ratings by virtue of his sex. Second, a woman who blatantly competes on "men's terms" might be perceived as particularly atypical (i.e., masculine) and there-fore suffer a loss in social attractiveness (Brown & Geis, 1984; Eagly et al., 1992). The results of Experiment 1 suggested that this might be particularly true for female interviewers.

A second objective was to assess whether male self-effacement would elicit social sanctions similar to those imposed on the self-pro-moting woman in Experiment 1. Toward this end, the male target was assigned to self-promote or self-efface during interviews, depending on random assignment. In contrast, the female target always self-pro-moted. In the past, both genders have experienced repercussions for violating gender-based expectancies (Cherry & Deaux, 1978; Costrich et al., 1975; Spence, Helmreich, & Stapp, 1975). It was therefore con-ceivable that the self-effacing man would be viewed as less socially attractive than his self-promoting counterpart. In any event, self-effacement was expected to decrease task aptitude ratings for the male target as it did for the woman in Experiment 1 (Miller, Cooke, Tsang, & Morgan, 1992). As a result, the woman was expected to be hired when she competed against the self-effacing man for practical, if not for social, reasons.

Experiment 2:
Can a Strong Woman Compete Against a
Strong Male Competitor?

To explore this hypothesis, participants (21 women and 19 men) conducted interviews with two targets: a self-promoting woman and either a self-promoting or a self-effacing man, depending on the male target's IM condition. Interview order was counterbalanced. Participants subsequently "hired" one candidate as their computer game partner under outcome-dependent goal conditions (i.e., to qualify for a cash prize drawing as part of an experimentwide competition). Thus, all participants had a vested interest in the skills of the partner they hired.

Following Experiment 1, participants selected 8 questions (out of 16 alternatives) prior to the interviews. Targets' answers were scripted and memorized in advance. The female target used the self-promoting script from Experiment 1. The male target's self-effacing script was based on feminine communication patterns, including the use of hedges and disclaimers (e.g., "I guess so"). In contrast, the self-promoting script was more direct and masculine (e.g., "I thrive in pressure situations"). In response to the question, "Are you by nature a competitive person?," the self-promoting man replied,

> Absolutely. Maybe I was born this way, but I've always been real competitive. I think everyone is competitive and if they were honest, they'd admit it. What is that Vince Lombardi quote again? Oh yeah: "If it doesn't matter if you win or lose, why do they keep score?"

By contrast, the self-effacing man replied,

> I don't think anybody likes to lose, but I don't think I'm naturally all that competitive, either. I mean, I do better when I'm playing a team sport, like soccer, than when I'm playing golf. So I'm probably not competitive by nature.

As in Experiment 1, targets self-promoted or self-effaced only when asked task-relevant questions (participants asked an average of 5.42 task-relevant questions of each target).[2] Following each interview, participants evaluated the targets on measures identical to those used in Experiment 1. Participants then selected a game partner from the two candidates. After completion of the dependent measures, participants were debriefed and compensated.[3]

Results

Manipulation Checks

As expected, the self-promoting man was rated as more self-promoting than the self-effacer, $p < .01$ ($Ms = 6.29$ vs. 5.01). In addition, the self-effacing man was rated as less typical than the self-promoting man, $p < .05$ ($Ms = 3.41$ vs. 4.28). The self-promoting woman was perceived as more atypical when the man self-effaced than when he self-promoted, $p < .01$ ($Ms = 4.35$ vs. 2.70). No differences emerged, however, between the two self-promoters on either the self-promotion or atypicality measure. Thus, it appears that the man was the standard to which the woman was compared in that she was assimilated (i.e., viewed as "typical") or contrasted (i.e., viewed as "atypical"), depending on his self-presentational style.

Task Aptitude Ratings

Results revealed an IM × Target Gender × Subject Gender interaction, $p < .05$ (Figure 13.2). In the self-effacing condition, participants predictably rated the woman higher than the man, $p < .01$ ($Ms = 6.50$ vs. 5.19). Gender differences emerged, however, in the self-promoting condition. Men rated the self-promoters equally ($M = 6.44$), whereas women rated the man higher than the woman, $p < .01$ ($Ms = 7.06$ vs. 6.30). Thus, the self-promoting woman suffered the predicted loss in competence ratings when paired with a self-promoting man, but only when interviewers were female.

Social Attractiveness Ratings

Results revealed a subject gender × target gender interaction, $p < .05$ (Figure 13.2). Overall, women found the man more socially attrac-

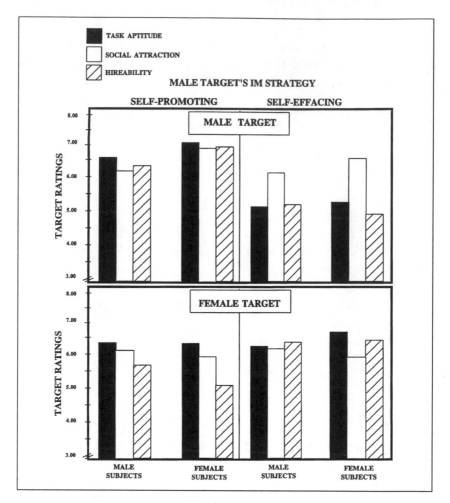

Figure 13.2. Task Aptitude, Social Attraction, and Hireability Ratings as a Function of the Male Target's IM Strategy, Target Gender, and Subject Gender (Experiment 2)

tive than the woman, $p < .05$ ($Ms = 6.70$ vs. 6.08). For men, no differences emerged ($M = 6.09$). A planned contrast revealed no differences between the self-promoting and self-effacing man, $F < 1.00$ ($Ms = 6.44$ and 6.34, respectively). Thus, the atypical man was not viewed as less socially attractive than his more normative counterpart. Finally, a measure of physical attractiveness revealed no differences across experimental conditions ($M = 5.24$).

TABLE 13.1 Game Partner Selection as a Function of the Male Target's IM
Condition, Target Gender, and Subject Gender in Experiment 2

	Self-Effacing Male Target		Self-Promoting Male Target	
Subject Gender	Male Target	Female Target	Male Target	Female Target
Male	1	9	4	5
Female	2	9	10	0

Note: Nonparametric tests analyzing partner choice as a function of the male target's IM tactic and subject gender revealed significant discrepancies from expected cell frequencies for both men (χ^2 [1, $N = 19$] = 4.55, $p < .05$) and women (χ^2 [1, $N = 21$] = 14.63, $p < .01$).

Hirability Ratings

Results revealed an IM × Target Gender × Subject Gender interaction, $p < .05$ (Figure 13.2). In the self-effacing condition, the woman was predictably assessed as more hirable than the man, $p < .001$ (Ms = 6.42 vs. 5.35). In the self-promoting condition, however, men rated the self-promoters equally (M = 6.00), whereas women favored hiring the man over the woman, $p < .01$ (Ms = 6.94 vs. 5.08). Thus, once again, the woman was devalued when competing against a strong man but only by women interviewers.

Partner Selection

Table 13.1 displays the outcome of the interview for the male and female candidates as a function of the man's IM strategy and interviewer gender. As can be seen, when choosing between two self-promoters, men selected evenly across target gender, choosing a man 4 times and a woman 5 times out of 9. In the self-effacing condition, however, men clearly favored the woman, selecting her 9 times out of 10. Women also favored hiring the woman over the man in the self-effacing condition, selecting her 9 times out of 11. In contrast, women uniformly awarded the self-promoting man the partnership, choosing him 10 times out of 10.

Summary

As predicted, the self-promoting woman was favored by both men and women when she competed against a self-effacing man. Rejection of the self-effacing man appeared to be based on devaluation of his competence rather than a dislike for him personally. This finding was surprising but is consistent with recent social attraction research demonstrating equal desirability ratings for prosocial and dominant men (Jensen-Campbell, Graziano, & West, 1995) and may point to relaxed standards regarding acceptable self-presentational tactics for men in our culture (but see Miller et al., 1992).

In contrast, the self-promoting woman was predictably discriminated against when she directly competed against a self-promoting man, but only by women interviewers. Women found her less qualified and less hirable than the man and uniformly selected him as their partner over her, whereas men displayed no preferences. Moreover, women uniformly rated the man as more socially attractive than the woman, irrespective of his IM strategy. Contrary to expectations, the woman was not socially devalued as a result of enhanced atypicality assessments. In fact, the self-promoting woman was most likely to be selected as a partner when she was viewed as particularly atypical (i.e., when competing against a self-effacing man; Glick et al., 1988). Thus, it appears that managing an impression of atypicality may overcome gender stereotypes for women, but whether the outcome is favorable or not may depend largely on the gender (and motivational set) of their audience and the nature of their competitors.

Discussion

The good news for women is that self-promotion almost universally led to a hiring decision for the female target when she competed against a self-effacing man. Given a choice between a "high-powered" woman and a relatively weak man, even female interviewers selected the woman. The sobering result, however, was that women uniformly rejected the self-promoting woman when the playing field included a strong male contender. This finding may be attributable to the fact that the task was stereotypically masculine and may have therefore signaled a "lack of fit" for the woman (Heilman, 1983). It does not explain, however, why women discriminated against the self-promoting female candidate more than did men.

The picture that emerges across both studies is that women were less receptive to the self-promoting woman than were men. In Experiment 1, women recognized that the woman was more qualified than a self-effacing woman, but they failed to reward her with increased hirability ratings, even when they had a vested interest in her performance. In Experiment 2, they uniformly rejected her as a partner when she competed against a self-promoting man. In addition, they rated her as less qualified and hirable than the self-promoting man and less socially attractive than the man (irrespective of his IM style).

These findings were unexpected for at least two reasons. First, women tend to be more egalitarian than men on direct measures of sexism (Glick & Fiske, 1996; Swim, Aikin, Hall, & Hunter, 1995; Williams & Best, 1990). Shouldn't these attitudes lead to less discriminatory behavior on the part of women? Second, women tend to be more receptive to powerful women speakers than are men (Carli et al., 1995). In that line of research, however, women are speaking persuasively about topics other than themselves. The results from both studies suggest that it may still be problematic for a woman to speak directly and confidently about her own qualifications, especially (though not exclusively) when evaluators are women (Powers & Zuroff, 1988).

Why were women more likely than men to react negatively when faced with a strong, self-confident woman?[4] The psychological underpinnings of the backlash effect exhibited by women remain to be investigated. The explanations proposed here are speculative but may provide direction for future research. They can be summarized as focused on socialization and similarity-attraction mechanisms.

Socialization

Throughout their lives, women are oriented toward modesty and self-effacement (Nelson, 1978). Moreover, women develop with an emphasis on similarities and connections, whereas men develop with the stress on individuality, leadership, and hierarchy (Bakan, 1966; Eagly, 1987). In addition, women are encouraged to advocate for others and not themselves (Janoff-Bulman & Wade, 1996). The result is that female self-promotion may violate deeply ingrained, interpersonal rules adopted by women since childhood—rules suggesting that women should seek connections with others and men superiority over others (Bakan, 1966). As a result, women may be uncomfortable when another woman presents herself as independent, "masterful," and self-assured (Powers & Zuroff, 1988). The differences between what is acceptable for men versus women in terms of power displays may be so ingrained in women that they may be unaware of the source of their discomfort when they are faced with a strong, self-confident woman (Heim, 1990). Consistent with this view, the results of open-ended measures and post-experiment interviews with women suggested that they were "annoyed" with the female self-promoter but unable to articulate the cause of their disturbance.

One implication of the current results is that women may be more averse to female power than men. A recent Gallup poll conducted in 22 countries showed that internationally, both men and women preferred having male versus female bosses (Gallup Organization, 1995). Among U.S. respondents, however, 37% of men and 57% of women responded "male" when asked which gender they preferred to work for. That is, women were less supportive than men of female authority figures. Interestingly, the poll reflected no sex differences in American respondents' advocacy of equal opportunities for women. Thus, women "vote for equality" in the workplace, but when it comes to female bosses, support for equality seemingly fades. One way to reconcile these two positions is to consider that women (and other disenfranchised members of society) may value status equalization more than status enhancement for social groups (Pratto, Stallworth, Sidanius, & Stiers, 1997). As the members of a traditionally oppressed class, women may not be as anxious for other women to be "in charge" as they desire for men and women to be "equals" in the workplace as well as the home. Thus, women may feel it does not behoove them to "switch places with men"—that is, for some women to take on traditionally masculine roles (and traits) associated with dominance and leadership. More preferably, women may want to change society's whole approach to hierarchy—specifically, to replace the dominant model with a partnership model (Filipczak, 1994). Although this is likely to be an unrealistic goal where men are concerned, women may nonetheless feel committed to keeping the power "dead even" when it comes to other women (Heim, 1990).

Similarity Attraction

Perceived similarity is a powerful predictor of social attraction (Byrne, 1971); it is therefore possible that men's and women's reactions were based on similarity differences (assuming that male interviewers were more likely to be self-promoters than were female interviewers). If similarity disparities were primarily responsible for the current findings, however, men should have reacted positively to the self-promoting woman irrespective of goal condition in Experiment 1, and atypicality ratings should have predicted partner rejection for women in Experiment 2. Instead, men responded positively under specific conditions (when outcome dependent), and women selected the woman as a partner when she was viewed as particularly atypical (in the self-effacing male target condition of Experiment 2). Nonetheless, it is left to future research to explore similarity-attraction and socialization factors as possible mechanisms underlying women's negative reactions to self-promoting women.

The negative reactions on the part of women toward female self-promotion would be less significant if a direct, self-confident style was unassociated with perceptions of competence. Taken together, however, the two experiments provide persuasive evidence that self-promotion, at least in a normative context (i.e., a job interview), effectively enhances a woman's perceived qualifications. It is conceivable that women do not give "popularity points" to other women for enhanced competence (Teague, 1973). A more benign view is that women were reacting more to the masculine attributes of the job when they considered hiring a female candidate and less to her self-promoting IM style per se. That is, women may have felt that the best way to augment their chances of success would be to hire a man because he would compensate for their own "lack of fit" (Heilman, 1983). Given no masculine options in Experiment 1, they rated the female candidates equally low. Given a masculine option in Experiment 2, they strongly preferred a self-promoting male versus female candidate, despite her strengths. Men may have felt more freedom to select equally among the strong candidates; they, after all, had the "gender base" covered. Perhaps women would have responded more favorably to female self-promotion if the task was feminine-linked. The research, however, was intended to model the real-world situation that is more problematic for women—one in which they must counter gender stereotypes when competing for masculine-linked positions. Under these conditions, self-promoting women may fare best when evaluators are male versus female. If men continue to be predominately responsible for hiring and promotion decisions, this might be viewed as a "silver lining" in the dark cloud of the glass ceiling for strong, self-confident women. As more women achieve organizational clout (e.g., as human resource managers), however, the reality is that female job candidates may be compelled to walk a tightrope—self-promoting enough to impress male interviewers but not enough to "turn off" female interviewers. Moreover, once hired, women may be forced to manage a "bilingual" impression for their male and female colleagues. Having to be direct and assertive on the one hand, and equivocal on the other hand, represents a particular type of "multiple audience problem" (Fleming & Rudman, 1993) that may be costly for women both economically and psychologically (Baumeister, 1989).

Conclusion

Work is a vital means by which people create and define themselves (Argyle, 1987). Given the importance of impression management in the contemporary workplace (Giacalone & Rosenfeld, 1989), self-presentational activities have taken a central role in defining life's meaning for many people (Baumeister, 1989). Thus, it is important that researchers seriously consider the types of impression management dilemmas that women face in performance settings, and particularly as they seek entry into previously male-dominated occupations. Self-promotion appears to represent a double-edged sword for women. On the one hand, it increased competence ratings; on the other hand, it decreased social attraction and hirability ratings, especially when perceivers were outcome independent or women. The situation represents a catch-22 in which women may be discriminated against for failing to counter gender stereotypes (i.e., for acting "as a woman") and discriminated against for countering gender stereotypes (i.e., for not acting "as a woman should"). Irrespective of whether evaluators who censure counterstereotypical behavior are doing so consciously or unconsciously, for reasons stemming from socialization or other factors, the implications are that women may be forced to choose between their gender identity and their professional identity—a choice that, ultimately, they cannot win (Riordan et al., 1994). To the extent that women continue to present a self-effacing "face" to the world, they may jeopardize professional success to avoid social reprisals (Sonnert & Holton, 1996; Wiley & Crittenden, 1992). The current research sought to call attention to the interpersonal barriers that may prevent women from fully engaging in equal opportunities for career advancement and success and to encourage future investigations that target the IM dilemma that women in performance settings face.

Notes

1. The means differed marginally for the outcome-dependent and accuracy-motivated groups (5.03 and 4.13, respectively; $p = .06$).

2. Participants were instructed to ask the same questions of both interviewees (all participants complied).

3. For both studies, a drawing was conducted at the end of the project and the cash prize was awarded. During debriefing, it was made clear to all participants that they were automatically eligible for the drawing.

4. One mundane possibility is that script differences between the male and the female target were responsible for the effect. In a follow-up experiment, 349 respondents (113 men and 236 women) rated the verbal scripts in a between-participants design that varied target gender, IM style, and response authenticity (actual vs. cross-gendered responses; Rudman, 1997). That is, half the participants rated the responses as they were actually spoken by the targets. The other half rated the female's responses as if they had been spoken by a man or vice versa. The primary result was a crossover interaction between script authenticity and target gender, $p < .001$. Follow-up tests revealed that both targets received higher ratings when their responses were derived from the female versus the male script, $ps < .01$. Thus, it appears that of the two scripts, the female target's responses were, if anything, superior to the male target's, negating the possibility that the effects of Experiment 2 were derived from scripts that differentially favored the male over the female target.

References

Argyle, M. (1987). *The psychology of happiness.* London: Methuen.

Bakan, D. (1966). *The duality of existence.* Chicago: Rand McNally.

Baumeister, R. (1989). Motives and costs of self-presentations in organizations. In R. A. Giacolone & P. Rosenfeld (Eds.), *Impression management in the organization* (pp. 57-72). Hillsdale, NJ: Lawrence Erlbaum.

Berger, J., Webster, M., Jr., Ridgeway, C. L., & Rosenholtz, S. J. (1986). Status cues, expectations, and behaviors. In E. Lawler (Ed.), *Advances in group processes* (Vol. 3, pp. 1-22). Greenwich, CT: JAI.

Brewer, M. B. (1988). A dual-process model of impression formation. In T. K. Srull & R. S. Wyer, Jr. (Eds.), *Advances in social cognition* (Vol. 1, pp. 1-36). Hillsdale, NJ: Lawrence Erlbaum.

Brown, V., & Geis, F. L. (1984). Turning lead into gold: Evaluations of men and women leaders and the alchemy of social consensus. *Journal of Personality and Social Psychology, 46,* 811-824.

Buss, D. M. (1988). The evolution of human intrasexual competition: Tactics of mate attraction. *Journal of Personality and Social Psychology, 54,* 616-628.

Byrne, D. (1971). *The attraction paradigm*. New York: Academic Press.

Carli, L. L., LaFleur, S., & Loeber, C. C. (1995). Nonverbal behavior, gender, and influence. *Journal of Personality and Social Psychology, 68*, 1030-1041.

Cherry, F., & Deaux, K. (1978). Fear of success versus fear of gender-inappropriate behavior. *Sex Roles, 4*, 97-101.

Costrich, N., Feinstein, J., Kidder, L., Marecek, J., & Pascale, L. (1975). When stereotypes hurt: Three studies of penalties for sex-role reversals. *Journal of Experimental Social Psychology, 11*, 520-530.

Crittenden, K. S. (1991). Asian self-effacement or feminine modesty? Attributional patterns of women university students in Taiwan. *Gender & Society, 5*(1), 98-117.

Deaux, K. (1976). *The behavior of women and men*. Belmont, CA: Wadsworth.

Deaux, K., & Emswiller, E. (1974). Explanations of successful performance on sex-linked tasks: What is skill for the male is luck for the female. *Journal of Personality and Social Psychology, 29*, 80-85.

Eagly, A. (1987). *Sex differences in social behavior: A social-role interpretation*. Hillsdale, NJ: Lawrence Erlbaum.

Eagly, A. H., Makhijani, M. G., & Klonsky, B. G. (1992). Gender and the evaluation of leaders: A meta-analysis. *Psychological Bulletin, 111*, 3-222.

Filipczak, B. (1994). Is it getting chilly in here? *Training, 31*(2), 25-30.

Fiske, S. T., & Neuberg, S. L. (1990). A continuum of impression formation, from category-based to individuating processes: Influences of information and motivation on attention and interpretation. In M. P. Zanna (Ed.), *Advances in experimental social psychology* (Vol. 23, pp. 1-74). New York: Academic Press.

Fiske, S. T., & Stevens, L. E. (1993). What's so special about sex? Gender stereotyping and discrimination. In S. Oskamp & M. Costanzo (Eds.), *Gender issues in contemporary society* (pp. 173-196). Newbury Park, CA: Sage.

Fleming, J. H., & Rudman, L. A. (1993). Between a rock and a hard place: Self-concept regulating and communicative properties of distancing behaviors. *Journal of Personality and Social Psychology, 64*, 44-59.

Gallup Organization. (1995). *Gender & society: Status and stereotypes*. Princeton, NJ: Author.

Giacalone, R. A., & Rosenfeld, P. (Eds.). (1989). *Impression management in the organization*. Hillsdale, NJ: Lawrence Erlbaum.

Glick, P., & Fiske, S. T. (1996). The ambivalent sexism inventory: Differentiating hostile and benevolent sexism. *Journal of Personality and Social Psychology, 70*, 491-512.

Glick, P., Zion, C., & Nelson, C. (1988). What mediates sex discrimination in hiring decisions? *Journal of Personality and Social Psychology, 55*, 178-186.

Gould, R. J., & Slone, C. G. (1982). The "feminine modesty" effect: A self-presentational interpretation of sex differences in causal attribution. *Personality and Social Psychology Bulletin, 8*, 477-485.

Heatherington, L., Daubman, K. A., Bates, C., Ahn, A., Brown, H., & Preston, C. (1993). Two investigations of "female modesty" in achievement situations. *Sex Roles, 29*, 739-754.

Heilman, M. E. (1983). Sex bias in work settings: The lack of fit model. *Research in Organizational Behavior, 5*, 269-298.

Heilman, M. E. (1995). Sex stereotypes and their effects in the workplace: What we know and what we don't know. *Journal of Social Behavior and Personality, 10*, 3-26.

Heim, P. (1990). Keeping the power dead even. *Journal of American Medical Women's Association, 45*, 232-243.

Hilton, J. L., & Darley, J. M. (1991). The effects of interaction goals on person perception. In M. P. Zanna (Ed.), *Advances in experimental social psychology* (Vol. 24, pp. 236-267). San Diego: Academic Press.

Janoff-Bulman, R., & Wade, M. B. (1996). The dilemma of self-advocacy for women: Another case of blaming the victim? *Journal of Social and Clinical Psychology, 15*(2), 143-152.

Jensen-Campbell, L. A., Graziano, W. G., & West, S. G. (1995). Dominance, prosocial orientation, and female preferences: Do nice guys really finish last? *Journal of Personality and Social Psychology, 68*, 427-440.

Jones, E. E., & Pittman, T. S. (1982). Toward a general theory of strategic self-presentation. In J. Suls (Ed.), *Psychological perspectives on the self* (Vol. 1, pp. 231-262). Hillsdale, NJ: Lawrence Erlbaum.

Kacmar, K. M., & Carlson, D. S. (1994). Using impression management in women's job search processes. *American Behavioral Scientist, 37*, 682-696.

Kacmar, K. M., Delery, J. E., & Ferris, G. R. (1992). Differential effectiveness of applicant impression management tactics on employment interview decisions. *Journal of Applied Social Psychology, 16*, 1250-1272.

Lakoff, R. T. (1990). *Talking power: The politics of language in our lives.* New York: Basic Books.

Miller, L. C., Cooke, L. L., Tsang, J., & Morgan, F. (1992). Should I brag? Nature and impact of positive and boastful disclosures for women and men. *Human Communication Research, 18*, 364-399.

Nelson, K. (1978). Modesty socialization in sexual identity: The transition from infant to girl or boy (Doctoral dissertation, University of California, Berkeley, 1978). *Dissertation Abstracts International, 39*(2A), 760.

Powers, T. A., & Zuroff, D. C. (1988). Interpersonal consequences of overt self-criticism: A comparison with neutral and self-enhancing presentations of self. *Journal of Personality and Social Psychology, 54*, 1054-1062.

Pratto, F., Stallworth, L. M., Sidanius, J., & Stiers, B. (1997). The gender gap in occupational role attainment: The social dominance approach. *Journal of Personality and Social Psychology, 72*, 37-53.

Riordan, C. A., Gross, T., & Maloney, C. C. (1994). Self-monitoring, gender, and the personal consequences of impression management. *American Behavioral Scientist, 37*, 715-725.

Rudman, L. A. (1997). [Script data]. Unpublished raw data, University of Washington, Seattle.

Rudman, L. A. (1998). Self-promotion as a risk factor for women: The costs and benefits of counterstereotypical impression management. *Journal of Personality and Social Psychology, 74*, 629-645.

Sonnert, G., & Holton, G. (1996). Career patterns of women and men in the sciences. *Scientific American, 274*(1), 63-71.

Spence, J. T., Helmreich, R., & Stapp, J. (1975). Likability, sex-role congruence of interest, and competence: It all depends on how you ask. *Journal of Applied Social Psychology, 5*, 93-109.

Stevens, C. K., & Kristof, A. L. (1995). Making the right impression: A field experiment of applicant impression management during job interviews. *Journal of Applied Psychology, 80*, 587-606.

Strutton, D., Pelton, L. E., & Lumpkin, J. R. (1995). Sex differences in ingratiatory behavior: An investigation of influence tactics in the salesperson-customer dyad. *Journal of Business Research, 34*(1), 35-45.

Swim, J. K., Aikin, K. J., Hall, W. S., & Hunter, B. A. (1995). Sexism and racism: Old-fashioned and modern prejudice. *Journal of Personality and Social Psychology, 68,* 199-214.

Tannen, D. (1990). *You just don't understand: Women and men in conversation.* New York: William Morrow.

Teague, M. C. (1973). Competence and non-competency as determinants of interpersonal attraction in biased and unbiased women. *Dissertation Abstracts International, 35*(2B), 1031.

Tedeschi, J. T., & Norman, N. (1985). Social power, self-presentation, and the self. In B. R. Schlenker (Ed.), *The self and social life* (pp. 293-322). New York: McGraw-Hill.

Wasserstein, W. (1990). *The Heidi chronicles and other plays.* New York: Harcourt, Brace, Jovanovich.

Wiley, M. G., & Crittenden, K. S. (1992). By your attributions you shall be known: Consequences of attributional accounts for professional and gender identities. *Sex Roles, 27,* 259-276.

Williams, J. E., & Best, D. L. (1990). *Measuring sex stereotypes: A multination study.* Newbury Park, CA: Sage.

14

Women and Power

Conformity, Resistance, and Disorganized Coaction

JOANNE MARTIN
DEBRA MEYERSON

As women have moved into positions formerly held by men, researchers have begun to examine whether women's experiences of power are, in some contexts, different from those of men so that some of the conclusions of earlier, supposedly gender-neutral power research might have to be expanded or modified (Acker & Van Houten, 1976; Blau & Ferber, 1987; Calas, 1993; Calas & Smircich, 1992; Clegg, 1989; Ibarra, 1992; Karsten, 1994; Marshall, 1984; Mills & Tancred, 1992; Pfeffer, 1992). For example, studies have examined obstacles that block individual women from gaining power (Lee, 1993; Martin, 1994; Northcraft & Gutek, 1993) and strategies that individual women can employ to gain power (Cantor & Bernay, 1992; Lipman-Blumen, 1997;

AUTHORS' NOTE: We thank the women of Link.Com, who spoke so honestly and openly to us. We also thank Susan Okin, Jeff Pfeffer, and Ralph Stablein for helpful comments on earlier drafts of the chapter.

Morrison, White, Van Velsor, & the Center of Creative Leadership, 1992; Rosener, 1995).

Some studies of power and gender share the following implicit assumptions that merit critical examination: (a) that power in society lies in the labor market; (b) that the more women hold paying jobs, the more access to power women as a group will have; and (c) that as more individual women gain high-ranking positions, the more change will occur to benefit all women. This "add-women-and-stir" approach has conservative variants ("all that is needed is equal opportunity to enter the labor market") and liberal versions ("equal outcomes are what matters"), but in either case increasing numbers of women in certain kinds of jobs are seen as the key indicator of women gaining power.

With time, it has become clear that the add-women-and-stir approach has had mixed results. Whether one regards the glass as half full or half empty depends on the point of view of the author and the reader (Blum & Smith, 1988; Lord, Ross, & Lepper, 1979; Northcraft & Gutek, 1993). Studies documenting the entry of women into the labor market, and their rise into professional and managerial positions, have been countered by observations that the majority of working women are still segregated into low-level, female-dominated jobs with limited advancement opportunities (Baron & Morris, 1976; Bielby & Baron, 1986; Blau & Ferber, 1987; Catalyst, 1996; Ferguson, 1984; Harlan & Weiss, 1982; Hartmann & Reskin, 1986; Hartsock, 1985; Marshall, 1984). Furthermore, to the dismay of many who have invested in their recruitment and training, high-ranking women continue to exit mainstream corporations at a startling rate, often to found their own companies (Brush & Hisrich, 1986; Strober, 1982).

Researchers have tried to determine why this exodus has happened and why sex inequality persists with such tenacity. Because power lies not just in the public domain of work but also in the domain of the home and family, changes in the work domain will be short-lived and limited in their impact if they are not accompanied by equally substantial changes in the allocation of tasks and responsibilities at home (Hochschild, 1989; Okin, 1989; Olsen, 1983). In addition, add-women-and-stir remedies cannot suffice if the gendered practices of organizational cultures foster, reinforce, and therefore reproduce inequalities between men and women in ways that many do not see as gender related (Cockburn, 1991; Ferguson, 1991; Ferree & Martin, 1995; Leidner, 1991; Martin, 1994; P. Martin, 1990; Mills & Tancred, 1992;

Pettigrew & Martin, 1987). As long as the gendered bases of inequality are obscured, they run the risk of being ignored. Many women and men are reluctant to raise "women's issues" because they fear harming their reputations and career prospects (Ashford, Dutton, & Edwards, 1997). Women who achieve high-ranking positions have often been either selected or socialized, like their male colleagues, to act just like their male predecessors (Blum & Smith, 1988; Ferguson, 1984; Kanter, 1977; Pfeffer, 1977; Schein, 1978). The costs of such conformity pressures are particularly high for women whose personal values, experiences, and family commitments are likely to differ from those of otherwise comparable men. Even in relatively supportive organizations, many women feel sufficiently uncomfortable that they eventually stand aside from the competition for advancement, quit, seek more conventionally gendered jobs, or create new organizations in which they can affect, if not control, the working environment.

In this chapter, we explore an additional reason for the exodus and the persistence of gender inequality in organizations. This chapter's focus on high-ranking executive women allows us to separate the effects of formal power and gender. These women occupy positions of considerable formal power, but they are disempowered, in some ways, by their gender. We examine a configuration of microprocesses that undermine the formal power of high-ranking women in a male-dominated organization, showing how these women's capacities to reduce systemic causes of gender inequality are therefore more limited than it might appear. In the following section, we introduce Foucault's exploration of the microprocesses that enforce dominant views of appropriate language and behavior and feminist theory's observations that these dominant practices are not gender neutral but rather reflect socially constructed images of masculinity.

Women and Power:
An Uneasy Relationship

Foucault and Feminism:
Power Is in the Details

Foucault focuses on the "microprocesses"—that is, the everyday details of normal working life that appear power neutral—the taken-for-granted "way things are." Foucault shows how microprocesses, such as the physical arrangements of desks in a classroom or cells in a prison, provide nonobvious ways of disciplining and surveilling organizational members, whether they be students or prisoners, into complying voluntarily with the demands of authority figures (Foucault, 1973, 1975, 1979; Gordon, 1980). Foucault (as quoted in Sheridan, 1980, p. 217; cited in Martin, 1988) stated,

> When I think of the mechanics of power, I think of its capillary form of existence, of the extent to which power seeps into the very grain of individuals, reaches right into their bodies, permeates their gestures, their posture, what they wear, how they learn to live and work with other people. (p. 6)

Foucault is adept at analyzing how microprocesses are shaped by the discourse of experts, who define "normal" ways of behaving in language that appears neutral but in fact excludes whole ways of life or habits of behavior as marginalized, inappropriate, and deserving of discipline. Biddy Martin (1988) notes,

> Foucault is able to deconstruct some of the last vestiges of the self-evident and apparently natural, exposing the workings of power in any will to or pretense at truth, finality, or nature. All categories of the natural or the normal, as well as the unnatural or abnormal, are exposed as social constructs rather than distinctions given at the level of the body or individual psyche, categories that have been produced discursively. (p. 10)

According to Foucault, discourse shapes what can be considered "knowledge" and "truth," creating a desire for compliance so that the standard of behavior normalized by experts and reinforced by the surveillance of authorities seems voluntary, is internalized as "natural," and therefore comes to be seen as unchangeable and perhaps even desirable.

Power has many faces (Bachrach & Baratz, 1962; Blau, 1964; French & Raven, 1968; Pfeffer, 1992): It can be vested in a central point, in particular positions of formal authority, in dominant individuals, or in the acquisition of rank in particular hierarchies. In addition, power is inherent in the institutionalized practices and language—the discourse

(Boden, 1994)—we expect and accept as neutral and which we therefore do not even see. Foucault acknowledges the full range of these aspects of power, but he focuses on institutionalized practices and discourse. He argues that power gains its force precisely because it is dispersed, its workings made invisible by the social construction of perceived realities that seem natural and appropriate (Martin, 1988).

Of course, some people and some knowledges are more disempowered than others by a dominant discourse. Although Foucault attended to the ways in which the workings of power systematically subordinate some discourses and privilege others (e.g., prisoners and prison wardens and students and teachers), he virtually ignored gender as an axis of power (Diamond & Quinby, 1988). Despite this shortcoming, feminists have found Foucault's approach to power useful, in part because of his emphasis on the exclusionary effects of experts' systems of classification. In organizations, such classifications are transformed from rhetoric, text, and cognition into material conditions of work (Foucault, 1979). To Foucault's analysis, feminist theory has added consideration of gender, showing how it can be seen as an axis of classification wherein men and all that is masculine can be seen as having power over women and all that is feminine (Kamuf, 1988; Sawicki, 1988). In organizations, gender acts as an ordering principle, creating boundaries between what is considered appropriately masculine and feminine, occupationally and socially dividing men from women, and separating some men from other men and some women from other women (Kerfoot & Knights, 1993, pp. 660-661). These boundaries and classifications are not just cognitive categories; they have the power to affect what people do, where they do it, and how much they are rewarded for their work.

In addition to emphasis on socially constructed and formally institutionalized forms of domination and control, feminists have been drawn to Foucault's analysis of the conformity pressures inherent in the microprocesses of everyday life. Feminist theories analyze the ways men and women, and the systems in which they are embedded, have been shaped by apparently gender-neutral microprocesses to behave in ways that foster and reflect gendered ideas of inequality (Acker, 1990; Alvesson & Billing, 1992; Hearn & Parkin, 1987; Hochschild, 1989; J. Martin, 1990; Meyerson, 1998; Mumby & Putnam, 1992), creating organizational cultures that can be described as "masculine." Conformity in such a context would present particular stress

for many women and some men who do not fit traditional male stereotypes (Ferguson, 1984; Marshall, 1984; Martin & Knopoff, 1997).

Feminists have had one other major criticism of Foucault: his
deemphasis of opportunities for successful resistance and system
change. Foucault stresses the pervasiveness of the microprocesses that
reinforce the power of authorities and underplays the potential impact
of resistance. From his perspective, resistance is mental, hidden, or
transient. To the extent that this type of resistance would occur on a
collective level, it would be fragmented, dispersed, and uncoordinated—a far cry from sociological conceptions of organized collective
action, such as riots or protests (Smelser, 1980).

In contrast to Foucault, feminism is a political as well as a theoretical movement, with the aim of combating the subordination of women.
Feminist versions of resistance move beyond the definitions of resistance as relatively passive, defensive activities that implicitly depict
the resistors as disempowered, such as when workers on a shop floor
engage in work slowdowns, sabotage, or subversive jokes with other
low-ranking employees (Collinson, 1992; Collinson & Hearn, 1996;
Jermier, Knights, & Nord, 1994). Feminists conceptualize resistance as
including proactive, subjective reactions to disadvantage, such as
learning to see gender inequality as unjust (Crosby, 1982; Martin,
Scully, & Levitt, 1990) and refusing to accept subjectivities and identities defined by those in power (Hartsock, 1987; Hooks, 1984).

Although the women's movement has emphasized resistance (especially through consciousness-raising), and some forms of organized
collective action (such as the National Organization for Women, *Ms.*
magazine, and various organized protests; Farrell, 1994), it has been
criticized as being a relatively disorganized social movement, with few
long-term, generally accepted leaders, specific goals, or coordinated
strategies for action (Martin, 1988). Nevertheless, the women's movement, in its dispersed and disorganized fashion, has had some success
in combating the subordination of women. Foucault's insights regarding power may offer a way of conceptualizing the aspects of this social
change effort that are not explained by such familiar concepts as resistance and collective behavior. From a Foucauldian perspective, all
people have power, although all do not have equal formal power
positions. Microprocesses reflect and constitute power in action. Also,
microprocesses can add up to change (Cantril, 1941).

To extend Foucault's ideas with a feminist slant—slow, subtle, but pervasive change can take place as women act, speak, or think in ways that challenge or resist the assumptions of the dominant discourse (Meyerson, Ely, Kolb, Coleman, & Rapoport, 1997; Meyerson & Scully, 1995). Women, especially high-ranking women, may be isolated and have little contact with each other. Their actions may be subtle and unremarkable. These women, however, proactively (and with the help of male allies) may attempt to change a system by helping others see sex and gender issues where previously these concerns were invisible. Meyerson and Scully used the term "tempered radicals" to describe people who attempt to effect change in these ways and who simultaneously struggle with their dual "insider-outsider" identities. Tempered radicals are people who work within an organization or a system for change while seeking to avoid cooptation, false consciousness, burnout, and ineffectiveness as a professional within the system. Despite Meyerson and Scully's emphasis on the common struggles of individual tempered radicals, however, they only hint at the implications for change on a more collective level.

Because high-ranking women are reacting to similar problems of disempowerment (they are all "not men" in an organization dominated by men), their varied individual reactions and solutions may have important commonalties and potential collective implications. When these acts are viewed on a collective level, they appear—or disappear—as fragmented, dispersed, and uncoordinated. These behaviors, however, can be described as the "disorganized coaction" of individuals who are doing somewhat similar things without explicit coordination (Thompson, 1967). The women we studied were not passive, and they were not alone in their struggles. Although they did conform to dominant norms, they also resisted and engaged in disorganized coaction as they struggled to find a place for themselves (and sometimes others) in an organizational culture they all experienced as masculine.

Masculinities at Work

Recent research on masculinities helps explain why and how these women would perceive an organizational culture as masculine. (The plural, "masculinities," acknowledges differences in expectations due, for example, to class and context.) The study of masculinities explores the microprocesses through which organizations come to define men and masculinity as the standard by which normality is defined, creating meanings, policies, and practices that seem gender neutral but are not (Connell, 1995). The meanings and images of masculinities become ordering devices, bases of classification and power. Understanding how these images play out in a particular context provides insight into how "gendering" is accomplished in that context, even if its members are generally unaware of this process (such as when men think gender is a "woman's issue," disregarding the fact they too have a gender). Hearn and Morgan (1991) (as quoted in Kerfoot & Knights, 1993) note,

> Common sense assumptions about men and masculinity in everyday conversation, for example, in pubs, workplaces, on street corners, and in the home, frequently become generalized into implicit notions of how men behave or to what extent individual men are more or less masculine than others. . . . Masculinity, then, from a common-sense perspective is unproblematically what men do and what men are; consequently, men need no more theorize masculinity "than a fish need theorize water" (p. 660)

Research on masculinities is an important development in feminist theorizing (Jardine & Smith, 1987). Although feminists have historically focused their critiques on the ways in which women have been subordinated, theories of masculinity focus primarily on men and offer new insight into the microprocesses that reproduce and normalize power relations between the sexes. (Theories of masculinities also show how men who do not fit dominant images of masculinity are subordinated through microprocesses that reproduce these images.)

Of particular relevance to this chapter is research that has explored the behaviors of men in jobs held predominantly by men (whether on the shop floor, in technical positions, or in executive suites). In such contexts, men enact particular, class-related versions of what it means to seem masculine, take charge, and be in control. Hierarchies provide arenas for a Darwinian struggle for dominance, an overt competition that focuses on actual or perceived competence (Kerfoot & Knights, 1993; Wajcman, 1991). In jobs in which the basis for evaluation is abstract rather than physical (i.e., knowledge rather than strength), criteria for supremacy often entail technical expertise (Zuboff, 1988). Also, because such expertise usually cannot be viewed directly, self-promotion skills and displays of confidence become crucial (Cockburn, 1985):

> Male self-identity is won in a costly tussle with other men for status and prestige, and this applies in technical work no less than in other situations. Those men who seek their masculine identity in technological competence find themselves obliged to maneuver for position and negotiate their rank relative to other men. There are comparisons of competence: the cognoscenti versus the rest. (pp. 178-179)

If apparently gender-neutral organizational cultures can be masculine, in the sense described previously, this may explain some of the difficulties experienced by high-ranking women who try to thrive in the masculine bastions of the executive ranks. Whereas many men in such a context might see themselves as simply doing business in the usual (gender-neutral) way, women in this context might be more likely to see their male colleagues as men acting like men (Martin, 1997). Furthermore, boundary-heightening displays of masculinity (such as sexual joking, physical acting out, interrupting each other, and bragging contests about "who knows more about X," where X could be any topic) are more likely in contexts, such as male-dominated technical environments and executive teams, in which women are present but proportionately rare (Kanter, 1977). In such an environment, some women may feel uncomfortable, from time to time, in ways that many men and women will find it difficult to see as gender related.

This difficulty raises a series of questions. In such a context, what are the ways in which high-ranking women can gain power and advance change? Should women mimic norms of masculinity to acquire power? Would this not present a double threat to male colleagues, who might react strongly to being "one-upped" by a woman? Alternately, should women step aside from the contest? How do high-ranking women successfully challenge and resist norms of masculinity? Also, what might this suggest about possibilities for system-level change?

The following discussion addresses these questions by drawing on the experiences of individual women who hold high-ranking executive positions in a large computer company. Their jobs require technical skills, which seem to shape how masculinity plays out in this context. At the same time that these women are empowered by their formal positions, they are disempowered by the gendered associations that come with being a woman in this context, where—as in most industries—high-ranking women are rare.

This chapter does not attempt to represent the views of the vast majority of women who occupy low-ranking positions in organizations, and it does not assess the validity of claims of relatively measurable unfairness, such as pay and promotion inequality. Instead, we use women's descriptions of their own experiences to illustrate how they perceive the microprocesses of their everyday organizational lives as they struggle to survive in executive positions in which men outnumber women, valued behaviors sometimes have distinctly masculine overtones, and experts urge conformity in apparently gender-neutral terms.

The Link.Com Case Histories

The Corporation and the Women Executives

Link.Com is a pseudonym for a remarkably successful company that supplies high-performance computer products, both hardware and software. The firm has become a legend in a legendary location: the Silicon Valley in California that has spawned many entrepreneurial triumphs in the high-technology industry. Employees throughout the organization benefited from Link.Com's phenomenal financial success through the company's generous stock option policies. Among the beneficiaries were the firm's highest ranking female executives, all but one of whom participated in the current study. At the time our study was conducted, one of these women was both a vice president and corporate officer, another had been promoted to vice presidential (executive committee) status, three others were high-level divisional managers, and the seventh had just been promoted to a middle-level management position. To protect the anonymity of these women and the company, we have changed their names.

We interviewed each of these women in-depth, sometimes more than once. In addition, group interviews among some participants were held, and lengthy telephone and e-mail conversations were used to clarify ambiguous issues. Documentary evidence about the company, when available, was studied. The women gave vivid, frank, and detailed descriptions of the ways they experienced their own power and powerlessness at Link.Com. Page limitations make a full description of these data impossible. We cite a small subset of quotations, drawn from these individual case histories (Martin & Meyerson, 1997),[1] selecting those most germane to the theoretical focus of this chapter.

A Male-Dominated Industry

Although Link.Com's financial success has been exceptional, its proportion of female senior executives and scientific and engineering professionals is not at all unusual for the industry. For example, a study of 100 companies in the computer industry (Hannan, Burton, & Baron, 1996) found that, in 1994 and 1995, the percentage of female employees was as follows:

	Link.Com	Sample Mean
In senior management positions	15%	13.5%
In engineering and scientific positions	26%	16.5%

Using a variety of measures, Link.Com fell approximately in the middle of the distribution of computer industry companies for which sex ratio data were available. This was a male-dominated industry and, within that industry, Link.Com did not have an unusually high or low percentage of women in the top executive or technical ranks.

We have no reason to believe that, in its gender relations, Link.Com was atypical for its industry or perhaps other, male-dominated industries. As will be shown, Link.Com's employee sex ratios were congruent with the ways in which the women we interviewed experienced the gendered nature of its organizational culture. These comparative statistics, however, should not be construed as a claim that insights drawn from studying these seven individuals are a valid source for generalizing to female executives at other companies within or outside of this industry.[2] This is a bounded case study and, as such, it necessarily has a detailed and in-depth focus (Yin, 1989): In this instance, a small number of select individuals who worked at a single company in 1994 and 1995. What we can do is to quote these individuals' expressed points of view with accuracy, interpret them with some understanding of the company and industry in which they worked at that time, and place them in a broader context by drawing on related research.

The women's descriptions of their own experiences, and comparisons across these experiences, provide rich illustrations of the ways in which power and gender intersect within this organizational culture. These data are presented in two parts. The first illustrates, through the women's descriptions, ways in which a culture of masculinity was enacted in a patterned configuration of normalized microprocesses— practices, norms, language, and expressed values. The second part illustrates the variety of ways these women responded to the culture, including conformity, resistance, and disorganized coaction. In each part, we elaborate the illustrations with theory.

Perceptions of the Dominant Culture

Competition and Threats to Individual Identity

Although the senior female executives we interviewed sometimes described the Link.Com culture in gender-neutral terms, explicit references to gender issues were sprinkled throughout their interview transcripts. For example, Masako Hirada, who said she was comfortable and accepted by her male coworkers, used words such as "macho" to interpret the behavior of some of her coworkers (Martin & Meyerson, 1997):

> One on one these men were fine. They were intelligent, logical, and they didn't think women were inferior. But when a conference room became filled with these men, they changed. Their voices got deeper and their chests got bigger. It was a jock thing, very macho. One of them would say, "I worked 50 hours this week," and another would respond, "I worked 60," and all of

a sudden the numbers got bigger and bigger. Each time the fight was harder, longer, and more exhausting. (p. 3)

This instance can be understood as a prototypical struggle for dominance through self-promotion, as the men vied to claim that each worked longer hours than his competitors. Furthermore, although Masako did not mention her presence, the quotation implies that she witnessed this kind of competitive behavior repeatedly; her female presence in such a male-dominated context might well have encouraged the men to act in an exaggerated macho manner (Kanter, 1977).

It is also significant that time acts as the medium of competition—the way "power is done"—in this context. In organizations, time often becomes a symbol of commitment and contribution (Bailyn, 1993) and, accordingly, a basis of classification, reward, and recognition. Time, however, is not a gender-neutral criterion. Because women do a disproportionate share of the housework and dependent care (Hochschild, 1989), it is more difficult for most women, in comparison to most men, to work exceptionally long hours. Women are therefore particularly disadvantaged when time becomes the medium of competition.

Several of the women noted the prevalence of this kind of competitive behavior and called attention to the confrontational norms that prevailed in meetings of the executives at Link.Com. Masako Hirada stated (Martin & Meyerson, 1997),

It was an environment that was brutal—brutally honest. I don't think that it was bad if you could handle it. You had to have a thick skin. There weren't that many women, but it was actually some of the women who had the thickest skin of all. . . . You said what you thought. People screamed at each other. It was quite chaotic and yet very effective. (p. 3)

Some women were more discomforted by these norms. Patricia Sullivan stated (Martin & Meyerson, 1997),

I would walk past that executive staff meeting room, and listen to all the yelling and screaming that was going on, and think, "Why do these people hate each other so much? What could

they possibly be talking about that could require such vitriol?
There is nothing in this company going on that is so important
that they should be yelling like this." (p. 1)

Patricia saw the shouting as indicative of the emotion of anger, but it
was a sanctioned expression of controlled anger—a playacting of violence—that, in the right circumstances, she saw as effective. She said
(Martin & Meyerson, 1997),

> The other thing that was so frustrating was that when these men
> were being violent, they were totally in control. Some of it was
> even orchestrated. So you knew that the worst thing you could
> do was to lose control, because if you tried to be emotional or
> aggressive when you were out of control, it didn't have the
> same impact. (p. 2)

Patricia believed that certain ways of being ("lose control" and "emotional") would be ineffective in this context. Although she did not mention sex differences in this regard, lack of emotional control is often
associated with women and femininity, in contrast to rationality and
control, traits typically associated with men and masculinity (Martin,
Knopoff, & Beckman, in press; Mumby & Putnam, 1992).

At Link.Com, both male and female senior executives were expected to conform to dominant norms: brutal honesty and controlled
anger—which often coalesced in the form of screaming arguments that
had a scripted, playacting quality. Those who failed to conform were
advised to change their behavior. This advice, even when it came from
a supposedly sympathetic expert, was phrased in terms that were apparently gender neutral. Natalie Kramer stated (Martin & Meyerson,
1997),

> Marvin [a consultant hired by Link.Com] told me that as an
> open, participative, and collaborative person, it would be hard
> for me to survive at the company. In this environment, these
> characteristics would be perceived as weakness and put me at
> a disadvantage. They were not qualities valued by this culture.
> So, very early in my career at Link.Com, I was directly con-
> fronted with a problem. I had come to believe that one has to

be authentic to be an effective manager. It takes too much energy to pretend to be someone other than who you are. Now here was somebody advising me to be less open, less participative, less cooperative—to be not the way I am. It was a real dilemma for me. (p. 4)

Feminist researchers have explored the problems women and minorities face when they seek ways of adapting to white male organizational cultures while simultaneously preserving values that are central to their own personal identities (Bell, 1990; hooks, 1984; Meyerson & Scully, 1995). For example, Ibarra (1992, 1993), in a series of studies of such fields as advertising, consulting, and investment banking, found that employees who are demographically different from the norm often found it difficult to create an effective mode of work behavior that felt personally authentic. Natalie illustrates these problems, as she ties herself in knots seeking a way to remain authentic while conforming enough to succeed.

Recent research has challenged the idea that a person can be "authentic" in the sense of remaining congruent with a unified self-conception. Instead, and particularly for women and minorities who work in a white male environment, the self may be more appropriately conceptualized as fragmented, containing overlapping, nested, possibly contradictory components that reflect various aspects of one's identity: race, occupation, working experience, religion, educational background, rank, and so on (Bell, 1990; Flax, 1990; Rosaldo, 1989). With this more complex version of self-identity, it becomes more complicated to ask what it means, and what it costs, for women to conform to the norms of a masculine culture.

The entry of women into male-dominated environments also can raise problems related to male identity and competence. In a controversial paper, Wajcman (1991, p. 38) argues that, for most men, technical skills are a critical part of male identity, creating the potential for widespread insecurity in technically skilled occupations. If a man's technical competence is challenged, he may experience a fear of being unmasculine. Such feelings of threat might have intensified contests for dominance at Link.Com, making men feel they needed to discredit others to preserve their own self-respect, particularly if women were present.

Competition Between Groups

At Link.Com, competitive, aggressive norms were present at the group as well as the individual level of analysis. Individuals were strongly encouraged to become loyal members of groups that then competed, fiercely, in struggles for dominance. Groups protected members of their own teams while attacking members of other coalitions. Patricia remarked (Martin & Meyerson, 1997),

> Loyalty was also part of the dominant culture. I watched senior executives place people in jobs they weren't qualified to do. People made strategic placements around themselves, and that became part of the management culture. . . . There was a pro-Ricardo faction and an anti-Ricardo faction. There was the pro-Ben and the anti-Ben camp. There were all of these camps forming. Every time you tried to have a conversation with anybody on the executive staff, before you were allowed to, you had to declare where you stood in this line-up. . . . The reason why I seemed to be getting pushed further and further to the outside of the inner circle was because I wouldn't commit. I didn't want to take sides. (pp. 4, 5)

Anyone who wanted to stand aside from these warring factions became isolated and excluded from powerful circles. If someone did not belong to a coalition, he or she was constantly scrutinized and tested. Cultural fit, networking, finding mentors, and building alliances are problems for both men and women (Pfeffer, 1992; Schein, 1978), but these problems take a particular shape and intensity for women who work in male-dominated cultures. Most men at this level seemed to align themselves relatively easily with sponsors and coalitions. The senior women we interviewed, however, like women in other organizational settings (Ely, 1991; Ibarra, 1992), found it more difficult to find willing mentors (high-ranking women role models and sponsors were rare), and they were often unaligned or not central in these coalitions and alliances. In addition, Patricia experienced the requirement to declare loyalty to one side or another as a particularly alienating demand. She could not bring herself to form such an alliance (and thus create enemies), even when she was given the opportunity to do so. To her, creating allies and enemies necessarily colored her personal relationships with these people. This process felt alien and artificial. She suspected that this process was more normal and less personal for her male counterparts.

Conformity, Resistance, and Confrontation: The Women's Reactions

Although women vary considerably, they share the experience of being outsiders in male-dominated contexts. As outsiders, they may be particularly sensitive to the ways apparently gender-neutral micro-processes have male overtones and implications (Alcoff, 1988). It is from this outsider position that women may be able to resist and challenge as well as conform to the various microexpressions of masculinity and power. It is to these responses that we now turn, exploring how they vary depending in part on situational factors and in part on the individual preferences of the women executives.

Masako Hirada:
Conformity Within Limits, With Wit

Masako took considerable pleasure in being accepted as a member of a team by her male colleagues. She was willing to conform, to a carefully calibrated extent, to gain acceptance and work effectively in this male environment. She noted (Martin & Meyerson, 1997),

> I wouldn't sit back and let them say horrible things, but I would conform in the sense that I learned to be more willing to take credit for things that I had done. Women generally don't take credit because we believe in working in a team. Men naturally tend to be more aggressive than women. [For a man] it's OK to play hard; it's OK to compete. Whereas, for me, competition with peers is not the focus; the job is. But I've learned to compete. Very few people can be the exception and survive in a company without conforming to some extent. If I came across as not aggressive or competitive, they would think I wasn't interested in challenging projects. However, the men were sometimes threatened by the same aggressiveness they expected from themselves. (p. 4)

In this quotation, Masako suggests she conforms by taking more credit for herself in instances in which she would be inclined to give more credit to her team. In explaining her conformity, she uses the word "naturally" to legitimate her characterization of men as aggressive. Foucault has drawn attention to this word, explaining that it can signal an attempt to frame an observation as an unassailable truth. In this case, what is claimed to be natural is an implicit dichotomy: Men are "naturally" aggressive and competitive, whereas women are not. Any dichotomy exaggerates difference and ignores commonalties, and when such dichotomies are used to speak of sex, this is an instance of what feminist theory terms "essentialist" thinking: All members of one sex are similar to each other and different from members of an opposite sex. Masako uses this dichotomy to say that she, like other women, is more focused on doing a good job than on competing aggressively with others. She explains her willingness to conform to self-promotional norms in terms congruent with this female self-image: She competes not to dominate her male colleagues but to get challenging work. Presumably, this explanation might make her willingness to compete less threatening to them as well as to her self-image as an Asian American and as a woman.

In the last line of the quotation, Masako's apparent contentment with these gendered patterns of behavior disappears, however, as she notes that her male peers saw her "aggressiveness" differently than they saw their own aggression; she was seen as threatening. Thus, conforming to male norms was not a complete solution for Masako because she saw that the same behavior, coming from a woman, was interpreted differently than when it came from a man. She could not win by not conforming to the company's competitive and aggressive cultural norms because she would be seen as not wanting challenging work, but she could not win by conforming because her behavior would be seen as threatening. This dilemma is one of several characterized by Jamieson (1995) as double binds that face women who enter masculine organizational cultures. When men conform to behavioral norms associated with masculinity, their behaviors are seen as men behaving normally or naturally. When women attempt to conform to masculinity norms, however, their behaviors are viewed more skeptically as women trying to act "like men."

Masako was relatively understanding of her male colleagues but not blind to their biases. Hers was a resigned acceptance, almost to say "boys will be boys." She stated (Martin & Meyerson, 1997),

> The men I've worked with tended to be open-minded and fair.
> I don't think they had a problem with women but they tended
> to do things that came naturally to them. You naturally gravi-
> tate toward what you know. If there were some things that
> weren't necessarily fair, I think that [this] was probably the
> cause. Young men coming out of business schools and colleges,
> people of my generation, treated women fairly; it was equal.
> But in this environment the traditional men hired and influ-
> enced the younger guys. After the young guys went through
> the socialization process, I would have to kick them and say,
> "Wait a minute, you weren't like that before. Why are you be-
> having like that? What happened?" And they would say, "Oh,
> yeah, you're right." If I gave them a reminder, then they started
> thinking straight again. It took constant reinforcement. (p. 3)

Masako excused some of this behavior, and even what she saw as unfairness, by characterizing it as men (or at least older men) behaving
naturally. She was willing, however, to confront her colleagues about
what she saw as macho behavior. In another instance, Masako framed
her confrontation as a (successful) joke and used a concept, in this case
the word "testosterone," to attribute the behavior to natural (based in
male physiology) origins (Martin & Meyerson, 1997): "In a smaller gathering, when the men put on their 'macho act,' I said, 'I guess I don't have
enough testosterone for this meeting.' They were used to that from me,
and they laughed" (p. 7). Masako's language again reflects essentialist
assumptions that characterize stereotypically masculine behavior as
natural for men and not for women, even though she had said that she
saw such behavior as something the younger men had to learn during
their socialization into the company's norms. Masako reacts to these
contradictions and double binds by blending conformity with confrontation, using humor to convey dual messages and to take the sting out
of her words.

Kathleen Casey: Rejecting Protection and Reacting With Restraint

In the first years of Link.Com's existence, Kathleen had not been
invited to off-site retreats and other top-level meetings. She believed
that Jim Nelson (the company's chief executive officer [CEO] at the

time) was trying to shelter her and another woman, Diane Caldwell (then manager of human resources), from the yelling and fighting characteristic of these gatherings. She noted (Martin & Meyerson, 1997),

> The impression I got from talking to Jim was that he wanted to protect Diane and myself by keeping our exposure to these confrontational meetings to a minimum. I didn't feel protected; I felt left out. I wanted to see how things worked and I wanted to be able to develop my own understanding of who was saying what and what some of the issues were. (p. 2)

Although Kathleen wanted to be included in executive-level meetings, as befit her title, she was not comfortable with confrontation. Unlike some of the other executive women, Kathleen avoided public discussions of gender-related issues. She noted (Martin & Meyerson, 1997):

> There were times I felt uncomfortable and I would just let it slide—probably more so in the older days before I was a vice president. I did sit in executive staff meetings, but as a director-level person, I didn't feel I had the same level of contribution to make as a lot of the executives there. I would let things pass or sometimes I would speak to people afterwards. Natalie's style was different. I knew there was a story about her saying, "Go to hell," to Jim Nelson. That was not my style. It sounds a little conceited, but I was probably a little bit more personally respectful, no matter what. Natalie was always much more . . . she would make herself stand out. She put her feet on the table in executive staff meetings. I would think, "That's interesting—she's got a dress on, but she's got her feet on the table." (p. 3)

Although Kathleen tried to avoid conflict, when essential, she would confront—but privately so that her colleagues would not be embarrassed. She saw this mode of behavior as respectful and contrasted it with the more confrontative behavior of Natalie Kramer: swearing at more senior executives, drawing attention to herself, and putting her feet on the table. Kathleen refused to conform to these norms, and she apparently disapproved of Natalie doing so. Although it appears to be an insignificant "side comment," Kathleen's calling attention to the image of Natalie wearing a dress and putting her feet on the table frames this as a gender issue. As long as Kathleen disapproves of women engaging in traditionally masculine behaviors, she locates Natalie and herself in a double bind; if women should conform to norms of appropriately respectful, modest, quiet behavior, in accord with traditional feminine stereotypes, these limited behavioral options may impede women's abilities to make their competence evident in a competitive, aggressive environment such as Link.Com.

Patricia Sullivan:
Adjusting to Double Binds

Like Masako, Patricia was conscious of these kinds of double binds, and like Natalie, Patricia eloquently described the difficulty of finding a way to behave that felt personally authentic (Martin & Meyerson, 1997):

> One of the things that would happen in an environment like that was that you would run into these tremendous personal conflicts. You wondered if you had to adapt to that kind of environment in order to survive. You could learn to yell and scream, in which case you knew you were going to hate yourself because you just hated being put into positions where you did things that were inconsistent with your own values about civility. Or, you were faced with not being able to succeed because the rules of engagement were such that you didn't have any weapons that could have helped. (pp. 1-2)

Patricia responded in a variety of ways to the conflict between her "authentic" self-image and the firm's practices and norms. At times she adapted or conformed, at times she resisted and refused to play by the rules, and occasionally she engaged in direct confrontation. Patricia also developed a management style that was different from the more controlling styles of her male peers (Martin & Meyerson, 1997):

> I provided a very high degree of autonomy for most of the people who worked for me. My management style was basi-

cally to give advice about how they could best do their jobs. I
would let them run with it and use me as a last resort or as a
way to get additional guidance. . . . Certainly, in a group like
Peter's, there was only one place where autonomy lay, and that
was with [Peter]. (p. 6)

Over time, according to Patricia, Link.Com's norms of aggressiveness
that had once been so salient seemed to fade from awareness: "It became
like working in the heat without air-conditioning. You just learned to
get used to it" (p. 3). It is hard to tell whether Patricia's resistance and
confrontation had had any effect in changing the culture or whether the
dominant masculine discourse came to seem increasingly normal to
Patricia as she increasingly identified herself as an organizational
insider.

At Link.Com, most forms of emotional expression were viewed as
signs of weakness. The expression of anger, however, seemed to be an
accepted part of the dominant culture. As indicated previously in her
descriptions of "orchestrated" aggression, Patricia believed that anger
was more effective when it was controlled. She eventually learned to
"become violent under control" and claimed that, under the right
circumstances, it was effective (Martin & Meyerson, 1997, p. 3).

This conformity is described as if it were easy, but it required that
Patricia modify her own experienced emotions. Patricia learned to
reinterpret her anger and retool how she expressed it, using her expressed emotions strategically (Martin & Meyerson, 1997):

You could not personalize it. What I found was that the things
that I really felt emotional about were the things that I could
not afford to show emotion or be animate about. . . . You
couldn't show that you were weak and vulnerable. (p. 2)

This is emotional labor (Hochschild, 1983), and it can take a toll.
Hochschild delineates the physiological and psychological stress that
ensues from this kind of emotional labor, including the emotional dead-
ening and distancing that is caused by repeatedly suppressing felt
emotions while expressing contradictory, unfelt feelings. Under such
conditions, if emotional laborers cannot change the emotional demands
of the environment, they sometimes attempt to change the emotions
they spontaneously feel, eventually running the risk of "losing them-

selves" in a corporate persona. This is a deeply personal form of disempowerment, one that, in this case, might have gender implications because "weak and vulnerable" are stereotypical feminine characteristics.

Denise Brousseau:
Learning to Play the Men's Game

Like Patricia, Denise had to learn to refrain from interpreting competition, expressions of anger, and overt aggression as personal attacks. Initially, she felt like an outsider at Link.Com and invested inordinate amounts of time and effort in trying to establish good working relationships with her male peers. She expressed feelings of insecurity (Martin & Meyerson, 1997):

> Before the training program, I had been taking everything personally. I wanted everybody to like me and respect my abilities; that was just partly me—the way I did things. Guys, they liked to go to work, hang around the guys, and then go home. I felt I had to spend so much more energy than most people, getting to know the guys, and trying to make them respect me. One false move and that was one less person I could count on. I really needed resources to do my job. (p. 2)

During a company training program, Denise experienced a moment of illumination (Martin & Meyerson, 1997):

> Then I took a class with about 30 Link.Com managers. The class compared business to a war game, with flanking strategies, a competitor. . . . I had a blast! In fact, I was blowing all these guys away. There was an instructor who defined everything—kind of refereeing it all. We'd have an exercise and I'd be finished before everybody. Guys asked me questions. We would be talking about scenarios and I just wasn't as inhibited as I might have been. I thought, "I'm just as good as they are. I can do this." It was all a game, so I didn't care if I stepped on their toes or hurt them. Once I realized that business is just a game to all these men, it completely changed my outlook. After the war games, I came to the realization that, for the guys, there was nothing

personal involved. It was just like a game. I thought, "Well, I can play games." (p. 2)

The image of a "war game" is a vivid depiction of a competitive struggle for dominance emblematic of a culture of masculinity. Once Denise defined the competition as a game, she could even beat the men at it but still keep her status as an outsider, as long as she could refrain from taking the fight personally.

Where does the power lie in this description? During the war game, Denise exhibited expertise, she was asked for advice, and she showed she could win the game. She gained this credibility and power, however, by entering the game and conforming. To Denise, the game was play and not work. It was unfamiliar and not part of her extensive repertoire of professional and technical education, and it required the ability to depersonalize interpersonal interaction, which was not her preferred way of interacting. Denise believed that this way of competing was experienced as relatively normal and natural by her male peers, but it was a behavior with which she had to learn to become comfortable.

By learning to play this game, however, Denise may have paid a price. Conformity demands are disempowering, in that they suggest that there is nothing problematic or biased about the status quo; it is the individual who is different who must change. This kind of adjustment takes psychological as well as behavioral effort.

In defining her conformity as a game—play and not work—Denise may have escaped the double bind and the limited behavioral options that the other women confronted. Denise was playacting, whereas Patricia was trying to control and retool deeply felt emotions. In some ways, however, the reactions of the two women were similar. Patricia talked of "learning to be violent under control," an "orchestrated" form of anger enactment that could also be interpreted as acting in the sense of learning to disguise one's felt emotions. To conform, even partially, to the norms of this organizational culture, these women had to learn to act roles and (dis)play feelings that were not congruent with their inner emotional states. Everyone faces some conformity pressures in an organization, but when the culture of that firm is masculine and the conformer is a woman, the degree of adjustment—in emotions and cognitions as well as behavior—tends to be greater and the costs of conformity, and nonconformity, are correspondingly high.

Mariana Torcelli:
A Reluctant Warrior

Mariana's story echoes many of the same themes as the women quoted previously. She too saw the competition for power take place in rituals of aggression and machismo: "The higher you screamed, the more powerful you were, and the more you proved your point" (Martin & Meyerson, 1997, p. 4). Mariana was reluctant to "rock the boat," but once she accepted that confrontation was the only way her achievements and competence were going to get recognized, she engaged in conflict with the frankness characteristic of the company norms. For example, when she felt that she was unfairly passed over for promotion, Mariana confronted the decision makers:

> They never explained why they [hired him as a director and kept me as regional manager]. Which to me meant that this happened because I was a woman. That's what I think. I went to Jerry [the vice president who hired my boss] and said, "Why wasn't I considered for that position? Do you think I am not capable?" And he said, "No, you are capable. Mariana, we really have to consider many people" and so on. And I said, "Was I considered?" He as much as said "No." I said, "Why? You've seen me perform—I've been at Link.Com for over 4 years. Why? Why wouldn't you even have that thought?" And then I said, "Were my [male] counterparts considered?" He said, "Yes." (p. 8)

This is a direct confrontation, in some ways, but Mariana refrained from mentioning the central issue in this matter: the accusation of sex discrimination. In a masculine culture, in which the demographics of sex are clearly unequal, women often feel pressured not to raise the systemic issue that lies at the center of their difficulties, even when they recognize it (Ashford et al., 1997). Instead, they allow attributions to be made about individuals, and systemic sex bias (and the sex of different subjects) goes unmentioned, as when Mariana refers simply to "my counterparts." The outcome of such a censored discussion can only be at the individual level because discussion of systemic problems encountered by all members of a group—such as women executives—is absent. This analysis of the discourse of a confrontation reveals how power operates between the lines of a text, emerging in the silences as well as in what is said.

Natalie Kramer:
The Rewards of Confrontation

Natalie was famous, among the women executives at Link.Com, for having told her boss, who happened to be the CEO, Jim Nelson, to "Go to hell" on her first day at Link.Com. On that fateful day, Natalie arrived a little after 9 a.m. Jim greeted her by saying, "What have we here—the mommy track?" Natalie turned to Jim's secretary and said, "How do you say 'Go to hell' to your new boss?" Natalie immediately saw, from Jim's reaction, that this was hardly an auspicious start, and she made a conscious effort to seek a better fit between her language and Jim's preferences (Martin & Meyerson, 1997):

> I could see I had made him uncomfortable. When I said "Go to hell" it was clear he didn't like women using that kind of language. He didn't like aggressiveness in women—"pushy broads." I changed my language. I did not swear or use foul language at Link.Com. I rarely expressed anger to him, although others did. (p. 1)

Although Natalie tempered her language, she remained an outspoken advocate for women and, relatively rare at Link.Com, a willing confronter when sex and unfairness collided. Natalie's unwillingness to collude in silence about the gendered nature of the culture—to pretend that it was natural, normal, or appropriate—made her less than popular among some of her male peers. These difficulties were exacerbated by her direct style of confrontation. Natalie's executive assistant, Ana Ibarra, was an astute observer of the company's gendered norms, and she saw a clear contrast between Natalie's style of confrontation and that of most of her male colleagues in the executive committee (Martin & Meyerson, 1997):

> Natalie was very outspoken when she thought the company was not going in the right direction. [In contrast] the men would go with the trend—with the consensus. Or if they were going to disagree, they would do it in a softer way so they weren't

really being confrontational. . . . The men didn't like her out-
spokenness. It was as if they were saying, "You are going to be
put in your place. And this is not your place." I think a lot of it
was because she was a woman. I think they would have taken
that style from a man. (p. 5)

Natalie openly engaged in conflict and thereby conformed to masculine norms of confrontation, and she violated expectations of appropriate "feminine" behavior, such as deference and avoidance of conflict.
Even if she wore a dress, she also put her feet on the table. This carefully
calibrated balance of conformity and nonconformity, congruent with
the double bind experienced by many of the other women executives,
had its personal and professional costs for Natalie. Ana's predictions of
trouble proved to be prescient (Martin & Meyerson, 1997):

So Natalie did fight for herself. It was so hard to watch it, week
after week, month after month. And to see the toll it took on
her. I would think, "This is going to destroy her." I didn't see
how she could come in every day. I would never have done that.
You couldn't pay me enough to put up with that. There were
some weekends when I would go home on Friday, and I didn't
know if on Monday she would be there. (p. 5)

As soon as her stock options matured, Natalie quit Link.Com and
formed her own organization. Natalie's boss Jim and his wife Susan
arranged a party, at which Natalie received an award in recognition of
her accomplishments and devotion to the company. Natalie stated
(Martin & Meyerson, 1997),

When Jim Nelson moved from being president and CEO to
chairman of the board of Link.Com, his wife, Susan, organized
a "repotting" party. Jim gave a speech and had plaques made
for some of the original corporate officers, including me. My
plaque was inscribed with letters that said, "Natalie Kramer,
Building Gender Awareness at Link.Com, 1989-1993." I felt
some ambivalence about this plaque. On the one hand, I had
worked hard to be the best I could be in my job. I wanted to be
recognized for my professional contributions to the success of
the company. I believed that Nelson's intent was to acknowl-

edge the impact I had on his own development and his awareness of gender issues in the workplace. He thought he was recognizing me for something that was important to me, and it
was. I believed it was also important to him. Still, I would rather
have had him say, "Natalie, she was a great marketer." (p. 1)

Natalie's plaque illustrates how work gets valued and devalued in a
masculine culture. She was getting thanked for what must have been,
at times, a thankless task, and there was considerable evidence that
Jim's appreciation for Natalie's efforts to improve gender inequality
was genuine and heartfelt. Furthermore, the presentation of the plaque
was a way of honoring Natalie and her work at Link.Com.

Nevertheless, this was a company and a culture that rewarded
technical expertise. By calling attention in a very public forum to
Natalie's efforts in the less valued arena of gender awareness, the
plaque both revalued that arena positively and devalued Natalie's
technical contributions (as head of marketing) to the company's success. In a sense, Natalie's expertise had been "feminized," disconnect-
ing her from other well-established aspects of her expertise that were
more generally valued. Although the intention may have been to value
a central and authentic part of Natalie as a person, she felt as if her
other contributions to the company—the ones valued by those in
power—simply were discounted. What both Jim and Natalie failed to
consider is that both aspects of her performance could have been
praised—at the same time.

Women, Power, and Change:
Implications for Theory

This examination of the experiences of high-ranking women has
provided a leverage point for examining the intersection of power and
gender. Although these women had considerable formal power, examination of informal power resources (such as mentors, central positions
in networks, and coalition membership) revealed widespread evidence
of disempowerment. Although such a disjunction between formal and
informal power resources is congruent with prior research (Pfeffer,
1992), these women exhibited a pattern of disempowerment directly
related to their status as women working in a male world.

Theories of Masculinities

Link.Com had a masculine culture, characterized by self-promotion, overt struggles for competition, and interpersonal norms that condoned yelling and other forms of controlled aggression. As the masculinity literature predicts for technical occupations, these competitive struggles were intense at Link.Com. It is possible, although we cannot confirm this given the limitations of the data, that these competitions were particularly fierce when one or more of these high-ranking women were present. Under such conditions, stereotypically masculine behavior intensifies, heightening differences between the sexes (Kanter, 1977) (as well as creating discomfort for some men) and shoring up male identities threatened, perhaps, by the presence of women with equal technical skills (Kerfoot & Knights, 1993; Wajcman, 1991). These norms were reinforced by ostensibly gender-neutral organizational practices that worked to the advantage of men and created a context in which women engaged as "not men." For example, long hours were viewed as evidence of corporate commitment, a norm that worked against women, who usually carry a disproportionate share of the responsibilities for dependent care (Bailyn, 1993; Hochschild, 1989).

Foucault and Feminism:
Microprocesses That Disempower

In accord with a feminist extension of Foucault's ideas, power relations between the sexes in this context were enacted and reinforced by a myriad of microprocesses. Thus, in this context gender inequality was not attributed to specific actions of individual, malevolent discriminators. Instead, gender inequality was seen as the product of a series of institutionalized practices, including the placing of allegedly unqualified group members in desirable jobs as a reward for loyalty; the need for forceful, brutally honest, even semiviolent argumentation in meetings; and the allocation of challenging work to those who promoted themselves most actively. These ostensibly gender-neutral practices were gendered. Conformity to these norms was generally more problematic for women, in part because many men and some women, like Kathleen, disapproved when women engaged in the stereotypically male behaviors, such as aggression and competition, that were expected in this context.

Microprocesses, according to Foucault, also include habits of discourse, especially attempts to naturalize certain behaviors, thereby excluding alternative behavioral options. For example, aggressive, competitive behavior was labeled by Masako as "natural" for men but not for women. She excused discriminatory behavior by men in similar terms, saying they "naturally gravitate" to the familiar. Without using the word natural, Patricia expressed a similar sentiment when she described acclimation to the company's aggressive culture as similar to the process of gradually becoming unaware of air-conditioning.

Foucault urges attention particularly to the discourse of experts. In this context, one outside expert counseled Natalie, in ostensibly gender-neutral language, that her preference for open, participative, and collaborative relations should be abandoned because it would be perceived as weakness. Instead, he urged her to conform to the company's competitive norms to enhance her chances of success and acceptance. Taken as a patterned whole, these microprocesses reinforce the masculine tone of the environment at Link.Com.

These executive women had formal power; they were insiders. They worked in contexts dominated by men and masculinities, however, and, to greater and lesser extents, experienced the culture as outsiders. It is from this outsider stance of being not men (Alcoff, 1988) that the women could see the ways in which ostensibly gender-neutral microprocesses enhanced the power of their male colleagues.

Conformity, Resistance, and Disorganized Coaction

As each of the women described her reactions to this working atmosphere, she included a complex mixture of conformity, resistance, and confrontation to gendered norms. These women faced a double bind: If they simply conformed to the norms of this culture, they would be departing from stereotypically feminine behavior. As Masako explained clearly, some of the men would not have welcomed women behaving the same way men were expected to behave. The women, therefore, could not simply conform because these demands were contradictory. Most of the women conformed in some ways, such as when Masako learned to take credit for her accomplishments, Patricia exhibited controlled violence, Denise dared to compete with male colleagues, Mariana confronted her boss, and Natalie stopped swearing in front of her boss. The women varied in their conformity to traditionally feminine stereotypes, with most exhibiting a contradictory mix of behaviors, such as when Natalie wore a dress but put her feet on the table. The women were generally expected to be silent about gender-related difficulties (although a few men, such as Jim Nelson and some of Masako's colleagues, were sometimes open to these issues). Most of the women tended, most of the time, to conform to these expectations of silence, such as when Kathleen said she tended to let such things "slide." Even when Mariana confronted the reasons for her failure to be promoted, she did not say that she thought her sex was a cause.

Resistance in this context was primarily subjective. We had no evidence that these women engaged in overt kinds of resistance, such as sabotage or work slowdowns, although even if they had wanted to do so, they lacked the necessary numbers for this kind of collective behavior. These women did not blind themselves, however, to difficulties caused by sex. They noticed when women were treated unfairly or with disrespect (Ana, Patricia, and Masako were particularly acute analysts of these issues). They all mentioned times when men, or men's ways, were given undue preference. Even when the environment clearly pressured them to conform, they kept a sense of how their own values differed (e.g., Patricia's enduring commitment to civility). Patricia and Natalie, in particular, agonized about finding ways to survive at Link.Com and retain a sense of personal authenticity (Bell, 1990; Ibarra, 1993).

Their subjective resistance to conformity pressures entailed various forms of personal distancing. Here, Kelman's (1964) distinction among three degrees of conformity is germane. Compliance is external, without altering internal beliefs. Identification entails copying a role model, also without deep internal change. In contrast, internalization requires a realignment of one's internal beliefs with external demands. Of these three modes of conformity, identification was not much of a force in this context in part because role models for these high-ranking women were rare. These women generally refrained from internalization because they did not approve of the norms of aggression, brutal honesty, and yelling. Instead, they complied in limited ways, trying to distance themselves from conflict by "not taking it personally."

The distancing entailed in not taking things personally was most evident in Patricia's role playing of controlled violence while refraining from expressing deeply felt emotions that would be perceived as weak. Similarly, Denise distanced her internal self from her outward compliance with competitive norms by defining the expected behavior as a game she was playing. By defining their behavior using metaphors from playacting and theater, these women psychologically protected their difference, and preserved their integrity, while complying enough to perform effectively in this environment. Their subjective resistance was a crucially important mental component of this delicate balancing act.

Finally, these women did sometimes refuse to conform. They were generally reluctant to engage in confrontation, particularly on issues of gender in which costs were perceived as high (Ashford et al., 1997). On occasion, however, most of them did so. Masako used jokes, Kathleen preferred private, one-on-one discussions, Mariana confronted as a last resort, and Patricia tried to model a different kind of management behavior in the realms under her control. Only Natalie argued gender issues openly and often, despite the personal costs she had to bear.

These women did not, to any significant extent, coordinate these acts of confrontation, and their numbers were so small that their actions did not fit the definition of collective behavior as this term is used by sociologists. Although they knew of each other's existence, and even occasionally got together in pairs or small subgroups, these meetings were infrequent and close friendships were rare. Only Natalie made an attempt to serve as a mentor or organize group activities, but these activities were notable for being exceptional. These women did engage in individual acts of nonconformity, however, and these acts stemmed from a shared problem: being not men in a masculine working environment. Therefore, to some extent, their uncoordinated efforts had a common effect of raising gender awareness. It was as if they were, each working separately, trying to kill sex discrimination with a thousand pin pricks. This uncoordinated reaction by a group of individuals who share a social identity is an example of what we term disorganized coaction.

The Question of Effectiveness

Is disorganized coaction ultimately a successful strategy? In this context, as in numerical studies of gender inequality in other contexts, the answer is yes and no. The "no" component is easy to determine. Fighting a dominant culture takes considerable persistence and the willingness to keep fighting despite great odds and no-win double binds. Eventually, anyone would get discouraged and tired, psychologically and physiologically. Given these high costs and great difficulties, it is not surprising that as of 1997, three of these seven women had left Link.Com, in accord with the national exodus of high-ranking women from large corporations. One woman took an extended leave. Another quit to form her own organization. A third got a coveted promotion—at a competing firm. The remaining four decided to stay at Link.Com, and these four seemed to be doing well, most getting promoted. By 1997, a few new women had been promoted to the highest executive ranks at Link.Com, so the percentage of women in high-ranking positions remained virtually the same. From this viewpoint, the more things changed, the more they stayed the same.

A more optimistic assessment of the effectiveness of disorganized coaction is also plausible. The women of Link.Com all prospered financially—a material sign of success that is crucially important in the battle for change in gender inequality—and all were promoted, some more than once. Those who left Link.Com are continuing disorganized coaction in their new organizational contexts. These women changed the working environment at Link.Com in individual, fragmented, and subtle ways that affected others as well as themselves. They created wedges in the dominant discourse and demonstrated the viability of alternate ways of behaving. Just pointing to the gendered nature of norms, as when Masako labeled behavior as testosterone-induced, is a refusal to allow the illusion of gender neutrality to prevail. Such a proactive stance teaches gender awareness in a context in which, to some, the advantages awarded to men may seem invisible, like air-conditioning to people or water to a fish.

Meyerson and Scully (1995) claimed that tempered radicals often become discouraged because it is so difficult to see any concrete results of their actions. Similarly, it may be easy to underestimate the impact—and power—of disorganized coaction because its effects are usually small scale and subtle—often surfacing in microprocesses. Some efforts are easy to dismiss as not important, such as subjective forms of resistance or rhetorical acts that entail a refusal to accept dominant ways of thinking—or not thinking—about gender (Hartsock, 1987; Hooks, 1984). Disorganized coaction is not integrated and overt, like a strike or riot, but it is also harder to combat and less likely to trigger backlash (Weick, 1984). Disorganized coaction may be an important component of the success of social movements, which spread by contagion and can trigger large-scale change, often by a series of small wins rather than a single, major victory (McCarthy & Zald, 1977; Smelser, 1980). The women's movement has made some progress in the past few decades, and some of that progress is due not just—and perhaps not even primarily—to isolated acts of collective behavior, such as organized protests or class action suits. Instead, much of the progress is the result of disorganized coaction as large numbers of men and women, in homes and organizations across the globe, struggle against gender inequality without coordination (Martin, 1988). This is why it is important that the women of Link.Com were not always silent when their gender proved disempowering. Increasingly, researchers are also interested in breaking silence on this subject and coming to understand when claims of gender neutrality are appropriate and when they are not.

Notes

1. This collection of cases, written in a style suitable for classroom use, includes a description of the company as well as individual cases for each of the seven women.
2. Silicon Valley may be an extreme or even unique context.

References

Acker, J. (1990). Hierarchies, jobs, bodies: A theory of gendered organizations. *Gender & Society, 4,* 139-158.

Acker, J., & Van Houten, D. (1976). Differential recruitment and control: The sex structuring of organizations. *Administrative Science Quarterly, 19,* 152-163.

Alcoff, L. (1988). Cultural feminism versus poststructuralism: The identity crisis in feminist theory. *Signs, 13,* 405-436.

Alvesson, M., & Billing, Y. (1992). Gender and organization: Towards a differentiated understanding. *Organization Studies, 13*(2), 73-102.

Ashford, S., Dutton, J., & Edwards, J. (1997, August). *Decomposing demographic effects: The impact of gender proportions on issue-selling initiation.* Paper presented at Academy of Management, Boston.

Bachrach, P., & Baratz, M. (1962). Two faces of power. *American Political Science Review, 56,* 947-952.

Bailyn, L. (1993). *Breaking the mold: Women, men and time in the new corporate world.* New York: Free Press.

Baron, R., & Morris, G. (1976). Sexual divisions and the dual labour market. In D. L. Barker & S. Allen (Eds.), *Dependence and exploitation in work and marriage* (pp. 47-69). London: Longman.

Bell, F. (1990). The bicultural life experience of career-oriented black women. *Journal of Organizational Behavior, 11,* 459-478.

Bielby, W., & Baron, J. (1986). Men and women at work: Sex segregation and statistical discrimination. *American Journal of Sociology, 91*(4), 759-799.

Blau, F., & Ferber, M. (1987). Occupations and earnings of women workers. In K. Koziara, M. Moskow, & L. Tanner (Eds.), *Working women: Past, present, future* (pp. 37-68). Washington, DC: BNA Books.

Blau, P. (1964). *Exchange and power in social life.* New York: John Wiley.

Blum, L., & Smith, V. (1988). Women's mobility in the corporation: A critique of the politics of optimism. *Signs, 13*(3), 528-545.

Boden, D. (1994). *The business of talk: Organizations in action.* Cambridge, MA: Polity.

Brush, C., & Hisrich, R. (1986). *The woman entrepreneur: Starting, financing, and managing a successful new business.* Boston: Lexington Books.

Calas, M. (1993). Deconstructing charismatic leadership: Re-reading Weber from the dark side. *Leadership Quarterly, 4,* 305-328.

Calas, M., & Smircich, L. (1992). Re-writing gender into organization theorizing: Directions from feminist perspectives. In M. Reed & M. Hughes (Eds.), *Re-thinking organizations: New directions in organizational research and analysis.* London: Sage.

Cantor, D., & Bernay, T. (1992). *Women in power: The secrets of leadership.* Boston: Houghton Mifflin.

Cantril, H. (1941). *The psychology of social movements.* New York: John Wiley.

Catalyst. (1996). *Measuring up for women in business and the professions* [Annual report]. New York: Author.

Clegg, S. (1989). *The frameworks of power.* London: Sage.

Cockburn, C. (1985). *Machinery of dominance: Women, men and technical know-how.* London: Pluto Press.

Cockburn, C. (1991). *In the way of women: Men's resistance to sex equality in organizations.* Ithaca, NY: ILR.

Collinson, D. (1992). *Managing the shopfloor: Subjectivity, musculinity, and workplace culture.* Berlin: de Gruyter.

Collinson, D., & Hearn, J. (1996). "Men at work": Multiple masculinities in multiple workplaces. In M. M. A. Ghaill (Ed.), *Understanding masculinities: Social relations and cultural areas* (pp. 61-76). Buckingham, UK: Open University.

Connell, R. (1995). *Masculinities.* Cambridge, MA: Polity.

Crosby, F. (1982). *Relative deprivation & working women.* Oxford, UK: Oxford University Press.

Diamond, I., & Quinby, L. (Eds.). (1988). *Feminism & Foucault: Reflections on resistance.* Boston: Northeastern University Press.

Ely, R. (1991). Gender difference: What difference does it make? *Academy of Management Best Paper Proceedings,* 363-367.

Farrell, A. (1994). A social experiment in publishing: *Ms.* magazine, 1972-1989. *Human Relations, 47,* 707-730.

Ferguson, K. (1984). *The feminist case against bureaucracy.* Philadelphia: Temple University Press.

Ferguson, K. (1991). *The man question: Visions of subjectivity in feminist theory.* Berkeley: University of California Press.

Ferree, M., & Martin, P. (Eds.). (1995). *Feminist organizations*. Philadelphia: Temple University Press.

Flax, J. (1990). *Thinking fragments: Psychoanalysis, feminism, and postmodernism in the contemporary west*. Berkeley: University of California Press.

Foucault, M. (1973). *Madness and civilization: A history of insanity in the age of reason* (R. Howard, Trans.). New York: Vintage/Random House.

Foucault, M. (1975). *The birth of the clinic: An archaeology of medical perception* (A. M. Sheridan Smith, Trans.). New York: Vintage/Random House.

Foucault, M. (1979). *Discipline and punishment: The birth of the prison* (A. Sheridan, Trans.). New York: Vintage/Random House.

French, J., Jr., & Raven, B. (1968). The bases of social power. In D. Cartwright & A. Zander (Eds.), *Group dynamics* (3rd ed., pp. 259-269). New York: Harper & Row.

Gordon, C. (Ed.). (1980). *Power/knowledge: Selected interviews and other writings, 1972-1977*. New York: Pantheon.

Hannan, M., Burton, D., & Baron, J. (1996). Inertia and change in the early years: Employment relations in young, high technology firms. *Industrial and Corporate Change, 5*, 503-536.

Harlan, A., & Weiss, C. (1982). Sex differences in factors affecting managerial career advancement. In P. Wallace (Ed.), *Women in the workplace* (pp. 59-100). Boston: Auburn House.

Hartmann, H., & Reskin, B. (Eds.). (1986). *Women's work, men's work: Sex segregation on the job*. Washington, DC: National Academy Press.

Hartsock, N. (1985). *Money, sex, and power: Toward a feminist historical materialism*. Boston: Northeastern University Press.

Hartsock, N. (1987). Foucault on power: A theory for women? In M. Lejnaar, K. Davis, C. Helleman, J. Oldersmaa, & D. Vos (Eds.), *The gender of power*. Leiden: University of Leiden Press.

Hearn, J., & Morgan, D. (Eds.). (1991). *Men, masculinities and social theory*. London: Unwin Hyman.

Hearn, J., & Parkin, W. (1987). *"Sex" at "work": The power and paradox of organization sexuality*. New York: St. Martin's.

Hochschild, A. (1983). *The managed heart*. Berkeley: University of California Press.

Hochschild, A. (1989). *The second shift: Working parents and the revolution at home*. New York: Viking.

hooks, b. (1984). *Feminist theory from margin to center*. Boston: South End.

Ibarra, I. (1992). Homophily and differential returns: Sex differences in network structure and access in an advertising firm. *Administrative Science Quarterly, 37*, 422-447.

Ibarra, I. (1993). Personal networks of women and minorities in management: A conceptual framework. *Academy of Management Review, 18*(1), 56-87.

Jamieson, K. (1995). *Beyond the double bind: Women and leadership*. New York: Oxford University Press.

Jardine, A., & Smith, P. (Eds.). (1987). *Men in feminism*. New York: Routledge.

Jermier, J., Knights, D., & Nord, W. (1994). *Resistance and power in organizations*. New York: Routledge.

Kamuf, P. (1988). Penelope at work: Interruptions in a room of one's own. In I. Diamond & L. Quinby (Eds.), *Feminism & Foucault: Reflections on resistance* (pp. 149-164). Boston: Northeastern University Press.

Kanter, R. (1977). *Men and women of the corporation*. New York: Basic Books.

Karsten, M. (1994). *Management and gender: Issues and attitudes*. Westport, CT: Praeger.

Kelman, H. (1964). Compliance, identification, and internalization: Three processes of attitude change. *Journal of Conflict Resolution, 2,* 51-66.

Kerfoot, D., & Knights, D. (1993). Management, masculinity and manipulation: From paternalism to corporate strategy in financial services in Britain. *Journal of Management Studies, 30*(4), 559-677.

Lee, B. (1993). The legal and political realities for women managers: The barriers, the opportunities, and the horizon ahead. In E. Fagenson (Ed.), *Women in management, 4* (pp. 219-245). Newbury Park, CA: Sage.

Leidner, R. (1991). Serving hamburgers and selling insurance: Gender, work, and identity in interactive service jobs. *Gender & Society, 5,* 154-177.

Lipman-Blumen, J. (1997). *The connective edge: Leading in an interdependent world.* San Francisco: Jossey-Bass.

Lord, C., Ross, L., & Lepper, M. (1979). Biased assimilation and attitude polarization: The effects of prior theories on subsequently considered evidence. *Journal of Personality and Social Psychology, 37,* 2098-2109.

Marshall, J. (1984). *Women managers: Travellers in a male world.* Chichester, UK: Wiley.

Martin, B. (1988). Feminism, criticism, and Foucault. In I. Diamond & L. Quinby (Eds.), *Feminism & Foucault: Reflections on resistance* (pp. 6-13). Boston: Northeastern University Press.

Martin, J. (1990). Deconstructing organizational taboos: The suppression of gender conflict in organizations. *Organizational Science, 4,* 339-359.

Martin, J. (1994). The organization of exclusion: Institutionalization of sex inequality, gendered faculty jobs, and gendered knowledge in organizational theory and research. *Organization, 1,* 401-431.

Martin, J., & Knopoff, K. (1997). The gendered implications of apparently gender-neutral theory: Re-reading Weber. In E. Freeman & A. Larson (Eds.), *Ruffin lecture series Vol. 3: Business ethics and women's studies.* Oxford, UK: Oxford University Press.

Martin, J., Knopoff, K., & Beckman, C. (in press). An alternative to bureaucratic impersonality and emotional labor: Bounded emotionality at The Body Shop. *Administrative Science Quarterly.*

Martin, J., & Meyerson, D. (1997). *Executive women at Link.Com* [Teaching cases]. Cambridge, MA: Harvard Business School Press, Stanford University Case Number 0B33.

Martin, J., Scully, M., & Levitt, B. (1990). Injustice and the legitimation of revolution: Damning the past, excusing the present, and neglecting the future. *Journal of Personality and Social Psychology, 59*(2), 281-290.

Martin, P. (1990). Rethinking feminist organizations. *Gender & Society, 4,* 182-206.

Martin, P. (1997, February). *The mobilization of masculinities.* Paper presented at Interdisciplinary Conference of Organizational Studies, University of Michigan, Ann Arbor.

McCarthy, J., & Zald, M. (1977). Resource mobilization and social movement: A partial theory. *American Journal of Sociology, 82,* 1212-1241.

Meyerson, D. (1998). Feeling stressed and burned out: A feminist reading and revisioning of stress-related emotions in medicine and organization science. *Organization Science, 9,* 103-118.

Meyerson, D., Ely, R., Kolb, D., Coleman, G., & Rapoport, R. (1997, April). *Toward gender equity: A framework of organizational change and a report on work in progress.* Paper presented at Stanford Law School Faculty Seminar, Stanford University, Stanford, CA.

Meyerson, D., & Scully, M. (1995). Tempered radicalism and the politics of ambivalence and change. *Organization Science, 6,* 585-600.

Mills, A., & Tancred, P. (Eds.). (1992). *Gendering organizational analysis.* Newbury Park, CA: Sage.

Morrison, A., White, R., Van Velsor, E., and the Center for Creative Leadership. (1992). *Breaking the glass ceiling: Can women reach the top of America's largest corporations?* Reading, MA: Addison-Wesley.

Mumby, D., & Putnam, L. (1992). The politics of emotion: A feminist reading of bounded rationality. *Academy of Management Review, 17,* 465-485.

Northcraft, G., & Gutek, B. (1993). Point-counter-point: Discrimination against women in management—Going, going, gone or going but never gone? In E. Fagenson (Ed.), *Women in management, 4* (pp. 219-245). Newbury Park, CA: Sage.

Okin, S. (1989). *Justice, gender, and the family.* New York: Basic Books.

Olsen, F. (1983). The family and the market: A study of ideology and legal reform. *Harvard Law Review, 96*(7), 1497-1578.

Pettigrew, T., & Martin, J. (1987). Shaping the organizational context for black American inclusion. *Journal of Social Issues, 43,* 41-78.

Pfeffer, J. (1977). The ambiguity of leadership. *Academy of Management Review, 2,* 104-112.

Pfeffer, J. (1992). *Managing with power: Politics and influence in organizations.* Boston: Harvard Business School.

Rosaldo, R. (1989). *Culture & truth: The remaking of social analysis.* Boston: Beacon.

Rosener, J. (1995). *America's competitive secret: Utilizing women as a management strategy.* New York: Oxford University Press.

Sawicki, J. (1988). Identity politics and sexual freedom: Foucault and feminism. In I. Diamond & L. Quinby (Eds.), *Feminism & Foucault: Reflections on resistance* (pp. 177-191). Boston: Northeastern University Press.

Schein, E. (1978). *Career dynamics: Matching individual and organizational needs.* Reading, MA: Addison-Wesley.

Sheridan, A. (1980). *Michel Foucault: The will to truth.* New York: Tavistock.

Smelser, N. (1980). Theoretical issues of scope and problems. In M. Pugh (Ed.), *Collective behavior: A source book* (pp. 7-11). St. Paul, MN: West.

Strober, M. (1982). The MBA: Same passport to success for women and men? In P. Wallace (Ed.), *Women in the workplace* (pp. 25-55). Boston: Auburn House.

Thompson, J. (1967). *Organizations in action.* New York: McGraw-Hill.

Wajcman, J. (1991). Patriarchy, technology, and conception of skill. *Work and Occupations, 18*(1), 29-45.

Weick, C. (1984). Small wins: Redefining the scale of social problems. *American Psychologist, 39,* 40-49.

Yin, R. (1989). *Case study research: Design and methods.* Newbury Park, CA: Sage.

Zuboff, S. (1988). *In the age of the smart machine.* New York: Basic Books.

15

Championing Charged Issues

The Case of Gender Equity Within Organizations

SUSAN J. ASHFORD

Organizations are collectives with a purpose. They exist to get things done (Barnard, 1968). Their purpose at any moment is reflected in the organization's agenda. This agenda of issues represents the firm's priorities (Dutton, 1997). The agenda is constantly shifting incrementally at its margin, however, in both the content of the issues contained within it (i.e., what is considered relevant to the organizational purpose) and in the relative priority of the various issues.

One relevant question about this agenda of issues is who creates (defines) it and who maintains and alters it through time. If recent

AUTHOR'S NOTE: I thank Paula Caproni, Jane Dutton, and Jim Walsh for their comments on earlier drafts of this chapter. I also thank the University of Michigan Business School, the Interdisciplinary Committee on Organizational Studies, and the vice president for research, University of Michigan, for their financial support for the research. I also thank Mari Sederdal for her help with data coding and the initial analyses.

strategy researchers (Langley, Mintzberg, Pitcher, Posada, & Saint-Macary, 1995) are correct that the essence of organizations is the processing of issues, then who controls the agenda is critical. As Pfeffer (1992, p. 245) notes, "Perhaps the scarcest resource in organizations is attention. Time spent attending to one issue is time not devoted to other concerns." Therefore, what issues make it onto the agenda matters for what actions organizations take (Kingdon, 1984). Traditionally, the control and maintenance of the agenda has been considered to be the province of the top management group. Dutton and Ashford (1993) and others (Burgelman, 1990; Noda & Bower, 1996), however, have pointed out that issues are also raised from within by lower-level managers. In fact, these authors argue that middle managers fight to get the attention of top management for deserving issues.

In this fight, not all issues are created equally. Some issues (e.g., a financial development that will save the firm millions) may easily get on the agenda, whereas other issues may have difficulty getting a hearing in an organization. In fact, organizations develop routines that defend members against disquieting messages (Argyris, 1985). As Schein (1986, p. 175) stated, "In every organization, cultural rules will evolve that make certain issues undiscussable . . . there will be conditions under which the truth will not be told." Sellers too collude in this process out of their fears about raising controversial or radical ideas (Meyerson & Scully, 1995). This chapter generates some ideas and observations about how the nature of an issue might affect middle managers' decisions to engage in the fight for the attention of top management for their issues. My specific focus will be on issues that I believe are particularly problematic for organizations. These may be issues that challenge prevailing ideology, issues that are divisive, or issues that are outside of the business mainstream (although a business reason for their consideration can be articulated).

For lower-level managers and employees, engaging in this process is an attempt at upward influence. It is also an attempt to define some condition (event, development, or trend) occurring within the environment or within the firm as an issue or a problem worthy of the firm's attention. Dutton and Ashford (1993) label this upward-influence and social-definition process "issue selling." By issue selling, middle mangers attempt to bring about organizational change. It is notable that this perspective gives a different view of the impetus and energy for organizational change. Traditionally, depictions of organizational change focus on top-management-initiated change that is of fairly large scale, preplanned, and pushed down the hierarchy. Issue selling, in contrast, raises the possibility of change initiatives from those within the organization (and often closer to the action) that occur in a more haphazard, opportunistic fashion as conditions demand and concern topics that may be new (and, on occasion, even offensive or seemingly irrelevant) to those in the top organizational levels. The choice to engage in such change efforts, however, may be a very difficult one regarding some issues. These choices, however, are important due to the adaptive value of this behavior for the organization.

The Adaptive Value of Issue Selling

Dutton and Ashford (1993) argued that as today's business environments become more complex (Kiernan, 1993) and as organizations become more complex internally (with hierarchy replacing teams, spans of control increasing, and a more diverse workforce), top-management groups lack the cognitive and attentional capacity to fully monitor and represent the factors that must be accounted for in making effective decisions. Therefore, top-management groups that obtain input from multiple sources (including lower levels of their organizations) will create and work from issue agendas that better reflect the complexity in the environment (both external and internal) (Dutton & Ashford, 1993). These firms should have an adaptive advantage over firms that ignore such input (Dutton & Ashford, 1993).

Issue selling has adaptive value because it allows the organization to hear about issues not on top-management's agenda. Organizations may suffer if they do not allow for the expression of potentially contentious issues. A milieu that stifles issue selling may delay resource investments in potentially important issues, contributing to confusion and the elevation of costs. Well-known disasters, such as Union Carbide's chemical leak at Bhopal (Shrivastava, 1992), the struggle with the health risks of breast implants at Dow Chemical (Ginzel, Kramer, & Sutton, 1993), and the Challenger disaster (Starbuck & Milliken, 1988), provide vivid accounts of the difficulties individuals and organizations encounter when trying to direct attention toward contentious issues. Dutton and Dukerich (1991) described the Port Authority of New York and New Jersey's delay in treating homelessness as a serious strategic issue, and they delineate the damage that this time delay created for the organization's reputation. For these organizations, issue sellers' unwillingness to raise challenging issues translated into real organizational consequences.

Although issue selling can be a source of organizational learning and change (Weick & Ashford, 1997), organizations also defend against such learning because it can be a threat. As Trice and Beyer (1993) point out, organizations embody ideologies in which members become invested over time. Some issues can represent a challenge to the organization's dominant ideology. As a result, the top-management group may be conflicted. The group may be overwhelmed by environmental complexity and, therefore, dependent on input from below but also invested in a certain ideology and uninterested in input that challenges it. In the latter case, one defense is to not allow challenging issues to surface at all. As Bacharach and Baratz (1962) noted, simply preventing an issue from becoming a focus of decision making in the first place can squelch it. Thus, in addition to the drama frequently associated with organizational actors making big decisions on tough problems, there is also the more subtle, behind-the-scenes drama over what issues will surface onto the agenda in the first place. Kingdon (1984, p. 1) summarized this as follows: "We're talking here not about how issues get decided, nor about how decisions are implemented and what impacts they have, but rather how issues come to be issues in the first place." For the issues that I am interested in, this tension (between learning and defending) can be particularly pronounced.

If there is adaptive value for the organization in a flow of issue up the hierarchy, then it is important for upper management to (a) understand the barriers that those below them in the organization perceive to getting issues on the agenda, (b) understand their own defenses against such input, and (c) take steps to create avenues for issue input. These steps might include the establishment of specific means by which employees might suggest important issues or a more general attempt to create an environment that fosters interaction, disagreement on occasion, and input. This latter strategy is consistent with Bower's (1970) suggestion that managers should attend to the environment that they create within the firm and its effects (Noda & Bower, 1997). Undertaking task a or c above (my emphasis in this chapter) will be facilitated by understanding the social psychology that guides lower-level employees' decisions about whether and how to participate in the agenda-setting process.

To gain insights into that psychology, I use illustrative data collected from women managers regarding their decisions to raise the inequitable treatment of women employees as an important issue for their firm. I label this issue "gender equity."[1] I argue that this issue is one of a certain type in organizations and, at face value, is an "undiscussable" in many organizations. I suggest how the nature and constructed meaning of issues such as this may tend to inhibit interested parties from advocating for them within organizations.

Lessons From the Influence Literature

The literature on power and influence comes in several guises. For many years, this was considered to be an underresearched (and underdiscussed) topic in management. Recently, scholars have engaged in case study and anecdotal descriptions of the use of power in organizations (Allison, 1971; Pfeffer, 1992); laboratory work in social psychology has uncovered some of the mechanisms by which certain acts have influence (Benson, Karabenic, & Lerner, 1976), and an empirical literature on influence tactics has considered how influence is undertaken. This latter literature has primarily focused on what individuals will do to exert influence.

Findings suggest that individuals use a variety of tactics (the number and nature of these tactics vary depending on what instrument was used to collect the data). One popular instrument or conceptualization is Yukl's (Yukl & Falbe, 1990; Yukl, Falbe, & Youn, 1993; Yukl & Tracey, 1992), which measures rational, inspirational, or personal appeals along with consultation, ingratiation, exchange, coalition, and legitimacy tactics. Yukl and colleagues found that rational appeals are used more when trying to influence upward (as is the case in issue selling), whereas ingratiation, exchange, consultation, and pressure are used less in upward influence. In general, tactic choice is influenced by the prevailing social norms and roles, the nature of the influencer's power base, the appropriateness of the tactic for the influence objective, the level of resistance encountered or expected, and the costs in relation to benefits.

A second measurement or conceptual scheme has produced an additional set of results. Kipnis, Schmidt, and Wilkinson (1980) developed a measure that tapped rational, ingratiation, upward appeal, assertiveness, sanctions, and exchange. Using these same measures, Ansari and Kapoor (1987) found that how one might exert upward influence depends on one's goal. People use more rational, upward appeal, and blocking for organizational goals (e.g., getting others to perform or introducing a new procedure) and more ingratiation for personal goals (e.g., to get a better assignment or advancement). They also found that leaders invited a certain style of influence; authoritarian leaders drew more blocking, ingratiation, and upward appeals, and participative and nurturing managers drew more reason and persuasion.

Personality has also been shown to affect tactic choice, with internal locus of control individuals using more overt tactics (reason and persuasion) and external locus of control individuals using more covert tactics (ingratiation) (Kapoor, Ansari, & Shukla, 1986). Those high in need for approval selected more rational and indirect tactics, whereas those high in Machiavellianism were more flexible in their tactic use and selected more nonrational and indirect tactics (Grams & Rogers, 1990).

Three conclusions from this literature are relevant for my current purpose. First, this literature's emphasis and evolution, with its focus on how influence is exerted, ignores the question of what causes a person to engage in influence in the first place. Given the arguments in the beginning of this chapter concerning the adaptive value for the firm of generating influence from below, the question of what leads people to exert upward influence (and blocks them from exerting the same) is as critical as the question of how they might exert that influence.

Second, this literature pays little attention to the subject matter (content) of the influence attempt. Beyond Ansari and Kapoor's (1987) investigation of influence on own goals (e.g., to obtain better work assignments) versus organizational goals (e.g., to promote new ideas), the literature has treated the subject matter of the influence attempt as irrelevant. In this chapter, I raise the following question: Does the topic about which one is influencing affect the choice to exert influence? My argument is that it does.

Third, the influence-tactics literature's emphasis across several studies on the role that power differences play in the choice of how to influence suggests an important vertical distinction in influence-tactic choice (upward vs. downward influence) (Farmer, Maslyn, Fedor, & Goodman, 1997; Kapoor et al., 1986). Indeed, studies on this topic have often contrasted the ways that individuals influence in an upward direction with how they influence those below them in a hierarchy and, rarely, with how they influence their peers. This emphasis provides a contrast for a quite different distinction made here—that of influencing from the center versus the margin. This distinction is similar to the one that Van Maanen and Schein (1979) drew for organizational socialization in which the newcomer's task is to master the hierarchical transition of changing levels but also the task of moving from the periphery to the center of some new social group. They called this transition the task of crossing the inclusionary boundary.

A similar distinction may be made about influence: Individuals are not simply oriented hierarchically and affected by the hierarchical position of their influence target, but rather individuals also attend to the centrality versus marginality dimension. This dimension can pertain to the position (formal or informal) of the seller himself or herself (he or she could be central within a group or peripheral). It could also pertain to the issue of interest. The issue could be in the center or margin of some collectively endorsed sphere of legitimacy or acceptability (with issues in the center being the most consensually legitimate and with issues at the margin of the sphere being the least consensually legitimate). Trice and Beyer (1993) might say that issues are central to the firm's dominant ideology or peripheral. In this chapter, I focus primarily on the latter sense of marginality and centrality. I argue that the choice to influence, when that influence is about an issue that is marginal to the collective ideology, is a problematic choice for the potential seller or influencer. My initial hunch is that the choice to exert influence is determined in large part by the meaning such issues have for the seller and by the anticipated results of raising them (e.g., the potential career benefits or costs of raising an issue).

The Meaning of Issues

I began this chapter with the contention that different issues will be perceived differently by their potential sellers. They will have different meanings associated with them. It is also my contention that certain issue meanings are more problematic in some organizational settings than are other meanings. They are problematic in that they raise concerns and fears about discussing and promoting certain issues within the organization. The semantic differential is a useful technique for capturing the meaning of a concept (or, in this case, issue). Osgood (1952) argued that the semantic differential is well suited for tapping the connotative meaning of words or "the relationship between signs and their users." This distinction is important because the meaning of an issue is a function of the issue and the individual. An issue is not pleasant, troubling, or dangerous in and of itself but only in the eyes of a particular individual or set of individuals. My goal is to describe the meaning that the gender-equity issue has for my respondents to understand why this issue (and, by extrapolation, a larger set of issues) might be a very reluctant focus of influence.

The Study

The data were collected as part of a larger examination of how female managers view gender-equity issues and what prompts or deters them from raising these issues within their organizations. As part of this examination, I[2] collected a set of qualitative and semantic-differential data from 218 women managers. The managers were all graduates of the University of Michigan Business School working in a variety of organizations.[3] The average full-time work experience of the sample was 11.32 years (SD = 6.66) and 90% were white; 64% worked in staff positions and 36% in line positions. They worked in various fields, including marketing (21.4%), finance (17.8%), and accounting (11.7%).

Before posing the questions of interest, I described the gender-equity issue to the respondents. I labeled it the women's issue and described it as follows:

> Sometimes women experience an eroding sense of worth and place due to the atmosphere of the organization; sometimes women tend to feel unwelcome or unimportant due to events or incidents that, on their own, would be small things, but together and in repetition are quite powerful; and sometimes women feel that their ability to get ahead within the organization is limited.

Examples were given following each component of this issue description. This description was based on the situation presented in a Harvard Business Review case (Reordon, 1993). Although it may not be the way that every respondent would have described the issue on her own, I felt that it was critical that the respondents were reacting to the same issue description in all their responses.

I used 31 semantic differential items to capture the possible meanings that the gender-equity issue might have for the women respondents. Several of these items were taken from research by Osgood and colleagues (Heise, 1965; Osgood & Suci, 1955). I included established adjective pairs to tap evaluation, potency, and activity (Osgood & Suci, 1955) because these have been well documented and supported by previous research. Evaluation taps the perceived goodness or badness of a stimulus object. Potency captures the strength of the stimulus object, and activity taps the level of liveliness or activity associated with the stimulus object. See Table 15.1 for the adjective pairs tapping these dimensions. Table 15.1 also includes additional adjective pairs pulled from research by Dutton and colleagues (Dutton & Jackson, 1987; Dutton, Walton, & Abrahamson, 1989) to tap the dimensions that might differentiate strategic issues. Respondents rated the gender-equity issue on all 31 adjective pairs with 7-point response scales anchored by opposite work meanings on each end (e.g., "tough" and "tender"). Respondents were asked to put a check mark between the demarcations that best reflected the meaning that the issue had for them.

From these data, I developed a clear picture of how the respondents viewed this issue and began some informed speculation as to how and why this issue might be a troubling one to discuss. This picture does not tell me anything about how different issues are viewed, however. To get at the comparative question in an exploratory, suggestive manner, I compared my semantic differential results to some results collected by Jane Dutton and I in 1990. In that unpublished study, 62 human resource vice presidents provided semantic differential ratings of five issues that might arise in a fictitious bank. The issues were flexible scheduling, AIDS, child care, continuing education, drug use, and health and fitness. In this chapter, I focus on two issues—AIDS and continuing education.[4] The AIDS issue concerned whether or not an organization should take steps to address issues related to the rising incidence of AIDS and employees' concerns about

TABLE 15.1 Semantic Differential Results[a]

| | Gender-Equity Issue | | AIDS Issue | Continuing Education Issue |
Attribute	Mean	SD	(Mean)	(Mean)
Evaluation				
Good	2.89	1.51	3.45	5.90
Pleasant	1.65	1.33	1.26	4.61
Beautiful	1.65	1.24	2.52	4.82
Positive	2.05	1.53	2.87	5.00
Dimension	2.42		2.52	5.08
Potency				
Strong	4.41	1.59	5.34	4.73
Tough	4.86	1.16	4.13	3.68
Large	4.03	1.52	3.92	3.62
Dimension	4.43		4.46	4.01
Activity				
Active	4.25	1.69	5.33	5.37
Lively	4.17	1.42	5.33	5.07
Hot	3.58	1.32	4.70	3.66
Dimension	4.00		5.12	4.70
Other attributes				
Abstract/concrete	4.90	61.72	4.80	5.20
Simple/complex	5.81	1.22	6.05	3.85
Urgent/not urgent	2.94	1.47	2.36	3.53
Internal/external	3.48	1.46	4.30	3.31
Independent/dependent	3.98	1.55	4.34	3.53
Specific/general	4.01	1.65	2.76	3.57
Opportunity/threat	4.32	1.56	4.56	2.12
Controllable/uncontrollable	4.15	1.52	4.64	2.56
Important/unimportant	1.89	1.28	2.10	2.12
Unemotional/emotional	5.75	1.31	6.23	3.72
Personal/impersonal	2.60	1.51	2.26	3.12
Legitimate/illegitimate	2.49	1.65	2.13	2.20
Potential loss/gain	3.38	1.70	3.31	5.97
Predictable/unpredictable	3.84	1.59	5.39	2.92
Topical/not topical	3.09	1.49	2.30	3.53
Political/apolitical	2.55	1.59	2.87	4.39
Masculine/feminine	3.92	1.60	3.62	4.00
Short term/long term	5.58	1.31	5.41	5.85
Divisive/uniting	2.58	1.33	2.67	5.10
Involved/detached	3.23	1.54	2.95	2.87
Boring/interesting	5.06	1.41	5.20	5.27

a. All attributes measured with 7-point semantic-differential scales. Means for the AIDS and continuing education issues from Dutton and Ashford (1993).

AIDS exposure. The continuing education issue was whether the organization should take steps to address issues related to employees' continuing education needs. The comparison between the meanings attributed to the gender-equity issue by my respondents and the meaning that the human resources vice presidents attributed to the AIDS and continuing education issues are illuminating.

Results

Table 15.1 presents the semantic differential results. The three dimensions documented in prior research are presented first; then the other attributes are presented in random order. To get a sense of the patterns in the data, I first looked down the column of means that represent the meaning attributed to gender-equity issues. Here, I picked out the extreme responses (ratings >5 or <3). The most striking finding is how negatively the gender-equity issue is viewed. All four of Osgood and Suci's (1955) evaluation dimension items anchored the negative end of the scale, and their mean, 2.42 (on a 7-point scale), is quite low. In contrast, this issue is viewed as slightly above the mean in its potency and its activity. The issue is viewed as complex, emotional, interesting, and long term (all scores >5 on a 7-point scale). These respondents also view the issue as important, personal, and legitimate. Therefore, although this issue may be at the margins of the collective ideology, these female respondents view it as quite legitimate. It is perhaps not surprising that they view it as legitimate because I asked the sample about the way that they and others like them are treated in an organization. Finally, these respondents viewed the issue as divisive and political.

A picture emerges of this issue from these results. It is negatively evaluated and is seen as charged. Its political and divisive nature makes up part of the high charge on this issue as does its perceived emotionality and perhaps its personal nature. It may be that this issue is one of a type that exists on the margins of organizations—issues that are charged: personal and emotional for their perceivers and divisive and political in their contexts.

If this issue is one of a type, how does it relate to other issues? Table 15.1 provides suggestive data regarding this question. First, comparing across the rows, the means presented for the gender-equity issue and the AIDS issue are striking in their similarity. These two groups of respondents view these two issues similarly. If a 1-point difference is considered to be an interpretable difference, then these two sets of means differed on only 5 attributes. They essentially had the same pattern across the 31 attributes. Interestingly, 3 of the 5 differences were on the three items that make up the activity dimension. AIDS was viewed as a more "active" issue; it was seen as higher on the "active," "lively," and "hot" attributes than was gender equity. The other two differences were in specificity-generality (AIDS was viewed as more specific) and predictability-unpredictability (AIDS was viewed as more unpredictable). Therefore, these two issues were viewed more or less similarly. At face value, if the national debate on AIDS is an indicator of how this issue might be viewed in organizations, AIDS too might be expected to have the same "charged" quality that was seen with gender equity. It is an issue about which people feel emotional; it is an issue that is seen as negative, and it is also divisive and extremely political. How different is it (and, by implication, gender equity) from other issues?

For a contrasting issue, compare the means for gender equity and AIDS with the means for the continuing education issue. It is first instructive to focus on the attributes on which the issues were viewed similarly. For example, all three issues were veiwed as important, they were all viewed as similar in their abstractness, they were viewed as similarly interesting and involving, and they were viewed as similar in their perceived legitimacy. Thus, it is not the case that any of these issues were viewed as illegitimate, uninteresting, or unimportant within an organization. These meanings should not dissuade an interested party from raising any of these issues (and to be able to justify their importance). There were, however, several differences in how the three issues were viewed on other dimensions. In fact, the continuing education issue differed from the other two issues (taking an average of the other issues' means) on 11 of the 31 dimensions. Furthermore, although I used the same criterion to call a difference between two means a notable difference (criterion = means must differ by 1 point), here the average difference was 2.41 points and the smallest difference over 1 was 1.87. Therefore, the differences between the continuing education issue and the average score for the other issues were substantial. The most noteworthy differences were in Osgood and Suci's (1955) evaluation dimension. The continuing education issue differed from the other issues on all four of the evaluation attributes and on the total evaluation mean. This issue was viewed in a substantially more positive light than were either the AIDS or the gender-equity issues.

There were seven other differences as well. When compared to the AIDS and gender-equity issues, the continuing education issue was viewed as simpler, less of a threat, more controllable, less emotional, more of a potential gain, less political, and less divisive. Many of these attributes were also rated extremely on the gender-equity issue. It appears that these attributes differentiate people's perception of issues.

Issue Meaning:
Summary and Conclusions

The results suggest a portrait of what a charged issue might look like in organizations. Such issues are evaluated negatively, they are emotion laden, they are politically "hot" in that they are seen as having a divisive quality, and they are complex. Their meaning appears to be dominated by a general evaluative dimension (e.g., good-bad, pleasant-unpleasant, and positive-negative) and is supplemented with a sense of emotionality, complexity, and divisiveness. It is striking to note that when Dutton et al. (1989) reviewed the environmental scanning, issue management, and issue formulation/diagnosis literatures to see how issues are viewed, they found only one of the charged-issue attributes mentioned here—divisiveness. It may be that by studying the question of what issue dimensions matter from the perspective of the strategy process, which is typically focused on the top group and the legitimated, rationalized, espoused procedures, these authors failed to pick up on the qualities that seem most notable in my study. Dutton et al. may have picked up on dimensions of issues within the dominant ideology. As postmodernists note, however, there are many realities (truths) from which our scientific process selectively picks and legitimates only a certain few (Jacobson & Jacques, 1997; Kilduff & Mehra, 1997). The danger is that we begin to think of these legitimated realities as truths, whereas if we had asked different questions (e.g., What do these issues mean?) of different people (e.g., those lower down in the organization rather than those at the top) and on different topics (e.g., topics that may be more contested or ambiguous), then different "truths" might emerge. Certain issues become problematized in some organizations not because no one thinks they are important or that everyone thinks that they are illegitimate (remember that these means were similar) but because these issues have become imbued with meanings that make the raising of them problematic. What kind of person would raise a divisive, emotional, complex issue that is typically viewed as negative?

In a study of issue interpretation, Dutton and Dukerich (1991) suggest that how top-management groups within organizations respond to issues is a function of their issue interpretations. The issue that they studied, homelessness, was also emotionally laden. Their qualitative results suggest that top management's evolving interpretation of this issue led it to send signals that either invited or suppressed organizational initiatives of various kinds. The findings presented above suggest that in addition to top-management issue interpretations, the interpretations of those at lower organizational levels also have their effects. Specifically, the ways that they interpret charged issues may block them from raising the issues within the organization. Thus, just as top management shapes the agenda via its interpretation of various issues, so do those below by their choices not to become involved with and promote the issue. Without managerial involvement with an issue—that is, without managers persuading, cajoling, and pushing for the issue—its chances of landing on the organizational agenda are slim (Noda & Bower, 1996; Weick & Ashford, 1997).

Anticipated Outcomes of Issue Selling

The Dutton and Dukerich (1991) study suggested that organizations and their leaders influence managers' willingness to raise charged issues. Organizational context was also found to be important in Ashford, Rothbard, Piderit, and Dutton's (1997) study. Their data suggested that women are willing to raise this issue when it is important to them and when they strongly identify with women as a social category. It is not known if these women "see" the issue differently (i.e., it has different meaning for them) or if they view it similarly to the sample used here but are simply more willing to wade into the raising of such a charged issue due to its personal importance. More relevant to the question posed here, Ashford et al. (1997) showed that settings also have an influence. In settings in which the gender-equity issue is pervasive, managers express more willingness to raise it. Also, managers are more likely to raise the issue in settings in which the organization is supportive and in which managers have a specific supportive relationship with the person or group with which they are raising the issue. Key in the process, though, appears to be women's assessments of their likely success in being heard on the issue and, more important, their sense that their images will not be hurt in the process of raising the issue. This latter variable was important in that it both directly affected expressed willingness and affected assessments of the probability of success (Ashford et al. attributed this to a cognitive defense mechanism: "If I am afraid to raise it, I justify that fear by also stating that 'I probably wouldn't be too successful anyway'.").

The Study

What outcomes do women worry about when they think about raising gender-equity issues? What is image risk all about? What do women think might happen to their public images if they raise and promote this charged issue within their organization? Ashford et al.'s (1997) study is silent on these questions. An examination of these concerns should provide insight into what it feels like to exert influence on charged issues and what fears, founded or unfounded, might deter people from initiating such influence. To explore these issues, the same respondents who provided issue-meaning ratings were asked two open-ended questions: (a) "Assuming that you did sell this issue, how would this action affect you?" and, as a more specific follow-up, (b) "All managers develop an image or reputation that capture others' impressions of them as a manager. How would selling this issue affect your image in your work organization?" The answers to these questions should provide an inductive sense of what anticipated outcomes might be prompting women toward or holding women back from selling the issue.

To analyze the responses collected, I followed standard practices for qualitative data analysis described in Miles and Huberman (1984) and Glaser and Strauss (1967, 1970). My goal was to suspend a priori expectations of findings and maintain the richness of the data while creating sense and order. To accomplish this, I worked with a research assistant to build inductive code categories by first reading all the responses and generating an exhaustive list of all the perceived possible outcomes mentioned by the respondents that might result from selling this issue. Two coders analyzed the full set of responses and coded all distinguishable word phrases. For example, if someone stated that three different outcomes were possible, all were coded. Responses were also coded for attributes that described their full set of responses (e.g., mentioning both positive and negative effects was coded). An agreement of 96% between coders was achieved. When coders did not agree or were uncertain about which theme an example fit, they consulted (and debated) with one another until an agreement was reached, following the example of other qualitative researchers (Rafaeli & Sutton, 1991). Typical disagreements had to do with different levels of abstraction at which to consider the response.

Results

It is worth noting that respondents had a fairly easy time answering these questions. Of 209 respondents, only 15 said that they did not know or were unsure of the effect that selling this issue might have on them. Several respondents did, however, state that selling the issue would have no impact on them. They had various ways of characterizing this lack of impact. Fourteen women stated that, in general, selling the gender-equity issue would have no impact. Fifteen stated that it would have no impact on tangible outcomes, and 10 said more specifically that no change would occur in their image (these often were the same people stating that "no impact" would occur in response to both questions). Some described the no-impact response as relative to their current image. For example, two women commented,

> It wouldn't change my image or reputation much. I am viewed as very open-minded and competent in my line of work. Besides, I have always been active in volunteer works and community services. I am on the board of a few civic and community organizations. My supervisor and coworkers all know that I am an advocate of many civil rights matters.
>
>   It would not affect it. It is not uncommon for me to air concerns, confront issues, etc.

Others attributed their no-impact response to their level in the organization. For example, one respondent noted,

> I don't think I'm high enough in the organization that it would affect my future negatively, and I have no ambition to be president, so I'm ok. My guess is that few women in the company would be willing to make a big issue out of it.

Finally, others attributed their response to the importance or attention already being given to the issue in their organization. One woman stated,

> With some of the more traditional male managers, my image could be viewed as that of a troublemaker or one who rocks the boat. I believe, however, given the diversity seminars currently in place, my image would not suffer from selling the issue.

For those stating that raising the issue would have an impact, their answers were of a few basic types. First, respondents mentioned impacts on tangible outcomes (e.g., "I might get a raise") and on image (e.g., "I might be seen as wasting others' time"). Within these two general categories, respondents distinguished positive and negative outcomes. A final category of "other effects" was also coded. This category was composed of effects present in the data that did not fit well in other categories.

Regarding effects on tangible outcomes, the respondents equally mentioned positive and negative outcomes when speaking generally. When describing specific possible positive outcomes, however, respondents were almost twice as likely to emphasize that the likelihood of positive outcomes depended on the sellers' approach than did the likelihood of negative tangible outcomes. These comments exemplify respondents' sense that this issue can be raised safely if it is done so in an appropriate manner. For example, one woman commented, "I believe this may potentially enhance my career, if I'm successful in articulating my point without allowing the issue to hold emotional charge that is offensive to management."

Thirty-three positive tangible outcomes were mentioned by at least one respondent. Of these, the possibility of getting respect, of getting a promotion, and of getting recognition were mentioned most frequently. Examples of positive tangible outcomes are provided in the following quotes: "I'd get access to resources and people that I don't have right now, e.g., more equitable pay [the squeaky wheel syndrome]," "Many people, especially other women, would respect me for standing up for what I believe and for being fair," and "[I would receive a] large raise in salary [and the] 'go ahead' to act on decisions such as staffing changes and reengineering plans." One woman spoke of her hopes for how selling the gender-equity issue would be seen, but blended within her statement are also her fears about its mixed reception: "I would hope that it would make me a more valuable manager willing to take on risk to improve the corporation. Some of my male managers would view it positively, most would not."

Other outcomes mentioned with lesser frequency were the possibility of creating career opportunities, doing better work, increasing morale, and creating an atmosphere in which people would be more careful about their comments when around the seller. The rest of the tangible outcomes were mentioned by only a couple of respondents each. They included hopes for having a positive effect on the firm (e.g., "The firm would become more family friendly") and the seller (e.g., "My salary would rise," "I would feel empowered," and "Women would want to work for me"). From these responses, it is clear that women see a variety of possible positive outcomes stemming from their selling efforts for this issue. It is also apparent that there is not a consensual view on what might happen. Although three outcomes (getting respect, promotions, and recognition) were frequently mentioned, many others were foreseen by different people.

Negative tangible outcomes were also mentioned but with less frequency (37 possible outcomes mentioned as opposed to 77 positive outcomes). There was also less differentiation among the negative outcomes (22 unique categories as opposed to 33 for positive outcomes). Here, there were two dominant responses: that such selling would be career limiting, and, more specifically, that it would lower promotional opportunities for the seller and for all women. Only one or two respondents mentioned each of the other negative tangible outcomes. It appears that women have a more fine-grained sense of the positive potential of selling this issue than they do of the possible negative outcomes. Alternatively, it may be that the positive outcomes are more specific to a particular organizational context. Given this, there were a wider variety of positive outcomes mentioned by the sample (who were drawn from a diverse set of contexts). Those anticipating negative tangible outcomes tended to focus on the quite general—that this act would be career limiting. The following quotes reflect this concern:

> I would become known as the "women's issue" person and would lose all chance for promotion. My entire function would be pigeon-holed into this box.
>
> I would not sell—if I did, I feel it would be equivalent of giving up on [my] career.
>
> These are touchy issues to raise in the male-dominated legal profession where you don't want to focus attention on what may be perceived as "small issues" or "women's issues" for fear of indirect repercussion on merit raises or promotions, or being viewed as someone raising gender to somehow benefit themselves. Part time or flexible work arrangements in the last several years became available on a limited basis (of which I am a participant). I never want to draw attention to this so others will take me seriously and continue to respect me. Anything which could be viewed as a benefit to women only or a "women's issue" is difficult to champion for fear of your colleagues feeling you are receiving an unfair advantage.

The last quote is suggestive of how intertwined the tangible and image concerns are for this issue. The respondent fears repercussions on tangible outcomes, such as raises and promotions, but sees these as stemming from how she might be viewed differently for having raised the issue. This quote also highlights a tension associated with this issue—that of raising concerns about the treatment of one's own group (what Harquail [1996] labels advocacy). Although anyone might observe and comment on an inequity, being in the group that will benefit from any changes that address the inequity makes it difficult to rule out a self-serving quality in one's issue selling. Sellers feel that they cannot speak up "for women" because it will be viewed as speaking up for themselves. This tension may serve as a deterrent to issue selling. For example, one woman noted quite bluntly, "[It would impact my image] negatively. I would be viewed as a pushy 'libber' wanting 'special' attention and rights for women." Another commented that she would be seen as "not able to get ahead on my own so I need an excuse."

This tension is not unique to women and this issue. It is felt to some degree by anyone raising concerns about a set of conditions that hurt a group in which he or she is a part. Young turks who feel unheard, minority group members who feel discriminated against, members of a functional group that fared poorly in the last budget cycle are all examples. Finley (1996) describes a similar tension felt by African American employees as a double bind, with the two unattractive choices being to stay silent about painful realities or to bring them up and be branded an opportunist (among other things). Will these sellers be seen as raising the issue for the importance of the issue or to better protect or promote themselves? Concerns over how selling will be perceived in some of these situations may deter the airing of important concerns within the organization. This aspect may be part of the reason why this issue is emotionally charged. Other charged issues may get their emotional "kick" from other sources.

For image outcomes, the pattern is somewhat different than that for tangible outcomes. Here, twice as many respondents saw possible negative image consequences than positive. For those stating that their image would be hurt, however, nearly all stated or implied that it depended on their approach in selling the issue. For example, two women commented,

> [I] would probably be viewed as a rebel, unless I handled it very carefully, such as part of a diversity initiative—where there could be an open dialogue and others [other groups—men, blacks, etc.] were able to air their perceptions/complaints simultaneously.
>
> It has the potential to affect my image and negatively depending on how positive/upbeat/constructive I am in selling the issue. How least threatening [to men] and seemingly most "objective" I can make the selling.

This pattern again suggests that women believe they can influence, to some extent, the outcomes that might occur when they sell gender-equity issues by the way that they go about selling them. The following quote, however, exemplifies how ambiguities in the organizational and interpersonal context add a sense of fragility to that sense of control:

> It [reactions] would take one of two extremes—[I would] either
> be seen as a troublemaker and then I'd be stuck in that level
> forever, or be seen as someone who's proactive, creating posi-
> tive change, increasing diversity. . . . It all depends on politics,
> how well I'm liked by my superiors and who likes me or who
> doesn't. It would be a gamble.

For those who believed that selling would help their image, many suggested that it depends on their approach, but even more suggested that
it depends on the actual results of their efforts for the organization.
Their responses either stated or implied that if the issue is sold successfully and the organization sees good things coming from it, then their
images would not be hurt. Nearly all respondents who noted positive
image outcomes appeared to be responding as if the issue had been sold
successfully.

Respondents mentioned several specific image consequences of
selling this issue. Examples include being seen as having a hidden
agenda, being less desirous of career advancement, being seen as
having excessively high expectations, being seen as oversensitive, and
being seen as being difficult to work with. In addition, respondents
mentioned a host of different labels (Table 15.2) that they felt would be
applied to them as a result of selling this issue. A panel of five "experts"
(doctoral students trained in organizational behavior—a mixture of
men and women, with no discernable differences found along sex
lines) rated these labels as to their positivity or negativity. Of the 88
labels mentioned, this panel of experts rated only 14 as positive. Sixty
were rated as negative and 14 received mixed ratings (with some raters
viewing the label as positive and others as neutral or negative). The
two most frequently endorsed labels were "feminist/women's libber,"
which is perhaps understandable given the nature of the issue, and
"troublemaker." Other highly endorsed labels were "complainer" and
"whiner." The following respondents' comments are quite specific
regarding potential labels:

> I would be seen as a complainer and just the kind of abrasive
> person the organization dislikes. Some abrasive men are toler-
> ated—not women.
>
> I would probably wear the whiner label. A particularly
> scarlet letter for a female. There might be no outward, overt

TABLE 15.2 Labels Mentioned by Respondents as Potential Outcomes of Issue Selling and Their Ratings[a]

Negatively Rated Labels	Positively Rated Labels	Mixed Rated Labels
Whiner/troublemaker	Confident	Aggressive
Bitch/chip on shoulder	Serious about career	Outspoken
Complainer/flaky	Forward thinking	Rebel
Unreliable/dangerous	Resource/solution	Liberal activist
Oversensitive/overreacting	Role model	Activist
Crybaby/weak	Assertive	Hard
Noncontributor/extremist	Bridge builder	Tough
Bitter/negative	Leader	Women's-issue person
Militant/man-hating	Competent	Yankee
Abrasive/uptight	Alert	Boat rocker
Insecure/nonprofessional	Strong woman	Risk taker
Ingrate/loud mouth	Concerned person	Woman pusher
Uppity/disruptive	Brave	Powerful
Traitor/problem person	Fair-minded	Underdog
Cop-out/uncooperative		
Too strident female/arrogant		
Too emotional/unreasonable		
Griping/inept		
Less competent and needing excuse		
Self-centered		
Lacking political savvy/weak		
Difficult to work with		
Too emotional		
One who blows things out of proportion		
Not a fit for my company		
Unable to compete without a handicap		
Feminist/women's libber		
Pushy/controversial		
Rabble-rouser/radical		
Difficult to approach		
Ax to grind/opportunist		
Squeaky wheel/biased		
Sexual harassment police		
Less desirous of career advancement		
Having a hidden agenda		
Having too high of expectations		
Unreasonable		
Not willing to pay same dues as those who went before		

a. Ratings provided by three coders naive to the purpose of the study.

mention of this, but in an indirect way, I might be treated more as an outsider, or someone with a chip on her shoulder.

[I would be seen as a] troublemaker. Looking for a way to move to another area of organization, must not be getting along with others—"No one else seems to have this problem."

I'd get a lot of attention. (Adverse labeling—militant, whiny, and man-hating. These labels were actually used for a woman in my system who did "sell" women's issues. She quickly stopped).

Within the "other effects" category, three themes are worth noting. First, 48 respondents, more than for any other theme, stated that their raising of this issue would generate both positive and negative reactions. For example, respondents noted, "I would earn the respect of other women in the organization, while irritating some of the older, high-level men," "At this time I think it would have a negative impact on my reputation by upper management. Your reputation with staff, especially women, however, would be positively affected," and "[I] would be admired by some for speaking out and being proactive to correct a situation. Would be seen by some as not being a 'team' player." This finding reinforces the perceived divisive nature of this issue. Respondents appear to be able to easily visualize different stakeholders responding differently to their potential selling of this issue.

Second, many respondents mentioned that they would be concerned about feeling apart from the group if they raised this issue. Respondents talked about this in different ways, including being shunned by the organization, fear that they would be seen as not a team player, and fears that they would alienate others and that they would undermine team spirit. For example, respondents noted,

I doubt that it would affect my relationship with them [my peers] unless it put me on the political outs with top management. Then, I imagine, I would be shunned by many of my male peers, who must protect their political position.

My concern is that I would be viewed as a troublemaker and then no one would want to affiliate with me on projects. Talk about a fear of rejection!

A third theme, mentioned by fewer respondents, is that by raising the gender-equity issue, they would heighten awareness of themselves in the organization. The fears expressed included that people would be more guarded around the seller, that it would call attention to the seller, and that people would walk on eggshells around the seller. For example, one respondent noted,

> A lot of attention would be directed at me and people would scrutinize if I ever was a valid/prospective manager choice. If I slipped up on a job a very big deal would be made. Males at my level might shun me.

This theme echoes Finley's (1996) observation about the double-binding nature of being African American in white-dominated firms. She notes that being different is frequently equated with being undesirable or deficient. Given this, African Americans (or women in this case) may stay silent and profess not to see race or gender issues. Recognition of this potential outcome may drive advice from Catalyst (1996) and others (Lancaster, 1997) that a critical skill for women and people of color is to make others feel comfortable. "Making others feel comfortable" may be the underlying theme in these respondents' contention that the way one raises these types of issues is critical. If it is done in a way that does not cause discomfort, it can be done successfully (it can be heard and leave the seller with the credibility to raise issues in the future) (Dutton & Ashford, 1993).

Lessons for Issue Selling

If information and change initiatives from within have adaptive value for organizations, then top-level managers should have an interest in gaining information from below about issues of potential strategic importance. They should have an interest in hearing about the pleasant and the possible, the negative and the uncomfortable, the central and consensually "business" issues, and about what are sometimes defined as more marginal concerns. Clearly, this is not always the case. Top management's defenses against troubling input are well documented (Argyris, 1985; Hornstein, 1986). Hornstein describes the defensive mechanism quite dramatically:

Organizations are the site of an inevitable and eternal conflict. On one side are the forces of maintenance and continuity, which strive to create and sustain an orderly, predictable succession of human exchanges. Opposing them are the forces of innovation and discontinuity, which seek to alter established practices. In this struggle, neither of the two regularly wears the "black hat." The protagonists are both seeking an organization's survival but in different ways. In everyday experience, it comes down to a conflict between those folks who dutifully work to manage established routines in order to ensure the successful functioning of their organization, and those who courageously challenge routines in order to do the very same thing. (p. 8)

What this chapter highlights is the collusion of middle- and lower-level managers in this defensive process. Many of these managers, because of the meanings they give to some issues (e.g., that they are negative and divisive) and the anticipated consequences of raising them (e.g., that they will draw attention to themselves and cause themselves to be seen in a negative way), are not likely to raise and promote certain issues. The question for them is not how to best influence but whether it is worth undertaking influence in the first place. If the troubling conditions continue, however, then the issue will continue to fester and dissatisfy—individuals will suffer. If these same individuals fail to bring up important and legitimate issues because the costs are seen as too high, then "change from within" efforts will take a fairly narrow, limited path with a focus on the already acceptable and on positively evaluated issues—organizations will suffer. Besides the cost of this general narrowing of the scope of issues raised within the organization, there are more specific costs if issues such as the one studied here are not heard. For example, Wright, Ferris, Hiller, and Kroll (1995) found significant correlations between the number of affirmative action and discrimination suits and stock price. Another cost might be the "brain drain" as talented women leave firms for more hospitable environs. Given these costs, research efforts must be undertaken to better understand the question of when will individuals attempt influence (issue selling) in addition to how they go about it.

Both the influence and the issue-selling literatures also need to begin to take into account the subject matter of the influence (issue selling) attempt in their empirical investigations. The analysis here has shown that issues take on multiple meanings. The meaning attributed to gender-equity issues, for some variables, also seemed to color the anticipated consequences (e.g., along the dimension of divisiveness). It is an easy next step to argue that those meanings should affect the choice to go to bat for an issue and the process by which a person might sell various issues (or exert influence). For example, we might speculate that the negative evaluation associated with the gender-equity issue may lead women to raise it more subtly and informally in behind-the-scenes ways (as opposed to in public, formal settings such as presentations). The emotional charge for this issue may lead sellers to try to legitimate the issue with facts and data, thereby depersonalizing the issue and distancing themselves from it. The divisive quality of this charged issue may lead sellers to use a more flexible, tailored approach to their various constituencies. For example, they may use a moral appeal for the issue with one person while cloaking the issue in hard-core business logic with another. Meyerson and Scully (1995) also suggest a potential advantage of mixing linquistic appeals (e.g., using a moral appeal at times with a "bottom-line" person). They argue that such mixing allows the change agent to find unexpected allies. They also note that language has the power to coopt. A change agent that learns well how to speak the bottom-line language of the firm may lose his or her sense of the moral reason for action (Meyerson & Scully, 1995). These speculations are worth researching to develop a better understanding of why certain issues are seldom raised formally in organizations and so that leaders could take systematic action to address them.

What an issue means to a person seems interwoven with what the person expects to happen if he or she sells it. That is, given the meaning attributed to the gender-equity issue, the anticipated consequences were not surprising. Although respondents could name possible positive tangible and image consequences, these were predominantly couched in contingency language along the lines of, "If I am successful in selling this . . . [if positive things happen for the organization, then positive things will happen to me]." In essence, these comments represent more hopes than anticipated realities (the seller hopes for the successful sale, and then the positive consequences follow, almost by definition). Also striking in these respondents' comments is how they describe successful selling. These descriptions note aspects such as coming across as positive and nonthreatening with great frequency (Finley's [1996] point about keeping people comfortable). How one looks to others while selling (one's image) appears to be interwoven throughout all decisions about this issue.

The basic point is that the nature of the issue matters. The manner of selling the gender-equity issue and, indeed, the willingness to sell it in the first place is due in part to the negative, emotional, and divisive meanings that this issue has for women. This is not to say that we need to study issue selling issue by issue. Rather, there may be some basic issue types that stand out for people in organizations. Charged versus not charged issues may be one important dimension along which issues vary. Although some issues may take on a charged quality in specific contexts (e.g., "issue X in our organization is negative, emotional, and divisive"), other issues appear to be significantly more charged at face value. AIDS and gender equity, for example, were rated as significantly more negative, emotional, and divisive by samples drawn from a wide variety of contexts. These issues may simply feel, in general and without reference to context, more marginal and more explosive to raise than do others.

If image is critical, how will it look for individuals to raise highly charged issues within organizations? Although there were some positive image consequences mentioned, our respondents' comments predominantly suggest that if they sold gender-equity issues, they would look like they were troublemakers, whiners, and complainers and like they were self-serving and after rewards for themselves. These are important image concerns for someone considering raising an issue in an organization. They also serve as a particularly effective defensive routine for an organization. The organization can discount this issue as self-serving if sellers raise it, and the seller, anticipating that response, self-censors herself from raising the issue in the first place. Both parties collude in not communicating about the issue.

Conclusions

Given the anticipated labels and consequences of selling (e.g., the general fear that such selling would be "career limiting"), raising the gender-equality issue is an act of managerial courage. As Hornstein

(1986) points out, managers act courageously when they identify with an organization. Greater organizational identification motivates managers to take more risks (display more courage) for the good of the organization. With gender-equity issues, I suspect that the identification is not with the organization per se (which is causing the seller some pain) but with an envisioned "possible organization" in which women are treated equitably. The identification is also with women as a social group. Given this dual identification, sellers of this issue probably are best characterized by Meyerson and Scully's (1995) tempered radical label. Courageous enough to step forward to try to influence an issue important to them (the treatment of women in organizations) but savvy enough to undertake that persuasion in ways that leave them alive and able to influence again another day. Clearly, given the tone of many of the comments expressed in this chapter, for many women, as in Finley's (1996) description of corporate African Americans, the struggle is between the perception of the existence of a problem and their personal desire for safety. It is not clear, however, what a victory in this struggle would be. Although staying quiet may seem like the best short-term response, this response is not an effective long-run solution for the organization (in which the problem continues to fester) and perhaps not for the seller herself. Given this tension, women wrestle with the need for and fears about raising gender-equity issues. For example, one of my respondents sadly commented,

> I never saw myself as someone who would/could tolerate sexism and I am ashamed to be so passive. I want to stick it out to prove as a woman I can make it in the auto industry—I don't want defeat. On the other hand—not much change is going to occur in my company and to truly come to terms I will eventually have to leave.

The struggle over how much to influence, when to speak up, and when to stay quiet is ongoing. The desire for career success that deters influence is reflected in the previous comment ("I want to . . . prove as a woman I can make it in the auto industry"), as is the cost of making it in a system that leaves one on the short end of personal or group inequity ("I will eventually have to leave"). Three factors appear to affect the resolution of this struggle; the personal valuing of this issue ("I am responsible and should raise it"; Harquail, 1996), the nature of the context (supportive contexts yield more voice about this issue) (Ashford et al., 1997), and the seller's self-perceptions of her interpersonal skills in raising the issue in such a way that others remain comfortable with both the discussion and the seller herself. Managers who feel personally called on to speak up, who work in supportive contexts, and who have accomplished interpersonal skills are far more likely to resolve the struggle in favor of speaking up than staying quiet. Firms interested in opening up the corporate conversation to include discussion of charged issues such as the treatment of employees (in all its various guises) need to work hard to make the context appear supportive and to establish communication avenues that deemphasize interpersonal skills. Such moves are first steps in breaking down the collusion between top- and middle-level managers that keeps issues such as gender-equity undiscussable.

Notes

1. Although either men or women could raise this issue, this chapter focuses on women only for two reasons. First, although clearly men can be concerned about gender-equity issues affecting women and may directly experience them if they work in female-dominated firms, my prior expectation is that these issues would be more relevant for women. Given the state of organizations today (predominantly male dominated and with males in power positions), women are more likely to experience gender-equity concerns. Second, although either group could sell this issue and men could speak up on behalf of women, I did not want to assume that the risks faced or the dynamics in play would be the same for those selling on behalf of their own group as for others selling on behalf of another group.

2. Two graduate students, Nancy Rothbard and Sandy Piderit, Jane Dutton, and I collected these data. I use the pronoun "I" for simplicity. The data collection was a collective effort. The analysis and writing were done by me.

3. These two issues were chosen for illustrative purposes. Within the human resource vice president sample, the AIDS issue was viewed quite similarly to the drug-use issue and the continuing education issue was viewed quite similarly to the health and fitness issue. I chose two comparison issues for simplicity.

4. One-fifth of the female graduate population of the University of Michigan Business School was randomly selected to receive the qualitative survey. Of the 887 surveys mailed, 111 were excluded and 218 were returned, for a response rate of 28%. Ninety percent of the respondents were white. Their average full-time work experience was 11.32 years ($SD = 6.66$). sixty-four percent worked in staff positions. The respondents worked in various fields, including marketing (21.4%), finance (17.8%), and accounting (11.7%).

References

Allison, G. T. (1971). *Essence of decision: Explaining the Cuban missile crisis.* Boston: Little, Brown.

Ansari, M., & Kapoor, A. (1987). Organizational context and upward influence tactics. *Organizational Behavior and Human Decision Processes, 40,* 39-49.

Argyris, C. (1985). *Strategy change and defensive routines.* Boston: Pittman.

Ashford, S. J., Rothbard, N. P., Piderit, S. K., & Dutton, J. E. (1997). *Out on a limb: The role of context and impression management in selling gender-equity issues.* Working Paper, University of Michigan, Ann Arbor.

Bacharach, P., & Baratz, M. S. (1962). Two faces of power. *American Political Science Review, 56,* 947-952.

Barnard, C. I. (1968). *The functions of the executive.* Cambridge, MA: Harvard University Press.

Bower, J. L. (1970). *Managing the resource allocation process: A study of corporate planning and investment.* Boston: Harvard Business School Press.

Benson, P. L., Karabenic, S. A., & Lerner, R. M. (1976). Pretty pleases: The effects of physical attractiveness on race, sex, and receiving help. *Journal of Experimental Social Psychology, 37,* 1387-1397.

Burgelman, R. A. (1990). Strategy-making and organizational ecology: A conceptual integration. In J. V. Singh (Ed.), *Organizational evolution: New directions* (pp. 164-181). Newbury Park, CA: Sage.

Catalyst. (1996). *Women in corporate leadership: Progress and prospects.* New York: Author.

Dutton, J. E. (1997). Strategic agenda building in organizations. In Z. Shapria (Ed.) *Organizational decision making* (pp. 81-107). Cambridge, UK: Cambridge University Press.

Dutton, J. E., & Ashford, S. J. (1993). Selling issues to top management. *Academy of Management Review, 18,* 397-428.

Dutton, J. E., & Dukerich, J. (1991). Keeping an eye on the mirror: Image and identity in organizational adaptation. *Academy of Management Journal, 34*(3), 517-554.

Dutton, J. E., & Jackson, S. E. (1987). Categorizing strategic issues: Links to organizational action. *Academy of Management Review, 12*(1), 76-90.

Dutton, J. E., Walton, E. J., & Abrahamson, E. (1989). Important dimensions of strategic issues: Separating the wheat from the chaff. *Journal of Management Studies, 26*(4), 379-396.

Farmer, S. M., Maslyn, J. M., Fedor, D. B., & Goodman, J. S. (1997). Putting upward influence strategies in context. *Journal of Organizational Behavior, 18,* 17-42.

Finley, J. A. (1996). *Communication double binds: The catch-22 of conversations about racial issues in workgroups.* Doctoral dissertation, University of Michigan, Ann Arbor.

Ginzel, L. E., Kramer, R. M., & Sutton, R. I. (1993). Orgaizational impression management as a reciprocal influence process: The neglected role of the organizational audience. *Research in Organizational Behavior, 15,* 227-266.

Glaser, B., & Strauss, A. L. (1967). *The discovery of grounded theory.* New York: Aldine.

Glaser, B., & Strauss, A. L. (1970). Discovery of substantive theory: A basic strategy underlying qualitative research. In W. Filstead (Ed.), *Qualitative methodology* (pp. 288-297). Chicago: Rand McNally.

Grams, W. C., & Rogers, R. W. (1990). Power and personality: Effects of Machiavellianism, need for approval, and motivation on use of influence tactics. *Journal of General Psychology, 117*(1), 71-82.

Harquail, C. V. (1996). *When one speaks for many: The influence of social identification on group advocacy in organizations.* Unpublished doctoral dissertation, University of Michigan, Ann Arbor.

Heise, D. R. (1965). Semantic differential profiles for 1,000 most-frequent words. *Psychological Monographs, 79*(8), 1248-1263.

Hornstein, H. (1986). *Managerial courage: Revitalizing your company without sacrificing your job.* New York: John Wiley.

Jacobson, S. W., & Jacques, R. (1997). Destabilizing the field: Poststructuralist knowledge-making strategies in a postindustrial era. *Journal of Management Inquiry, 6*(1), 42-60.

Kapoor, A., Ansari, M. A., & Shukla, R. (1986). Upward influence tactics as a function of locus of control and organizational context. *Psychological Studies, 31*(2), 190-199.

Kiernan, M. J. (1993). The new strategic architecture: Learning to compete in the twenty-first century. *The Executive, 7*(1), 7-21.

Kilduff, M., & Mehra, A. (1997). Postmodernism and organizational research. *Academy of Management Review, 22*(2), 453-481.

Kingdon, J. W. (1984). *Agendas, alternatives, and public policies.* Boston: Little, Brown.

Kipnis, D., Schmidt, S. M., & Wilkinson, I. (1980). Intraorganizational influence tactics: Explorations in getting one's way. *Journal of Applied Psychology, 65,* 440-452.

Lancaster, H. (1997, March 4). Black managers often must emphasize building relationships. *Wall Street Journal,* p. B1.

Langley, A., Mintzberg, H., Pitcher, P., Posada, E., & Saint-Macary, J. (1995). Opening up decision-making: The view from the black stool. *Organizational Science, 6,* 260-279.

Meyerson, D. E., & Scully, M. A. (1995). Tempered radicalism and the politics of ambivalence and change. *Organization Science, 6*(5), 585-600.

Miles, M. B., & Huberman, A. M. (1984). *Qualitative data analysis: A sourcebook of new methods.* Beverly Hills, CA: Sage.

Noda, T., & Bower, J. L. (1996). Strategy making as iterated processes of resource allocation. *Strategic Management Journal, 17,* 159-192.

Osgood, C. E., & Suci, G. J. (1955). Factor analysis of meaning. *Journal of Experimental Psychology, 50,* 325-338.

Pfeffer, J. (1992). *Managing with power: Politics and influence in organizations.* Boston: Harvard Business School Press.

Rafaeli, A., & Sutton, R. I. (1991). Emotional contrast strategies as means of social influence: Lessons from criminal interrogators and bill collectors. *Academy of Management Journal, 34*(4), 749-775.

Reordon, K. (1993, March/April). The memo every woman keeps in her desk. *Harvard Business Review,* 3-8.

Schein, E. H. (1986). International human resource management: New directions, perpetual issues and missing themes. *Human Resource Management, 25,* 169-176.

Shrivastava, P. (1992). *Bhopal: Anatomy of a crisis* (2nd ed.). London: Paul Chapman.

Starbuck, W. H., & Milliken, F. (1988). Challenger: Fine-tuning the odds until something breaks. *Journal of Management Studies, 25,* 319-340.

Trice, H. M., & Beyer, J. M. (1993). *The cultures of work organizations.* Englewood Cliffs, NJ: Prentice Hall.

Van Maanen, J., & Schein, E. H. (1979). Toward a theory of organizational socialization. In B. M. Staw (Ed.), *Research for organizational behavior* (Vol. 1). Greenwich, CT: JAI.

Weick, K., & Ashford, S. J. (1997). Learning in organizations. In L. Putnam & F. Jablin (Eds.), *Handbook of organizational communication* (2nd ed.). Thousand Oaks, CA: Sage.

Wright, P., Ferris, S. P., Hiller, J. S., & Kroll, M. (1995). Competitiveness through management of diversity: Effects on stock price valuation. Special issue: Intra- and inter-organizational cooperation. *Academy of Management Journal, 38*(1), 272-287.

Yukl, G., & Falbe, C. (1990). Influence tactics and objectives in upward, downward, and lateral influence attempts. *Journal of Applied Psychology, 75,* 132-140.

Yukl, G., Falbe, C., & Youn, J. Y. (1993). Patterns of influence behavior for managers. *Group and Organization Management, 18*(1), 5-28.

Yukl, G., & Tracey, J. B. (1992). Consequences of influence tactics used with subordinates, peers, and the boss. *Journal of Applied Psychology, 77*(4), 525-535.

Index

About the Contributors

Susan J. Ashford is the Michael and Susan Jandernoa professor on the business school faculty at the University of Michigan. She received a MS and a PhD in organizational behavior from Northwestern University. Her research focuses on the ways that individuals are proactive in their organizational lives, whether it is in assessing their own performance by seeking feedback, enhancing their managerial effectiveness by staying "tuned in" to various constituents, facilitating their own socialization during organizational entry, or attempting to sell particular issues to top management from the middle ranks of organizations. Her work has been published in a variety of journals.

Blake E. Ashforth is Professor of Management at Arizona State University-Tempe. He received a PhD from the University of Toronto. His research interests include the adjustment of newcomers to work, the dysfunctions of organizational structures and processes, and the links between individual-, group-, and organization-level phenomena. His recent work has focused on socialization, identity, and labeling processes. He is a consulting editor for the *Academy of Management Review* and is on the editorial boards of *Administrative Science Quarterly* and the *Canadian Journal of Administrative Sciences*.

Samuel B. Bacharach is Professor of Industrial and Labor Relations in the Department of Organizational Behavior, New York State School of Industrial and Labor Relations and also director of the Smithers Institute. He is also a Lady Davis Fellow in the faculty of Industrial Engineering and Management at the Technion Israel Institute of Technology.

Robert J. Bies is Associate Professor of Management in the School of Business, Georgetown University. He received both a BA in business administration and MBA from the University of Washington. He received a PhD in business administration (organizational behavior) from Stanford University. His research interests include the delivery of bad news, revenge in the workplace, and organizational (in)justice. He is coeditor of *The Legalistic Organization* (1993) and *Research on Negotiation in Organizations*, a biannual series of analytical essays and critical reviews. He is a member of the Academy of Management and the American Psychological Association and is on the editorial boards of *Journal of Applied Psychology, Journal of Management*, and *The International Journal of Conflict Management*.

Ronald S. Burt is a Hobart W. Williams Professor of Sociology and Strategy at the University of Chicago and codirector of the Chicago Management Council. His interests concern network theory applied to the social organization of competition. He received a PhD in sociology from the University of Chicago.

Robert B. Cialdini received undergraduate, graduate, and postgraduate education in psychology at the University of Wisconsin, University of North Carolina, and Columbia University, respectively. He has held Visiting Scholar appointments at Ohio State University, the universities of California at San Diego and at Santa Cruz, the Annenberg School of Communications, and at both the Psychology Department and the Graduate School of Business of Stanford University. He is currently Regents' Professor of Psychology at Arizona State University, where he has also been named Distinguished Graduate Research Professor. His book, *Influence*, which was the result of a three-year program of study into the reasons that people comply with requests in natural settings, has appeared in numerous editions and seven languages.

Benjamin A. Hanna is a doctoral candidate in organizational behavior at the Stanford University Graduate School of Business. His interests include the effects of media scrutiny on organizations and the role of social identity and self-categorization in sensemaking and trust behavior. His dissertation will examine the relationship between leader communication and media scrutiny during organizational crisis.

David Krackhardt is Professor of Organizations and Public Policy at the Heinz School of Public Policy and Management, Carnegie Mellon University. He received a BS degree from the Massachusetts Institute of Technology and a PhD from the University of California, Irvine. He has held positions as a Marvin Bower Fellow at Harvard Business School and a visiting professor of organizations at the University of Chicago. His research has focused on how the theoretical insights and methodological innovations of network analysis can enhance our understanding of how organizations function. He pioneered the concept of "cognitive social structure." He developed a set of measures for studying the shape and structure of organizations as a whole. His published works have appeared in a variety of journals.

Roderick M. Kramer is Associate Professor of Organizational Behavior at the Graduate School of Business, Stanford University. He received a PhD in social psychology from the University of California, Los Angeles. His current interests are trust and distrust in organizations, conflict and cooperation, and organizational decision making. His research has appeared in many journals. Recent publications include *Negotiation as a Social Process* (with David Messick; 1995), *Trust in Organizations* (with Tom Tyler; 1996), and *The Psychology of the Social Self* (with Tom Tyler and Oliver John).

Edward J. Lawler is Professor of Organizational Behavior and of Sociology, and Dean of the School of Industrial and Labor Relations at Cornell. He received his PhD in sociology from the University of Iowa for more than 20 years before moving to Cornell in 1994. He served a term as editor of the *Social Psychology Quarterly* and currently is series editor of *Advances in Group Processes*. His research interests include power, negotiation, social exchange, and organizational politics. His most recent work, published in the *American Sociological Review* over the last few years, is on the role of emotion and emotional processes in the development of commitment in exchange relations. He is co-author with Samuel B. Bacharach of two books—*Power and Politics in Organizations* (1980) and *Bargaining: Power, Tactics and Outcomes* (1981)—and as the article in this volume suggests, they are returning to this theme after a hiatus of several years.

Fred A. Mael is Senior Research Scientist at the American Institutes for Research in Washington, D.C., and an adjunct professor in the psychology and management departments at Loyola College. He received a PhD in industrial/organizational psychology from Wayne State University and a master's degree in counseling psychology. His areas of research expertise include individual commitment to and identification with work and nonwork organizations; personnel selection methods, especially biographical data; invasion of privacy in personnel selection; and career development and varieties of career trajectories. He is author of more than three dozen journal articles, book chapters, and conference presentations. His current research centers on the process of determining inability to work because of physical or psychological disability and a comparative analysis of various work and nonwork identities.

Elizabeth A. Mannix is Associate Professor of Organizational Behavior at the Graduate School of Business, Columbia University. Her research and teaching activities include negotiation, teams, and power and politics in organizations. She is also interested in international negotiation and management and has taught at Chulalongkorn University in Bangkok. In addition, she is the recipient of two grants from the Center for International Business Education to study bargaining behavior in Japan and in the People's Republic of China. Her research has appeared in many journals. She is currently at work on the first in a series of volumes (coedited with Margaret Neale and Deborah Gruenfeld) titled *Research on Managing in Groups and Teams*.

Joanne Martin is a Fred H. Merrill Professor of Organizational Behavior at the Graduate School of Business and, by courtesy, in the Department of Sociology, Stanford University. She received a PhD in social psychology from the Department of Psychology and Social Relations, Harvard University. Her current research interests include the following: organizational culture, with particular emphasis on subcultural identities and ambiguities; and diversity in organizations, with a particular interest in subtle barriers to acceptance and advancement for women. Recent books include *Reframing Organizational Culture* (coedited and cowritten with Peter Frost, Larry Moore, Meryl Louis, and Craig Lundberg; 1991) and *Cultures in Organizations* (1992).

David M. Messick is the Morris and Alice Kaplan Professor of Ethics and Decisions in Management in the Kellogg Graduate School of Management of Northwestern University. He received a BA in psychology from the University of Delaware and a MA and PhD in psychology from the University of North Carolina, Chapel Hill. He is an experimental social psychologist who has published extensively on a variety of problems having to do with decision making in social environments. His current research and teaching involves the application of psychological theory and methods of ethical aspects of business decision making.

Debra Meyerson is a Visiting Scholar at the Institute for Research on Women and Gender at Stanford University and a Fellow at Simmons Institute of Leadership and Change. She received a PhD in organizational behavior from Stanford University. Her research focuses on the processes and politics of change directed at gender and race equity, the identity processes related to these changes, feminist reconstructions of organizational theory and practice, and "tempered radicalism" in organizations. She is co-principle investigator of an action research project aimed at increasing gender equity in organizations and is writing a book on tempered radicalism.

Margaret A. Neale is Academic Associate Dean and Professor of Organizational Behavior at the Graduate School of Business at Stanford University. She received her PhD in business administration from the University of Texas. Her research includes bargaining and negotiation, the allocation of burdens and benefits, behavioral decision theory, and group performance. She is author of more than 60 articles and coauthor of *Organizational Behavior: A Management Challenge* (2nd ed.) (with G. B. Northcraft; 1994), *Cognition and Rationality in Negotiation* (with M. H. Bazerman; 1997), *Negotiating Rationally* (with M. H. Bazerman; 1992), and *Research on Managing in Groups and Teams* (with E. Mannix; 1998).

Rafal K. Ohme is Assistant Professor at the Institute of Psychology at the Maria Curie-Sklodowska University in Lublin, Poland. Within the field of social psychology, Ohme focuses his attention on the areas of social influence and implicit social cognition. In addition, he teaches courses on social communication and advertising. In 1995 and 1996, Ohme visited the Kellogg Graduate School of Management as a Fulbright scholar. He also has research affiliations at Stanford University and the University of North Florida.

Jeffrey Pfeffer is the Thomas D. Dee Professor of Organizational Behavior at the Graduate School of Business, Stanford University. He has authored eight books, including *The Human Equation: Building Profits by Putting People First, New Directions for Organization Theory: Problems and Prospects,* and *Managing With Power: Politics and Influence in Organizations,* as well as more than 95 articles and book chapters. He has served as director of executive education at Stanford and has presented executive seminars in 20 countries as well as to numerous companies and associations in the United States.

Laurie A. Rudman is Assistant Professor in Psychology at Rutgers, The State University of New Jersey. She received a PhD from the University of Minnesota. In 1995, she received the Gordon Allport Intergroup Relations Award (with Gene Borgida). Her research interests include social cognition, impression management, and implicit attitude assessment.

Philip E. Tetlock is the Harold Burtt Professor of Psychology and Political Science at the Ohio State University. His experimental research program on judgment and choice explores the implications of thinking of people as intuitive politicians, theologians, and prosecutors. He also does research in a variety of nonexperimental settings, including work on counterfactual thought experiments (how experts think about what might have been as well as what might yet be). He has received a variety of professional awards, including the American Association for the Advancement of Science's Behavioral Science Research Prize and the Woodrow Wilson Book Award from the American Political Science Association.

Tracy A. Thompson is Assistant Professor in the Business Administration Program at the University of Washington, Tacoma. She received a PhD in organization behavior from Northwestern University. Her research focuses on strategic management, organization change, and corporate governance. Her work has appeared in *Administrative Science Quarterly, Corporate Governance,* and the *Journal of Managerial Education.* As an academic affiliate to the Newspaper Management Center at Northwestern University, she conducts research on the newspaper industry and teaches in executive education programs. She is also an active member of the Academy of Management's Business Policy and Strategy Division.

Thomas M. Tripp is Associate Professor of Management at Washington State University. He received a PhD in organization behavior from the Kellogg Graduate School of Management at Northwestern University. He has specialized in the study of organizational injustice, power in negotiations, measuring negotiator performance accurately, and workplace revenge. His research has appeared in many journals. He is a member of the Academy of Management and serves on the executive committee of its Conflict Management Division.

Tom R. Tyler is Professor of Psychology at New York University. His research examines social justice and the psychology of authority. He is the author of several books, including *The Social Psychology of Procedural Justice* (with Allan Lind), *Why People Obey the Law: Trust in Organizations* (with Roderick Kramer), and *Social Justice in a Diverse Society* (with Robert Boeckmann, Heather Smith, and Yuen Huo).

Kathleen L. Valley is Associate Professor at the Harvard Business School. She received a PhD from the Kellogg Graduate School of Management at Northwestern University. Her research is focused on interpersonal relationships and their role in decisions, conflict, and resource allocation within organizations. Her investigations into the way people interact, both personally and professionally, in the workplace have resulted in numerous journal articles and book chapters. Currently, she is exploring the ways in which personal and professional relationships affect and are affected by organizational change. She has presented her work at universities and conferences across North America and Europe. She has designed and taught numerous courses in organizational behavior, negotiations, and decision analysis. She currently teaches negotiations to MBAs at the Harvard Business School and to professionals at Harvard Law School's Program on Negotiation.

Ruth Wageman is a professor on the faculty of the Columbia Business School. She received a BA from Columbia College and a PhD from the Harvard Joint Doctoral Program in Organizational Behavior. Her teaching and research interests include designing and leading effective task force performing teams, reward system design for groups, human motivation, and structural and individual influences on group and interpersonal behavior. Current projects include "How Leaders Foster Team Self-Management," "Toward a Theory of Team Coaching," and "Equalitarian Values and Member Responses to Team Failures." Her recent research has appeared in such journals as *Administrative Science Quarterly*, *Organizational Dynamics*, and *Journal of Organizational Behavior*.